| ...M | AMOUNT | SUGGESTED SERVING TEMP. | POWER LEVEL | APPROX. TIME MINS. |
|---|---|---|---|---|
| **...ndwiches** | | | | |
| **...st Filling;** such | 1 serving | 110° | M. High | 1-1½ |
| ...sloppy joe, | 2 servings | 110° | M. High | 1½-2½ |
| ...rbecue, ham | 4 servings | 110° | M. High | 2½-4 |
| ...ad, etc. in bun ⅓ cup / serving | | | | |
| **...ick Meat-Cheese ...ing;** with firm ...ead | 1 serving | 110° | M. High | 1½-2½ |
| | 2 servings | 110° | M. High | 2½-3½ |
| | 4 servings | 110° | M. High | 5-7 |
| **...up** | | | | |
| ...ter Base ...cup /serving | 1 serving | 150°-170° | High | 2½-3½ |
| | 2 servings | 150°-170° | High | 4-5½ |
| | 4 servings | 150°-170° | High | 7-9 |
| | 1 can 10-oz. reconstituted | 150°-170° | High | 5-7 |
| ...lk Base ...cup / serving | 1 serving | 140° | M. High | 3-4 |
| | 2 servings | 140° | M. High | 5-7 |
| | 4 servings | 140° | M. High | 10-12 |
| | 1 can 10-oz. reconstituted | 140° | M. High | 8-10 |

...: Use paper towel or napkin to cover sandwiches. Cover ...ups with wax paper or plastic wrap.

| **...EGETABLES** | | | | |
|---|---|---|---|---|
| **...mall Pieces** such | 1 serving | 150°-160° | High | 1-2 |
| ...peas, beans, | 2 servings | 150°-160° | High | 2-3 |
| ...rn, etc. | 4 servings | 150°-160° | High | 3-4 |
| ...½ cup / serving | 1 can 16-oz. | 150°-160° | High or M. High | 4-4½ |
| **...rge pieces** or | 1 serving | | High | 2-2½ |
| ...hole such as | 2 servings | | High | 3-3½ |
| ...sparagus spears, | 4 servings | | High | 4-4½ |
| ...rn on the cob, etc. | 1 can 16-oz. | | High | 4-4½ |
| **...ashed** | 1 serving | 150°-160° | High | 1-2 |
| ...½ cup / serving | 2 servings | 150°-160° | High | 2-3 |
| | 4 servings | 150°-160° | High | 6-7 |

...: Cover vegetables for most even heating.

| **...AUCES** | | | | |
|---|---|---|---|---|
| **...essert** such as ...hocolate, butterscotch | | | | |
| ...oom Temp | ½ cup | 125° | High | ¼-½ |
| | 1 cup | 125° | High | ½-1 |
| ...ef. Temp. | ½ cup | 125° | High | 1-1½ |
| | 1 cup | 125° | High | 2-2½ |
| **...eat or Main Dish** | | | | |
| ...hunky type such | ½ cup | 150°-160° | High | 1½-2 |
| ...s giblet gravy, | 1 cup | 150°-160° | High | 2½-3½ |
| ...paghetti sauce, | 1 can 16-oz. | 150°-160° | High | 5-6 |
| ...tc. | | | | |
| **...reamy Type** | ½ cup | 140°-150° | High | 1-1½ |
| | 1 cup | 140°-150° | High | 2-2½ |

...ip: Cover food to prevent spatter.

---

| ITEM | | SUGGESTED ...R ... LEVEL | | APPROX. TIME MINS. |
|---|---|---|---|---|
| **BAKERY FOODS** | | | | |
| Room Temperature | | | | |
| **Cake, Coffee Cake, Doughnuts, Sweet Rolls, Nut or Fruit Bread.** | 1 piece | 90° | Low | ½-1 |
| | 2 pieces | | Low | 1-1½ |
| | 4 pieces | | Low | 1½-2½ |
| | 9-in. cake or 12 rolls or doughnuts | 90° | Low | 2-4 |
| **Dinner Rolls, Muffins** | 1 | 90° | Medium | ¼-½ |
| | 2 | | Medium | ½-¾ |
| | 4 | | Medium | ½-1 |
| | 6-8 | | Medium | 1-1¾ |
| **Pie,** Fruit or Nut ⅛ of 9-in. pie = 1 slice | 1 slice | 110° | High | ½-1 |
| | 2 slices | | High | 1-1½ |
| | 4 slices | | M. High | 2½-3½ |
| | 9-in. pie | 110° | M. High | 5-7 |
| **Pie,** Custard ⅛ of 9-in. pie = 1 slice | 1 slice | 110° | M. High | ½-1 |
| | 2 slices | | M. High | 1½-2 |
| | 4 slices | | M. High | 2½-3½ |
| | 9-in. pie | 110° | M. High | 5-7 |
| **GRIDDLE FOODS** | | | | |
| Room Temperature | | | | |
| **Pancakes** | | | | |
| Plain, no topping | Stack of 3 | 120° | High | ½-1 |
| Syrup & butter | Stack of 3 | 120° | High | 1-1¼ |
| With 2 sausage patties | Stack of 3 | 120° | High | 1¼-1½ |
| **French Toast** | | | | |
| Plain, no topping | 2 slices | 120° | High | ½-1 |
| With syrup & butter | 2 slices | 120° | High | 1-1¼ |
| **Waffles** 3" x 4" | | | | |
| Plain, no topping | 2 | 120° | High | ½-1 |
| With syrup & butter | 2 | 120° | High | 1-1¼ |
| **BEVERAGES** | | | | |
| **Coffee, Tea, Cider,** other water based | 1 cup | 160°-170° | High | 1½-2½ |
| | 2 cups | | High | 3½-4½ |
| | 4 cups | | High | 6-7 |
| **Cocoa,** other milk based | 1 cup | 140° | M. High | 2-3 |
| | 2 cups | | M. High | 4-5 |
| | 4 cups | | M. High | 7-8 |

Tip: Do not cover bakery foods, griddle foods (pancakes, etc.) or beverages.

# How to Use This Book

This unusual, new book is both a guide and a cookbook. It grew out of nationwide cooking schools and extensive consumer research, from which we learned what people need to know to become confident, successful and expert microwave cooks.

To make the most effective use of this book, first read the introductory guide, which teaches you the principles and techniques of microwaving. Many will be familiar, some, new. All are clearly illustrated with photographs.

Then go on to the recipe chapters where Microlessons demonstrate how to cook specific foods. We show you what to do, what to expect, how the food should look, and how to tell when it's done. You'll soon learn that successful microwaving is not only faster, but often 'easier than conventional cooking.

Diana Williams Hansen
Manager-Home Economics
Range Marketing Department

Many thanks
to home economists,
Jean E. Kozar
Joyce Elliott Blair
Brigid Lally Bowles
Marita A. Duber
Paula Cooper Matthews

D.W.H.

The photographs in this book were designed to help you learn by seeing examples of foods and cooking techniques. All foods were microwaved according to recipes in the book, and photographed exactly as they came from the oven, using Kodak's new, no pollution E & G film and processing system.

# Contents

# Microwaving: A New Cooking Term

**Water Boils** in a paper cup. One of the remarkable characteristics of microwave energy is that it heats the food, not the utensil. Utensils become warm only when heat from food has transferred to them.

**Television** is radio waves converted to a picture on the screen. Microwave energy is very short radio waves converted to heat in food.

The microwave oven has added a new term to our cooking language. "Microwaving" means to cook, heat or defrost foods with microwave energy. Microwaving is a new type of cooking, which has its own special benefits, and produces its own food characteristics. Some microwaved foods may be different from what you expect when cooking in a conventional oven or on the range top. The difference may be in appearance, in improved flavor and juiciness, or in cooking technique.

The microwave oven is called an "oven" because it looks more like an oven than any other conventional appliance, but it can take over many of your top-of-range jobs with less time, attention and clean-up. Foods which you used to bake in a conventional oven will taste the same, but may look different. For example, a casserole will heat through quickly, but will not crust over, because the air in a microwave oven is room temperature, not hot and dry.

Like any new skill, microwaving takes a little practice. Until you are used to its speed, you may overcook. Some foods will be removed from the oven before they look done, because they finish cooking with internal heat. This book is designed to teach you what to expect, and how to achieve successful results with microwaving. You'll find learning to microwave easy and exciting.

## HOW MICROWAVE WORKS

Microwaves are very short, high-frequency radio waves, and your microwave oven is similar to a miniature broadcasting system. Microwaves are the same type of energy as AM, FM or CB radio, but the wave length is much shorter.

Where other types of radio waves broadcast over a distance, the microwave broadcasting system is self-contained. When the door is closed and the oven is turned on, a transmitter, called a magnetron, sends a signal to a receiver within the oven. The moment you open the door, the microwave oven stops broadcasting, just as your radio will not play if the station has "signed off". No energy will be received from the oven while the door is open.

The receiver deflects the microwave energy into the metal-lined oven cavity, where it agitates food molecules. Since microwaves cannot penetrate metal, all the energy remains inside the oven, where it turns to heat in the food.

# "HEAT" PHOTOS SHOW HOW MICROWAVES COOK

A new process, called thermography, which makes images of heat, demonstrates the different ways in which foods cook. At the General Electric Major Appliance Laboratory, potatoes were heated on a range top, in a conventional oven, and in a microwave oven, then cut in half and thermographed to show how heat is distributed in each cooking method.

On the thermograph scale, blue stands for cool areas, red represents warmth and yellow indicates the hottest area. The "halo" of blue around the potatoes is thermal reflection and occurs when the potatoes are removed from heat to room temperature for photography.

## RANGE TOP

**Cut Potato** in a skillet is placed on a range surface unit set at medium heat. Potato was sliced so that a large flat surface could be exposed.

**After 3 Minutes** some heat from the surface unit has transferred through the pan to the cut side of the potato. On a range top, the bottom part of the food is always hottest.

**After 8 Minutes** the hot yellow area has increased and heat is being conducted into the red, warm portions. The top of the potato is still cool.

## CONVENTIONAL OVEN

**Whole Potato** is placed on the shelf of a conventional oven preheated to 400°. The air inside the oven is hot and dry.

**After 7 Minutes,** thin yellow areas indicate that air in the oven has heated the surface of the potato. Prolonged exposure to hot, dry air will make the outside dry and crusty.

**After 15 Minutes,** heat is gradually spreading to the interior through conduction, although the center is still cool. It takes about 1 hour to bake a potato conventionally.

## MICROWAVE

**Potato** is placed on the oven floor with a paper towel or napkin to absorb moisture, and is microwaved at High Power. Air in the oven is room temperature.

**After 1 Minute,** yellow areas of heat appear inside the potato, showing that microwave energy penetrates ¾ to 1¼-in. through food surfaces. Heat is then conducted inward and outward.

**After 4 Minutes,** potato is heated throughout, although it is not ready to serve. During a brief standing time, heat within the potato cooks it thoroughly.

## COMPARISON OF MICROWAVE & CONVENTIONAL COOKING

**Range Top.** On the range top, heat from the surface unit transfers through the pan to the bottom of the food. Stirring the food while it cooks brings heated portions to the top and prevents scorching. Covering the pan holds in steam and speeds cooking. Rearranging or turning foods over helps them cook evenly. Because the bottom of the pan is hot, fried or griddled foods become crisp or crusty.

**Conventional Oven.** In a conventional oven, the heating units heat the air inside the oven. The oven may be preheated until the air reaches the proper cooking temperature. Heat from this hot dry air enters the food through its exterior surfaces, and gradually spreads to the interior

through conduction. The process is usually slow, so by the time the center is done, the surfaces have become dry and crusty.

**Microwave Oven.** Microwaves penetrate ¾ to 1¼-in. through all food surfaces; top, bottom and sides. At this depth they are absorbed by moisture, sugar or fat molecules, which begin to cook. Heat is then conducted into the center and out to the surfaces. The food cooks by internal heat, not by contact with hot air or a hot pan. Because microwaves penetrate foods and cook them below the surface, cooking is faster for most foods, but the surface remains moist, not dry and crusty. Occasionally, the surface is the last place to cook.

## COMPARISON OF MICROWAVE & CONVENTIONAL ENERGY CONSUMPTION

Microwaving can save energy and reduce electric bills, but savings depend on what, and how much, you cook. Some foods make efficient use of microwave energy. Others, such as popcorn, use less energy when cooked conventionally.

The amount of food cooked affects energy consumption, too. Four baked potatoes require 61% less energy when microwaved, but about 12 potatoes bake more efficiently in a conventional oven. Greatest savings result when heating medium or small quantities of dense foods.

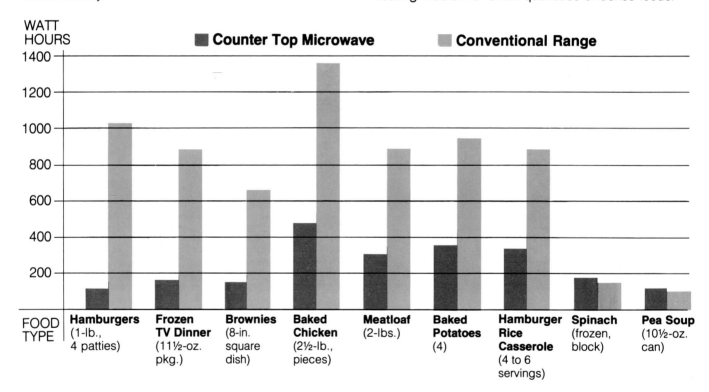

## PRECAUTIONS TO AVOID POSSIBLE EXPOSURE TO EXCESSIVE MICROWAVE ENERGY

1. **Do Not Attempt** to operate the oven with the door open since open-door operation can result in harmful exposure to microwave energy. It is important not to defeat or tamper with the safety interlocks.
2. **Do Not Place** any object between the oven front face and the door or allow soil or cleaner residue to accumulate on sealing surfaces.
3. **Do Not Operate** the oven if it is damaged. It is particularly important that the oven door close properly and that there is no damage to the (1) door (bent), (2) hinges and latches (broken or loosened), (3) door seals and sealing surfaces.
4. **The Oven Should** not be adjusted or repaired by anyone except properly qualified service personnel.

## SOME FOODS MICROWAVE WITH EXCEPTIONAL QUALITY

Some foods microwave so well that you may never want to cook them any other way. Foods which demand constant stirring on the range top, such as sauces, puddings, frostings and candies, need only an occasional stir in the microwave oven. Many can be measured, mixed and cooked in the same utensil for easy clean-up.

The excellent flavor and texture of microwaved fish, vegetables and fruits makes superior flavor the principle reason for cooking them by microwaves. Saving in time, while important, becomes a secondary advantage. In addition, there are some things unique to microwaving which cannot be done any other way.

**Vegetables** retain their fresh, crisp texture and bright color when microwaved according to chart, page 204.

**Baked Potato** microwaves fluffy, moist and tender. As an added benefit, you save time and energy. A potato microwaves in about 5 minutes.

**Leftovers** stay moist and taste freshly cooked. Roasted meats don't have a "leftover" flavor, rice reheats without overcooking.

**Defrost** foods rapidly. 1 pound of ground beef is ready to cook in 8 to 9 minutes. "I forgot to defrost", is never an emergency.

**Melt Chocolate** right in its paper wrapper. You have nothing to clean up and no danger of scorching or overcooking.

**Eggs** scramble fluffy, with greater volume. Compare 1 egg, cooked conventionally, left, with 1 microwave scrambled egg.

**Reheat** a meal right on the serving plate. If family members eat at different times, cook once and serve everyone a hot meal.

**Fish** steam tender and moist in their own natural juices, without additional water, for delicate flavor and pleasing texture.

**Bacon** microwaves crisp, brown and flat on paper towels. You don't have to turn it over, drain it, or scour a crusty pan.

## MORE FOODS THAT MICROWAVE WITH EXCEPTIONAL QUALITY

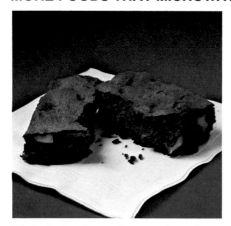

**Rich,** fudgy brownies can be microwaved in 6 minutes for a quick dessert or impromptu treat.

**Casseroles** can be microwaved, refrigerated and reheated in the same dish. They'll taste just as fresh the second day.

**Hot Appetizers** and snacks microwave in seconds on a paper napkin. They're so easy you can treat your family or guests to a variety.

**Cakes** rise higher and cook moist and tender when microwaved. Compare microwaved cake (right) with conventionally baked (left).

**Puddings** and custards cook smooth and creamy with no more than an occasional stirring. Cook and serve them from one dish.

**Blanch** vegetables for the freezer when they are at the peak of flavor. You and your kitchen will keep cool.

**Candies** that used to take constant stirring and attention are simplified by microwaving. The real, old-fashioned flavor is the same.

**Hot Fruit** desserts take less water to cook, so juices have true fruit flavor. Fruit keeps its fresh color and texture.

**Heat** frozen entrees rapidly whether you buy them ready-made or freeze leftovers in single servings for quick meals.

## THESE MICROWAVED FOODS SAVE TIME AND RESULTS COMPARE TO CONVENTIONAL COOKING

**A Hamburger** microwaves in 1 to 2 minutes, right on a paper or microwave ovenproof plate. It won't stick to the dish, so you save clean-up time.

**Chicken** pieces are tender, juicy and ready to serve quickly. A cut up broiler-fryer microwaves in about 20 minutes. Skin will not be crispy.

**Meatloaf** takes about 15 to 20 minutes to microwave. Add another 8 to 9 minutes if you must defrost the meat first.

**Upside-down Cake** becomes a last-minute dessert or afternoon snack when it takes only about 10 minutes.

**Sirloin Tip** roast will be tender and medium-rare when microwaved at Medium Power for 11 to 16 minutes per pound.

**Coffee Cake** microwaves in 5 to 7 minutes when neighbors drop in for coffee. It also makes an easy surprise for family breakfast.

## SOME FOODS DO NOT MICROWAVE WELL

No single appliance does everything well, and your microwave oven is no exception. Some things should not be done, either because results are not satisfactory, or because conventional cooking is more efficient.

**Eggs in Shells** and shelled boiled eggs can burst.

**Pancakes** do not crust, however, they reheat well.

**Popcorn,** other than popcorn especially labeled "Microwave Popcorn", is too dry to attract microwave energy.

**Canning** requires prolonged high temperatures.

**Deep Fat** frying could cause burns.

**Bottles** with narrow necks may shatter if heated.

**Large** food loads, such as a 25-lb. turkey or a dozen potatoes cook more efficiently in a conventional oven.

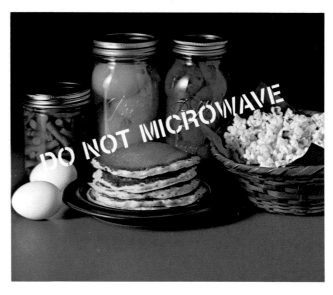

# Microwaving Techniques

Many of the techniques used in microwaving are the same ones you use in conventional cooking. Most of them either speed cooking or promote even heating. While the techniques may be familiar, their application may be somewhat different because of the unique way in which microwave energy cooks.

**Stirring.** In range-top cooking, you stir foods up from the bottom to help them heat evenly. When microwaving, you stir cooked portions from the outside to the center. Foods which require constant stirring conventionally will need only occasional stirring.

**Turning Over.** In range top cooking you turn over foods such as hamburgers, so both sides can directly contact hot pan. When microwaving, turning is often needed during defrosting, or when cooking foods such as hamburgers without a cover, or from frozen state.

**Arranging on Oven Shelf.** In conventional baking, you position foods, such as tomatoes or potatoes, so that hot air can flow around them. When microwaving, you arrange foods in a ring, so that all sides are exposed to microwave energy.

**Rearranging.** In conventional cooking, you reposition foods in the pan, especially when there are several layers. When microwaving, you also rearrange foods part way through the cooking period.

**Standing Time.** In conventional cooking, foods such as roasts or cakes are allowed to stand to finish cooking or set. Standing time is especially important in microwave cooking. Note that the microwaved cake is not placed on a cooling rack.

**Shielding.** In a conventional oven you shield turkey breasts or baked foods to prevent over-browning. When defrosting, you use small strips of foil to shield thin parts, such as the tips of wings and legs on poultry, which would cook before larger parts were defrosted.

**Covering.** In both conventional and microwave cooking, covers hold in moisture and speed heating. Conventionally, partial covering allows excess steam to escape. Venting plastic wrap or covering with wax paper serves the same purpose when microwaving.

## SOME TECHNIQUES ARE UNIQUE TO MICROWAVING

**Arranging in Dish.** When microwaving, arrange foods with the thickest portions to the outside of the dish. This enables them to cook through without overcooking the thinner areas. Arrange foods of equal size in a ring, leaving the center empty.

**Rotating.** Repositioning a dish in the oven helps food cook evenly. To rotate ½ turn, turn the dish until the side which was to the back of the oven is to the front. To rotate ¼ turn, turn the dish until the side which was to the back of the oven is to the side.

## MICROWAVING BAKED POTATOES DEMONSTRATES SEVERAL TECHNIQUES

**Prick** potatoes in several places to allow steam to escape.

**Arrange** potatoes in a ring so that all sides can be exposed to equal amounts of microwave energy.

**Turn Over** and rearrange potatoes half way through cooking.

## COVERING TECHNIQUES FOR RETAINING MOISTURE IN FOODS

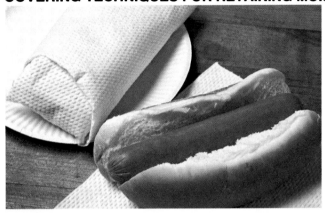

**Porous Cover,** such as paper towel or napkin, allows steam to escape while it promotes even heating and prevents spatters. Use to cover bacon, sandwiches and some vegetable custards.

**Light Cover** of wax paper holds in heat for faster cooking without steaming food. It is frequently used to cover some fruits and meats, such as chicken, hamburgers or roasts, which do not need steam to tenderize them.

**Tight Cover** of plastic wrap holds in steam as well as heat. Turning back one edge as a vent allows excess steam to escape, so wrap will not split during cooking. Vegetables and fish should be steamed.

**Utensil Cover** can be used instead of plastic wrap when you are microwaving vegetables, saucy casseroles and meats which require moisture and steam to tenderize them.

**Cooking Bags** also hold in steam. If the bag has a foil strip on the end, remove it. Cut a ½-in. wide strip from the open end of the bag to serve as a tie. Do not use metal twist ties. Make an X-shaped slash to vent.

**Freezer Bags** hold moisture in foods and serve as both cooking utensil and cover. Pierce the top of the bag with a knife to vent. Package leftovers in single portions for easy-to-heat homemade frozen entrees.

## HOW TO ADD MOISTURE TO FOODS

**Sprinkle** a little fruit juice or water over dried fruits, cover with plastic wrap and microwave ½ to 1 minute at High to moisten and plump them.

**Wet Paper Towel,** with excess water squeezed out, provides enough moisture to steam fish fillets and scallops. Wrap tortillas or crepes in damp towel and microwave at High ½ minute or more to soften them.

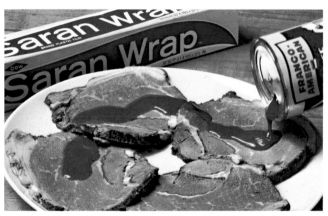

**Add Water** or sauce when reheating dry leftovers. A tablespoon of water or sauce is sufficient, and will not change the flavor of food or cause overcooking. Moisture creates steam for even reheating.

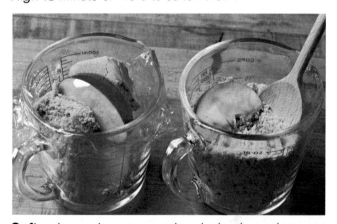

**Soften** lumpy brown sugar by placing in a microwave ovenproof container with a slice of apple. Cover or seal tightly and microwave ¼ minute or more, until moisture from the apple has softened the sugar.

## HOW TO REMOVE MOISTURE FROM FOODS

**Freshen Snacks,** chips, pretzels, etc. by microwaving them, uncovered, for a few seconds. Let stand a minute or two to crisp. Dry a quart of bread crumbs or croutons at High 6 to 8 minutes, stirring every 2 minutes.

**Paper Napkin** or towel will absorb excess moisture. Dry herbs between 2 layers of towel or napkin until they can be crumbled. Watch carefully after ½ minute-small amounts overheat and can catch fire easily. Paper towels absorb bottom moisture of cakes (see page 258).

## FACTORS WHICH AFFECT COOKING

Several factors which influence timing and results in conventional cooking are exaggerated by microwave speed. From conventional cooking you are familiar with the idea that more food takes more time. Two cups of water take longer to boil than one. Size of food is important, too. Cut up potatoes cook faster than whole ones. These differences are more apparent in microwaving, since energy penetrates and turns to heat directly in the food. Knowing what affects the speed and evenness of cooking will help you enjoy all the advantages of microwaving.

**Piece Size.** In both conventional and microwave cooking, small pieces cook faster than large ones. Pieces which are similar in size and shape cook more evenly.

**Starting Temperature.** Foods taken from the refrigerator take longer to cook than foods at room temperature. Timings in our recipes are based on the temperatures at which you normally store the foods.

**Density of Food.** In both conventional and microwave cooking, dense foods, such as a potato, take longer to cook or heat than light, porous foods, such as a piece of cake, bread or a roll.

**Quantity of Food.** In both types of cooking, small amounts usually take less time than large ones. This is most apparent in microwave cooking, where time is directly related to the number of servings.

**Shape of Food.** In both types of cooking, thin areas cook faster than thick ones. This can be controlled in microwaving by placing thick pieces to the outside edge with thin pieces to the center.

**Height in Oven.** In both types of cooking, areas which are closest to the source of heat or energy cook faster. For even microwaving, turn over or shield vulnerable foods which are higher than 5 inches.

**Boiling.** Microwaves exaggerate boiling in milk-based foods. A temperature probe turns off the oven before foods boil over. Use a lower power setting and watch carefully when not using a probe.

**Prick Foods to Release Pressure.** Steam builds up pressure in foods which are tightly covered by a skin or membrane. Prick potatoes (as you do conventionally), egg yolks and chicken livers to prevent bursting.

**Round Shapes.** Since microwaves penetrate foods to about 1-in. from top, bottom and sides, round shapes and rings cook more evenly. Corners receive more energy and may overcook. This may also happen conventionally.

**Bury Vulnerable Foods.** Foods which attract microwave energy, such as cheese or meat, should, when possible, be buried in sauce or other ingredients. In conventional stewing or pot roasting, meat not covered with liquid dries out.

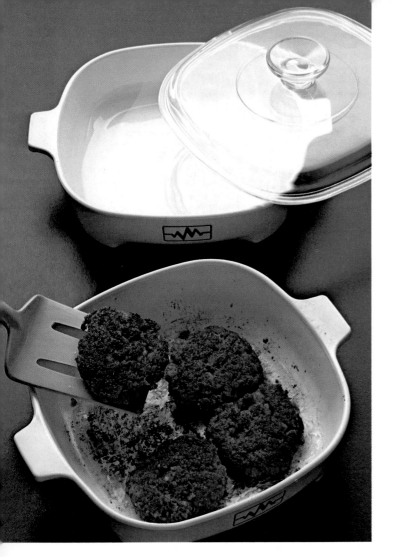

# Microwave Utensils

**Special Utensils** for microwaving are now available because of the increasing popularity of microwave ovens. These utensils are made of microwave ovenproof materials and satisfy some of the special needs of microwave cooks.

Many manufacturers are designing utensils which can be used both in microwave and conventional ovens. Special utensils also include many everyday items of glass, pottery, plastic and paper which were never considered cooking utensils until microwaving made it possible to use them.

**Brown 'N Sear Dish** (9-in. square) has a special coating on the bottom which attracts microwave energy. When preheated, it fries eggs and browns hamburgers or chicken. A cover controls moisture and spatters.

## BROWN 'N SEAR COOKING CHART    POWER LEVEL: **High (10)**

Preheat Brown 'N Sear Dish before each use. Use potholders and avoid touching bottom. If cooking many foods consecutively, preheat dish 1 to 1½ minutes between foods. Use the cover when cooking the foods listed on the chart below.

| ITEM | AMOUNT | PREHEAT TIME/MINUTES | FIRST SIDE TIME/MINUTES | SECOND SIDE TIME/MINUTES |
|---|---|---|---|---|
| **Steaks, Rib Eye or Delmonico** (6-oz. each, ½-in. thick) | 2 | 7 to 8 | 1 | 1½ to 2 |
| **Hamburgers,** (¼-lb. each, ½-in. thick) | 1 or 2 | 4 to 6 | 2 to 2½ | 1 to 1½ |
| | 3 or 4 | 6 to 8 | 2½ to 3 | 1½ to 2 |
| **Pork Chops** (5-oz. each, ¾-in. thick) | 1 | 3 to 4 | 2 | 4 to 6 |
| | 2 | 5 to 6 | 4 | 4 to 6 |
| **Pork Sausage Links** (Uncooked, 8-oz.) | 6 to 8 | 4 to 5½ | 1 | 2 to 2½ |
| **Ham Slice** (¼ to ½-in. thick) | 1 | 3½ to 4½ | 1 to 2 | 1 to 2 |
| **Chicken, Fried** (pieces coated with seasoned flour and paprika) | 3 | 6 to 7 (add 1 tablespoon oil after preheat) | 3 | 3 to 4 |
| | 6 | 7 to 8 (add 1 tablespoon oil after preheat) | 4 | 3 to 5 |
| **Fish Fillets** (6-oz. each, ½-in. thick) (seasoned flour on outsides) | 2 | 5 to 6 (add 1 tablespoon oil after preheat) | 1½ to 2½ | 2 to 3 |
| **Lamb Chops** (4-oz. each, ¾-in. thick) | 2 | 5 to 6 | 3 | 3 to 4 |
| | 4 | 6 to 8 | 3 to 4 | 4 to 5 |

**Browning Griddle** (11½×14-in.) browns larger pieces or more items than the Brown 'N Sear Dish. A well around the outside of the griddle catches drippings. The griddle has no cover.

**Microwave Trivet** fits in its own plastic dish or may be placed in a 12×8×2-in. cooking dish. Like a conventional roasting rack, it holds meat out of its juices to prevent stewing.

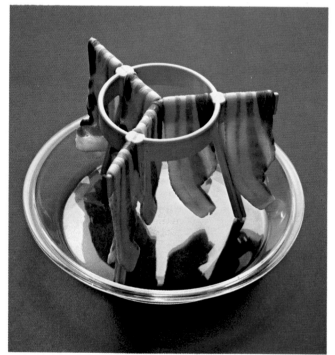

**Bacon Tree** holds up to 6 slices. Set in a dish or 1-qt. measure to catch the fat as bacon microwaves.

**Cupcaker** arranges and spaces muffins and cupcakes in the ring shape recommended for even microwaving.

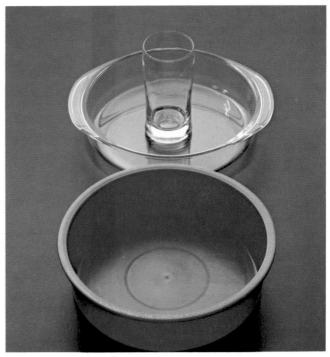

**Ring Molds** (fluted and straight sided) of plastic or ceramic are ideal for cakes, quick breads and meatloaves. They give them the ring shape preferred for microwaving, as well as an attractive appearance.

**High Sided Cake Pans** of plastic, glass or ceramic are especially designed for cake mixes, which rise higher in the microwave oven. Pans hold half of the cake mix batter. Make your own ring mold by placing a 3-in. diameter glass in an 8-in. round dish or casserole.

**Utensils You Already Have** may be suitable for microwaving. Oven glass casseroles, cooking dishes, measuring cups and custard cups are common household utensils. Pottery or china dinner ware which does not have gold or silver trim or glaze with a metallic sheen can be used. Most glass ceramic oven-to-table ware is labeled "suitable for microwave". If you are uncertain about a dish or container, use the dish test described below.

## WHAT TO LOOK FOR WHEN BUYING UTENSILS FOR MICROWAVING

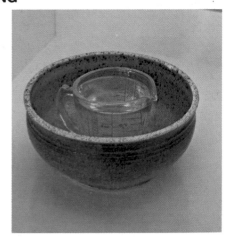

**"Suitable** for Microwave" or "Microwave Safe" may appear on the label or sticker, or may be stated in the warranty.

**Lugs and Handles** make dishes easier to use. While microwave energy does not heat the dish directly, heat from foods will transfer to the bottom and sides of it. Lugs and handles generally do not become hot.

**Test Dishes.** Measure 1 cup of water in a glass cup. Place in oven on or beside dish. Microwave 1 minute at High. If water becomes hot, dish is microwave safe. If dish heats, it should not be used for microwaving.

# MICROWAVE UTENSIL GUIDE

Use this guide to help you evaluate and select utensils for microwaving. Some items can only be used for heating. Others are suitable for cooking. Many microwave utensils are designed both for cooking and attractive serving. Brands listed are among those recommended by their manufacturers for microwaving.

| TYPE OF UTENSIL | **Paper Towels and Napkins, Wax Paper** | **Paper Plates and Cups (plain and plastic coated), such as:** Chinet, Diamond International, Dixie, St. Regis. |
| --- | --- | --- |
| MICROWAVE USES | Cooking Bacon. Absorbing moisture and preventing spatters. Heating and serving sandwiches or appetizers. Light covering to hold in steam. | Heating and serving foods and beverages. |
| COMMENTS | Recycled paper products can contain metal flecks which may cause arcing or ignite. Paper products containing nylon or nylon filaments should be avoided, as they may also ignite.<br><br>Dye from some colored paper products may bleed onto food. | Use plastic coated plates for moist or saucy foods. Use "hot drink" cups for soups and beverages.<br><br>Also, see column to left. |

| **Plastic Foam Plates and Cups, such as:** Sweetheart | **Plastic Wrap, Cooking Bags, Boil-in-bags, Storage Bags, such as:** Glad Wrap, Handi-Wrap, Saran Wrap, Cooking Magic, Reynolds, Baggies, Ziploc. | **Boilable Hard and Soft Plastics, such as:** Rubbermaid. |
| --- | --- | --- |
| Short term heating to low temperatures and serving. | Covering to hold in steam (wrap). Cooking (cooking and boil-in-bags). Heating (storage bags). | Cooking ground beef (colander). Defrosting. Heating. |
| Distort when used with bacon and foods with high fat content. | Storage bags can melt at high temperatures. | May discolor from fat. May distort when used with foods with high fat content (except colander). |

| TYPE OF UTENSIL | **Microwave Plastics such as:** Anchor Hocking Microwave, Bangor Plastics, Mister Microwave, Nupac | **Oven Glass such as:** Anchor Hocking, Fire King, Glassbake, Heller, Jena, Pyrex | **Glass-Ceramic (Pyroceram), such as:** Corning Ware, Progression G. by Noritake |
|---|---|---|---|
| MICROWAVE USES | Specialized cooking (see pages 17 and 18 for details.) | Cooking and heating. | Cooking and heating. |
| COMMENTS | Some pieces may be available from appliance or housewares departments. | Inexpensive and readily available in supermarkets, hardware and department stores. | Attractive for serving. Plastic storage lids, available with individual casseroles, should not be used for microwaving. |

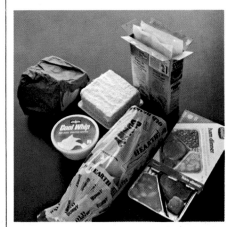

| TYPE OF UTENSIL | **Specialty Glass-Ceramic and Porcleain, such as:** El Camino, F. B. Rogers, Heller, Marsh Industries, Pfaltzgraff, Shafford | **Straw and Wood** | **Boxes lined with paper or plastic, Paper or plastic packages, Styrofoam base, Shallow frozen dinner tray.** |
|---|---|---|---|
| MICROWAVE USES | Recommended for microwave oven-to-table cooking of special foods. | Short term heating (baskets and boards). Cooking (spoons, whisks, picks and skewers). | Refresh foods, defrost meat and baked goods. Cook vegetables. Heat frozen foods. |
| COMMENTS | Microwave ovenproof ceramics may be sold with metal holders. Ceramic part, but not holders, may be used in microwave oven. | Spoons and whisks may be left in foods while microwaving. | Do not use foil trays higher than ¾-in. |

**Handmade Pottery, Porcelain, Stoneware**

Cooking and heating.

Avoid glazes with metallic sheen. Use the dish test, page 18, to determine if hand-made pottery is microwavable.

**Regular Dinnerware, such as:** Corelle by Corning, Dansk Generation, Denby, El Camino, Franciscan, International Stoneware, Lenox Temperware, Marsh, Mikasa, Pfaltzgraff

Heating and some cooking.

Check for "Recommended for microwave" seal, or use dish test. Avoid metal trim.

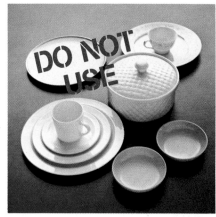

**Unsuitable Dinnerware, such as:** Corning Centura, Fitz and Floyd Oven-to-table Ware, Malamine, Dishes with metal trim

None

Warranty for Centura and Fitz and Floyd dishes states unsuitability for microwave.

**Foil-lined Paper Bags, Boxes and Baking Trays**

Avoid

Check for foil lining before attempting to microwave food in original packages.

**Metal or part metal pots, Pans, Thermometers, Skewers and Foil Trays**

Avoid

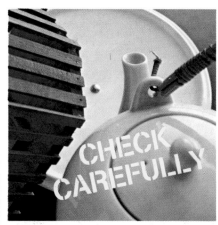

**Glass, pottery, pyroceram, wood or straw with metal fittings (screws, handles, clamps, etc.)**

Avoid or remove metal parts.

**Block of Ice** was defrosted for several minutes. Melted water has tunneled through ice, leaving some areas intact.

## HOW TO DISTRIBUTE MICROWAVE ENERGY EVENLY DURING DEFROSTING

**Stir** vegetables, casseroles and saucy foods part way through defrosting time.

**Turn Over** or rotate foods which cannot be stirred, such as meats, layered casseroles or cakes.

**Separate Pieces,** such as chicken parts or fish fillets, as soon as possible. Let large items stand to complete defrosting.

# Defrosting

Ice absorbs microwave energy slowly, while water and moisture respond rapidly. Where microwaves penetrate frozen foods and moisture appears, melting is exaggerated. Defrosting techniques which redistribute microwave energy help foods defrost evenly and speed defrosting as well. If you try to defrost food without any attention, vulnerable spots, such as edges and thin areas, will start to cook before centers or thick areas are defrosted. Step-by-step instructions for defrosting specific foods are included throughout the recipe sections. Be sure to observe standing time where directed. Some microwave ovens allow you to program standing time.

## TIPS FOR MICROWAVING FROZEN DINNERS

**Remove** food from trays over ¾-in. high and arrange on plate. Peel off foil lid from shallow trays. Return tray to box. (Check box for microwave directions.)

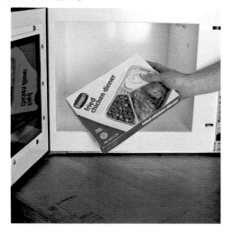

**Place Box** in oven 1-in. from sides. Microwave at Medium High 8 to 12 Minutes, or at High 5 to 8 Minutes. (Rotate ½ turn after ½ of time at High.) Plated foods take less time.

**Avoid** French fries, doughs and foods which do not microwave well, or remove them and cook conventionally.

## HOW TO FREEZE FOODS FOR MICROWAVING

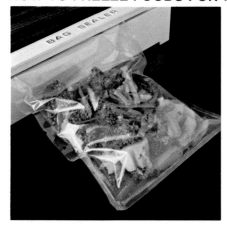

**Package** single portions for future heating in pouches. Make additional servings or use leftovers.

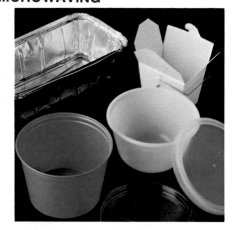

**Freeze** and defrost foods in plastic or cardboard cartons from deli foods, sour cream, etc. Pop out foods from foil pans.

**Freeze** and heat homemade dinners in shallow foil trays. Select foods which microwave well, and follow directions above.

# Heating

Heating is one of the advantages of microwaving. Food can be prepared earlier in the day, when cooking may be more convenient, and reheated at serving time. Plates of food can be set aside and heated to give late comers a hot meal. Leftovers will taste freshly cooked when reheated.

Consult the chart on the inside front cover for times and power levels recommended for various types and quantities of food. When heating by time, stir, turn over or rotate foods as needed.

**Starting Temperature.** Foods taken from the refrigerator take longer than foods stored on your pantry shelf.

**Quantity.** One serving heats faster than several. Heat large amounts at Medium High and rotate or stir after ½ of time for even heating.

**Automatic Temperature Probe.** Heat foods by temperature for accuracy. Moist casseroles heat well. Serve at 150° to 160°.

**Soften Ice Cream** for easy scooping. Remove any foil and microwave at Defrost ½ minute per pint, or 1½ to 2 minutes for ½ gallon.

**Soften Butter** to spreadable stage. Unwrap ¼ lb. and place on plate. Microwave at Defrost ½ minute (refrigerated) or 1 minute (frozen).

**Melt Butter** in small bowl or glass measure, using High Power. To clarify, heat until bubbly and pour off clear liquid.

## HEATING SINGLE PLATES OF FOOD

Arrange plates with hardest to heat foods on the outside of dish. Make a depression in dense foods like mashed potatoes, to give them a ring shape. Where possible, spread foods out to keep a low, even profile.

When assembling plates from leftovers, start with foods of the same temperature; all refrigerated or all room temperature. Fast heating items can be added at the end.

Cover most foods with wax paper to hold in heat and prevent spatters without steaming. When more moisture is desired, cover with plastic wrap. Be careful of steam when removing wrap.

For accurate heating, use the temperature probe inserted into the largest piece of food and set to 150° to 160°, which is serving temperature.

When heating by time at High, you may want to rotate the plate after ½ the time. Heat for 2 to 3 minutes and test by feeling the bottom of the plate. If plate is warm, it indicates that food is hot enough to transfer heat to the plate. If plate is cool, food may be warm, but will lose heat to the plate and taste cool when served.

**Arrange** thick areas and dense foods to the outside of dish, with easy-to-heat foods on the inside.

**Speed** heating of uniform foods like beef stew by stirring from edges to center while heating.

**Spread** saucy, moist foods, such as chow mein or creamed tuna with noodles flat for absorption of energy. Rotate layered foods.

**Add Sauce** to sliced meat and a pat of butter to dry pasta or rice, to speed heating. Add frozen roll last ½ to 1 minute.

**Delicate** foods which can overheat, such as macaroni and cheese or seafood, may be microwaved at Medium to keep them tender.

**Use** temperature probe for accurate, carefree reheating of moist, saucy foods. Cover plate with plastic wrap.

# The Automatic Temperature Probe

The automatic temperature probe takes the guesswork out of timing. Factors which influence time cooking, such as the amount, type and starting temperature of food are automatically adjusted in temperature cooking. Foods cook to a pre-set internal temperature, then the oven signals you and turns off. With Automatic Simmering the probe regulates temperature so that foods cook slowly.

With temperature cooking, roasting most meats and poultry becomes carefree. If you follow directions for covering, probe placement and power level, the roast will need no attention during cooking.

Probe placement is important for accurate results. Throughout this book you will find pictures and instruc-

tions for positioning the probe in different types of food. Here are a few general rules:

Insert probe into foods as directed in recipes, making sure the disc does not touch food. Probe is easiest to use when inserted from the front. Use the clip to keep probe in place while heating. Cover foods as directed for moisture control and speedy, even heating. When simmering automatically, submerge the tip of the probe in liquid.

Where choice of power levels is given, lower setting will heat more evenly, but requires a little more time.

If food has been frozen, make sure it is completely defrosted before inserting the probe. Do not use the probe with TV dinner trays or with the Brown 'N Sear Dish.

## ACCURATE COOKING

**Roast Beef** to rare, medium or well done at Medium or Low Power. Insert probe into center of meaty areas, without touching fat or bone.

**Roast Poultry** at Medium or Medium High to an internal temperature of 190°. Insert probe into meatiest area of inner thigh, from below the end of, and parallel to the leg.

**Cook Casseroles** at High to Medium, to accurate internal temperature as directed in recipes. Insert probe so tip is in center of casserole.

**Cook Meatloaves** without special attention, following recipes for power levels and internal temperatures. Insert probe into center of loaf or ring.

# The Cook Code

Many of the recipes in this book include a two or three-digit "Cook Code." This handy code is a time-saving short-cut method for entering time and power level desired for the dish you are preparing. Cook Codes are only used for recipes which need little or no attention, and which require no change of power level during cooking. Recipes which require additional ingredients, attention or change of power level during microwaving should be cooked in the usual manner. Also, recipes with cooking time of less than one minute or more than 99 minutes do not carry Cook Codes.

The Cook Code feature is easy to use. If your microwave oven is equipped with Cook Code, use it by simply touching the Cook Code pad. The readout display will display O and "Enter Code" will flash, indicating that the oven is ready to be programmed with the numerals designating cooking time and power level desired. Now you touch the number pads which correspond to the three-digit Cook Code given in the recipe you are using. The first two digits indicate the time in whole minutes. The last digit shows the selected Power Level setting. The code for High Power is "0", meaning Power Level 10. Be sure to enter any zeros that are given in the code. For single digit minutes, there is no need for entering a "0" before, but make sure you enter double digits with "0" after the numeral, as in 20 minutes. You must enter at least two digits and no more than three for the oven to carry out the Code that you desire for your cooking. If you enter an incorrect number and need to start over,

simply touch "Clear Off" and then "Cook Code" pad and later new numerals. When you have made the correct Cook Code entry for your recipe, just touch the "Start" pad to begin cooking. The microwave oven will automatically decode your instructions. The readout display will show "Cook Time Left" and display area will count down in seconds, showing time remaining. The Power Level being used will also be displayed.

It's easy to invent Cook Codes for your own recipes. Just select one or two digits representing the length of cooking time desired, and a final digit for the Power Level required. Then program your new "Cook Code" in the same way as shown above. You can also change the codes given in a recipe in order to suit your individual taste. Cook Codes are given for the minimum time needed, to avoid overcooking which can dry out food and make it tasteless and tough. If you feel that more cooking is needed, add additional time by changing the Cook Code. You cannot add seconds to the cycle time—Cook Codes are for whole minutes only. If your recipe calls for Power Level changes or different amounts of time needed between addition of ingredients, you may set one Cook Code for the first part of the recipe, then after completion, set another Cook Code for that period of time and Power Level.

Remember that Cook Codes are for microwaving by time only. If you are microwaving by temperature, you must use the Temp Cook or Auto Roast functions.

**TIME "COOK CODE"**

Time in Minutes / Power Level High (10)

**TYPICAL TIME COOK RECIPE**

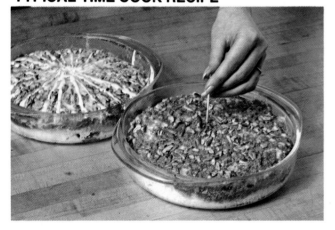

**Coffeecake** microwaves at High 5 to 7 minutes, 5 (5 minutes), 0 (High).

# Menu Planning

As with any meal, microwave menus begin with balanced nutrition and contrast of color, texture and taste for eye and appetite appeal. As with conventional cooking, plan your meals so that all the foods will not need last-minute cooking or attention at the same time.

Some special features of microwaving make it easy to serve meals with every food piping hot. Cooking of some foods may be interrupted while you start others, without harm to the food.

A recipe which requires standing time can be microwaved first, and another food cooked while it stands. Dishes prepared in advance can be reheated briefly before serving.

Use these sample menus as a guide to planning microwave meals. They are well-balanced, good tasting dinners made with every-day, popular foods. Follow the step-by-step microwaving order to have everything hot and ready to eat at the same time.

Chicken Dinner

### CHICKEN DINNER

Crumb Coated Chicken
page 138

Frozen Beans
page 204

Tossed Salad

Warm Rolls
page 229

Fruit-Topped Cake
page 258

45 minutes before serving time:

Prepare Fruit-Topped Cake

While cake is cooking, skin chicken (if desired). and coat with crumbs.

When cake is ready, microwave chicken. While chicken cooks, prepare and refrigerate salad greens and get beans ready to microwave.

When chicken is done, set it aside to keep warm and microwave beans.

Toss salad and warm rolls just before serving.

## MENU PLANNING TIPS

**Appetizers.** Early in the day, get appetizers ready to microwave and refrigerate them if necessary. At serving time, microwave them and serve them hot. If you must remove another food from the oven while you heat appetizers, it will not harm the food.

**Meats and Main Dish Casseroles.** As a general rule, start cooking the meat or main dish casserole first. Meats cooked with a sauce or other ingredients improve in flavor if allowed to stand a few minutes before serving. Many meats and main dishes require standing time to finish cooking.

**Vegetables.** We recommend a short standing time of 4 to 6 minutes for frozen vegetables and most fresh vegetables. During this time, heat rolls or microwave a beverage.

**Desserts.** Many desserts such as cakes, brownies or refrigerated pies may be microwaved several hours ahead of serving time. Others, such as baked apples or defrosted frozen cakes and pastries, may be prepared while dishes from the main course are being cleared from the table.

**Baked Breads and Rolls.** Warm breads and rolls for only a few seconds just before serving dinner.

Meatloaf Dinner

## MEATLOAF DINNER

Lemon Lovers Meatloaf
page 94

Baked Potatoes
with Bacon Crumbles and Sour Cream
page 206

Frozen Carrots and Peas
page 205

Apple Graham Pie
page 253

Early in the day:

Make Apple Graham Pie. Refrigerate if made more than 4 hours in advance.

About 50 minutes before serving time:

Microwave Bacon.

Prepare and microwave meatloaf.

While meatloaf cooks, scrub potatoes and prick them in several places with fork. Crumble bacon.

When meatloaf is done, set it aside in a warm place to stand while microwaving potatoes. When potatoes are done (still slightly firm to the touch), set them aside. Microwave carrots and peas.

Reheat pie while clearing the table.

# Power Levels

Microwave ovens vary in the number of power levels available, depending upon the model selected. Each power level serves a definite purpose, and should be used when recommended, if possible.

Where a choice of power levels is given, the lower setting will cook and heat more evenly, although it will take a little more time.

If your oven does not have the recommended setting, you will not get the same results. Some foods may be cooked at a higher power level with additional attention, such as frequent stirring, turning over or rotating. Other foods, especially those which are delicate or require slow simmering, should not be attempted at higher settings.

**High Power** is full (100%) power and used for fast cooking, and for foods which tolerate heat and speed. Many recipes in this book call for High Power.

**Medium High Power** is about ⅔ (70%) the oven's full power and used for ease in heating and cooking amounts or types of food which require extra attention at High Power.

**Medium Power** is about ½ (50%) the oven's full power and used for slower cooking and most meat cookery.

**Low Power** is about ⅓ (30%) the oven's full power and recommended for delicate foods which are not tolerant of fast cooking, or for foods which require slow simmering to tenderize them.

**Warm** is about 1/10 (10%) the oven's full power and used for extremely gentle cooking or for holding foods at serving temperature.

**Additional Settings** of up to 10 levels offer greater flexibility. You can match the power to the food by lowering or increasing the setting.

## HOW TO ADAPT OUR RECIPE TIMES

These recipes were developed for microwave ovens of 625 watts. However, house power varies from one part of the country to another, or during periods of peak consumption, such as early evening or extremely hot or cold weather. To prevent overcooking, recipes which are cooked by time direct you to check for doneness after the minimum cooking time, then add more time if needed. Fluctuations in power do not affect cooking with the temperature probe.

If you are uncertain about your house power, or have purchased this book for use with a different microwave oven, you can determine wattage with the following test. You will need a 1-qt. measure, a 1 cup measure and a watch or clock with a second hand.

Bring tap water from cold to boil as shown in pictures below. Time how long it takes. If your oven has 625 watts, timing will be approximately 3½ minutes, and recipe times in this cookbook should be correct for you. If your timing is significantly longer, expect recipe times to be about maximum or more. If your timing is shorter, use minimum or less time.

**Combine** 1 cup cold tap water with 8 ice cubes. Stir together for 1 minute.

**Pour Off** 1 cup of water without ice cubes. Temperature of water will be about 38°.

**Timing Carefully,** microwave water at High until many bubbles break on the surface (212°).

## HOW TO CONVERT CONVENTIONAL RECIPES FOR MICROWAVING

Before converting your recipe, study it in terms of microwaving. Is it one of the many foods which microwave well? Look for cooking techniques which are similar to microwaving techniques, such as covering, steaming or cooking in sauce or liquid. If the food requires a crisp, fried crust or very dry surface, you will prefer to cook it conventionally. Some recipes may not be exactly the same when microwaved, but you will be pleased with the results.

If the food is suitable for microwaving, refer to a Microlesson or similar recipe for cooking techniques, power level, timing and possible changes in ingredients.

Many recipes will not need changing. Moist, rich cakes, candies and moist meatloaves are examples.

Since liquids do not evaporate when microwaved, reduce the amount or add more thickening to sauces and gravies. Reduce seasonings; lack of evaporation intensifies flavors. Salt meats and vegetables after cooking. If an ingredient takes longer to microwave than the others, substitute one which is precooked or quick-cooking, as we have done in the following example.

### CONVENTIONAL SPANISH RICE

COOKING TIME: 45 to 50 min., total

*Use Chuck*

**1 lb. ground beef** . . . . . . In 10-in. skillet crumble ground beef. Cook over medium high heat 10 minutes, uncovered.

*Use 3 qt. casserole*
*Skip*

*Omit*
*Substitute 1 cup precooked rice*
*Reduce*

**1½ cups water** . . . . . . . . . Add water, rice, chili powder, onion, salt pepper and tomatoes. Stir very well. Cover and cook over medium heat 35 to 40 minutes.
**¾ cup long grain rice**
**2 tablespoons chili powder**
**2 tablespoons instant minced onion**
**2 teaspoons salt**
**⅛ teaspoon pepper**
**1 can (1-lb. 12-oz.) tomatoes**

*Microwave at High, 12 to 14 minutes, stirring after 6 minutes*

Makes 4 to 6 servings

### MICROWAVE SPANISH RICE

POWER LEVEL: High
MICROWAVE TIME: 12 to 14 min., total

**1 lb. ground chuck beef** . . Into 3-qt. casserole crumble beef. Add remaining ingredients and mix well, cutting tomatoes to distribute evenly. Cover. **Microwave at High 12 to 14 Minutes,** stirring after 6 minutes. If top of food appears dry during cooking, stir again, then return to oven to finish cooking.
**1 cup packaged precooked rice (minute)**
**1 can (1-lb. 12-oz.) tomatoes**
**1 tablespoon instant minced onion**
**2 tablespoons chili powder**
**2 teaspoons salt**
**⅛ teaspoon pepper**

Makes 4 to 6 servings

# Guide to Automatic Step-by-Step Microwaving

Automatic Step-by-Step cooking makes microwaving even more versatile and carefree. A micro-computer allows you to program a series of up to three cooking steps which the oven carries out automatically. All you do is push "Start".

This chapter shows you how to use computerized microwaving to advantage. The meal pictured at the left illustrates a few of the things you can do.

1. Chocolate Cake, Defrosting Chart, page 38
2. Split Pea Soup, page 208, Adapted for Two-Step Microwaving as in Vegetable Beef Soup, page 40
3. Chicken, How to Defrost and Cook

Prepare a hearty split-pea soup by automatic two-step microwaving. It requires no stirring, is faster than slow-simmering, and produces a creamier soup. Freeze any leftovers for future freezer-to-table microwaving.

The main course is tender, flavorful chicken. Take the individually frozen pieces from the freezer, cover with a savory sauce, and set the oven. Automatically, the oven defrosts the chicken, holds it to equalize temperature, then cooks it. No rotating is needed.

For dessert, serve a frozen cake, defrosted and held to the proper temperature for cutting and serving. The Defrost setting is so gentle, frosting doesn't start to melt, even though the cake is given no attention.

# Automatic Freezer to Table Microwaving

Step-by-step freezer to table microwaving is completely automatic, so the food is given no attention during defrosting and cooking or heating. It may take a little longer than regular microwaving since food is not turned over or broken up to speed defrosting, and lower power levels may be required for cooking or heating. Once raw food is defrosted, the actual cooking time is about the same as for fresh food. Choose foods which cook or heat well without attention, such as saucy dishes containing small or flat pieces, or foods which can be arranged in a ring.

---

## TIPS FOR FREEZING FOODS

1. Use fresh, high quality food. Freezing will not improve food of inferior quality.

2. Make sure the food, utensils and containers are clean. Freezing does not kill bacteria.

3. Undercook food slightly. Fully cooked meat, vegetables and pasta can overcook when reheated.

4. Season food lightly. Some seasonings become strong when frozen. Add more seasoning before serving, if necessary.

5. Omit crumb and cheese toppings. Add them after the food has been defrosted and heated.

6. Bake two-crust fruit or meat pies conventionally before freezing. Raw pastry does not reheat well.

7. Cool food quickly. Spread it in shallow containers and let stand 30 minutes at room temperature. Do not pour boiling hot food in pans lined with plastic film. Cool soup before packing in bulky 1-quart containers.

8. Pack food firmly and evenly to prevent air pockets. Wrap and seal tightly to avoid freezer burn.

9. Freeze at 0° or below. Place packages in coldest part of freezer with 1-inch space around them.

10. In general, store cooked food up to 6 months.

---

## RAW FOODS SUITABLE FOR FREEZER TO TABLE MICROWAVING

Italian Style Chicken, Use 'N' Care Book, p. 25

**Individually frozen** peeled, deveined shrimp, chicken parts, meatballs, Salisbury steaks or appetizers can be packaged in plastic bags and used as needed. Pieces must be separate and in a single layer for freezer-to-table microwaving. Meatloaf should be frozen in a ring. Fish steaks and separate fish fillets are good, too.

Favorite Stuffed Peppers, p. 85

**Stuffed peppers,** mushrooms, zucchini or cabbage rolls should be filled with stuffing, then frozen individually. Package in plastic bags. To conserve freezer space and for best microwaving results, sauce should be added to these foods when they are arranged in the dish for defrosting and cooking.

## COOKED FOODS SUITABLE FOR FREEZER TO TABLE MICROWAVING

Round Steak Stew, p. 97

**Soups and stews** are excellent because they contain small pieces and plenty of liquid. For convenience, freeze in single portions. If you package in plastic bags, do not freeze bags flat. Place them in serving bowls until frozen, and return to bowls for microwaving.

Chicken Ala King, p. 140

**Saucy main dishes** and vegetable casseroles provide moisture which absorbs microwave energy, shields vulnerable food and helps it heat evenly. Top slices of cooked meatloaf generously with sauce for added moisture and flavor.

Lasagna, p. 196

**Pasta and rice** casseroles with plenty of sauce freeze and reheat easily. Freeze lasagna in square dish no more than half full. Since it does not have sides or edges covered with sauce, reheat at low power or shield.

See Chart, p. 38

**Desserts** can be defrosted and warmed to serving temperature without attention. Choose fruit and nut pies or cakes and cupcakes with butter or fudge icing. Cream-filled cakes need a short Defrost and long Hold time.

# How to Freeze Foods for Microwaving

Foods cooked at home and raw foods can be frozen for later defrosting and cooking in the microwave. Certain techniques should be used in preparing the foods for freezing to assure even cooking later. Undercook pasta and rice for casseroles, as they will complete cooking when defrosted and heated. Add crumb or cheese toppings after removing from the freezer for defrosting and heating. Saucy foods work well for freezing and microwave cooking. Anything without a sauce should have moisture added (e.g., oil on chicken) to prevent drying out. If cornstarch is used as a thickener, substitute flour because cornstarch breaks down when frozen, and the resulting sauce may be too thin. Arrange foods in the best microwave shapes as identified earlier in this book.

Check page 23 to be sure that containers are appropriate for the freezer. Some paper containers, for example, are recommended only for short term freezing. Cover the container well.

Unless your freezing container is microwave-safe, pop the food out of the container before defrosting and heating. Freeze food in individual serving containers for faster defrosting and reheating.

The pictures and chart (opposite) show favorite foods you prepare often and might want to freeze for microwave cooking. Recipes for all these foods are included in this book.

**MICROLESSON: HOW TO FREEZE FOODS FOR MICROWAVING**

**Cut wings and drumsticks** from breasts and thighs. Wash and spread separately on cookie sheet to freeze, package in freezer bags.

Basic Meatloaf, p. 93

**Shape meatloaf** in a ring, using a 2-quart casserole with a paper cup in the center. Freeze slices or wedges of cooked meatloaf individually.

Basic Meatballs, p. 86

**Freeze** stuffed peppers, mushrooms, cabbage rolls and meatballs on cookie sheet, with space between. Package in plastic bags.

Chow Mein, p.118, Quick 'N' Easy Macaroni & Cheese, p. 194

**Spread foods** evenly in shallow dishes, (pie plates, 8-in. round, square or 12×8×2-inch dishes), up to 1 inch from top. Keep casseroles half full.

Round Steak Stew, p. 97

**Omit** potatoes from stews and soups. After defrosting and heating food, add canned or microwaved potatoes and reheat briefly, if needed.

Round Steak Stew, p. 97

**Submerge** pieces of meat and vegetables in broth when freezing soups and stews. Freeze pouches in dishes so they will be bowl shaped.

## TIPS FOR EVEN DEFROSTING AND HEATING

Fish with Clam Chowder

**Defrost** 1 lb. of fish fillets 4 minutes. Quarter, place in 8-in. dish; coat with 1 can undiluted soup; cover with plastic wrap. Defrost 10 minutes. Let stand 5 minutes. Cook 10 to 12 minutes at Medium.

Basic Meatloaf, p. 93  Round Steak Stew, p. 97

**Add** ½ cup water, bouillon or tomato juice to top of stew or whole cooked meatloaf before defrosting and heating. Top slices or wedges of meatloaf with sauce.

Chicken with Sauce, p. 138

**Arrange food** with saucy or frosty area on top to prevent drying or overcooking. Exceptions are lasagna and one crust pot pies, which cannot be turned over. Two crust pot pies are not recommended.

**HOME-FROZEN FOODS:** Foods prepared from recipes in this book may be defrosted and cooked or heated according to the chart below. Directions are for full or half recipes. For single servings, follow the convenience food chart for similar amounts. When possible, stir food before serving.

### FOOD YOU PREPARE YOURSELF

| ITEM | AMOUNT | DEFROST TIME | HOLD TIME | COOK TIME | COMMENTS |
|---|---|---|---|---|---|
| **Meat Balls** Raw | 1 recipe (12) 9-in. pie plate | 5 | 2½ | 7-9 High | Arrange in a circle. Cover with plastic wrap. Let stand covered 5 minutes before serving. |
| **Meatloaf** Raw | 1 recipe, round 9-in. pie plate or 8-in. round | 30 | 15 | 25-30 High | Cover with plastic wrap. Let stand 10 minutes before serving. |
| | 1 recipe, ring shape | 25 | 12½ | 15-20 High | |
| Cooked* | 1 recipe, round 9-in. pie plate or 8-in. round | 30 | 15 | 23-28 Medium High | Add ½ cup liquid. Cover with plastic wrap. Let stand 10 minutes before serving. |
| **Lasagna** | 1 recipe 12x8x2-in. | 30 | 15 | 25-30 High | Omit cheese topping. Shield as directed. Cover with wax paper. Let stand 10 minutes before serving. |
| | ½ recipe 8-in. square | 20 | 10 | 15-20 High | |
| **Chicken Ala King,*** **Chili,*** **Spaghetti Sauce.*** | 1 recipe (1½-qts.) 12x8x2-in. | 25 | 12½ | 25-30 Medium High | Cover with plastic wrap. Stir and let stand 5 minutes before serving. |
| | ½ recipe (3 cups) 1-qt. casserole | 15 | 7½ | 14-16 High | |
| **Soup** Chunky | 1-qt. in plastic freezer container or 2-qt. casserole. | 20 | 10 | 15-18 Medium High | Cover. Stir and let stand 5 minutes before serving. |
| Thin* | | 20 | 10 | 20-25 High | |
| **Beef Stew** | 1 recipe (2-qts.) 13x9x2-in. | 25 | 12½ | 25-30 High | Using 2 or 3-qt. casseroles, increase Defrost and Hold time by 5 minutes each. Add ½ cup liquid. Cover with wax paper. |
| | ½ recipe (1½ qts.) 12x8x2-in. | 25 | 12½ | 20-25 High | |
| **Fish** Frozen, raw | 1-lb. block 8-in. square dish | 10 | 5 | 10-12 Medium High | |
| **Stuffed Peppers** Raw | 1 recipe (6) 3-qt. casserole | 35 | 17½ | 24-28 High | Arrange in circle. Cover with sauce. Cover dish. Baste, then let stand 10 minutes before serving. |
| | ½ recipe (3) 1½-qt. casserole | 20 | 10 | 15-18 High | |

*Hold time is optional for these foods. Use automatic step by step combination programming.

# How to Use Defrost and Hold

Most frozen foods need to stand after the Defrost period. During this time they complete defrosting without starting to cook. Foods which are not to be cooked or heated come to proper serving temperature.

The low Defrost setting is so gentle that many foods do not require attention during defrosting. You can set the oven to Defrost, then Hold, and it will signal when the program is completed. This is especially useful for foods which you wish to serve or refrigerate immediately.

If you wish to warm pies, coffeecakes or breads for a just-baked flavor, program the oven to Defrost, Hold and Time Cook at Power Level Low (3). Set a warming time equal to the Defrosting time.

Some foods require attention during defrosting, even with the low power setting. Among them are packaged hamburger, whole chickens, roasts and custard, meringue or whipped cream pies. Follow the defrosting instructions given in other sections of this book.

## FROZEN BAKED GOODS CHART

| ITEM | DEFROST | HOLD | TIME COOK, LOW (3) |
|------|---------|------|--------------------|
| **Bread, white** | | | |
| (16-oz. loaf) | 5 | 15 | |
| **Bread, whole grain** | | | |
| (16-oz. loaf) | 7 | 20 | |
| **Dinner rolls (?)** | | | |
| **Coffeecake** | | | |
| (10- to 20-oz.) | 3-4 | 10 | 3-4 |
| **Sweet rolls** | | | |
| (7- to 10-oz.) | 2 | 5 | 2 |
| (11- to 16-oz.) | 4 | 10 | 4 |
| **Muffins** (6) | 3 | 15 | 3 |
| **Doughnuts** | | | |
| 2 | 1 | 5 | |
| 6 | 2 | 5 | |
| 8 | 3 | 5 | |
| **Cakes, iced** | | | |
| 1 layer | | | |
| (13- to 14-oz.) | 2 | 15-20 | |
| 2 layer | | | |
| (10- to 11-oz.) | 2 | 5 | |
| (24- to 30-oz.) | 6-7 | 15-20 | |
| 3 layer | | | |
| (12- to 17-oz.) | 1½-2 | 15-20 | |
| Bundt | | | |
| 3" high | 12 | 25 | |
| 4" high | 15 | 30 | |
| **Cupcakes** (6) | 1½ | 15 | |
| **Crumb cakes** | 2 | 10 | |
| **Pound cake** | | | |
| (10- to 16-oz.) | 3-4 | 5 | |
| (17- to 30-oz.) | 5-7 | 10 | |
| **Cheesecake** | | | |
| (17- to 19-oz.) plain or fruit | 3 | 10-15 | |
| (23½- to 26-oz.) plain or fruit | 4 | 15 | |
| **Pies** | | | |
| Nut (20- to 22-oz.) | 4 | 15 | 4 |
| Fruit | | | |
| (8-oz.) | 3½ | 10 | 3½ |
| (22-oz.) | 8 | 15 | 8 |
| (44-oz.) | 14 | 20 | 14 |
| Pumpkin | | | |
| (6½-oz.) | 3 | 10 | 3 |
| (24-oz.) | 12 | 20 | 12 |

# TIPS FOR DEFROST AND HOLD

**Arrange** iced cupcakes, crumb cakes or muffins 6 at a time in a circle on a plate. Warm muffins, if desired.

**Place** rectangular rolls on a trivet or paper towels to eliminate moisture. Ring placement is not needed.

**Remove** 6 to 8 plain, glazed or jelly filled doughnuts from box and place them flat on a plate.

**Defrost** 9-oz. container of whipped topping 1½ minutes, Hold 5 to 6. Spoon onto desserts or refrigerate.

**Push out** 6-oz. frozen juice concentrate from can into pitcher. Defrost 2 minutes, Hold 5; add cold water.

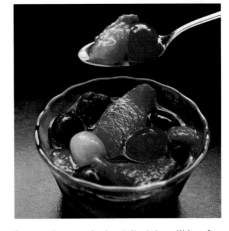

**Serve** frozen fruit while it is still icy for fresh, cool flavor. Defrost 10-oz. pouch 2 minutes, Hold 5.

**Warm** nut pies after defrosting and holding for home-baked flavor. Try fruit and pumpkin pies, too.

**Place** rectangular coffeecake lengthwise in oven. If desired, warm after defrosting and holding.

**Slice** cheesecake while it is still slightly icy; place on serving plates. Let stand a few more minutes.

# How to Use Automatic Two-Step Microwaving

If the power level of your defrost setting can be changed, you can set the oven to start microwaving at High (10), then change automatically to Medium (5). Bringing food to a boil and then simmering is a familiar cooking technique which is excellent for soups, stewed chicken, small picnic hams, briskets and corned beef. It takes less time than slow simmering.

Automatic two-step microwaving should be used only for very saucy foods. Delicate foods, like cakes, which need attention during cooking, should be microwaved in the regular way, even though the recipe may call for a change in power level. The oven's audible beep is a helpful reminder when food needs attention.

## TIPS FOR AUTOMATIC TWO-STEP MICROWAVING

**Use** 4 to 5-qt. casserole. Cover food with water to 1 inch below top of dish.

**Keep** brisket in 1 layer and weigh with plate or inverted dish cover.

**Cover.** Due to extra water, add ⅓ more time to each cooking step.

## HOW TO MICROWAVE VEGETABLE-BEEF SOUP

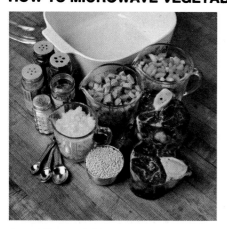

**Combine** 1 cup chopped onion, 2 cups each diced celery and carrot, ½ cup barley, 2 teaspoons salt, 1 teaspoon each celery salt and parsley flakes, ½ teaspoon each pepper and marjoram in a 5-quart casserole. Add 1 meaty soup bone.

**Add** 1 can (6-oz.) tomato paste, 8 cups water; stir and cover. Set the oven to Defrost at High (10) for 60 minutes, then Time Cook at Medium (5) for 99 minutes.

**Dice** meat from soup bone and return to soup. Stir in 4 cups water and 2 teaspoons salt. If desired, skim fat from soup before serving. Freeze leftovers in single servings for freezer-to-table microwaving.

# How to Cook and Keep Warm

If your defrost setting can be changed to a higher power level, you can program the oven to microwave with Defrost, then keep food warm with Time Cook set at power level 1. If your oven is not equipped with a warm setting, use low setting for up to ½ hour. If food requires standing time, program a Hold between Defrost and Cook.

Keeping foods warm after cooking is a technique familiar to you from conventional cooking. It can be convenient,

especially if the dinner hour is delayed or if you wish to microwave a dessert during dinner and have it ready to serve as soon as it is needed.

Do not keep foods warm longer than one hour. Sauces may thicken or foods become dry. Remember that your microwave oven reheats food rapidly without loss of moisture or flavor. Reheated food may taste fresher.

## TIPS FOR KEEPING FOODS WARM

Classic Italian Sauce, p. 192

**Choose** saucy foods with meat and vegetables well-coated with sauce.

Fresh Green Beans (add Ham as desired), See Chart, p. 204

**Select** foods which mellow and develop flavor while standing.

**Have** hot beverages, such as cider or cocoa ready to serve after cold weather activities.

**Prepare** and keep warm cherry sauce for cake or ice cream while eating main course. Stir 1 can (11-oz.) mandarin oranges into 1 can (20-oz.) cherry pie filling in 1½-qt. casserole. Set oven to Defrost at High (10) for 8 minutes, then Warm (1) about 1 hour.

Stewed Dried Fruit, p. 241

**Select** baked apples, stewed fruits or fruit sauces when you plan to keep dessert warm. Fruits retain their moisture and improve in flavor.

Chewy Spare Ribs, p. 113

**Rearrange** or stir some foods as recipe directs, then program final cooking time and keep warm time in 1 step.

# How to Delay Cooking with the "Hold" Feature

The micro-computer allows you to program a delay before the start of cooking, so you can set the oven, push the "Start" bar, and have dinner ready when you want it. You don't have to be there when microwaving starts.

Whether you cook conventionally or microwave, you should not allow food to stand at room temperature more than 2 hours. The Maximum "Hold" time of 99 minutes, 99 seconds, has been selected to keep within the safety recommended range.

If you are Time Cooking, the length of time food is held outside the refrigerator may affect cooking time. Small quantities or small pieces, such as meatballs, will need shorter cooking time than refrigerated foods.

Large or dense foods, such as chicken or roasts, will not be affected by a short "Hold" time of 30 minutes. If you hold them 99 minutes, they may need 1 or 2 fewer minutes per pound. Adjust your program to allow for this.

For delayed Time Cooking, choose foods which do not need attention. If a recipe calls for stirring or rotating halfway through the cooking time, you may eliminate this step by lowering the power level to the next named point. (For example, if your oven has 10 levels, lower High (10) to Medium-High (7).) Cook for the maximum time given in the recipe. You may have to add a little more time if the Hold period has been short.

If you are delaying Temperature Cooking, the amount of Hold time will not affect cooking, because the oven shuts off automatically when preset temperature is reached. When planning your program, you may want to allow for the fact that, if food has stood for 99 minutes, it will reach finished temperature sooner than the recipe estimates for refrigerated food. The most important thing to remember when delaying Temperature Cooking, is to insert the probe and attach it to the oven. If you fail to do this, the oven will Hold, but it cannot cook without the Probe.

## HOW TO HOLD AND TIME COOK

**Prepare** lasagna as directed on page 196. Program the oven to Hold as needed, up to 99 minutes, 99 seconds. Set Time Cook for 26 minutes; change Power Level from High (10) to Medium-High (7).

## HOW TO HOLD AND TEMPERATURE COOK

Roast Beef, See Chart, p. 110, Whole Chicken, p. 142

**Insert** Probe into prepared roast as directed in the microlesson. Program oven to "Hold" as needed, up to 99 minutes, 99 seconds, then Temperature Cook to recommended internal temperature.

# How to Time Cook and Hold

Many foods require standing time after microwaving. During this time they continue to cook, due to internal heat. Throughout this cookbook you will find pictures illustrating the use of standing time to complete cooking.

If your defrost setting can be changed to a higher power level, you can set the oven to microwave at Defrost, then Hold. The oven will signal when the food is ready. If the recipe calls for stirring, rotating or additional ingredients part way through cooking, set this time first. After you have attended to the food, program the oven to Defrost at the proper power level for time needed to complete the cooking, then Hold.

## FOODS WHICH NEED STANDING TIME

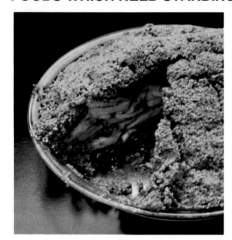

**Before standing,** Apple Graham Pie is mounded. The apple slices are loose and not layered. Their shape is defined, and they look opaque and slightly undercooked.

**After standing,** the pie has settled and is firm and easy to cut. The apple slices are layered, translucent and fully cooked. Pat crumbs around edges lightly to prevent cracking.

**Most vegetables,** especially those which have been blanched or frozen, will be tender but not overcooked after standing. Be sure peeled vegetables are covered to hold in steam.

Basic Meatloaf, p. 93

**Meatloaf** firms up and slices better after standing. Some of the juices are reabsorbed. The surface becomes dryer and appears browner.

Not The Same Old Chicken, p. 139

**Casseroles** are more savory after standing. The meat absorbs flavor from the sauce, which thickens to proper consistency.

Cake Mix Chart, p. 259

**Tube cakes,** brownies, breads and coffeecakes set during standing. Trapped heat finishes cooking on the bottom while the top surface dries.

# How and When to Use the Double-Duty™ Shelf

Whether you use the Double-Duty shelf to cook several foods at once, or microwave them in the regular way, one at a time, depends on the type of food and the amount of attention you wish to give it. Shelf cooking requires more care than regular microwaving, so you may prefer to cook a roast by itself, without attention, using the temperature probe. Microwave the potatoes and vegetables while the roast is standing. It will stay warm until sliced.

Two foods which microwave well at high power may save time when cooked on the shelf with a third food on the oven floor. Because microwave timing depends on quantity, two plates of food or two TV dinners take the same time either way; however both are ready to serve together when you use the Double-Duty shelf.

**Use** the shelf when you want several foods hot at the same time without standing or reheating.

**Heat** many small dishes of leftovers simultaneously. Small amounts can cool if heated one at a time.

**Increase** oven capacity when you have more food than will fit on the oven floor.

# How to Select Foods

## FOODS FOR THE SHELF

Always place meat, poultry, fish, main dish casseroles, stews or hearty soups on the shelf. The remaining space can be used for hard vegetables or side dishes which need more energy and can be rotated or stirred.

**Meats and Main Dishes.** Chicken pieces, ground meat, fish and casseroles need no special treatment. Roasts and whole poultry should be no higher than 4½ inches and require shielding with foil. Microwave less tender cuts, such as pot roast, at 50% of power.

## FOODS FOR THE OVEN FLOOR

The arrangement and cooking time of foods on the shelf determine what you select for the oven floor. This could be an accompaniment or dessert which microwaves easily, is rich, moist or delicate, or needs only defrosting or heating.

**A Second Accompaniment.** Foods like tomatoes, pudding or sandwiches are too delicate for the shelf, but do well on the oven floor. Frozen peas cook rapidly. Potato salad and canned vegetables are pre-cooked.

**Shelf Accompaniments.** Select hard or dense vegetables and fruits which require high energy or are not prone to overcooking. The dressing and macaroni casseroles are pre-cooked but need more energy to heat because of the deep loaf dish.

**Desserts.** Rich, moist cakes and bars microwave easily but need an open arrangement or long cooking time. Sugar added to apples attracts microwave energy. Defrost or heat fruits and pies under a closed arrangement.

# How the Shelf Works for Double-Duty™ Cooking

**The Open Arrangement** acts like a sieve. Part of the energy is absorbed by foods on the shelf, but the spaces between them allow some energy to reach the oven floor. With an open arrangement of individual pieces of meat or fish, meatballs or patties, potatoes or small dishes, it is possible to cook raw foods in the lower position.

Begin by arranging foods such as bacon, scrambled eggs, soup, potatoes, rice, meat rings or loaf, or vegetables on the oven shelf. Then place such foods as frozen coffee cake, other cakes or bars, vegetables (canned), fruit desserts or sandwiches on the oven floor. Position foods on oven floor where most microwave energy will reach it.

**The Closed Arrangement** fills most of the shelf with food. Items can be warmed on the oven floor. If you wish to cook foods in this position, you must give them additional time after foods have been removed from shelf, or choose foods for the shelf which absorb little energy.

Foods such as chicken 'n dressing, chicken

pieces, potatoes, rice, or casseroles should be used on the shelf. Fruit desserts, bakery pies, or frozen fruit are microwaved best on the oven floor when using the closed arrangement shelf cooking.

**The Staggered Arrangement** allows you to microwave two foods at the same time. Place one to the rear of the shelf and the other to the front of the oven floor. If foods are dissimilar, place the one which requires most energy on the shelf. Rotate the dishes after half the cooking time and reverse similar foods.

In this arrangement foods such as pot roast with vegetables, beef stew, turkey, TV dinners, plates of leftovers, or a layer cake are best positioned on the shelf. Another plate of leftovers, layer of cake, or TV dinner microwave well on the oven floor. Special desserts such as Apple Graham Pie, Fruit Compote, Bread Pudding or Lemon Squares can be microwaved on the oven floor with the meat dishes suggested for the oven shelf.

**An Open** arrangement of salmon ring, baked potatoes and baked apples microwaves in about 35 minutes.

**A Closed** arrangement of chicken, dressing and frozen peas and carrots cook on the shelf in about 30 minutes, while a pecan pie warms on the oven floor.

**A Staggered** arrangement of TV dinners heats in 10 to 12 minutes. Position of the dinners was reversed after half the time so they received equal energy.

# Techniques for Double-Duty™ Microwaving

Select High Power for Double-Duty microwaving. Foods cook at a slower rate because there are more of them in the oven. The exception is less tender meat, which must be microwaved at 50% of the power.

Stirring, turning, rotating or rearranging are needed for even cooking. Check often for indications that food needs attention, such as areas on batters which are more set than others, boiling in some spots, or change in color.

Remove foods from the oven when they appear done. If a food needs more cooking, microwave a little longer.

## TECHNIQUES FOR EVEN HEATING

**Stir,** rotate, rearrange or turn food over frequently.

**Cover** foods to hold in heat, speed cooking and prevent spattering.

**Shield** roasts and whole chickens to prevent overcooking. Foil helps deflect energy to other foods.

**Check** meat with probe after cooking. Set OR dial 200°. Oven will read out temperature or you can dial back until oven turns off.

# Variables that Affect Double-Duty™ Microwaving

Characteristics of food vary and affect the way they microwave. This is especially true of Double-Duty microwaving, since the ability of one food to absorb energy can change another food's rate of cooking.

In order to have all foods done at one time, you may have to start some of them earlier than others. If you substitute canned vegetables for frozen on the oven floor, you should add them later and reduce the cooking time for foods on the shelf since more energy will be available.

**Distribution and Amount of Fat.** Well-marbled meat microwaves more evenly than meat with heavy or irregular streaks of fat. Since fatty drippings attract energy, removing them speeds cooking of other foods.

**Similar Fat and Moisture Content.** Low fat or moisture foods, like carrots, take longer to cook when paired with an energy attracting food, like chicken. Dressing and chicken are similar and microwave at the same rate.

**Moisture Content.** Moisture attracts microwave energy. Dry foods, like carrots, need added water and covering. A potato's skin holds in steam produced by natural moisture. Be sure to prick potato with a fork.

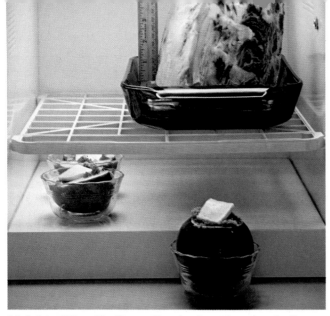

**Height of Food in Oven.** Foods placed on the shelf must be no higher than 4½ inches, or they will receive too much energy. Foods higher than 3 inches will not fit under the shelf for cooking on the oven floor.

**Quantity of Food.** Match quantities when substituting foods. Four 6-ounce baked potatoes equal one creamed potato casserole. If you change the number of potatoes, add or subtract 5 minutes cooking time per potato.

**Amount of Pre-cooking.** Canned vegetables are cooked and heat rapidly. Partially cooked and frozen vegetables need less time than blanched and frozen ones. Start fresh vegetables 5 minutes early if substituted for frozen.

**Similar Cooking Times.** Foods which have similar cooking times when microwaved separately, generally cook well together, unless they vary greatly in fat or moisture content.

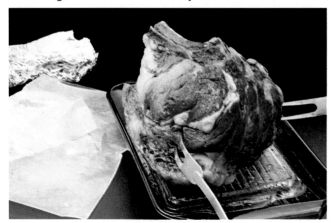

**Closeness to Oven Walls.** Energy is reflected off the walls. Food areas close to them cook faster than center. Turn roasts over to bring outside areas to the center. Rotate, rearrange or stir other foods.

**Position of Food in the Oven.** Some foods can be microwaved on either the shelf or the oven floor. The position used determines the length of cooking time.

**Uncovering During Standing.** Saucy casseroles which stand covered after regular microwaving should be uncovered after Double-Duty™ microwaving. Greater amount of steam in oven reduces evaporation of liquid.

**Covering.** Cooking time of foods not requiring covering, like potatoes or hamburgers, can be shortened by covering. This helps control rate of cooking with dissimilar foods.

Whole Roast Chicken, Rice, and Chopped Broccoli.

# Chicken Dinner

**1.** Whole Roast Chicken or
Chicken Pieces

**2.** Plain Rice* or
Corn Pudding or
Squash Combo

**3.** Frozen Chopped Broccoli (10-oz.) or
Cherry Cobbler or Streuseled Apples

(serves 4)

For recipes or cooking directions of foods above refer to the Recipe Section of this Cookbook.
*For extra flavor, add 3 Chicken Bouillon Cubes to water.

## HOW TO PREPARE CHICKEN

**Use** 12×8-in. dish. Arrange chicken breast side down. Add ¼ cup water. Cover with vented plastic wrap. Arrange chicken pieces in dish with thickest parts to the outside. Drizzle with ¼ cup melted butter; sprinkle with paprika. Cover with wax paper.

## HOW TO MICROWAVE CHICKEN DINNER

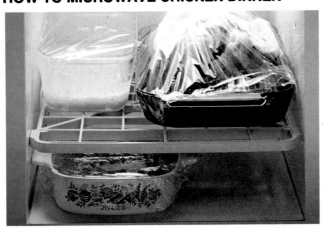

**Place** chicken on right side of shelf and top accompaniment to left rear. Arrange oven floor accompaniment below open area. Microwave at High for 15 minutes.

**Turn** whole chicken over. Brush with melted butter; sprinkle with paprika. Shield breast with 2-inch wide strip of foil. (Rotate chicken pieces ½ turn.) Stir or rotate accompaniments. Microwave 15 minutes. Remove chicken and let stand covered. Microwave accompaniments 5 minutes more. Let rice stand covered 5 to 10 minutes.

# Meatloaf Dinner

**1.** Basic Meatloaf or
Salmon Loaf or
Classic Ham Loaf

**2.** 4 ears frozen corn on cob or
4 baking potatoes or
Potato-Cheese Hurry Up

**3.** Brownies from a mix or
Frozen cut corn or peas or
chopped broccoli (10-oz.)

(serves 4)

For recipes or cooking directions of foods above refer to the
Recipe Section of this Cookbook.

## HOW TO PREPARE LOAF

**Pat** loaf mixture in 9-inch pie plate. Place a custard cup
in center of Salmon Loaf to form ring. When brownies are
included in meal, use custard cup in meat or ham loaves,
too. Cover with plastic wrap, turning back edge to vent.

Basic Meatloaf, Corn on the Cob and Brownies

## HOW TO MICROWAVE MEATLOAF DINNER

**Place** corn or potatoes to front of
shelf or casserole to right of front.
(Wrap each ear of corn in wax paper. Prepare Potato Hurry-Up in
9x5x3 glass loaf dish.) Microwave
at High for 4 minutes.

**Arrange** loaf to right rear of shelf and
brownies on oven floor under open
area. Microwave 15 minutes.

**Rotate** loaf ½ turn. Turn over and rearrange corn or baking potatoes. Stir
or rotate other accompaniments. Microwave 10 to 15 minutes. Beef or ham
loaf may need additional 2 to 3 minutes.

# Breakfast

Old Fashioned Oatmeal
Cocoa
Grapefruit
or
Bacon
4 Eggs, Scrambled
Coffee Cake

Old-Fashioned Oatmeal, Grapefruit and Cocoa.

## HOW TO MICROWAVE OATMEAL BREAKFAST

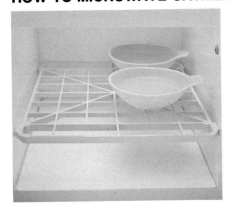

**Place** water and salt for 2 servings of old fashioned oatmeal on right of shelf. Microwave at High 5 minutes.

**Stir** oatmeal into water. Place 2 cups of cocoa on left of shelf and grapefruit halves on oven floor. Microwave 5 minutes.

**Remove** oatmeal and grapefruit. Float a marshmallow in each cup of cocoa. Microwave 1 minute.

## HOW TO MICROWAVE BACON AND EGG BREAKFAST

**Arrange** 4 strips of bacon on trivet in 12x8-inch dish. Cover with paper towel. Place to right of shelf. Microwave 3 minutes at high.

**Rotate** bacon ½ turn. Place eggs to left of shelf. Microwave 2 minutes, stirring eggs after 1 minute.

**Place** frozen coffee cake on oven floor. Stir eggs and rotate bacon. Microwave 2 to 3 minutes.

# Hot Lunch

Cups of Soup &
Sandwiches
or
Leftovers

Hot Dog and Chicken Noodle Soup.

## HOW TO MICROWAVE HOT LUNCH

**Refrigerated** soup, pictured at left takes twice as long to heat as room temperature soup, right.

**Cover** soup with plastic wrap; place to rear of shelf. Microwave 1 minute for each 5 to 6-oz. cup. (Allow 1 minute more per cup if soup is refrigerated.

**Wrap** sandwiches in paper towel. Arrange at front on oven floor. Stir soup. Microwave 1 minute per sandwich.

## HOW TO MICROWAVE LEFTOVERS

**Arrange** plates with thick or dense foods to outside and easy-to-heat foods on the inside. Cover with wax paper. Place in oven.

**Add** total time for all foods, using your cookbook heating guide. Microwave for ½ of time. Reverse position of plates. Heat for ½ of time.

**Arrange** covered bowls of leftovers with larger amounts or dense foods on shelf and smaller amounts or delicate foods below. Check often.

**Beef Stew** simmers 6 to 8 hours, controlled automatically by the temperature probe.

**In the Morning,** prepare vegetables and combine with beef, liquid and seasonings in the casserole. Place the probe with its tip submerged in liquid.

**In the Evening,** serve savory, tender beef stew. Microwave a dish of brownies in 6 to 7 minutes for a popular family dessert.

# Auto Roast Code 6 or Automatic Simmering & Slow Cooking

If your microwave oven is equipped with a simmer or slow cook setting, or Auto Roast Code 6, use it to prepare delicious, old-fashioned in-a-pot dishes. Most of these hearty foods are a meal in themselves made from popular, yet inexpensive, meats and vegetables.

In-a-pot meals are versatile enough to serve as a sustaining family dinner or easy-on-the-hostess party fare. Just add a crisp green salad, crusty French bread and microwave a quick dessert.

Slow cooked dishes, except for tall or chunky roasts, need no attention during microwaving. The temperature probe controls cooking automatically, keeping foods at a slow simmer to develop rich homemade flavor and fork tender texture. If desired, however, you may check or stir the food at any time while it's cooking.

Our recipes call for refrigerated meat, but you may also start with frozen meat. Adjust the cooking time according to the chart below. Fresh vegetables in large chunks may be started with frozen meat and will not overcook in the minimum time.

Recipes for crocks and slow cookers may be used for microwave simmering. Reduce cooking time by about 2 hours less than minimum time given in the slow cook recipe. Check food and continue as necessary.

## AUTOMATIC SIMMERING AND SLOW COOKING CHART

Always add at least ½ cup liquid when simmering foods. Place the temperature probe IN THE LIQUID with the tip submerged. It should rest on the bottom of the utensil, about halfway between the center and side of dish.

Unlike regular microwave recipes, automatic simmer recipes can microwave one or even two hours beyond their minimum time. At minimum time, food will be very tender but firm enough to hold its shape when lifted from the pot. At this point in cooking, you may wish to stir the food or even if it is a roast, turn it over. Maximum time will produce "fall off the bone" tenderness.

For soups and stews, select a microwave-proof casserole which is roomy enough to allow all the liquid in the recipe. Where large amounts of water are called for, it is important to add all of it to prevent overcooking the meat or vegetables. Also follow the tip for chili and stew for "floating" a layer of water over the top to keep it moist.

Remember, that microwave energy comes into the oven from the top and the top surfaces of tall foods are vulnerable to overcooking. Follow the utensil directions given in recipes here, but if in doubt, arrange the food in a flat even layer in a low sided dish such as a 13x9x2 in. size. This low flat arrangement works best for most of the saucy meat casseroles in this section.

Do not use a lid on the casserole. Instead, cover with plastic wrap, folding or gathering it loosely around the probe to allow steam to escape.

| ITEM | APPROXIMATE AUTOMATIC SIMMER TIME/HOURS |
|---|---|
| **Beef Chuck Roast** (5-lb.) | |
| Fresh | 6 to 8 |
| Frozen | 9 to 11 |
| **Beef Stew** | 6 to 8 |
| **Chicken, Stewing** (4 to 6-lb.) | |
| Fresh | 11 to 12 |
| Frozen | 12 to 14 |
| **Chicken, Broiler-Fryer** (2½ to 3½-lb.) | |
| Fresh | 4 to 6 |
| Frozen | 6 to 8 |

| ITEM | APPROXIMATE AUTOMATIC SIMMER TIME/HOURS |
|---|---|
| **Chili and other Saucy Hamburger Mixtures** | 11 to 13 |
| **Ham or Pork Roast** (5-lb.) | 4 to 6 |
| **Pork and Beans** | 9 to 11 |
| **Punch or Cider** (your favorite recipe) | 4 to 6 |
| **Soup Stock** | 4 to 6 |
| **Split Pea Soup** | 13 to 15 |
| **Vegetable Soup** | 3 to 4 |

# Beef

Savory stews, tender pot roasts and hearty casseroles microwave carefree with automatic simmering. To keep these meats tender and juicy, bury them beneath vegetables or cover them with liquid or sauce.

## HOW TO MICROWAVE BEEF STEW WITH AUTOMATIC SIMMERING

**Combine** 1 can undiluted beef broth, 1½ cups liquid, ½ cup minute tapioca and 2 tablespoons brown bouquet sauce in casserole.

**Bury** stew meat and vegetables under liquid. Gently pour water over surface. Insert the temperature probe and cover with plastic wrap.

**Vary** the recipe with different meats and vegetables. Special seasonings such as curry give stews international flavor.

## BASIC BEEF STEW

*To lengthen cooking of all beef stews by 1 or 2 hours, add one more can of beef broth and increase tapioca to ½ cup.*

POWER LEVEL: Automatic Simmer
MICROWAVE TIME: 6 to 8 hr.

| | |
|---|---|
| **2 lb. beef stew meat,** cut in 1-in. cubes | In 4 qt. casserole place beef, potatoes, carrots, onions, celery, broth, water, tapioca, brown bouquet sauce, salt, pepper and garlic powder. Mix together very thoroughly. Press chunks of meat to submerge under liquid. Insert temperature probe so tip rests on bottom of dish, halfway between center and side. Cover tightly with plastic wrap, arranging loosely around probe to vent. Attach cable end at receptacle. **Microwave at Automatic Simmer 6 to 8 Hours.** Stir before serving. |
| **2 large potatoes,** peeled, cut into chunks | |
| **5 medium carrots,** peeled, sliced | |
| **2 medium onions,** sliced | |
| **2 stalks celery, sliced** | |
| **1 can (10½-oz.) beef broth** | |
| **1½ cups water** | |
| **½ cup minute tapioca** | |
| **2 tablespoons brown bouquet sauce** | |
| **2 teaspoons salt** | |
| **¼ teaspoon pepper** | |
| **¼ teaspoon garlic powder** | |

Makes about 6 servings

**For Larger Amount of Beef Stew:** Use a 5-qt. casserole. Increase the above recipe by ½ the amount, except reserve 1 cup water. Invert a microwave oven proof saucer over stew to hold meat and vegetables under liquid. Gently pour reserved water around edge of dish. **Automatic Simmer 9 to 11 Hours.**

VARIATIONS

**Beef Curry:** Prepare Beef Stew, omitting potatoes and carrots. Blend ½ cup raisins and 3 tablespoons curry powder into mixture and microwave as in recipe. Serve over rice.

**Beef Goulash:** Prepare Beef Stew, omitting potatoes and carrots. Stir 2 tablespoons paprika into mixture and microwave as in recipe. Just before serving, stir in 1 cup (8-oz.) sour cream. Serve over noodles.

**Irish Stew:** Substitute lamb for beef. Just before serving, stir in 1 pkg. (10-oz.) frozen peas. **Microwave at High 5 to 10 Minutes,** until peas are tender.

## BEEF STEW WITH WINE

*This French beef stew is also called Boeuf Bouguignon. Serve with buttered wide noodles.*

POWER LEVEL: Automatic Simmer
MICROWAVE TIME: 6 to 8 hr.

Make Basic Beef Stew (left), except omit potatoes and celery. Add 1 can (6-oz.) tomato paste, 1 can (8-oz.) mushrooms, drained and substitute 1 cup red burgundy for 1 cup of the water.

Insert temperature probe so tip rests on bottom of dish, halfway between center and side. Cover tightly with plastic wrap, arranging loosely around probe to vent. Attach cable end at receptacle. **Microwave at Automatic Simmer 6 to 8 Hours.** Stir before serving. If desired, garnish each serving with crumbled bacon, (Microwave 4 to 6 strips bacon at High 4 to 6 minutes), and chopped parsley.

Makes 8 to 10 servings

# CHILI

POWER LEVEL: High (10) and Automatic Simmer
MICROWAVE TIME: 11 to 13 hr.

**To Prepare Beans:** In 3-qt. casserole place **½ lb. dry pinto beans** and **2 qt. water.** Soak overnight. Before finishing chili, drain beans and add **6 cups fresh water. Microwave uncovered at High 60 Minutes.** Drain.

| | |
|---|---|
| **2 lb. ground chuck beef** | In 4-qt. casserole crumble beef. **Microwave at High 8 to 10 Minutes,** stirring after 4 minutes. Drain off fat. |
| **2 cans (1-lb. each) tomatoes**<br>**1 can (6-oz.) tomato paste**<br>**2 medium onions, coarsely chopped**<br>**1 green pepper, coarsely chopped**<br>**2 cloves garlic, crushed**<br>**2 to 3 tablespoons chili powder**<br>**½ teaspoon pepper**<br>**½ teaspoon cumin**<br>**2 teaspoons salt**<br>**1 cup water** | Add drained beans, to-matoes, tomato paste, on-ions, peppers, garlic, chili powder, pepper, cumin and salt. Stir well. Over back of spoon, gently pour water onto top surface; do not stir in. Insert tempera-ture probe so tip rests on bottom of dish, halfway be-tween center and side. |

Cover tightly with plastic wrap, arranging loosely around probe to vent. Attach cable end at receptacle. **Microwave at Automatic Simmer 10 to 12 Hours.** Stir before serving.

Makes 8 to 10 servings

NOTE: 2 cans (1-lb. each) pinto or kidney beans, drained, may be substituted for the dry beans. No overnight soak-ing or cooking of beans is needed.

Chili

TIP: Before automatic simmering chili or stew, pour water over the back of a spoon to form a layer over surface to keep the top from drying out. Stir water into mixture before serving.

# GERMAN MEATBALLS

POWER LEVEL: Automatic Simmer
MICROWAVE TIME: 6 hr. to 8 hr.

| | |
|---|---|
| **2 lb. ground veal, pork and beef mixture**<br>**1 medium onion, finely chopped**<br>**2 eggs**<br>**2 tablespoons flour**<br>**2 tablespoons dry onion soup mix**<br>**1 teaspoon salt**<br>**¼ teaspoon pepper**<br>**Boiling water**<br>**2 bay leaves**<br>**2 tablespoons dry onion soup mix**<br>**1 teaspoon salt**<br>**1 teaspoon brown bouquet sauce (optional)** | In mixing bowl mix to-gether ground meat, on-ion, eggs, flour, soup mix, salt and pepper. Form into medium sized balls (up to ¼ cup per ball). Set aside. Pour 1-qt. boiling water into 3-qt. casserole. Add bay leaves, soup mix, salt and brown bouquet sauce. Carefully add meatballs. Add more boil-ing water if needed to cover. Insert temperature probe so tip rests in liquid on bottom of dish, half-way between center and side. |

Cover tightly with plastic wrap, arranging loosely around probe to vent. Attach cable end at receptacle. **Microwave at Automatic Simmer 6 to 8 Hours.** Thicken broth (below), if desired.

**To Thicken Broth:** Remove meatballs from broth and keep warm. Into hot broth in dish, stir mixture of ¼ cup cornstarch and ¼ cup water. Add additional dry onion soup mix for onion gravy. **Microwave at High 4 to 6 Minutes,** stirring every 2 minutes.

Makes 16 to 18 meatballs

## AUTOMATIC SIMMERING POT ROASTS

*Depending on your time schedule, select a flat roast, like beef chuck or blade roast, or a chunky roast, such as rolled rump or sirloin tip. Flat roasts may be simmered for 6 or more hours while chunky roasts must be checked after 3 to 4 hours.*

## CHUCK ROAST

*Arrange vegetables as flat as possible in dish. If vegetables cover roast, microwave for minimum time.*

POWER LEVEL: Automatic Simmer
MICROWAVE TIME: Fresh 6 to 8 hr. - Frozen 9 to 11 hr.

**1 fresh or frozen beef chuck or arm roast, about 5-lb.**
**2 to 3 potatoes, peeled and cut in large chunks**
**4 to 6 carrots, scraped and cut in chunks**
**2 large onions, cleaned and quartered**
**1 can (10½-oz.) beef consomme or beef broth**

In 13×9×2-in. dish place roast. Arrange vegetables around edges of dish. Pour consomme over top. Insert temperature probe so tip is in liquid on bottom of dish. Cover tightly with plastic wrap, arranging loosely around probe to vent. Attach cable end at receptacle. **Microwave at Automatic Simmer 6 to 8 Hours,** for fresh meat, or **9 to 11 Hours,** for frozen.

Makes 6 to 8 servings

VARIATIONS:

**Pot Roast with Wine:** Use above recipe except omit vegetables and consomme. Sprinkle 1 cup chopped onions over top of roast; top with mixture of 1 can (10-oz.) beef gravy and ½ cup red cooking wine.

**With Other Vegetables:** Fresh rutabagas, turnips, and parsnips, peeled and cut in large chunks, or 1 pkg. (32-oz.) frozen stew vegetables may be substituted for carrots and potatoes in basic recipe.

**Place** probe, with tip submerged in liquid, next to meat in microwave ovenproof cooking dish.

Chuck Roast

# Pork & Ham

Pork and ham products are delicious when simmered slowly, but they can become dry on top and care must be taken to prepare them properly for automatic simmering. Small pieces, such as ribs, chops, bacon or sausages can be buried beneath vegetables or in liquid.

Pork roasts and hams may be simmered in 13x9x2-in. dish with 3 cups water, using probe and tight cover of plastic wrap as for chuck roasts (see picture on opposite page). Simmer time will be 4 to 6 hours, but meat must be checked and if needed turned over after half the time. Look for a thick rind when you buy hams for automatic simmering.

## SMOTHERED PORK CHOPS

POWER LEVEL: High (10) and Automatic Simmer
MICROWAVE TIME: 5 to 7 Hours

| | |
|---|---|
| **6 pork rib or loin chops (¾ in. thick)**<br>**¼ cup Worcestershire sauce** | Score fat on chops and brush both sides with Worcestershire sauce. Arrange in 13 x 9 x 2-in. dish so "tails" are in center. Cover with plastic wrap, turning back one corner to vent. **Microwave at High 14 Minutes, rearranging after 7 Minutes.** Drain off liquid. |
| **2 cans (10-¾ oz. each) cream of mushroom soup**<br>**2 tablespoons water**<br>**½ teaspoon salt**<br>**¼ teaspoon pepper**<br>**1 cup chopped onion** | In small mixing bowl, combine soup, water, salt and pepper. Spread evenly over chops. Top with chopped onion. Insert temperature probe so tip is in liquid on bottom of dish. Cover tightly with plastic wrap, arranging loosely around probe to vent. **Microwave at Automatic Simmer 5 to 7 Hours.** Check at minimum time. |

Makes 6 servings.

VARIATIONS:
**Soup:** Substitute 1 can cream of celery, onion or other favorite cream soup for 1 can of the cream of mushroom soup.

**Vegetables:** Substitute 1 cup sliced celery for 1 cup chopped onion.

**Cheese:** After automatic simmering has been completed, top with 1 cup shredded cheddar cheese and **Microwave** uncovered **at High for 1 to 2 Minutes** to melt cheese.

Sausage and Tomato Stew

## SAUSAGE AND TOMATO STEW

*Of Polish origin, sometimes called Hunters Stew. Very hearty. Sauerkraut becomes mild over the long cooking period.*

POWER LEVEL: Automatic Simmer
MICROWAVE TIME: 9 to 10 hr.

| | |
|---|---|
| **2 lb. polish sausage (kielbasa) sliced diagonally in 1-in. pieces**<br>**2 cans (4-oz. each) mushroom pieces, undrained**<br>**2 large apples, peeled, cored and sliced**<br>**3 cans (1-lb. each) sauerkraut, drained**<br>**2 medium onions, chopped**<br>**2 bay leaves**<br>**10 peppercorns**<br>**1 clove garlic, minced**<br>**2 cans (1-lb. each) tomatoes**<br>**5 strips microwaved bacon, crumbled** | In 5-qt. casserole layer ½ of each of the following, in the order listed: sausage, mushrooms, apple, sauerkraut, onion, bay leaves, peppercorns, garlic and tomatoes. Sprinkle with all of bacon. Repeat layers. Insert temperature probe so tip rests in liquid in bottom of dish. Cover tightly with plastic wrap, arranging loosely around probe to vent. **Microwave at Automatic Simmer 9 to 10 Hours.** |

Makes about 10 servings

## SPARERIBS APPLES AND SAUERKRAUT

POWER LEVEL: High (10) and Automatic Simmer
MICROWAVE TIME: 8 to 10 hr.

| | |
|---|---|
| **3 to 3½ lb. lean pork spareribs, cut in serving pieces** | In 3-qt. casserole place ribs. Cover. **Microwave at High 15 Minutes,** re-arranging meat after 7 minutes. Drain off liquid. |
| **1 teaspoon salt**<br>**¼ teaspoon pepper**<br>**1 teaspoon dill weed**<br>**2 apples, quartered, cored and sliced**<br>**2 large onions, thinly sliced**<br>**1 can (16-oz.) sauerkraut**<br>**1 cup water** | Sprinkle salt, pepper, and dill weed over ribs. Cover with apple slices, onion slices, undrained sauerkraut, then water. Insert temperature probe so tip rests in water on bottom of dish. |

Cover tightly with plastic wrap, arranging loosely around probe to vent. Attach cable end at receptacle. **Microwave at Automatic Simmer 8 to 10 Hours.**

Makes 3 to 4 servings

## HAM AND SHRIMP CREOLE

*Fresh onion and pepper, chopped, may be used; measure 1½ cups of each.*

POWER LEVEL: Automatic Simmer
MICROWAVE TIME: 6 to 8 hours

| | |
|---|---|
| **2 lb. cooked ham cut in ¾″ cubes**<br>**2 cans (4½ oz.) whole shrimp, drained, reserve liquid**<br>**2 cans (10-oz. each) condensed tomato bisque soup**<br>**1 cup dry red wine**<br>**1 pkg. (12-oz.) frozen chopped onion**<br>**1 pkg. (12-oz.) frozen chopped green pepper**<br>**1 pkg. (10-oz.) frozen chopped okra**<br>**1 teaspoon creole seasoning or chili powder**<br>**1 teaspoon salt**<br>**½ teaspoon brown bouquet sauce**<br>**¼ teaspoon pepper**<br>**½ teaspoon hot pepper sauce (tabasco)**<br>**Shrimp liquid plus water to total 1 cup** | In 4-qt. casserole, place the ham, shrimp, soup, wine, onion, pepper, okra, creole seasoning, salt, bouquet sauce, pepper and liquid pepper seasoning. Mix together very well. Press chunks of meat to submerge under liquid. Over back of spoon, gently pour shrimp liquid and water mixture onto top surface. Do not stir in. Insert temperature probe so tip rests on bottom of dish. Cover with plastic wrap, arranging loosely around probe to vent. Attach cable end at receptacle. **Microwave at Automatic Simmer 6 to 8 Hours.**<br><br>Stir before serving.<br><br>Makes about 6 servings. |

## OLD-FASHIONED BAKED BEANS

POWER LEVEL: High (10) and Automatic Simmer
MICROWAVE TIME: 9 to 11 hours, total.

**To Prepare Beans:** In 4-qt. casserole, place **1½ lb. (3½ cups) navy (pea) beans** with enough **water** to cover, about 2 qts. Let stand at room temperature to soak several hours or overnight.

After soaking, drain water from beans and add **1 teaspoon soda, 1 teaspoon salt** and **6 cups hot water.** Cover casserole with lid or plastic wrap. **Microwave at High for 1 hour,** stirring after 30 minutes until beans are almost tender. Drain.

| | |
|---|---|
| **1 cup brown sugar, packed**<br>**1 cup ketchup**<br>**2 cups hot water**<br>**½ cup chopped onion**<br>**¼ cup prepared mustard**<br>**¼ cup molasses**<br>**¼ cup vinegar**<br>**1 tablespoon salt**<br>**6 slices bacon** | In small mixing bowl stir together well the brown sugar, ketchup, water, onion, mustard, molasses, vinegar, and salt. Add and blend well into drained beans. Layer bacon on top of beans.<br>Cover tightly with plastic wrap, arranging loosely around probe to vent. Attach cable end at receptacle. **Microwave at Automatic Simmer 8 to 10 Hours.** Stir before serving. |

Makes 8 to 10 servings.

## BACON WITH FRESH GREEN BEANS

POWER LEVEL: High (10) and Automatic Simmer
MICROWAVE TIME: 10 to 11 hr.

| | |
|---|---|
| **9 slices bacon, cut in 1-in. pieces** | In 3-qt. casserole place bacon pieces. **Microwave at High 4 to 5 Minutes,** until just partially cooked. Do not drain. |
| **1 lb. fresh green beans washed and cut**<br>**2 onions, sliced**<br>**2 cups water**<br>**1 bay leaf, optional**<br>**1 clove garlic, minced**<br>**1 teaspoon salt**<br>**¼ teaspoon pepper** | To bacon and fat in dish, add beans and stir. Cover with onions. In 1-qt. measure stir together water, bay leaf, garlic, salt and pepper. Add to casserole. |

Insert temperature probe so tip rests in water on bottom of dish, halfway between center and side. Cover tightly with plastic wrap, arranging loosely around probe to vent. Attach cable end at receptacle. **Microwave at Automatic Simmer 10 to 11 Hours.**

Makes about 4 servings

VARIATION:
**With Ham:** Substitute ½ lb. ham cubes or pieces for bacon. Microwave as above.

# Poultry

Slowly simmered chicken is an international favorite. It's tender, tasty and economical, too. With automatic simmering you can microwave stewing chickens or broiler-fryers, either fresh or frozen, without attention. Just put them in the pot and forget about them until dinner time.

## STEWING CHICKEN

POWER LEVEL: Automatic Simmer
MICROWAVE TIME: 11 to 12 hr.

| | |
|---|---|
| **1 large onion,**.......................<br>**chopped**<br>**1 stewing chicken (4 to<br>6-lb.) cut up**<br>**4 cups water**<br>**2 tablespoons chicken<br>bouillon granules**<br>**1 teaspoon salt** | In 5-qt. casserole, spread out onions in even layer. Cover with chicken pieces, bony-side-up, with meatiest pieces to edges of dish. In small bowl mix water, bouillon granules and salt. Pour over chicken. |

Insert temperature probe so tip rests in liquid on bottom of dish, halfway between center and edge. Cover tightly with plastic wrap, arranging loosely around probe to vent. Attach cable end at receptacle. **Microwave at Automatic Simmer 11 to 12 hours.** Let pieces stand in broth until cool. Strip off skin and remove meat from bones. Skim fat from broth.

Makes about 1 qt. meat (about 8 servings)

**CHICKEN 'N' DUMPLINGS:** Prepare dough for Fluffy Dumplings (recipe with Bohemian Steak, Meat Chapter) or use favorite recipe. To broth in casserole, add the de-boned and cut up chicken pieces along with a mixture of ¼ cup each cornstarch and cold water. **Microwave at High until hot and bubbly, 5 to 8 Minutes.** Drop dumplings around edges of dish. **Microwave at Medium 7 to 9 Minutes,** until dumplings appear set and dry.

**CHICKEN 'N' NOODLES OR RICE:** For noodle variation, prepare homemade noodles (recipe with Short Ribs, Meat Chapter) except do not dry them by microwaving; or use 1 to 1½ cups packaged egg noodles. After cooked meat has been removed, and fat skimmed off, **Microwave broth at High until boiling, 5 to 8 Minutes.** Add noodles or, for rice variation, add ¾ cup long grain rice and continue to **Microwave at High 10 to 12 Minutes,** for noodles or **15 to 20 Minutes** for rice, until tender, stirring after half of time. Add deboned and cut up chicken. **Microwave at High 10 Minutes more,** until thickened, well blended and bubbly.

## CHICKEN FRICASSEE

POWER LEVEL: Automatic Simmer and High (10)
MICROWAVE TIME: 11 to 12 hr.

| | |
|---|---|
| **1 stewing chicken (4 to<br>6-lb.), cut up**<br>**2 teaspoons salt**<br>**1 teaspoon paprika**<br>**1 bay leaf**<br>**2 medium onions,<br>sliced**<br>**3 stalks celery, sliced**<br>**2 carrots, pared and<br>sliced**<br>**1 cup chicken broth** | ..In 5-qt. casserole arrange chicken pieces. Sprinkle with salt, paprika and top with bay leaf. Add onions, celery and carrots. Pour chicken broth over top. Insert temperature probe so tip rests in broth on bottom of dish, halfway between center and side. |

Cover tightly with plastic wrap, arranging loosely around probe to vent. Attach cable end at receptacle. **Microwave at Automatic Simmer 11 to 12 Hours.** Cool. Strip off skin and remove bones from chicken. Skim fat from broth and thicken (see below) just before serving.

**To Thicken Broth:** Stir together ½ cup flour and ½ cup water well. Add chicken pieces to broth and stir in flour-water mixture. **Microwave at High 10 to 13 Minutes,** until hot and bubbly. Serve over mashed potatoes or noodles.

## HOW TO STEW CHICKEN WITH AUTOMATIC SIMMERING

**Submerge** chicken pieces in liquid and add seasoning. Place the probe with the tip in liquid halfway between the center and side of the dish.

**Strip Meat** from bones after microwaving. Use meat in cooked chicken recipes or return it to the casserole.

**Vary** chicken in broth by dropping dumplings on top or adding rice or noodles. Microwave as directed in the recipes below.

Simmered Chicken

## SIMMERED CHICKEN

*One of the simplest of ways to cook chicken, and one of the best.*

POWER LEVEL: Automatic Simmer
MICROWAVE TIME: Fresh 4 to 6 hr.—
                    Frozen 5 to 7 hr.

| | |
|---|---|
| 1 whole chicken (2½ to 3½-lb.)<br>Paprika<br>1 cup chicken broth | In 3-qt. casserole place chicken. Rub chicken with paprika. Add broth. |

Insert temperature probe so tip is in liquid on bottom of dish. Cover tightly with plastic wrap, arranging loosely around probe to vent. Attach cable end at receptacle. **Microwave at Automatic Simmer 4 to 6 Hours** for fresh chicken; or **5 to 7 Hours** for frozen.

Makes 4 servings

## SPANISH STYLE CHICKEN

*This is a version of the famous Arroz Con Pollo.*

POWER LEVEL: Automatic Simmer and High (10)
MICROWAVE TIME: 4 hr. to 6 hr.

| | |
|---|---|
| 1 chicken (2½ to 3½-lb.) cut up<br>1 teaspoon salt<br>¼ teaspoon pepper<br>¼ teaspoon chili powder<br>1 clove garlic, minced<br>⅛ teaspoon saffron powder<br>2 cups chicken broth<br>2 tablespoons sherry | In 3-qt. casserole, place chicken bony-side-up and meaty pieces around edges. Sprinkle with salt, pepper, chili powder, garlic and saffron. Add broth and sherry. Insert temperature probe so tip rests in liquid on bottom of dish, halfway between center and side. |

Cover tightly with plastic wrap, arranging loosely around probe to vent. Attach cable end at receptacle. **Microwave at Automatic Simmer 4 to 6 Hours.**

**TO FINISH:** To casserole, **add 2 cups cooked rice, 1 pkg. (10-oz.) defrosted frozen peas and ½ cup sliced stuffed olives.** Cover and **Microwave at High 5 Minutes,** until vegetables are hot.

Makes 4 to 6 servings

## CHICKEN IN ITALIAN SAUCE

*Sometimes known as Chicken Marengo.*

POWER LEVEL: Automatic Simmer and High (10)
MICROWAVE TIME: 4 to 6 hr.

| | |
|---|---|
| 1 chicken (2½ to 3½-lb.) cut up<br>1 pkg. (1½-oz.) spaghetti sauce mix<br>½ cup water or dry white wine | In 2-qt. casserole, place chicken bony-side-up and meaty pieces around edges. Stir together sauce mix and liquid; pour over top. |

Insert temperature probe so tip rests in liquid on bottom of dish, halfway between center and side. Cover tightly with plastic wrap, arranging loosely around probe to vent. Attach cable end at receptacle. **Microwave at Automatic Simmer 4 to 6 Hours.** Garnish as described below.

**To Garnish:** Stir **2 peeled fresh tomatoes,** cut in quarters and **¼ lb. fresh mushrooms,** cut in ½-in. slices, into chicken. **Microwave at High 5 Minutes** to heat. If desired, serve with ½ cup sliced black olives and ¼ cup snipped fresh parsley. Serve over rice.

## CHICKEN IN WINE

*Coq au Vin is its French name. This makes a delicious supper when served with rice and a salad.*

POWER LEVEL: Automatic Simmer
MICROWAVE TIME: 4 to 6 hr.

| | |
|---|---|
| 1 medium onion, chopped (¾ cup)<br>1 chicken (2½ to 3½-lb.) cut up<br>1 tablespoon paprika<br>3 tablespoons minute tapioca<br>Sauce (below) | In 3-qt. casserole, spread onion evenly. Rub paprika on chicken then arrange chicken bony-side-up with meaty pieces around edges. Sprinkle with tapioca. Pour sauce (below) over all. Insert temperature probe so tip rests in sauce on bottom of dish. Cover tightly with plastic wrap, arranging loosely around the probe to vent. Attach cable end at receptacles. **Microwave at Automatic Simmer 4 to 6 Hours.** |
| 1 lb. large fresh mushrooms, quartered<br>2 tablespoons fresh snipped parsley | Add mushrooms and parsley to casserole. Cover and **Microwave at High 5 minutes** to heat. |

Makes about 4 servings.

**Sauce:** In small bowl stir together **1 cup white wine, ½ bay leaf, ½ teaspoon thyme, 1 teaspoon salt and ⅛ teaspoon freshly ground pepper.**

# Soups & Sauces

With automatic simmering you can microwave good, old-fashioned soups, mellowed sauces and the full-bodied broth essential to many Italian, French and Chinese recipes. Freeze poultry carcasses, or roast bones with some meat on them, until you have enough for stock. If you bone meat before cooking, save these scraps, too. When making stock for soup, add extra chicken backs or beef soup bones for flavor.

Split Pea Soup

## BEAN SOUP

POWER LEVEL: High (10) and Automatic Simmer
MICROWAVE TIME: 13 to 15 hr.

| | |
|---|---|
| **1 lb. navy beans** . . . . . . . . <br> **Water** | Wash and sort beans. Place in 4-qt. casserole with water to cover and soak overnight. In the morning, drain beans and add 6 cups fresh water. **Microwave uncovered at High 60 Minutes.** |
| **1 meaty ham bone or 2 <br> cups diced cooked <br> ham** <br> **1 cup celery, finely <br> chopped** <br> **1 onion, finely chopped** <br> **2 tablespoons parsley, <br> finely chopped** <br> **1 teaspoon salt** <br> **¼ teaspoon pepper** <br> **1 bay leaf** | . . .To beans, add ham, celery, onion, parsley, salt, pepper and bay leaf. Insert temperature probe so tip rests in liquid on bottom of dish, halfway between center and side. Cover tightly with plastic wrap, arranging loosely around probe to vent. Attach cable end at receptacle. |

**Microwave at Automatic Simmer 12 to 14 Hours,** until beans are very tender. Remove ham bone and bay leaf. Cut meat off bone, return meat to bean soup. Add water to thin, if desired. Serve hot.

Makes 8 to 10 servings

## CHICKEN NOODLE SOUP

A very nice chicken soup may be made by adding about 1-qt. chicken broth to Chicken 'N' Noodles, page 59.

## SPLIT PEA SOUP

*For a creamy version of this chunky soup, puree in blender before adding ham.*

POWER LEVEL: High (10) and Automatic Simmer
MICROWAVE TIME: 13 to 15 hr.

| | |
|---|---|
| **1 lb. dried split peas** . . . . . . . . . . | In 4-qt. casserole place peas with water to cover. Soak overnight. Drain. Add 6 cups fresh water. **Microwave uncovered at High 60 minutes.** |
| **1 can (1-lb.) tomatoes, <br> cut up** <br> **1½ cups sliced carrots** <br> **1 cup chopped celery** <br> **¾ cup chopped onion** <br> **1 clove garlic, minced** <br> **1 teaspoon salt** <br> **1 meaty ham bone** | . . . . . Add tomatoes, carrots, celery, onion, garlic and salt. Stir well and add ham bone. Insert temperature probe so tip is in liquid touching bottom of dish. Cover tightly with plastic wrap, arranging loosely around probe to vent. |

Attach cable end at receptacle. **Microwave at Automatic Simmer 12 to 14 Hours.** Cut meat off bone and return to soup. Thin with water, if desired.

Makes about 12 servings.

## HOW TO MAKE BASIC STOCK

**Save** meat and bones until you have enough. (See Basic Beef Stock.) Add water, seasonings and carrots, onions and celery tops for flavor.

**Strip** meat from bones after microwaving and return it to stock when making soup. Or, strain stock and freeze for broth.

**Skim** fat if using immediately, or refrigerate stock until fat solidifies and can be lifted off.

## BASIC BEEF STOCK

Substitute 1 to 2 lb. bony chicken pieces for beef to make chicken stock.

POWER LEVEL: Automatic Simmer
MICROWAVE TIME: 4 to 6 hr.

**2-3 lbs. soup bones or** ........
  **beef shortribs**
**1 teaspoon salt**
**1 teaspoon celery salt**
**1 small onion,**
  **chopped**
**1 cup diced carrots**
**½ cup diced celery**
  **Water**

In 5-qt. casserole place meaty bones, salt, celery salt, onion, carrots, celery and water to cover. Insert temperature probe so tip rests on bottom of dish, halfway between center and side. Cover tightly with plastic wrap, arranging loosely around probe to vent. Attach cable end at receptacle. **Microwave at Automatic Simmer 4 to 6 Hours.** Remove fat from surface. Remove meat from bones; chop and return to broth.

Makes about 2½ quarts stock.

**Make Soup or Basic Stock** ahead and freeze in one cup containers. Defrost rapidly by microwaving when ready to use. Any main dishes which call for water will taste richer if you substitute stock.

## MINESTRONE

*The popular Italian vegetable soup.*

POWER LEVEL: Automatic Simmer
MICROWAVE TIME: Stock 4 to 6 hr.—
                    Soup 6 to 8 hr.

**Basic Beef Stock** ................
  **(recipe left)**
**1 medium onion,**
  **chopped**
**2 carrots, diced**
**2 stalks celery with**
  **tops sliced**
**1 cup diced leaks,**
  **optional**
**1 can (1-lb.) tomatoes**
**1 pkg. (10-oz.) frozen**
  **mixed vegetables**
**½ cup uncooked**
  **vermicelli, broken**
  **into 2-in. pieces**
**1 zucchini, sliced**
**1 cup shredded**
  **cabbage**
**2 teaspoons dried basil**
**1 clove garlic, minced**
**1 tablespoon salt**
**1 teaspoon oregano**
**1 can (6-oz.) tomato**
  **paste**
  **Water**

Prepare stock in 5-qt. casserole as in recipe. Cool and return meat and marrow from bones to stock. Add onion, carrots, celery, leeks, tomatoes, mixed vegetables, vermicelli, zucchini, cabbage, basil, garlic, salt and oregano. Add tomato paste for heartier flavor. Submerge the chunks beneath broth surface, add additional water if needed to cover. Insert temperature probe so tip rests on bottom of dish, halfway between center and side. Cover lightly with plastic wrap, arranging loosely around probe to vent. Attach cable end at receptacle. **Microwave at Automatic Simmer 6 to 8 Hours.** To serve, ladle into bowls and sprinkle with Parmesan cheese. Serve with crusty bread.

Makes 8 to 10 servings

## VEGETABLE BEEF SOUP

POWER LEVEL: Automatic Simmer
MICROWAVE TIME: Stock 4 to 6 hrs.—
Soup 3 to 4 hrs.

| | |
|---|---|
| **Basic Beef Stock** <br> **(recipe opposite page)** | Prepare stock in 5-qt. casserole as in recipe. Cool and return meat and marrow from bones to stock. |
| **2 cups diced, peeled potatoes** <br> **1 can (1-lb.) whole kernel corn, undrained** <br> **1 can (1-lb.) tomatoes, cut up** <br> **2 diced, peeled turnips** <br> **1 can (6-oz.) tomato paste** <br> **4 beef bouillon cubes** <br> **½ teaspoon marjoram** <br> **½ teaspoon salt** <br> **¼ teaspoon pepper** | Add potatoes, corn, tomatoes, turnips, tomato paste, bouillon, marjoram, salt and pepper. Stir. With back of spoon press meat and vegetable chunks to submerge under water. Insert temperature probe so tip rests in liquid on bottom of dish, halfway between center and side. Cover tightly with plastic wrap, arranging loosely around probe to vent. Attach cable end at receptacle. **Microwave at Automatic Simmer 3 to 4 Hours.** |

Makes 8 to 10 servings

## SPAGHETTI SAUCE

*If desired, you can omit sauteeing the onion in butter by lengthening simmering time 2 hours.*

POWER LEVEL: High (10) and Automatic Simmer
MICROWAVE TIME: 3 to 4 hr.

| | |
|---|---|
| **2 cups chopped onion** <br> **2 tablespoons butter** | In 3-qt. casserole, place onion and butter. **Microwave at High 4 to 5 minutes,** until onion is slightly cooked. |
| **2 cans (1-lb. 14-oz.) tomatoes, cut up** <br> **2 cans (6-oz.) tomato paste** <br> **½ cup snipped parsley** <br> **¼ cup brown sugar** <br> **2 teaspoons salt** <br> **1 tablespoon dried oregano, crushed** <br> **½ teaspoon dried thyme, crushed** <br> **2 bay leaves** | Add tomatoes, tomato paste, parsley, brown sugar, salt, oregano, thyme, and bay leaves. Mix together well. Insert temperature probe so tip is in liquid on bottom of dish. Cover tightly with plastic wrap, arranging loosely around probe to vent. Attach cable end at receptacle. **Microwave at Automatic Simmer 3 to 4 Hours.** |

Makes 2 to 3 quarts

TIP: Freeze in ice cube trays. When frozen hard, remove to plastic bags. Only amounts needed can be easily thawed and/or heated.

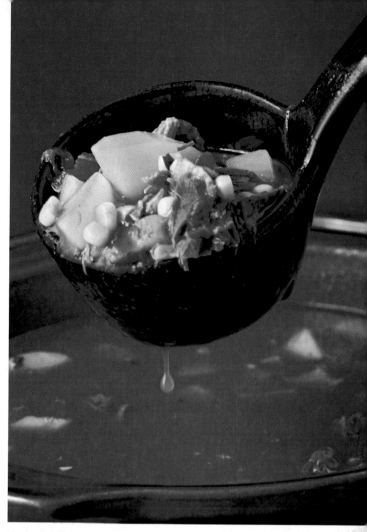

Vegetable Soup

## MARINARA SAUCE

*This sauce starts with convenience ingredients and results 3 to 4 hours later, in a rich homemade taste. Serve with meatballs, spaghetti or chicken.*

POWER LEVEL: Automatic Simmer
MICROWAVE TIME: 3 to 4 hr.

| | |
|---|---|
| **1 jar (2-lb) spaghetti sauce** <br> **1 can (28-oz.) tomatoes, cut up** <br> **1 can (16-oz.) stewed tomatoes, cut up** <br> **1 can (10½-oz.) tomato puree** <br> **1 cup onion, chopped** <br> **½ cup red cooking wine** <br> **1 tablespoon sugar** <br> **2 teaspoons garlic powder** <br> **1 teaspoon thyme** | In 4-qt. casserole mix together spaghetti sauce, tomatoes, stewed tomatoes, tomato puree, onion, wine, sugar, garlic powder and thyme. Insert temperature probe so tip rests on bottom of dish, halfway between center and side. Cover tightly with plastic wrap, arranging loosely around probe to vent. Attach cable end at receptacle. **Microwave at Automatic Simmer 3 to 4 Hours.** |

Makes 2 to 3 quarts.

# Appetizers & Hot Snacks

Microwaving makes exciting hot appetizers and snacks as easy to serve as the more ordinary cold ones. A minute or two after your guests arrive, you can offer them hot and tempting nibbles to stimulate appetites and conversation. Since all the preparation is done ahead, you can serve an unusual variety without last minute fuss.

1. Bacon Poles, page 71
2. Seaside Cheese Dip, page 69
3. Curried Pineapple and Piggies, page 73
4. Cheese Crock, page 70

**Arrange** pieces, such as meatballs, mushrooms or canapes in a circle for even heating. To serve, place a bowl of sauce or another snack, such as pretzels, in center.

## MICROLESSON:

Appetizers and snacks are among the easiest foods to microwave. On these pages you'll find the basic principles of microwaving which assure success, some possibilities unique to microwave, and helpful ideas for using your microwave oven to make entertaining easier and more varied.

**The Temperature Probe** heats dips, such as Chili Con Queso, page 69 to correct serving temperature. Stir dip well before serving.

**Dry Mixtures,** such as Party Mix, page 69, must be stirred, as in conventional cooking, but they cook much faster.

**Wooden or Plastic Picks,** even those with frills, may be used in the microwave oven. Use bamboo skewers instead of metal, when making kabobs.

**Cover** foods according to the amount of moisture needed. Paper towels absorb it, waxed paper holds in a little, plastic wrap and lids seal it in.

**Soften Cream Cheese** for spreads or dips. Remove foil wrap and microwave at Medium 1 to 1½ Minutes.

**Dry Croutons,** page 69, for snacks, using leftover bread, herbs and butter. Also great for salads and soups.

**Sloppy Joe Filling,** canned or deli, spooned on buttered bun, makes an easy snack in ½ Minute at High.

**Warm Cheese** from refrigerator ½ to 1 Minute at Medium High to make it easy to slice.

**Use Paper Plates** for heating and serving. Let guests microwave their own hors d'oeuvres.

**Shell Nuts** easily. Microwave 2 cups pecan or Brazil nuts in 1 cup water 4 to 5 Minutes at High.

**Soften Tortillas** and crepes in the package or damp towel by microwaving at High ½ to 1 Minute.

**Refresh Salty Snacks,** by microwaving a few seconds at High. Let stand to crisp.

**For Fast Canapes,** spread ham salad or cheese spread on crackers. Microwave at High a few seconds.

## SOUR CREAM DIPS WITH VARIATIONS

POWER LEVEL: Low (3)                    TEMP:  90°
APPROX. MICROWAVE TIME: 4 to 5 min.

1. Use **1 cup (8-oz.) dairy sour cream** as a basis for the following variations. In 1-qt. casserole or microwave ovenproof bowl, stir sour cream together with ingredients of one of the variations. Insert temperature probe so tip is in center of dip. Cover with plastic wrap, arranging loosely around probe to vent.
2. Attach cable end at receptacle. **Microwave at Low. Set Temp, Set 90°.** Stir before serving.

NOTE: Due to the delicate nature of sour cream, it is best microwaved at **Low.**

VARIATIONS:

### ONION DIP

**1 packet (½ of 2⅞-oz. box) onion soup mix**
**1 teaspoon lemon juice**
**1 tablespoon sherry wine (optional)**

Makes about 1 cup

### ZIPPY DIP

**2 tablespoons chili sauce**
**1 tablespoon minced green pepper**

Makes about 1 cup

### DEVILED HAM DIP

**1 can (4½-oz.) deviled ham**
**2 tablespoons chopped green olives**
**2 teaspoons instant minced onion**
**⅛ teaspoon pepper**

Makes about 1½ cups

### PUB DIP

POWER LEVEL: Medium (5)                    TEMP:  130°
APPROX. MICROWAVE TIME: 6 to 8 min.

**Cook Code:**   65

**2 jars (5-oz. each)** ...... In 1½-qt. casserole stir to-
**sharp Old English** gether cheeses, beer,
**cheese spread,** Worcestershire sauce and
**softened** pepper sauce. Insert tem-
**1 pkg. (8-oz.) cream** perature probe so tip is in
**cheese, softened** center of dip. Attach cable
**⅓ cup beer** end at receptacle. **Micro-**
**1 teaspoon** **wave at Medium. Set**
**Worcestershire** **Temp, Set 130°.**
**sauce**
**5 to 6 drops hot pepper**
**sauce (optional)**
**4 strips bacon,** ......... When oven signals, stir in
**microwaved crisp** crumbled bacon. Serve
**and crumbled** with pretzels, crackers or
other crisp dippers.

Makes about 1½ cups

## CREAM CHEESE DIPS WITH VARIATIONS

POWER LEVEL: Medium (5)                    TEMP:  130°
APPROX. MICROWAVE TIME: 4 to 7 min.

**Cook Code:**  45

1. Use **1 pkg. (8-oz.) cream cheese** as a basis for the following variations. In 1-qt. casserole place cream cheese. **Microwave at Medium 1 to 1½ Minutes,** to soften. Stir in ingredients of one of the variations. Insert temperature probe so tip is in center of dip. Cover with plastic wrap, arranging loosely around probe to vent.
2. Attach cable end at receptacle. **Microwave at Medium. Set Temp, Set 130°.** Stir before serving.

VARIATIONS:

### SHRIMP DIP

**1 can (7-oz.) broken shrimp, drained**
**2 teaspoons ketchup**
**1 teaspoon instant minced onion**
**1 teaspoon prepared mustard**
**1 teaspoon Worcestershire sauce**
**¼ teaspoon garlic salt**

Makes about 2 cups

### HOT CRAB DIP

**1 can (6 - 8-oz.) crab meat, drained and flaked**
**2 tablespoons milk**
**1 tablespoon instant minced onion**
**1 tablespoon lemon juice**
**1 tablespoon sherry wine (optional)**
**1½ teaspoons grated lemon rind**
**1 teaspoon cream-style horseradish**

Makes about 2 cups

## APPETIZER CONVENIENCE FOODS

Many pastry-style frozen appetizers can be microwaved rapidly at High Power. However, pastry will not be as crisp as when baked conventionally for longer time.

**Frozen Egg or Pizza Rolls:** For 1 pkg. of 6 rolls (12-oz.) place on plate suitable for microwave oven. **Microwave at High 3 to 4 Minutes,** turning rolls over after 2 minutes. Let stand to crisp about 5 minutes before serving. **Cook Code:** 30.

**Frozen Prepared Sandwiches:** Remove from foil package and wrap in paper towel. For each sandwich, **Microwave at High 1 to 1½ Minutes.** Let stand about 5 minutes to continue heating through. **Cook Code:** 10.

**Canned Sausages:** (About 5-oz.) Drain and cut into pieces of desired size. Place on plate suitable for microwave oven. Add ½ cup chili sauce or cocktail sauce as desired. Cover with wax paper. **Microwave at High 1 to 1½ Minutes. Cook Code:** 10.

## CHILI CON QUESO DIP

*Served fondue style, and accompanied by a salad, Chili Con Queso makes a nice informal luncheon. Dip is very thick and should be served with sturdy dippers such as large tortilla chips.*

POWER LEVEL: Medium High (7)      TEMP: 140°
APPROX. MICROWAVE TIME: 12 to 14 min.

**Cook Code: 127**

| | |
|---|---|
| **1 lb. block pasteurized processed cheese, diced in 1½-in. pieces**<br>**1 can (1-lb.) chili with beans** | In 1½-qt. casserole stir together diced cheese and chili. |

Insert temperature probe so tip is in center of dip. Attach cable end at receptacle. **Microwave at Medium High. Set Temp, Set 140°.**

When oven signals, stir well. Let stand a few minutes before serving. Serve with tortilla chips.

Makes about 3 cups

VARIATION: A smaller amount can be made by using a 1-qt. casserole, an 8-oz. block of cheese and 1 can (7½-oz.) of chili with beans. Approximate microwave time is 5 to 7 minutes.

## SEASIDE CHEESE DIP

POWER LEVEL: Medium (5)      TEMP: 130°
APPROX. MICROWAVE TIME: 11 to 14 min.

**Cook Code: 115**

| | |
|---|---|
| **1 can (6½-oz.) minced or chopped clams**<br>**2 jars (5-oz. each) sharp Old English cheese spread, softened**<br>**1 pkg. (8-oz.) cream cheese, softened**<br>**1 tablespoon Worcestershire sauce**<br>**½ medium green pepper, chopped (about ⅓ cup)**<br>**2 green onions, chopped (about 2 tablespoons)** | Drain clams, saving ¼ cup juice. In 1½-qt. casserole place drained clams, with reserved juice, along with sharp cheese spread, cream cheese, Worcestershire sauce, pepper and onion. Stir together well. |

Attach cable end at receptacle. **Microwave at Medium. Set Temp, Set 130°.**

When oven signals, stir before serving. Excellent with fresh raw vegetables such as celery, cucumbers, radishes and cauliflowerets.

Makes about 2 cups

## PARTY MIX

POWER LEVEL: High (10)
MICROWAVE TIME: 6 to 7 min., total

| | |
|---|---|
| **6 tablespoons butter**<br>**4 teaspoons Worcestershire sauce**<br>**1 teaspoon seasoned salt** | In 13×9×2-in. dish place butter, Worcestershire sauce and salt. **Microwave at High 1 Minute,** or until butter is melted. Stir well. |
| **2 cups corn chex**<br>**2 cups wheat chex**<br>**2 cups rice chex**<br>**2 cups thin stick pretzels**<br>**1½ cups (12-oz.) mixed nuts** | Add cereals, pretzels and nuts, mixing thoroughly to coat. **Microwave at High 5 to 6 Minutes,** stirring after 3 minutes, until evenly toasted. |

Makes about 2½ quarts

## CROUTONS ITALIANO

*This is a delicious snack food as well as a great way to use up dry bread. Croutons may also be used as soup accompaniment or topping for tossed salad.*

POWER LEVEL: High (10)
MICROWAVE TIME: 10 to 12 min., total

| | |
|---|---|
| **1½ qts. bread cubes (6 cups)** | In 12×8×2-in. dish place cubes. **Microwave at High 6 Minutes,** stirring after 2 minutes, until cubes begin to dry. |
| **2 tablespoons Italian herb seasoning**<br>**½ teaspoon garlic salt**<br>**½ cup (¼-lb.) melted butter** | Sprinkle herb seasoning and garlic salt evenly over bread cubes. Drizzle with butter, tossing to coat cubes. |

**Microwave at High 4 to 6 Minutes,** stirring every minute, until crisp and dry.

Makes 1½ quarts

## SPREADS ON CRACKERS

POWER LEVEL: High (10)
MICROWAVE TIME: ¼ to ½ min., per plate

| | |
|---|---|
| **12 crackers**<br>**¼ cup canned meat spread or deli filling** | Spread about 1 teaspoon spread on each cracker. Arrange in circle on a paper plate. **Microwave at High ¼ to ½ Minute,** rotating dish ½ turn after ¼ minute, if necessary. |

NOTE: If spread has a delicate mayonnaise base, Microwave at Low, increasing time by ¼ minute. Refrigerated spreads as well as larger amounts may take slightly longer to heat.

Soft Smokey Cheese Ball

## MEXICAN CORN CHIP SNACKS

*A version of the popular Nachos.*

POWER LEVEL: High (10)
MICROWAVE TIME: ¼ to ½ min., per plate

**Large corn chips (plain or taco flavored)**
**Jalapeno bean dip or refried beans**
**Hot pepper cheese**

Mound about 1 teaspoon bean dip or refried bean mixture on each tortilla corn chip. Top with ⅛-in. thick slice of cheese to cover bean dip. Place 8 to 12 pieces in circle on paper plate or small pottery plate. **Microwave at High ¼ to ½ Minute,** until cheese is melted.

## CRAB-SWISS CRISPS

POWER LEVEL: High (10)
MICROWAVE TIME: ¾ to 1 min., per plate

**1 can (7½-oz.) crab, drained and flaked**
**1½ tablespoons sliced green onion**
**1¼ cup shredded Swiss cheese**
**½ cup mayonnaise**
**1 teaspoon lemon juice**
**¼ teaspoon curry powder**
**36 crisp round crackers**

Combine crab, onion, cheese, mayonnaise, lemon juice and curry powder. Shortly before serving, place level teaspoonful on each cracker round. Place appetizers in circle on paper plates or other plates suitable for microwave oven. Cook about 12 at a time. **Microwave at High ¾ to 1 Minute,** rotating dish ¼ turn after ½ minute,

Makes 36 appetizers

## SOFT SMOKEY CHEESE BALL

*This cheese ball is soft and easily spreadable on crackers. For a more smokey flavor, add a few drops liquid smoke or smoke-flavored salt to taste.*

POWER LEVEL: High (10)
MICROWAVE TIME: 2 to 2¼ min., total

**1 roll-shaped pkg. (6-oz.) smokey cheese spread**
**2 pkgs. (3-oz. each) cream cheese**
**1 teaspoon Worcestershire sauce**
**1 cup (4-oz.) shredded sharp cheddar cheese**

Unwrap cheeses. In 1½-qt. casserole place smokey cheese. **Microwave at High 1 Minute.** Add cream cheese. **Microwave at High 1 to 1¼ Minutes** more, until cheeses can be mixed together. Add Worcestershire sauce and blend mixture well. Stir in shredded cheese. Mixture should remain gold-flecked.

**½ cup chopped fresh parsley**
**½ cup chopped pecans**

Chill cheese mixture about 15 to 30 minutes in freezer or about 1 hour in refrigerator, until it can be formed into a ball with the hands. Roll cheese ball in parsley, then pecans. Chill to set. Serve with crackers.

Makes 1 (14-oz.) cheese ball

## CHEESE CROCK

*Cheese Crock may be used immediately; however, aging truly improves the flavor. This makes an excellent gift.*

POWER LEVEL: Medium (5)        **Cook Code:   45**
MICROWAVE TIME: 4 to 6 min., total

**4 cups (1-lb.) shredded sharp cheddar cheese**
**1 pkg. (3-oz.) cream cheese**
**2 to 3 tablespoons brandy**
**1 to 2 tablespoons olive oil**
**1 teaspoon garlic salt**
**1 teaspoon dry mustard**

In large glass mixing bowl place cheeses. **Microwave at Medium 4 to 6 Minutes,** until soft, stirring after 2 minutes. Stir in brandy, oil, salt and mustard. Beat well until thoroughly blended. Mixture will be soft and creamy. Pack into a container with a tight-fitting lid or cover well. Refrigerate 1 week to age before using. Spread on crackers or cocktail rye rounds.

Makes about 3 cups

## BACON POLES

POWER LEVEL: High (10)
MICROWAVE TIME: See Recipe
**Cook Code** for 20 sticks:  100 — for 7 sticks:  30

| | |
|---|---|
| **10 strips bacon** | With scissors, cut bacon strips in half lengthwise, making 2 long, thin strips from each slice. Wrap one strip in a spiral "barber pole fashion" around each bread stick. |
| **20 long, thin garlic bread sticks or sesame bread sticks** | |

TO MICROWAVE ENTIRE RECIPE: Place 2 paper towels in bottom of 13×9×2-in. dish. Distribute wrapped bread sticks so they don't touch each other. Cover with paper towel. **Microwave at High 10 to 13 Minutes,** rotating dish ½ turn after 5 minutes, until bacon is cooked.

TO MICROWAVE 7 ON A PAPER PLATE: Makes 3 plates. Place 2 paper towels on a paper plate. Arrange wrapped bread sticks on top. Cover with paper towel. **Microwave at High 2½ to 4 Minutes,** until bacon is cooked.

Total recipe makes 20

## BACON-WRAPPED CHICKEN LIVERS

*This is often known by its Polynesian name of Rumaki.*

POWER LEVEL: High (10)
MICROWAVE TIME: 6½ to 7½ min., per plate

| | |
|---|---|
| **1 lb. thinly sliced bacon** | **Microwave at High 1 Minute,** in the package, until slices easily separate. Divide bacon slices between 4 paper towel lined paper plates. Cover with paper towel. Microwave one plate at a time. **Microwave at High 2½ Minutes.** Cut each partially cooked slice in half. |
| **1 can (8-oz.) water chestnuts** | Drain and cut each chestnut in half. |
| **½ lb. chicken livers (about 20)** | Rinse and drain livers. Cut in half. |

To assemble, sprinkle bacon strips lightly with ground cloves and brown sugar. Place one piece of chicken liver and one piece of water chestnut at the end of each bacon strip. Roll up, securing with a toothpick. Arrange 10 in a circle on each of 4 paper towel lined (1 sheet) paper plates. Cover with paper towel. Recipe may be refrigerated at this point if desired. Microwave one plate at a time. **Microwave at High 3 to 4 Minutes,** rotating dish ½ turn after 1½ minutes. When microwaving from refrigerator temperature, increase time for each plate ½ to 1 minute.

Makes 40 hors d'oeuvres

Tacos

## TACOS

POWER LEVEL: High (10)
MICROWAVE TIME: 11 to 13 min., total

| | |
|---|---|
| **1 lb. ground chuck beef** | In 2-qt. casserole break up ground beef in very small chunks. Add onion, green pepper and garlic. Cover. **Microwave at High 6 to 7 Minutes,** stirring every 2 minutes. Drain well. |
| **½ cup chopped onion** | |
| **½ cup chopped green pepper** | |
| **1 clove garlic, minced** | |
| **1 can (8-oz.) tomato sauce** | Add tomato sauce, Worcestershire sauce, pepper, chili powder and salt. Cover. **Microwave at High 5 to 6 Minutes,** stirring after 3 minutes. |
| **1 teaspoon Worcestershire sauce** | |
| **⅛ to ¼ teaspoon cayenne pepper** | |
| **½ teaspoon chili powder** | |
| **½ teaspoon salt** | |

Use meat to fill prebaked, packaged taco shells, filling about half full. Finish tacos by topping with 2 or more of the following: shredded lettuce, shredded cheese, chopped tomatoes and chopped onions. Add hot sauce if desired.

Makes 12 tacos

## EASY TACOS

POWER LEVEL: High (10)
MICROWAVE TIME: 9 to 11 min., total

| | |
|---|---|
| **1 lb. ground chuck beef** | In 2-qt. casserole crumble beef. **Microwave at High 6 Minutes,** stirring after 3 minutes. Drain well. Mix in tomato sauce and taco seasoning mix. **Microwave 3 to 5 Minutes.** Stir well and serve as above. |
| **1 can (8-oz.) tomato sauce** | |
| **1 pkg. (1⅛ - 1¼-oz.) taco seasoning mix** | |

## CURRIED BEEF BALLS

*For convenience, make meatballs ahead of time and refrigerate on cooking dish or paper plate. Microwaving time may be slightly longer.*

POWER LEVEL: High (10)
MICROWAVE TIME: See Recipe
  **Cook Code** for 24 balls:   40 — for 12 balls:   20

| | |
|---|---|
| **½ cup buttery flavored cracker crumbs or slightly crushed herb seasoned stuffing mix**<br>**⅓ cup evaporated milk**<br>**¼ teaspoon salt**<br>**1½ to 2 teaspoons curry powder**<br>**1 lb. ground chuck beef** | .In large mixing bowl thoroughly combine crumbs, milk, salt and curry powder. Add beef and blend well. Shape meat mixture into 48 (1-in.) balls. |

TO MICROWAVE ENTIRE RECIPE: In 12×8×2-in. dish place about 24 balls. Cover with wax paper. **Microwave at High 4 to 5 Minutes,** rotating dish ½ turn after 2 minutes. Repeat with other half of beef balls.

TO MICROWAVE A DOZEN BEEF BALLS IN CIRCLE ON PAPER PLATE: Cover plate with wax paper. **Microwave at High 2 to 3 Minutes,** rotating dish ½ turn after 1 minute.

Makes 4 dozen hors d'oeuvres

## EASY MEXICAN MEATBALLS

| | |
|---|---|
| **1 lb. ground chuck beef**<br>**1 egg**<br>**½ pkg. (1⅛ - 1¼-oz., about 2 tablespoons) taco seasoning mix** | .In large mixing bowl, thoroughly combine beef, egg and seasoning mix. Shape into 48 (1-in.) balls. Cook as directed above. |

Makes 4 dozen hors d'oeuvres

## APPETIZER FRANKS

*If desired, 2 cans (4-oz. each) Vienna sausages, drained and halved, may be substituted for frankfurters.*

POWER LEVEL: High (10)          **Cook Code:**   20
MICROWAVE TIME: 2 to 3 min., per plate

| | |
|---|---|
| **3 frankfurters**<br>**¼ cup apricot preserves or apple jelly**<br>**1 tablespoon prepared mustard** | Cut frankfurters into eighths and arrange in circle on plastic coated paper plate. Mix together preserves and mustard. Spread over pieces. Stick each piece with wooden pick. **Microwave each plate at High 2 to 3 Minutes,** until hot. |

**Chili Franks:** Substitute chili sauce for preserves and mustard.

Makes 24 hors d'oeuvres

## BEEF TERIYAKI BITES

POWER LEVEL: High (10)
MICROWAVE TIME: 1½ to 2 min., each plate

| | |
|---|---|
| **1 lb. beef tenderloin or sirloin** | .Cut tenderloin into ¼-in. slices, then into 1-in. squares to make about 90 pieces. |
| **¼ cup cocktail sherry**<br>**¼ cup honey**<br>**¼ cup soy sauce**<br>**30 thin bamboo skewers, 5-in. long** | .In a deep bowl stir together sherry, honey and soy sauce. Add meat and stir to coat all pieces with teriyaki mixture. Cover with plastic wrap and marinate at least 1 hour or overnight, stirring once or twice so all meat is marinated. |

On each skewer thread 3 pieces of meat, skewering each piece twice, in opposite corners, so it looks as though there are 3 diamond shapes on each skewer. Place 6 skewers on a plate suitable for microwave oven. **Microwave at High 1½ to 2 Minutes,** rotating dish ½ turn after ¾ minute until beef is just cooked. Repeat with rest of skewers.

Makes about 30 skewers

## SWEET-TART FRANKS FOR A CROWD

POWER LEVEL: High (10)
MICROWAVE TIME: 5 to 8 min., total

| | |
|---|---|
| **1 jar (10-oz.) currant jelly**<br>**1 jar (6-oz.) prepared mustard** | .In 3-qt. casserole stir together jelly and mustard. **Microwave at High 1 to 2 Minutes** until mixture can be stirred smooth. |
| **2 lbs. frankfurters cut into 1-in. pieces** | .Stir in franks stirring to coat each piece. Cover. **Microwave at High 4 to 6 Minutes,** stirring after 2 minutes, until franks are hot. Serve immediately, or transfer to chafing dish, if desired. |

Makes about 80 hors d'oeuvres

TIP: Other recipes which make excellent appetizers are:

Meatballs Hawaiian, page 87
Swedish Meatballs, page 86
Tavern Franks (cut in 6ths or 8ths), page 129
Barbecued Franks (cut in 6ths or 8ths), page 129
Sweet-Sour Spareribs (cut into small riblets), page 114

## SWEET 'N' SOUR HAM CUBES

POWER LEVEL: High (10)        TEMP: 160°
APPROX. MICROWAVE TIME: 11 to 14 min.
                                **Cook Code:** 110

**1 lb. ham cut into ½-in. cubes (60 to 70)**
**1 can (20-oz.) pineapple chunks, drained**
**1 large green pepper, cut into ½-in. squares or 2 stalks celery, diagonally sliced ½-in. thick**
**1 jar (10-oz.) sweet and sour sauce**

...In 2-qt. casserole stir together ham, pineapple, green pepper or celery and sweet and sour sauce, mixing well.

Insert temperature probe so tip rests on center bottom of dish. Cover with plastic wrap, arranging loosely around probe to vent. Attach cable end at receptacle. **Microwave at High. Set Temp, Set 160°.**

When oven signals stir mixture before serving. Serve with cocktail picks.
                 Makes about 12 appetizer servings

NOTE: If desired, ham mixture may be heated in individual 10-oz. paper bowls. Fill bowls ½ full and microwave with temperature probe as above. Approximate microwave time is 2 to 3 minutes per bowl.

KABOB VARIATION: Use 28 thin bamboo skewers, about 5-in. long. Before adding sauce, thread 3 pieces of ham and 4 other pieces onto each skewer, beginning and ending with ham. Place 6 on a plastic coated paper plate. Spoon sauce over kabobs to coat. Cover with wax paper. **Microwave at High 3½ to 4½ Minutes** rotating dish ½ turn after 2 minutes, until hot. Repeat with remaining kabobs.

## CURRIED PINEAPPLE AND PIGGIES

*A Brown 'N Sear dish recipe.*

POWER LEVEL: High (10)
MICROWAVE TIME: 6½ min., total

**1 pkg. (8-oz.) brown 'n' serve sausages, cut crosswise in halves**
**1 can (13-oz.) pineapple chunks in syrup, drained**
**Curry powder**
**Seasoned salt**

...Preheat Brown 'N Sear Dish by placing in microwave oven, uncovered. **Microwave at High 4 Minutes.** Add sausages and cover. **Microwave at High 1 Minute.** Turn sausages over. Add drained pineapple and sprinkle with curry powder and seasoned salt. Cover. **Microwave at High 1½ Minutes** more. Serve with toothpicks.
        Makes 8 to 12 appetizer servings

Beef Teriyaki Bites & Sweet 'N' Sour Ham Cubes

## ESCARGOTS MICROWAVE

POWER LEVEL: High (10)
MICROWAVE TIME: 2 to 2½ min., per plate

| | |
|---|---|
| **½ cup (¼-lb.) butter** | In 1-pt. glass measure, place butter, garlic and parsley. **Microwave at High 1 Minute,** or until melted. Stir well. |
| **1 teaspoon garlic powder** | |
| **½ teaspoon minced parsley flakes** | |
| **1 can (4-oz.) medium size escargot (about 24 snails) with shells** | Drain and rinse snails. Pour small amount of butter sauce into each shell, add snail, then a little more sauce. Snail should be placed into shell loosely, not plugging hole, because steam will cause it to pop out in heating. Place 6 snails on each of 4 plates. Microwave one plate at a time. **Microwave at High 1 to 1½ Minutes.** |

Makes about 24

NOTE: If snails come without shells place 6 snails each in 4 small sauce dishes with ¼ of sauce. Or, use the special glass or pottery snail dishes which have 6 small compartments. Half fill each compartment with sauce, then add snails.

## SHRIMP IN SPECIAL GARLIC BUTTER

POWER LEVEL: High (10)
APPROX. MICROWAVE TIME: 5 to 7 min.

Cook Code:    50

| | |
|---|---|
| **1 lb. raw, shelled, deveined shrimp** | In 2-qt. casserole place shrimp. |
| **½ cup (¼-lb.) butter** | Stir together butter, wine, chives, garlic and pepper seasoning. Pour over shrimp and stir to coat. (Butter mixture will solidify because of temperature of shrimp.) Insert temperature probe so tip rests on center bottom of dish. Cover with plastic wrap, arranged loosely around probe. Attach cable end at receptacle **Microwave at High. Set Temp, Set 180°.** |
| **2 tablespoons sauterne wine** | |
| **2 teaspoons freeze dried or frozen chives** | |
| **⅛ teaspoon instant minced garlic or 1 clove fresh garlic, crushed** | |
| **1 to 2 drops liquid pepper seasoning (tabasco)** | |

When oven signals, stir shrimp before serving with cocktail picks.

Makes about 1 pound

NOTE: If desired, shrimp can be cooked in individual 10-oz. paper bowls. Fill bowls ½ full and microwave with probe. Approximate time is 1 to 2 minutes per bowl.

## STUFFED MUSHROOMS

*Choose large or medium-sized firm, fresh mushrooms. When fresh, mushrooms are pale grey or white and the gills (the accordian-like vents on the underside of the cap) should be tightly closed and firmly attached.*

POWER LEVEL: See Recipe          Cook Code:    30
MICROWAVE TIME: 3 to 4 min., per plate

1. For each of the following stuffings, use **12 large, fresh mushrooms,** 2-in. in diameter.

2. Wash mushrooms well, removing stems. Dry.

3. Prepare one of the following stuffing recipes. Divide evenly among caps and mound slightly. Arrange caps in a circle on plate suitable for microwave oven.

4. **Microwave at High 3 to 4 Minutes,** rotating plate ½ turn after 2 minutes. If mushroom size is not uniform, smaller caps may cook in a shorter time.

NOTE: Mushroom stems may be finely chopped (about ⅔ cup) and added to stuffing, except Spinach Stuffing, if desired.

## MUSHROOM STUFFINGS:
### HAM OR BACON STUFFING          Cook Code:    40

| | |
|---|---|
| **Stems from mushrooms, finely chopped** | In 1½-qt. casserole place chopped stems and onion. Cover. **Microwave at High 4 Minutes,** stirring after 2 minutes. |
| **½ cup finely chopped onion** | |
| **1 pkg. (3-oz.) cream cheese** | To hot mixture above, add cream cheese, mashing and mixing well. Stir in crumbs and ham or bacon. |
| **¼ cup fine dry bread crumbs** | |
| **½ cup chopped, cooked ham or bacon (8 slices)** | |

Stuffs 12 large mushrooms

Stuffed Mushrooms

## CLAM STUFFING      Cook Code:   20

**1 pkg. (3-oz.) creamed cheese, softened**
**1 can (7-oz.) minced clams, drained**
**1 tablespoon minced parsley**
**½ teaspoon garlic powder**
. . .In small bowl mix together cream cheese, clams, parsley and garlic powder.

**¼ cup crushed French fried onions**
. . .Sprinkle onion pieces over top.

NOTE: If mushroom stems are used, in 1-qt. casserole place chopped stems, ⅓ cup finely chopped onion and 2 tablespoons butter. **Microwave at High 2 Minutes,** stirring after 1 minute. Add remaining ingredients.

Stuffs 12 large mushrooms

## CRUNCHY STUFFING      Cook Code:   30

**2 tablespoons butter**
**⅓ cup finely chopped or grated onion**
**½ cup finely chopped walnuts**
**1 tablespoon chili sauce**
**1 teaspoon lemon juice**
**⅛ teaspoon salt**
. . .In 1-qt. casserole place butter and onions. **Microwave at High 3 Minutes,** until onion is limp. Add walnuts, chili sauce, lemon juice and salt.

NOTE: If mushroom stems are used, add chopped stems to butter and onions. Microwave following recipe directions.

Stuffs 12 large mushrooms

## BREAD CRUMB STUFFING      Cook Code:   30

**¼ cup finely chopped onion**
**¼ cup finely chopped green pepper**
**¼ cup finely chopped celery**
**3 tablespoons butter**
. . . .In 1-qt. casserole place onions, green pepper, celery and butter. **Microwave at High 3 Minutes,** until slightly cooked.

**1 pkg. (3-oz.) cream cheese, softened**
**1 cup fine, soft bread crumbs (3 slices)**
**1 teaspoon lemon juice**
**½ teaspoon salt**
**⅛ teaspoon pepper**
. . .Add cream cheese, crumbs, lemon juice, salt and pepper. Mix together well.

NOTE: If mushroom stems are used, add chopped stems to butter and onions. Microwave following recipe directions.

Stuffs 12 large mushrooms

## SPINACH STUFFING      Cook Code:   15

**1 pkg. (12-oz.) frozen spinach souffle**
. . . .Remove from foil container. With sharp knife cut in half. Return half to freezer, place other half in 1-qt. casserole. **Microwave at Medium 1 to 1½ Minutes,** until partially defrosted. Mash with fork.

**½ cup softened bread crumbs (about 1 slice)**
**1 teaspoon lemon juice**
**½ teaspoon instant minced onions**
**¼ teaspoon salt**
. . .Mix in crumbs, lemon juice, onion and salt.

Stuffs 12 large mushrooms

Since it starts with triangles of dough, Pizza-On-A-Plate may be slightly irregular, but quick and good.

## PIZZA-ON-A-PLATE

POWER LEVEL: Medium High (7)
MICROWAVE TIME: 11 to 15 min., per plate

**1 can (8-oz.)** . . . . . . . . . . . .On each of two 12-in.
    **refrigerated crescent** pieces of wax paper, press
    **roll dough** ½ of dough to form a 9-in.
**2 teaspoons cooking oil** circle. Press perforations together to seal. Brush each lightly with cooking oil. Place wax paper on microwave ovenproof plates. Microwave one pizza at a time. **Microwave at Medium High 4 Minutes.** Holding wax paper. Flip dough over onto plate and carefully peel off wax paper. **Microwave at Medium High 3 to 4 Minutes** more, until set and crisp. There will be some brown spots.

**1 can (8-oz.) tomato** . . . . . .Divide tomato sauce even-
    **sauce** ly between crusts, spread-
**1 pkg. (4-oz.) pepperoni** ing to edges. Top each
**1 cup (4-oz.) shredded** with half of pepperoni and
    **mozzarella cheese** sprinkle with half of cheese. **Microwave at Medium High 4 to 6 Minutes,** rotating plate ½ turn after 2 minutes. Remove immediately to cooling rack for crisper crust.

Makes 2 (9-in.) pizzas

## REHEATING PIZZA

POWER LEVEL: High (10)
MICROWAVE TIME: See Recipe

Pizza, with the exception of Pizza-On-A-Plate, is best *reheated,* in the microwave oven *after* it has been cooked conventionally. A frozen, uncooked pizza, if microwaved, will not have a crisp crust and the center tends to be soggy as there is no hot air to dry out the crust or topping.

1. To reheat a 10" pizza, cut into 8 wedges. Place each wedge on a paper towel or paper plate. Microwave one wedge at a time. **Microwave at High** according to chart below.

|  | MINUTES PER WEDGE |
|---|---|
| Room Temperature | ¼ to ½ |
| Refrigerated | ½ to ¾ |
| Frozen | ¾ to 1 |

2. Time may vary due to the size of pizza and amount of topping. Pizza topped with pepperoni and cheese was used to determine times above.

TIPS: If more than 1 pizza wedge is heated at one time, use amount of time given for *each* wedge, rotating dish ½ turn after half of total time. Place points to center of plate, as they are usually the first to melt.

For more even heating, use a lower power and increase time slightly.

For crisper bottom crust, place on cooling rack immediately after heating so crust can dry out.

## CHEESE PASTRY SNACKS

POWER LEVEL: High (10)     **Cook Code:** 30
MICROWAVE TIME: 2¾ to 3¼ min., per plate

**1 cup shredded** . . . . . . . . In large mixing bowl mix to-
   **cheddar cheese** gether cheese, flour, cere-
**¾ cup unsifted** al, walnuts, garlic salt, but-
   **all-purpose flour** ter, bacon and water with a
**¾ cup coarsely crushed** fork until a dough forms.
   **crisp rice cereal** Drop 7 level tablespoon-
**½ cup chopped walnuts** fuls in a circle onto each of
**½ teaspoon garlic salt** 3 lightly buttered plates
**⅓ cup butter, softened** suitable for microwave.
**6 strips crisp cooked** (Butter plates only around
   **bacon, crumbled** edges, where dough will
**2 tablespoons cold** be placed.)
   **water**

**Paprika** . . . . . . . . . . . . . Sprinkle with paprika. Microwave one plate at a
time. **Microwave at High
2¾ to 3¼ Minutes.** Dough
will be slightly puffed when
done and will crisp on drying. Remove immediately
from plate. Serve hot or
cold. Repeat with remain-
ing mixture.

Makes 21 Snacks

TIP: Another pastry appetizer is Quiche. See page 180
for several variations.

## ALMOND FILLED CHEESE BALLS

POWER LEVEL: High (10)     **Cook Code:** 20
MICROWAVE TIME: 1¾ to 2¼ min., per plate

**2 tablespoons soft** . . . . . . . In small mixing bowl, mix
   **butter** together butter and
**1 cup (4-oz.) shredded** cheese until smooth. Add
   **sharp cheese** flour, pepper and celery
**½ cup unsifted** seed, blending well,
   **all-purpose flour** kneading dough with
**Dash cayenne pepper** hands if necessary to form
**½ teaspoon celery seed** a ball.

**1 pkg. (3-oz.) hickory** . . . . Measure dough by level
   **smoked, barbecue** teaspoonfuls and shape
   **or cheese flavored** smoothly around each al-
   **almonds** mond to form a ball.

Place 9 balls in a circle on each of 4 paper plates. **Microwave at High 1¾ to 2¼ Minutes,** rotating dish ¼ turn
after 1 minute. Dough will be slightly puffy and dry when
cooked. Remove from dish and cool a few minutes before serving. Repeat, cooking all cheese balls.

Makes about 3 dozen cheese balls

Sugar Glazed Walnuts & Toasted Butter Pecans

## SUGAR GLAZED WALNUTS

POWER LEVEL: High (10)
MICROWAVE TIME: 6 to 8 min., total

**½ cup (¼-lb.) butter** . . . . . . In 1½-qt. casserole place
butter. **Microwave at High
1 Minute,** or until melted.

**1 cup brown sugar** . . . . . Stir in brown sugar and
   **(packed)** cinnamon. **Microwave at
1 teaspoon cinnamon** **High 2 Minutes.** Mix well
to combine butter and
sugar.

**1 lb. walnut halves** . . . . . . Add nuts and mix to coat.
   **or large pieces** **Microwave at High 3 to 5
   (about 4 cups)** **Minutes.** Spread out onto
wax paper and cool slight-
ly. Serve warm or cold.

Makes 1 pound

## TOASTED BUTTER PECANS

POWER LEVEL: High (10)     **Cook Code:** 50
MICROWAVE TIME: 5 to 6 min., total

**1 lb. pecan halves** . . . . . . . In 1½-qt. casserole place
   **(about 4 cups)** pecan halves. Sprinkle
**1 tablespoon seasoned** with seasoned salt. Cut
   **salt** butter into 4 pieces and ar-
**¼ cup butter** range evenly over top

**Microwave at High 5 to 6 Minutes.** Mix to evenly distribute butter. Serve warm or cold.

Makes 1 pound

# Soup & Sandwiches

Hot soups or sandwiches are popular choices for a be-tween meal break, lunch, or, together, as a hearty sup-per. Microwaving makes both fast and easy-to-clean-up. Soups can be heated right in the serving dish or cup. Most sandwiches are heated in a paper napkin or towel, so if you serve them casually, there's no clean up at all!

Some sandwiches are such meal-time staples that we have featured them in other sections. See:

Frankfurters, page 128; Melted Cheese, page 184; Ham-burgers, page 88; Sloppy Joes, page 67 and 83; Bacon-Lettuce-Tomato, using your microwave oven to cook the bacon, page 125.

## TIPS FOR HEATING SOUPS BY MICROWAVE

When you're serving soup and sandwich together, don't heat them together. Do the soup first; it will stay hot during the short time it takes to warm the sandwich.

**Water-Based Soups** can be heated at High. A can of condensed soup, diluted with water in a 1½-qt. cas-serole takes 5 to 7 minutes. One cup (⅔ to ¾ full) takes 2½ to 3½ minutes; or use temperature probe. **Set Temp, Set 150° to 170°.**

**Cream Soups** should be heated at Medium because milk boils over rapidly so times will be slightly longer. For care-free heating, use the temperature probe. **Set Temp, Set 140°.**

## CORN CHOWDER SOUP

POWER LEVEL: High (10)          **Cook Code:** 170
MICROWAVE TIME: 17 to 19 min., total

| | |
|---|---|
| **1 can (10¾-oz.) cream of potato soup** **2 cans (1-lb. 1-oz. each) cream-style corn** **1 can (13-oz.) evaporated milk** **1½ cups milk** **¼ cup finely chopped green pepper (optional)** **1 tablespoon instant minced onion** **1 teaspoon salt** **¼ teaspoon pepper** | In 3-qt. casserole combine soup, corn, milks, green pepper, onion, salt and pepper. Cover. **Micro-wave at High 17 to 19 Minutes,** stirring after 10 minutes, until hot. |
| **Fresh frozen or freeze dried chives** | Add chives and serve. |

Makes 8 one-cup servings

## INTERNATIONAL SANDWICH

POWER LEVEL: High (10)          **Cook Code:** 20
MICROWAVE TIME: 2 to 3 min., total

| | |
|---|---|
| **1 thick (1-in.) slice French bread** **Butter** **1 slice bologna** **1 slice salami** **½ cup sauerkraut*** **½ cup grated mozzarella cheese** | Spread the bread with but-ter. Cut bologna and sala-mi in halves. Alternate the half-slices over bread, then top with sauerkraut. Sprinkle cheese over top. |

Place sandwich on paper or china plate. **Microwave at High 2 to 3 Minutes,** giving sandwich ½ turn after 1 min-ute.

Makes 1 sandwich

*8-oz. can sauerkraut, drained, makes 2 sandwiches, 1-lb. to 1-lb. 4-oz. can makes 5 to 6 sandwiches.

NOTE: To heat 4 sandwiches, place on plate or platter and heat 6 to 7 minutes, giving plate ½ turn after 3 min-utes.

## HOT HOAGIE SANDWICH

POWER LEVEL: Medium High (7)          TEMP: 110°
APPROX. MICROWAVE TIME: 5 to 7 min.

**Cook Code:** 57

| | |
|---|---|
| **½ loaf unsliced Italian or French bread (10 to 12-in. in length)** **Mayonnaise** **Mustard** **½ lb. meat\*\*** **3 to 4 oz. cheese\*\*** | Cut bread lengthwise to make two long, thin layers. Spread both cut sides evenly with mayonnaise and mustard, spreading completely to edges. Cov-er both sides with meat slices, then cover bottom of loaf with cheese. |

Place meat covered top half of bread over bottom half. This arrangement results in cheese in center of sand-wich with meat on either side. Place on board or platter with piece of paper towel over sandwich and tucked un-der edges. Insert temperature probe about ⅓ the length of bread loaf so tip is "sandwiched" into center of filling. Attach cable end at receptacle. **Microwave at Medium. Set Temp, Set 110°.** Let stand a few minutes before slicing.

Makes 3 to 4 servings

**\*\*Meat Fillings:** Choose thin sliced hard salami, pastra-mi, pepperoni, corned beef, boiled ham, or a combina-tion of these.

**\*\*Cheese Fillings:** Choose sharp or mild cheddar, brick, Monterey Jack, Swiss, or a combination of these.

Hot Hoagie Sandwich

## TIPS FOR MICROWAVING HOT SANDWICHES

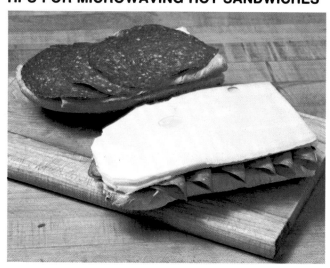

**Layer** filling with cheese in the center. Cheese attracts microwaves and by hiding it in the middle of the sandwich you promote rapid heating and avoid overcooking the cheese.

**Wrap** the sandwich in a paper towel or napkin, to absorb moisture from the bread. For an attractive presentation, microwave the sandwich on a wooden board. (Wood is not affected by short heating times.)

Microwaved meats cook tender and juicy in ⅓ to ½ the time it takes to cook them conventionally. Some meats are microwaved at High Power, but for most meats, the lower power settings allow you to cook with less care and attention. The automatic temperature probe gives you truly carefree microwaving. You simply set the dial for the finished temperature, and the oven signals you when the meat is ready.

Since meat continues to cook on standing, we recommend that you carve rare meats immediately. For well done meats, especially poultry, roast pork and meatloaf, the standing time is especially important, since it is ac-tually part of the cooking process. The meat finishes cooking while it stands.

In this chapter, we've included all your favorite types and cuts of meat, beginning with beef. Each section starts with small pieces and progresses to large, from simple recipes to the more complex, from hearty everyday food to party fare.

Each cut of meat has its own instructions for defrosting and microwaving, located where they will be most available and useful to you while cooking, plus special tips which will help you microwave all of them.

## GROUND BEEF DEFROSTING CHART

### POWER LEVEL: **Defrost**

| AMOUNT | FIRST SIDE | SECOND SIDE | SCRAPE OFF BREAK UP AND FINISH |
|---|---|---|---|
| 1 pound | 3 minutes | 3 minutes | 2 to 3 minutes |
| 2 pounds | 6 minutes | 6 minutes | 5 to 6 minutes |
| 5 pounds | 12 minutes | 12 minutes | 11 to 12 minutes* |

*Second scraping may be needed after minimum time.

1. Favorite Stuffed Peppers, page 85
2. Barbecued Franks, page 129
3. Sirloin Tip, page 106
4. Ham Slice, page 119

## HOW TO DEFROST GROUND BEEF

**Ground Beef** is packaged in a variety of shapes. Defrosting procedure is the same, but some shapes take more time and attention. Flat, circular packages, 1 to 1½-inches thick, are easiest to defrost. Tubes should be rotated frequently and broken up as soon as possible. The ends defrost rapidly and may cook before center is defrosted.

**Place Package** wrapped in plastic or paper in oven set at **Defrost.** Microwave first side. Turn package over. Microwave second side. With a fork, scrape softened meat onto wax paper and set aside. Scraping off defrosted meat is a very important step. Break remaining block into small pieces and return to oven. Continue defrosting, turning pieces over often.

**When Properly Defrosted,** crumbled beef should be cool, soft and glossy. Meat is red and fat still white. (Fat which turns transparent is beginning to cook.) It looks much like fresh ground beef, but feels colder. Some moisture may be apparent. It will make patties that hold together during cooking.

# Ground Beef Crumbled

Crumbled ground beef is the basic ingredient for a variety of popular main dishes, which take a minimum of time and attention when microwaved. Many can be mixed, cooked and served in the same casserole.

Our recipes were written for 1-step ease, but if you wish to lower calories, you may cook ground beef until it loses its pink color, then drain off fat. Add a little more water to the recipe if it seems dry.

To cook and drain fat from ground beef in one easy step, try our simple colander method. (Plastic colanders are widely available in the housewares section of department or hardware stores and supermarkets.)

Place crumbled ground beef in plastic colander, set over a casserole or bowl. For one pound of meat **Microwave at High 5 to 6 Minutes,** until meat loses its pink color, stirring after ½ the time. Discard fat and place meat in cooking dish.

## HOW TO DEFROST & COOK FROZEN GROUND BEEF IN 1-STEP

**Unwrap** 1 pound of frozen ground beef and place it in the same cooking utensil called for in the recipe you plan to follow. **Microwave at High 10 to 12 Minutes,** breaking up and stirring meat with a fork every 5 minutes. Some areas will still be pink. Let meat stand 1 to 2 minutes until the pink color disappears.

Sloppy Joes

## SLOPPY JOES

POWER LEVEL: High (10)
MICROWAVE TIME: 11 to 12 min., total

| | |
|---|---|
| **1½ lb. ground beef**<br>**⅔ cup finely chopped onion**<br>**½ cup diced celery**<br>**¼ cup diced green pepper** | In 1½-qt. casserole crumble beef. Add onion, celery and green pepper. Cover. **Microwave at High 6 Minutes,** stirring after 3 minutes. Drain meat well. |
| **½ cup ketchup**<br>**1 tablespoon Worcestershire sauce**<br>**½ teaspoon salt**<br>**⅛ teaspoon pepper** | To cooked meat mixture, add ketchup, Worcestershire sauce, salt and pepper. Cover. **Microwave at High 5 to 6 Minutes,** stirring after 3 minutes, until hot. To serve, spoon onto buns or crusty French rolls. |

Makes 6 to 8 sandwiches

**Sloppy Joes With Cheese:** Add 1 cup (4-oz.) shredded cheddar cheese to meat mixture along with ketchup.

**Sloppy Joes With Beans:** Add 1 can (16-oz.) pork and beans to meat mixture along with ketchup.

## BEEF AND CORN CASSEROLE

POWER LEVEL: High (10)
MICROWAVE TIME: 14 to 16 min., total

| | |
|---|---|
| **1 lb. ground chuck beef**<br>**¼ cup chopped onion**<br>**¼ cup chopped green pepper** | Into 2-qt. casserole crumble beef. Add onion and green pepper. **Microwave at High 6 Minutes,** stirring after 3 minutes. |
| **1 can (16-oz.) tomatoes**<br>**1 can (12-oz.) whole kernel corn, drained**<br>**1 can (8-oz.) tomato sauce**<br>**½ cup sliced stuffed olives**<br>**1 to 2 teaspoons chili powder** | Drain tomatoes, reserving ¼ cup juice. Dice tomatoes and add to meat mixture with reserved tomato juice, corn, tomato sauce, olives and chili powder. Cover. **Microwave at High 6 to 8 Minutes,** until hot. |
| **1 cup coarsely crushed corn chips**<br>**½ cup shredded cheddar cheese** | Remove cover, sprinkle corn chips and cheese over top. **Microwave at High 2 Minutes,** uncovered, until cheese melts. |

Makes 4 to 6 servings

## CHILI

*Microwaved with the temperature probe, this chili requires no stirring during cooking. Ground beef is softer with this 1-step method. For more texture, precook ground beef before combining with other ingredients.*

POWER LEVEL: High (10)          TEMP: 190°
APPROX. MICROWAVE TIME: 40 to 45 min.
                          **Cook Code:** 400

| | |
|---|---|
| **1½ lb. ground chuck beef** | Into 2½ to 3-qt. casserole crumble beef. |
| **1 can (28-oz.) tomatoes, undrained**<br>**1 can (6-oz.) tomato paste**<br>**2 cans (1-lb.) kidney beans, undrained**<br>**1 medium green pepper, finely chopped**<br>**3 teaspoons instant minced onion**<br>**1 to 2 tablespoons chili powder**<br>**2 teaspoons salt** | Mix in tomatoes, tomato paste, beans, green pepper, onion, chili powder and salt. Insert temperature probe so tip rests on center bottom of dish. Cover tightly with plastic wrap, arranging loosely around probe to vent. Attach cable end at receptacle. **Microwave at High. Set Temp, Set 190°.** When oven signals, stir and let chili stand about 10 minutes to blend flavors before serving. |

Makes 6 to 8 servings

## BEEFBURGER STROGANOFF

POWER LEVEL: High (10)          **Cook Code:** 150
MICROWAVE TIME: 15 to 18 min., total

| | |
|---|---|
| **1 lb. ground chuck beef**<br>**½ cup finely chopped onion**<br>**1 garlic clove, minced**<br>**1 can (8-oz.) mushrooms, undrained**<br>**1 can (10½-oz.) condensed cream of mushroom soup**<br>**3 tablespoons all-purpose flour**<br>**1 teaspoon salt**<br>**¼ teaspoon pepper** | Into 2-qt. casserole crumble beef. Add onion, garlic, mushrooms, soup, flour, salt and pepper. Mix thoroughly. Cover. **Microwave at High 15 to 18 Minutes,** stirring after 8 minutes. |
| **1 cup (8-oz.) dairy sour cream**<br>**½ teaspoon bottled brown bouquet sauce** | Stir casserole thoroughly, then stir in sour cream and bouquet sauce. Serve over cooked rice or chow mein noodles. |

Makes 6 servings

## CABBAGE ROLLS ITALIAN STYLE

POWER LEVEL: High (10)
MICROWAVE TIME: 22 to 26 min., total

| | |
|---|---|
| **8 large cabbage leaves (from outer layers of cabbage)**<br>**½ cup water** | In 3-qt. casserole place cabbage and water. Cover. **Microwave at High 7 to 9 Minutes,** until leaves are pliable. |
| **1 lb. ground chuck beef**<br>**1 egg**<br>**1 cup packaged precooked (minute) rice**<br>**3 tablespoons chopped onion**<br>**1 teaspoon salt** | While cabbage is cooking, mix together ground beef, egg, rice, onion and salt. Divide meat mixture into 8 equal portions. Place one portion on each partially-cooked cabbage leaf and roll meat into leaf, securing with toothpick if necessary. Return to 3-qt. casserole, placing rolls seam-side-down. |
| **2 cans (8-oz. each) tomato sauce**<br>**1 tablespoon sugar**<br>**1 teaspoon oregano** | Blend tomato sauce, sugar and oregano. Pour over cabbage rolls. Cover casserole. |

**Microwave at High 15 to 17 Minutes,** rotating dish ½ turn and basting with sauce after 9 minutes.

Makes 8 cabbage rolls

## FAVORITE STUFFED PEPPERS

*For crisper pepper and brighter color, remove cooked peppers from dish immediately. Separate them and let stand uncovered. Sprinkle top with grated, rather than sliced, cheese to assure melting.*

POWER LEVEL: High (10)          TEMP: 175°
APPROX. MICROWAVE TIME: 28 to 32 min.
**Cook Code:** 280

| | |
|---|---|
| **6 medium green peppers** | Cut off tops of green peppers; remove seeds and membrane. |
| **1½ lb. ground chuck beef**<br>**1 cup cooked long grain rice**<br>**1 small onion, chopped (about ½ cup)**<br>**1½ teaspoons salt**<br>**¼ teaspoon pepper**<br>**1 clove garlic, minced** | Mix beef with rice, onion, salt, pepper and garlic. Fill peppers with meat mixture. Arrange snugly in 3-qt. casserole so one pepper is in center of dish. |
| **1 can (10¾-oz.) condensed tomato soup**<br>**½ cup water** | Mix together soup and water; pour over and around peppers. Insert temperature probe so tip is in middle of center pepper. Cover tightly with plastic wrap, arranging loosely around probe to vent. Attach cable end at receptacle. **Microwave at High. Set Temp, Set 175°.** |
| **6 slices (1-oz. each) sharp cheese (optional)** | When oven signals, remove peppers and let stand, covered, 5 to 10 minutes before serving. If desired, cheese slices may be placed over tops of peppers to melt before casserole stands. Recover loosely with plastic wrap. |

Makes 6 servings

NOTE: Peppers should fit snugly in dish so steam and heat conduction help cook them evenly.

## HOW TO FORM CABBAGE ROLLS

Shape meat mixture into 8 rolls, each about 3-inches long. Place meat roll on the base of the cabbage leaf over heavy vein. Fold sides of leaf over meat and roll up. Secure roll with wooden pick if necessary and place in the casserole, seam side down.

## LAYERED TACO CASSEROLE

*With the exception of lettuce, this casserole has the texture and flavor of Mexican tacos.*

POWER LEVEL: High (10)
MICROWAVE TIME: 25½ to 29½ min., total

| | |
|---|---|
| **1 lb. ground chuck beef** | In 2-qt. casserole place beef. **Microwave at High 5 to 6 Minutes,** stirring after 3 minutes. Drain beef and remove from casserole. |
| **2 tablespoons butter**<br>**1 medium onion, chopped (about ½ cup)**<br>**2 tablespoons diced green chilies**<br>**1 can (8-oz.) tomato sauce**<br>**1 pkg. (1¼-oz.) taco seasoning mix**<br>**½ cup water** | In 1-qt. glass measure place butter, onions and chilies. **Microwave at High 2 to 2½ Minutes,** stirring after 1 minute. Add tomato sauce, taco seasoning mix and water. **Microwave at High 1½ to 2 Minutes** more. |
| **2 eggs**<br>**1 cup dairy half & half** | Beat eggs; blend in half & half. Add this mixture slowly to tomato sauce, stirring constantly. |
| **1 pkg. (6-oz.) corn chips**<br>**8 oz. Monterey Jack cheese, shredded or sliced** | Place half of corn chips in same 2-qt. casserole. Top with half of ground beef, half of cheese and half of sauce. Repeat layers. **Microwave at High 15 Minutes,** rotating dish ½ turn after 8 minutes. |
| **1 cup (8-oz.) dairy sour cream**<br>**½ cup grated cheddar cheese** | Top with sour cream and grated cheese. **Microwave at High 2 to 4 Minutes,** until cheese is melted. |

Makes about 6 servings

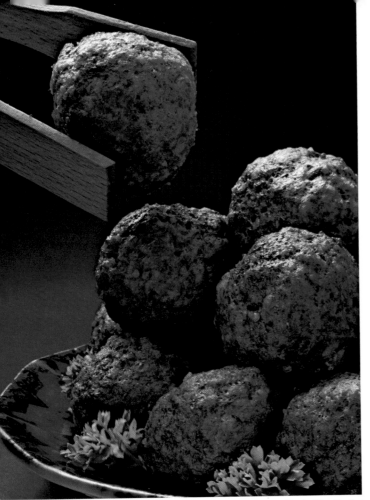

Basic Meatballs

# Ground Beef Meatballs

Meatballs microwave exceptionally well, and turn brown after a short standing time, so they need no special browning.

**For loose meatballs,** place about ¾" apart in dish. Rearrange them after half the cooking time. To cook meatballs with a minimum of attention, arrange them in a ring around the edge of a 9 or 10-in. pie plate, depending on size. After half the cooking time, rotate the dish ½ turn. These recipes are all well-tested favorites. Using them as models, you'll find it easy to adapt your own special recipes for microwaving.

## BASIC MEATBALLS

POWER LEVEL: High (10)　　　　**Cook Code:** 90
MICROWAVE TIME: 9 to 12 min., total

1 lb. ground chuck beef
1 egg
½ cup fine bread crumbs
1 teaspoon salt
¼ teaspoon paprika
⅛ teaspoon pepper

..Mix together beef, egg, crumbs, salt, paprika and pepper. Shape into 12 balls and arrange in a circle in 9 or 10-in. pie plate. Cover with wax paper. **Microwave at High 9 to 12 Minutes,** rotating dish ½ turn after 5 minutes, until done. If desired, serve with Italian Sauce, page 192.

Makes 12 meatballs

VARIATIONS:
Add one of the following flavor combinations:
1 tablespoon Worcestershire sauce and ¼ cup chopped onion
1 tablespoon steak sauce and 1 clove crushed garlic (or ½ teaspoon garlic powder)
1 tablespoon chili sauce and ¼ cup finely chopped green pepper
1 tablespoon ketchup and 1 teaspoon prepared mustard
2 tablespoons red wine and 1 teaspoon oregano

## SWEDISH MEATBALLS

POWER LEVEL: High (10)
MICROWAVE TIME: 16 to 22 min., total

2 lbs. ground chuck beef
2 cups soft bread crumbs
½ cup milk
1 egg
1 pkg. (½ of 2¾-oz. box) onion soup mix
½ teaspoon salt
½ teaspoon nutmeg

..Mix together beef, crumbs, milk, egg, soup mix, salt and nutmeg. Shape meat mixture into 40 balls. Cook 20 at a time in 13×9×2-in. dish. Cover with wax paper. **Microwave at High 6 to 8 Minutes,** rearranging meatballs after 3 minutes. Remove meatballs from dish and keep warm, reserving meat drippings. Repeat.

2 tablespoons unsifted all-purpose flour
1 cup milk
2 tablespoons brown bouquet sauce
1 cup dairy sour cream (8-oz.)

..To ¼ cup drippings in dish, add flour, stirring until smooth. Gradually stir in milk and brown bouquet sauce. **Microwave at High 3 to 4 Minutes,** stirring every minute, until thickened. Add sour cream. Stir well. Return meatballs to dish, mixing to coat evenly. **Microwave at High 1 to 2 Minutes,** until hot. Serve over noodles or rice.

Makes 40 meatballs (1-in.)

## PORCUPINE MEATBALLS

*Fast cooking rice is used in this recipe because the short cooking time does not allow regular rice to soften.*

POWER LEVEL: High (10)
MICROWAVE TIME: 9 to 13 min., total

| | |
|---|---|
| **1 lb. ground chuck beef** | . .Mix together beef, rice, ½ |
| **1 cup packaged precooked (minute) rice** | can of soup (about ½ cup), egg, water and onion salt. Shape into 12 balls and ar- |
| **1 can (10-oz.) condensed tomato soup (divided)** | range in a circle in 9 or 10-in. pie plate. Cover with wax paper. **Microwave at** |
| **1 egg** | **High 7 to 9 Minutes,** rotat- |
| **½ cup water** | ing dish ½ turn after 4 min- |
| **1 teaspoon onion salt** | utes. |

Spoon Topping over meatballs. **Microwave at High 2 to 4 Minutes** to heat. If desired, mound center of meatball ring with rice before serving.

**TOPPING:** Into remaining ½ can undiluted tomato soup, stir 2 tablespoons ketchup and 1 teaspoon prepared mustard.

Makes 4 to 6 servings

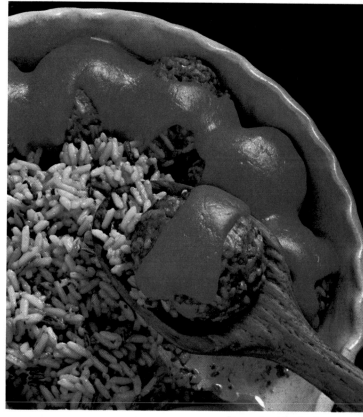

Porcupine Meatballs

## COLORFUL RING OF MEATBALLS

POWER LEVEL: High (10)
MICROWAVE TIME: 15 to 17 min., total

| | |
|---|---|
| **1 lb. ground chuck beef** | . . Mix together beef, egg, |
| **1 egg** | crumbs, paprika, salt and |
| **½ cup fine bread crumbs** | pepper. Shape into 12 balls and arrange in a cir- |
| **1 teaspoon salt** | cle in 9 or 10-in. pie plate. |
| **¼ teaspoon paprika** | Cover with wax paper. **Mi-** |
| **⅛ teaspoon pepper** | **crowave at High 8 Min-utes.** |

| | |
|---|---|
| **1 medium onion** . . . . . . . | . .While meatballs are cook- |
| **1 medium lemon** | ing, peel onion and lemon. |
| **1 medium green pepper** | Slice onion, lemon and |
| **1 cup dairy sour cream (8-oz.)** | pepper ¼-in. thick. Mix to-gether sour cream, chili |
| **½ cup chili sauce** | sauce and brown sugar. |
| **2 tablespoons brown sugar (packed)** | Rotate dish ½ turn. Distri-bute onion rings and lem-on and pepper slices over meatballs. Pour sour cream mixture evenly over slices. |

**Microwave at High 7 to 9 Minutes,** uncovered. Serve with buttered noodles, if desired.

Makes 4 to 5 servings

## MEATBALLS HAWAIIAN

*These meatballs microwave very quickly because of the moist pineapple filling.*

POWER LEVEL: High (10)
MICROWAVE TIME: 7 to 9 min., total

| | |
|---|---|
| **1 can (1-lb. 4-oz.)** . . . . . . . | .Drain pineapple well, re- |
| **pineapple chunks** | serving syrup. |
| **1 lb. ground chuck beef** | . .Mix together beef, egg, |
| **1 egg** | bread crumbs, onion, salt, |
| **2 slices fresh bread, crumbled** | cloves, allspice and syrup. Mold small amount of mix- |
| **1 tablespoon instant minced onion** | ture around each pine-apple chunk. Place meat- |
| **1 teaspoon salt** | balls in 12×8×2-in. dish. |
| **⅛ teaspoon cloves** | Cover with wax paper. **Mi-** |
| **⅛ teaspoon allspice** | **crowave at High 4 Min-** |
| **2 tablespoons reserved pineapple syrup** | **utes.** Pour off meat juices. |
| **⅓ cup reserved** . . . . . . . . . | .Stir together syrup, ketch- |
| **pineapple syrup** | up and brown sugar. Pour |
| **½ cup ketchup** | over drained meatballs. |
| **⅓ cup brown sugar (packed)** | **Microwave at High 3 to 5 Minutes** longer, until done. Serve with rice or noodles, or serve with toothpicks as an appetizer. |

Makes about 24 to 30 meatballs

# Ground Beef Hamburger Patties

Hamburgers are America's all-time favorite for lunch or supper. (Some people even like them for breakfast.) With microwaving, hamburgers defrost and cook so quickly and successfully that, if you keep a supply in the freezer, you can serve hamburgers at a moment's notice. You may microwave hamburgers in the Brown 'N Sear Dish or browning griddle, but they will be equally delicious when cooked on a paper or pottery plate suitable for microwaving; and you'll save even more cooking and clean up time.

## MICROLESSON:

Illustrated below are several ways additional browning can be achieved. Browning agents should be added before cooking.

**Cover** patties with wax paper for a juicy hamburger. Microwave at **High.** After half the cooking time, rotate dish ½ turn. For a drier surface, microwave uncovered and turn patties over after ½ the cooking time.

Plain hamburger immediately after microwaving    Barbecue Sauce    Teriyaki Sauce

**Let Patties Stand** a few minutes, covered with wax paper. On removal from the oven, hamburgers will look grey, but they will turn brown after standing.

**Serve** on buttered buns with your favorite condiments. Notice the change in appearance after standing time. This hamburger was cooked without a browning agent.

Onion Soup Mix        Brown Bouquet Sauce With Butter        Brown 'N Sear Dish

## TIPS FOR MICROWAVING GROUND BEEF PATTIES

**Thickness** and type of ground beef determine cooking time. The time chart is for medium-lean ground chuck. Fattier hamburgers might take less time, very lean ones, more.

**A Paper Plate** lined with a double thickness of paper towel gives you no-clean-up convenience. Cover patties with a single paper towel.

**For Lower Calorie** hamburgers, place patties on a trivet set over a plate or dish. Cover with wax paper and rotate dish ½ turn after half the cooking time. Fat drains into dish.

## GROUND BEEF PATTY COOKING CHART

**Timings** are based on medium-lean ground chuck shaped into 6, 4 or 2 patties per pound and microwaved to well done. Use paper, pottery or glass plate.

**Preheat** Brown 'N Sear dish or browning griddle when using this cooking method. Follow the timings given on the chart below, but turn fresh hamburgers over after ⅔ cooking time. For frozen hamburgers, turn as directed on the chart. Use the Brown 'N Sear dish cover to prevent spatters, but preheat dish uncovered.

**Extended Hamburgers.** Hamburgers may be extended with soy protein, following directions on the package.

You may also use oatmeal, crushed corn flakes or crackers, according to your favorite recipe. Extended hamburgers microwave in ½ to 1 minute less time per patty, and give greater volume per pound of meat. The following recipe uses bread as an extender.

**Meatloaf Burgers.** Mix together 1 pound ground chuck, 1½ cups cubed bread (2 slices), 1 egg and ½ teaspoon salt. Shape into size and thickness of patties preferred. Microwave ½ to 1 minute less time per pattie than for regular hamburgers.

POWER LEVEL: **High (10)**

| PATTY SIZE | NO. OF PATTIES | FRESH TIME/MINUTES | FROZEN TIME/MINUTES | | PREHEAT BROWNING DISH OR GRIDDLE TIME/MINUTES | |
|---|---|---|---|---|---|---|
| **6 per pound** | 1 | 1 to 1¼ | 2 | | 4 | |
| (about ½" thick) | 2 | 1½ to 2 | 4 to 4½ | Turn over after ½ of time | 4 | |
| | 3 | 2 to 2½ | 5 to 5½ | | 6 | |
| | 4 | 2½ to 3 | 6 to 6½ | | 6 | |
| | 5 | 3 to 4 | 7½ to 8 | Turn over every ⅓ of time | 8 | Griddle only |
| | 6 | 4 to 5 | 9 to 10 | | 8 | |
| **4 per pound** | 1 | 2 to 3 | 3 to 3½ | Turn over after ½ of time | 4 | |
| (about ¾" thick) | 2 | 3 to 4 | 4½ to 5½ | | 6 | |
| | 3 | 4 to 5 | 7 to 8 | Turn over every ⅓ of time | 6 | |
| | 4 | 5 to 6 | 10 to 11 | | 8 | |
| **2 per pound** | 1 | 2½ to 3½ | 5 to 7 | Turn over every ⅓ of time | 6 | |
| (about ¾" thick) | 2 | 6 to 7 | 12 to 14 | | 8 | – Griddle only |

## SALISBURY STEAKS

*If you prefer creamy gravy, substitute milk for water.*

POWER LEVEL: High (10)
MICROWAVE TIME: 10 to 13 min., total

| | |
|---|---|
| **1 lb. ground chuck beef**<br>**½ small onion, chopped**<br>**1 teaspoon seasoned salt**<br>**⅛ teaspoon pepper** | Combine beef, onion, salt and pepper. Shape into 2 large oval patties in 8-in. square dish. Cover with wax paper. **Microwave at High 7 to 9 Minutes,** rotating dish ½ turn after 3 minutes. Remove patties from dish and keep warm. |
| **3 tablespoons flour**<br>**½ cup water**<br>**½ teaspoon brown bouquet sauce**<br>**1 can (2-oz.) mushroom stems and pieces, undrained** | Mix flour and water to make a smooth paste. Add quickly to hot drippings, stirring until smooth. Add brown bouquet sauce and mushrooms, stirring well. **Microwave at High 2 Minutes,** stirring after 1 minute, until gravy thickens. Place patties in gravy, spooning some over the top. **Microwave at High 1 to 2 Minutes,** until hot. |

Makes 2 generous servings

## HAMBURGER PATTY STEW

*When arranging this casserole, be sure that the top layer of beef patties is well covered with vegetables or it will overcook.*

POWER LEVEL: Medium High (7)    **Cook Code:** 457
MICROWAVE TIME: 45 to 50 min., total

| | |
|---|---|
| **3 medium potatoes**<br>**3 medium carrots**<br>**3 medium onions** | Peel vegetables and slice into ¼-in. slices.  |
| **2 lbs. ground chuck beef**<br>**1 tablespoon salt**<br>**¼ teaspoon pepper**<br>**⅓ cup water**<br>**Paprika** | Form beef into 24 small flat patties. In 3-qt. casserole make 3 layers of beef with vegetables, sprinkling layers with salt and pepper, ending with vegetables. Add water. Press down into casserole. Sprinkle with paprika. Cover. **Microwave at Medium High 45 to 50 Minutes,** rotating dish ½ turn after 20 minutes. |

Makes 8 to 10 servings

Stuffed Hamburgers

## STUFFED HAMBURGERS

POWER LEVEL: High (10)    **Cook Code:** 70
MICROWAVE TIME: 7 to 9 min., total

| | |
|---|---|
| **1 lb. ground chuck beef**<br>**Salt**<br>**Pepper**<br>**Filling (below)** | Shape beef into 8 thin patties. Sprinkle with salt and pepper. Place selected filling over 4 patties and top with other 4 patties. Seal fillings inside by pinching firmly around edges. Arrange 4 stuffed patties in 8-in. square dish. Cover with wax paper. **Microwave at High 7 to 9 Minutes,** rotating dish ½ turn after 4 minutes. Serve on buttered buns. |

Makes 4 patties

FILLINGS:

**Ham 'N' Cheese:** Use a thin ham slice and 1 thin cheese slice per patty.

**Cordon Bleu:** Use ¼-in. thick slices Canadian bacon and 1 tablespoon crumbled bleu cheese per patty.

**Hot Dog Burgers:** Use ½ of a hot dog sliced lengthwise, 1 tablespoon ketchup and scant teaspoon mustard per patty.

**Maxi Burgers:** Use thin slice onion and thin slice tomato per patty. Before cooking raw, but filled patties, microwave 4 long bacon strips until barely done, but still limp. Quickly wrap strips around patties to encircle edges and secure with toothpicks. Place each patty on a slice of drained pineapple. Microwave as above, adding 1 additional minute for pineapple. Top Maxi Burgers with pimiento cheese slice after cooking. Allow to melt by returning to microwave oven few seconds.

# Ground Beef Meatloaf

In the microwave oven, meatloaf cooks in 15 to 20 minutes, instead of the hour, or hour and a half you expect conventionally. Microwaved meatloaves are round and flat. We do not recommend square or loaf shapes, because the corners absorb too much energy and will be overcooked by the time the center is done.

A conventionally baked meatloaf occasionally has areas on the top which are overbrown. When microwaved, these areas may appear on the bottom edges of the loaf. Because microwave energy is attracted to sweet mixtures, toppings which contain sugar, syrup or preserves can increase overbrowning if they come in contact with the bottom edges. When applied before microwaving, they should be brushed only on the top.

Plain meatloaf looks grey. It needs a topping, sauce or

browning agent for attractive color. For this picture, we brushed the left side of the meatloaf with a browning sauce, leaving the right side plain. Ketchup, chili or barbecue sauces make easy toppings. For delicious flavor variety, try one of our homemade toppings.

Basic Meatloaf

## HOW TO MICROWAVE PIE-SHAPED MEATLOAF

**Use** 1 to 2 pounds ground beef. If you are adapting a recipe, choose a moist mixture. Spread the mixture directly in a pie plate, not on a trivet. The top should be very flat and about even with the top of the dish.

**Brush** the top with a browning agent or sauce. If you are not using a probe, cover dish tightly with plastic wrap, turning back about 2-in. at edge to vent. After cooking, let loaf stand 5 to 10 minutes to complete cooking and make it easier to slice.

**Insert** temperature probe as horizontally as possible, so that tip is in the center of the loaf. Make sure disc does not touch the food. Cover tightly with plastic wrap, arranging loosely around probe to vent.

# BASIC MEATLOAF

*Add ¼ teaspoon herbs or dry mustard to vary flavor.*

POWER LEVEL: High (10)                 TEMP: 170°
APPROX. MICROWAVE TIME: 15 to 20 min.
                                    **Cook Code:** 150

| | |
|---|---|
| **1½ lbs. ground chuck beef** | Mix together beef, onion, crumbs, egg, ketchup, milk and seasonings. Mold into a rounded, flat loaf in 9-in. pie plate. |
| **¾ cup chopped onion** | |
| **½ cup fine dry bread crumbs** | |
| **1 egg** | |
| **2 tablespoons ketchup** | |
| **1 cup milk** | |
| **1 teaspoon salt** | |
| **¼ teaspoon pepper** | |
| **⅛ teaspoon paprika** | |
| **2 tablespoons ketchup** | Spread ketchup evenly over top of loaf. |

Insert temperature probe and cover as shown in picture on preceding page. Attach cable end at receptacle. **Microwave at High. Set Temp, Set 170°.**

When oven signals, remove meatloaf and let stand about 10 minutes to firm before serving. Serve in wedges.

Makes 6 servings

**1½-pound Loaf Shaped Meatloaf** can be microwaved at Medium High (7) to 170°, about 25 to 30 minutes.

# CHEESE STUFFED MEATLOAF

*This meatloaf tastes like a cheeseburger and will be popular with your family.*

POWER LEVEL: High (10)                 TEMP: 170°
APPROX. MICROWAVE TIME: 25 to 30 min.
                                    **Cook Code:** 250

| | |
|---|---|
| **1½ lbs. ground chuck beef** | Make meatloaf mixture: In large mixing bowl, mix together beef, bread, milk, salt and pepper. |
| **3 slices fresh bread, cubed** | |
| **1 cup milk** | |
| **2 teaspoons salt** | |
| **½ teaspoon pepper** | |
| **½ cup chopped onion** | Make cheese stuffing: In 1½-qt. casserole place onion, pepper, celery and lemon juice. **Microwave at High 3 Minutes,** until lightly sauteed. Add egg to hot vegetables and stir to blend well. Stir in cheese and fine bread crumbs. |
| **¼ cup chopped green pepper** | |
| **¼ cup chopped celery** | |
| **2 tablespoons lemon juice** | |
| **1 egg, slightly beaten** | |
| **1 cup (4-oz.) shredded cheddar cheese** | |
| **3 slices fresh bread, finely crumbled** | |

To assemble meatloaf: Pat half of meat mixture in bottom of 9-in. pie plate. Mound filling over meat leaving about 1-in. uncovered at edges. Spread remaining meat mixture over filling. (Meat mixture is soft and spreads easily.) Seal around edges. Brush assembled meatloaf with 1 tablespoon Worcestershire sauce.

Insert temperature probe so tip is in center of stuffing. Cover tightly with plastic wrap, arranging loosely around probe to vent. Attach cable end at receptacle. **Microwave at High. Set Temp, Set 170°.**

When oven signals, remove meatloaf and let stand about 10 minutes to firm before serving. Serve in wedges.

Makes 4 to 6 servings

# SOUPER MEATLOAF

POWER LEVEL: Medium High (7)           TEMP: 170°
APPROX. MICROWAVE TIME: 22 to 25 min.
                                    **Cook Code:** 227

| | |
|---|---|
| **2 lbs. ground chuck beef** | Mix together beef, crumbs, onion, egg, ½ of soup and bouillon. Shape into flat loaf in 10-in. pie plate. Insert temperature probe as shown in picture at left. Attach cable end at receptacle. **Microwave at Medium High. Set Temp, Set 170°.** When oven signals, let loaf stand 10 minutes. Serve with Topping. |
| **½ cup fine dry bread crumbs** | |
| **⅓ cup chopped onion** | |
| **1 egg, slightly beaten** | |
| **1 can (10½-oz.) condensed cream of mushroom soup, (divided)** | |
| **2 tablespoons beef bouillon granules** | |

**Topping:** Mix remaining soup with 1 teaspoon beef bouillon granules and ⅓ cup water. **Microwave at High 2 to 3 Minutes,** stirring every minute, until hot.

For best results, this loaf must be cooked in the 10-in. pie plate at Medium High Power.

## LEMON LOVERS' MEATLOAF

*Lemon juice and lemon slices add tang to this meatloaf.*

POWER LEVEL: High (10)                TEMP: 170°
APPROX. MICROWAVE TIME: 15 to 20 min.
**Cook Code:** 150

| | |
|---|---|
| ¾ **cup ketchup** | In small bowl mix together ketchup, brown sugar, dry mustard, allspice and cloves. Set aside. |
| ¼ **cup brown sugar (packed)** | |
| ¾ **teaspoon dry mustard** | |
| ¼ **teaspoon allspice** | |
| **Dash ground cloves** | |
| 1½ **lb. ground chuck beef** | Mix together beef, bread cubes, egg, lemon juice, onion and salt. Mold into rounded flat loaf in 9-in. pie plate. |
| 3 **slices day-old bread, cubed** | |
| 1 **egg, slightly beaten** | |
| ⅓ **cup lemon juice** | |
| ¼ **cup chopped onion** | |
| 2 **teaspoons seasoned salt** | |
| 6 **very thin lemon slices** | Spread half the reserved sauce over loaf and arrange lemon slices on top. |

Insert temperature probe so tip is in center of loaf. Cover tightly with plastic wrap, arranging loosely around probe to vent. Attach cable end at receptacle. **Microwave at High. Set Temp, Set 170°.**

When oven signals, remove loaf and let stand 5 minutes to firm before serving. Remove plastic wrap and spread remaining sauce over loaf before serving.

*Makes 6 servings*

**Mini Meatloaves:** Shape meat mixture into 6 individual loaves and arrange in 12×8×2-in. dish. Cover with wax paper. **Microwave at High 4 Minutes.** Evenly divide half of sauce over loaves. Top each loaf with a lemon slice. Recover with wax paper. Rotate dish ½ turn. **Microwave at High 7 to 9 Minutes,** until done. Heat and spoon remaining sauce over loaves before serving.

## HOW TO MAKE A MEATLOAF RING

## SAUERBRATEN BEEF RING

POWER LEVEL: High (10)                TEMP: 180°
APPROX. MICROWAVE TIME: 17 to 22 min.
**Cook Code:** 170

| | |
|---|---|
| 1¼ **cups finely crushed gingersnap cookies** | Reserve ½ cup gingersnap crumbs for meatloaf. In 1-qt. glass measure, mix together remaining ¾ cup crumbs, broth, brown sugar, raisins and lemon juice. **Microwave at High 8 to 10 Minutes,** stirring every 3 minutes, until thickened. Set aside. |
| 2 **cups beef broth** | |
| ½ **cup brown sugar (packed)** | |
| ¼ **cup raisins** | |
| ¼ **cup lemon juice** | |
| 2 **lbs. ground chuck beef** | In 2-qt. casserole mix together reserved crumbs, beef, bread crumbs, onion, lemon juice, water, salt and pepper. Invert 6-oz. custard cup in center of same 2-qt. casserole. Divide meat into 12 equal parts. Shape into ovals and arrange as shown below around custard cup. Pour 1 cup sauce over meat. |
| 1 **cup soft bread crumbs (1½ slices)** | |
| ½ **cup chopped onion** | |
| ¼ **cup lemon juice** | |
| ¼ **cup water** | |
| 1 **teaspoon salt** | |
| ¼ **teaspoon pepper** | |

Insert temperature probe so tip is in center of one meatball. Cover dish tightly with plastic wrap, arranging loosely around probe to vent. Attach cable end at receptacle. **Microwave at High. Set Temp, Set 180°.**

When oven signals, remove loaf from oven and let stand 10 minutes. Invert serving plate over casserole. Carefully but quickly invert beef ring onto serving plate. (*Caution:* custard cup in center of ring will be filled with hot meat liquid. Keep casserole over serving plate until meat and custard cup slip onto plate.) Remove custard cup full of liquid. Serve beef ring with remaining sauce, heated before serving, if necessary.

*Makes 6 to 9 servings*

**Place** inverted 6-oz. custard cup in center of casserole. Pack oval-shaped meatballs around it.

**Cover** casserole with serving plate after microwaving and standing for 10 minutes.

**Invert** casserole over plate. When meat and cup slip onto plate, remove casserole.

**Lift out** custard cup with tongs. Cup will be filled with hot meat liquid.

# Beef Convenience Foods

Canned convenience foods, or foods frozen in metal trays, should be removed from their containers to suitable microwave plates or casseroles. Small boil-in-bag pouches (about 5 to 10-oz.) can be placed directly in the oven. Slit or pierce the top of the pouch before microwaving and open carefully after heating to avoid burns from steam. Large boil-in-bags may be placed in a serving dish. When contents are partially defrosted, open the bag, slide food into the dish and stir before continuing to microwave.

## TIPS FOR MICROWAVING BEEF CONVENIENCE FOODS

**Stirring.** Part way through the heating period, stir food from the outside to the center of the dish. Foods which cannot be stirred, such as meatloaf, lasagna or salisbury steak, should be rotated, rearranged or turned over.

**Covering.** To shorten cooking time and prevent spatters, use a covered casserole. When heating foods on a serving plate, or in a dish without a cover, use wax paper or plastic wrap to cover the food. Prick or slash plastic wrap and remove carefully when stirring.

**Probe.** Before inserting temperature probe, make certain that frozen foods are completely defrosted. Heat fully cooked foods to 150° to 160°. For probe placement, and temperature of uncooked foods, follow instructions given with similar home-cooked recipes.

## CONVENIENCE GROUND BEEF COOKING CHART

**Main Dishes** such as canned or frozen barbecue beef, chili, hash, meatballs, patties or pieces with gravy, stew, meatloaf, salisbury steak, stuffed cabbage rolls and stuffed peppers can be microwaved following directions below.

**Dry Casserole Mixes.** Always use hottest tap water and 3-qt. casserole for dishes containing pasta or rice. Stir once or twice during cooking. Let them stand, covered, 5 minutes after cooking.

POWER LEVEL: **High (10)**

| CANNED AMOUNT | TIME MIN. | COOK CODE | COMMENTS |
|---|---|---|---|
| Up to 16-oz. | 3-5 | 30 | Stir after ½ of time or use temperature probe set for 150°. |
| Over 16-oz. | 5-8 | 50 | |
| **FROZEN AMOUNT** | | | |
| 8 to 16-oz. | 5-11 | 50 | Stir, redistribute or rotate after ½ of time. Use temperature probe only if completely defrosted. |
| 16 to 32-oz. | 11-22 | 110 | |

| CASSEROLE MIXES | TIME MIN. | COOK CODE | COMMENTS |
|---|---|---|---|
| Add Hamburger | 18-22 | 180 | Microwave crumbled ground beef 5 minutes, stirring after 3 minutes. Drain before adding remaining ingredients. |
| Add Cooked Beef | 18-22 | 180 | If milk is used for part of liquid add 2 to 3 minutes cooking time. |
| One-pot Main Dish (freeze-dried beef) | 11-13 | 110 | Add crumb topping just before serving. |

# Beef Strips & Chunks

Less tender beef, such as round or chuck, microwaves best when cut in small pieces and simmered gently at Low or sometimes Medium power setting. The temperature probe is not appropriate for small pieces of less tender meat. Recipes which call for Low power setting will not be as tender if cooked at Medium. Slower cooking allows the meat to simmer in its sauce until it is fork tender. When defrosting strips or chunks, place them in the cooking dish, separate and spread them out as soon as possible. Any juices which appear during defrosting can be added to the liquid in the recipe.

## HOW TO DEFROST STRIPS & CHUNKS

1. Place plastic or paper wrapped package in oven. **Microwave at Defrost** ½ the minimum total time.

2. Turn package over and defrost second ½ of time.

3. Separate pieces with a table knife and let stand to complete defrosting, or microwave 1 to 2 minutes more.

**DEFROSTING TIME: 4 to 8 minutes per pound**

Round Steak Stew

## TIPS FOR MICROWAVING BEEF STRIPS & CHUNKS

**Browning Agents** eliminate the pre-browning step associated with conventional cooking. These may be soy or teriyaki sauce, brown bouquet or steak sauce. Brown gravy mix, dry onion soup mix or bouillon may also be used.

**A Tight Cover** not only speeds cooking but holds in steam which helps tenderize meat. If your casserole does not have a tight cover, seal the top with plastic wrap, turning back about 2-in. at one edge to vent. Be careful when removing the cover to avoid scalding hot steam.

**Low Power Setting** cooks meat gently in liquid and steam until it becomes fork tender. Microwave time will be slightly shorter than conventional cooking. Some recipes may call for Medium power.

## SHORT RIBS AND HOMEMADE NOODLES

POWER LEVEL: High (10) and Low (3)
MICROWAVE TIME: 1½ hr. to 1 hr. 42 min., total

| | |
|---|---|
| **2 lb. short ribs, cut into 2 or 3 rib pieces**<br>**1 small onion, sliced**<br>**1 stalk celery with leaves, cut in half**<br>**2 teaspoons salt**<br>**3 cups water** | In 3-qt. casserole place short ribs, onion, celery, salt and water. Cover. **Microwave at High 20 Minutes.** Stir. Cover. **Microwave at Low 60 to 70 Minutes,** stirring after 30 minutes, until tender. |
| **Homemade Noodles or 1½ cups (½ of 6-oz. pkg.) narrow egg noodles** | Remove ribs and keep warm. Add dry noodles to broth. Cover. **Microwave at High 10 to 12 Minutes,** until tender. |

Makes 2 to 3 servings

## HOMEMADE NOODLES

Beat together 1 egg, 2 tablespoons milk and ½ teaspoon salt. Add 1 cup unsifted all-purpose flour and mix to make a stiff dough. Roll out very thin on floured surface; let stand 20 minutes. Roll up loosely; slice ¼-in. wide. Spread loosely in 13×9×2-in. dish. **Microwave at Low 10 to 12 Minutes,** stirring after 5 minutes, until noodles are dry.

Makes 3 cups cooked noodles.

## ROUND STEAK STEW

POWER LEVEL: High (10) and Low (3)
MICROWAVE TIME: 2 hr. 3 min. to 2 hr. 9 min., total

| | |
|---|---|
| **2 beef bouillon cubes**<br>**2 cups water** | In 3-qt. casserole place bouillon cubes and water. Cover. **Microwave at High 3 to 4 Minutes.** Stir. |
| **2 lbs. round steak, cubed** | Add round steak to bouillon. Cover. **Microwave at Low 1 Hour 45 Minutes,** stirring every 30 minutes. |
| **¼ cup cold water**<br>**3 tablespoons cornstarch**<br>**2 large potatoes, cut up**<br>**1 cup sliced carrots**<br>**½ cup sliced celery**<br>**1 tablespoon diced onion**<br>**1½ teaspoon salt**<br>**¼ teaspoon pepper**<br>**1 pkg. (10-oz.) frozen peas** | In small bowl stir together water and cornstarch. Slowly add to hot mixture, stirring well. Add potatoes, carrots, celery, onion, salt and pepper. Stir to distribute evenly. Cover. **Microwave at High 10 Minutes.** Add peas and stir well. Cover. **Microwave at High 5 to 10 Minutes,** until vegetables are tender. |

Makes 6 to 8 servings

## CUBE STEAK STEW

POWER LEVEL: Medium (5) and High (10)
MICROWAVE TIME: 49 to 58 min., total

| | |
|---|---|
| **4 cube steaks, cut in ½-in. strips**<br>**1 large onion, thinly sliced**<br>**1 teaspoon bottled brown bouquet sauce**<br>**1½ teaspoons salt**<br>**¼ teaspoon pepper**<br>**1 can (16-oz.) tomatoes**<br>**1 can (8-oz.) tomato sauce** | In 3-qt. casserole combine meat, onion, brown bouquet sauce, salt, pepper, tomatoes and tomato sauce. Stir well. Cover. **Microwave at Medium 35 to 38 Minutes.** Stir well. |
| **4 medium potatoes, peeled and cut in eighths** | Add potatoes to stew, stirring well. Cover. **Microwave at High 10 to 15 Minutes,** until potatoes are tender. |
| **1 pkg. (10-oz.) frozen peas, defrosted**<br>**½ medium green pepper, cut in strips** | Add peas and pepper to stew. Cover. **Microwave at High 4 to 5 Minutes,** until peas are tender but pepper still crisp. Stir well before serving. |

Makes about 6 servings

## STEWED BEEF WITH VEGETABLES

POWER LEVEL: Medium (5) and Medium High (7)
MICROWAVE TIME: 1 hr. 50 min. to 2 hr. 10 min., total

| | |
|---|---|
| **2 lb. beef stew meat, cut into 1-in. cubes**<br>**2 cups water**<br>**2 cans (6-oz. each) tomato paste**<br>**1 pkg. (½ of 2¾-oz. box) dry onion soup mix**<br>**¼ teaspoon garlic powder**<br>**¼ teaspoon pepper** | In 3-qt. casserole combine meat, water, tomato paste, onion soup mix, garlic powder and pepper. Stir well. If desired, marinate 3 to 4 hours or overnight. Cover. **Microwave at Medium 85 to 95 Minutes,** stirring every 30 minutes. |
| **2 medium potatoes, cut into 1-in. cubes**<br>**2 medium carrots, sliced**<br>**1 can (12-oz.) yellow kernel corn** | Add potatoes, carrots and corn to stew, stirring well. Cover. **Microwave at Medium High 25 to 35 Minutes** more, stirring after 15 minutes, until vegetables are tender. Stir well before serving. |

Makes 8 to 10 servings

# Beef Steaks Less Tender Cuts

Less tender steaks, such as round, flank or cubed should be microwaved in liquid at Low or Medium. Steam produced by the liquid softens the meat during its longer, slower cooking at the lower power settings. If power levels higher than medium are used, meat will not be as tender.

In some of our recipes, we recommend the traditional technique of pounding the meat, or having it processed through the butcher's tenderizing machine, before cooking.

Frequently, less tender steaks are cooked with a slightly acid liquid, such as tomato juice or wine, which helps tenderize them. Marinating both tenderizes and imparts a delicious flavor to steaks. Try one of the marinades on page 100, and use some of the marinade as the cooking liquid.

## HOW TO DEFROST STEAKS

POWER LEVEL: **Defrost**

### 4 to 8 Minutes Per Pound

1. Place plastic or paper wrapped package in oven. Microwave at Defrost ½ the minimum total time.

2. Turn package over and defrost second ½ of time.

3. Separate pieces with a table knife and let stand to complete defrosting, or microwave 1 to 2 minutes more.

**Separate** steaks as soon as possible and let stand until ice is no longer apparent. If meat is to be cut into strips, do this while it is still partially frozen. It will slice neatly and easily. Any juices which appear during defrosting can be added to the liquid in the recipe.

Swiss Steak

## SWISS STEAK

| POWER LEVEL: Medium (5) | **Cook Code:** 705 |
|---|---|

MICROWAVE TIME: 70 to 80 min., total

| 1½ lb. round steak, | Cut meat in 6 pieces, then |
|---|---|
| ½-in. thick, tenderized or pounded with meat mallet | coat with mixture of flour, salt and pepper. Place in 3-qt. casserole. Cover with |
| ¼ cup flour | onion. Break up tomatoes |
| 1½ teaspoons salt | with fork and pour over top. |
| ⅛ teaspoon pepper | Cover. **Microwave at Me-** |
| 1 medium onion, sliced thin | **dium 70 to 80 Minutes,** re- arranging meat after 40 |
| 1 can (1-lb.) tomatoes | minutes, until tender. |

Makes 6 servings

**Swiss Style Cube Steak:** Substitute 1½ lb. cube steaks, ½-in. thick (about 6), for round steak. Cut in half, if desired.

NOTE: If thicker gravy is desired, stir in 2 tablespoons of flour per cup of juices. Microwave 2 to 3 minutes.

## POLYNESIAN SWISS STEAK

*Be sure meat is covered with sauce throughout cooking time to prevent overbrowning.*

POWER LEVEL: Medium (5)          **Cook Code:** 705
MICROWAVE TIME: 70 to 80 min., total

| | |
|---|---|
| **2 lb. round steak, ½-in. thick, tenderized or pounded with meat mallet** | Trim fat from meat and cut into serving pieces. |
| **1 can (8-oz.) crushed pineapple, undrained**<br>**1 can (8-oz.) tomato sauce**<br>**1 pkg. (½ of 2¾-oz. box) dry onion soup mix**<br>**1 tablespoon prepared mustard** | In small bowl or 1-qt. measure, mix together undrained pineapple, tomato sauce, soup mix and mustard. In 3-qt. casserole, alternately layer meat and sauce. Cover. **Microwave at Medium 70 to 80 Minutes,** rearranging meat after 40 minutes, until tender. |

Makes 4 to 6 servings

## PEPPER STEAK

POWER LEVEL: Med. High (7), Med. (5) and High (10)
MICROWAVE TIME: 36 to 39 min., total

| | |
|---|---|
| **4 cube steaks (6-oz. each)**<br>**⅓ cup steak sauce** | In 12×8×2-in. dish place cube steaks, overlapping if necessary. Brush with steak sauce. Cover with wax paper. **Microwave at Medium High 10 Minutes.** |
| **1 can (10-oz.) beef consomme**<br>**1 teaspoon seasoned salt** | Transfer steaks to 2-qt. casserole. Add consomme and seasoned salt. Cover. **Microwave at Medium 20 Minutes.** |
| **¼ cup cold water**<br>**2 tablespoons cornstarch**<br>**1 medium green pepper, cut into strips**<br>**2 medium firm tomatoes, cut into chunks** | Mix together water and cornstarch. Add to sauce. Cover. **Microwave at High 2 to 3 Minutes,** until thickened. Stir well. Return meat to sauce and add green pepper and tomatoes. **Microwave at Medium 4 to 6 Minutes,** until hot. Let stand a few minutes before serving. Vegetables will be crisp-tender. |

Makes 4 servings

## BOHEMIAN STEAK

POWER LEVEL: Medium (5) and Medium High (7)
MICROWAVE TIME: 87 to 99 min., total

| | |
|---|---|
| **2 lb. round steak, tenderized or pounded with meat mallet**<br>**2 cups thinly sliced onion** | Cut round steak into 8 to 10 serving size pieces. In 3-qt. casserole layer meat and onion. |
| **½ cup water**<br>**1 can (12-oz.) beer**<br>**1 can (10-oz.) beef gravy**<br>**1 tablespoon sugar**<br>**2 teaspoons salt**<br>**½ teaspoon minced garlic**<br>**¼ teaspoon pepper** | Measure water into 1-qt. measure. Add beer, gravy, sugar, salt, garlic and pepper and mix well. Pour over meat and onions. Cover. **Microwave at Medium 80 to 90 Minutes,** rearranging meat after 50 minutes. |
| **¼ cup cold water**<br>**2 tablespoons unsifted all-purpose flour** | Stir together water and flour. Gradually add to stew, mixing well. **Microwave at Medium 3 to 4 Minutes,** uncovered, until thickened. Stir well. Top with Fluffy Dumplings (below). |

Makes 4 to 6 servings

**Fluffy Dumplings:** In small bowl mix together 2 cups buttermilk biscuit mix, ⅔ cup milk and 1 tablespoon parsley flakes just until moistened. Drop by tablespoonfuls around edges of hot stew. Cover. **Microwave at Medium High 4 to 5 Minutes,** until done.

## ROUND STEAK SAVORY

*A favorite recipe often made by our customers. A good variation is to use tomato soup in place of mushroom.*

POWER LEVEL: Low (3)
MICROWAVE TIME: 1 hr. 40 min. to 1 hr. 50 min., total

| | |
|---|---|
| **2 lb. round steak, ½-in. thick**<br>**1 teaspoon seasoned instant meat tenderizer** | Cut steak in serving size pieces (about 2 to 3-in. strips). Sprinkle pieces evenly with meat tenderizer. |
| **1 can (10½-oz.) condensed cream of mushroom soup**<br>**1 teaspoon beef bouillon granules** | In small bowl mix together soup and bouillon. In 3-qt. casserole layer meat and sauce, ending with sauce. Cover. **Microwave at Low 1 Hour 40 Minutes to 1 Hour 50 Minutes,** rearranging meat after 50 minutes. Let stand 10 minutes before serving so flavor can blend. |

Makes about 8 servings

## TOMATO MARINADE

| | |
|---|---|
| **1 cup tomato juice** . . . . . .| In cooking container or 1-qt. glass measure mix together tomato juice, onion, basil, sugar and garlic powder. Use as suggested. |
| **1 cup chopped onion** | |
| **1 teaspoon basil** | |
| **1 teaspoon sugar** | |
| **1 teaspoon garlic powder** | |

Makes 1½ cups

## TERIYAKI MARINADE

| | |
|---|---|
| **½ cup soy sauce** . . . . . . . .| In cooking container or 1-qt. glass measure mix together soy sauce, brown sugar, garlic, ginger, monosodium glutamate and pepper. Use as suggested. |
| **½ cup brown sugar (packed)** | |
| **1 clove garlic, minced** | |
| **2 teaspoons ground ginger** | |
| **1 teaspoon monosodium glutamate (accent)** | |
| **½ teaspoon pepper** | |

Makes ¾ cup

## LEMON OR VINEGAR MARINADE

| | |
|---|---|
| **½ cup lemon juice or white vinegar** . . . . .| In cooking container or 1-qt. glass measure mix together lemon juice, oil, parsley, bay leaves, garlic, onion, sugar, nutmeg, liquid pepper. Use as suggested. |
| **½ cup oil** | |
| **1 sprig parsley or 1 tablespoon chopped parsley** | |
| **2 bay leaves** | |
| **1 garlic clove, crushed** | |
| **2 slices onion** | |
| **1 tablespoon sugar** | |
| **Pinch of nutmeg** | |
| **2 drops liquid pepper seasoning (tabasco)** | |

Makes 1 cup

## WINE MARINADE

| | |
|---|---|
| **⅔ cup dry burgundy wine** . . . . .| In cooking container or 1-qt. glass measure mix together wine, oil, onion, garlic, pepper and thyme. Use as suggested. |
| **⅓ cup cooking oil** | |
| **1 medium onion, finely chopped** | |
| **1 clove garlic, minced** | |
| **½ teaspoon pepper** | |
| **¼ teaspoon dried thyme** | |

Makes 1 cup

## HOW TO MARINATE LESS TENDER STEAKS

POWER LEVEL: **Medium (5)**

**25 to 30 Minutes Per Pound**

*Flank steak, chuck steak, round steak and cube steak are good choices for marinating. Select desired marinade, left.*

*For convenience, mix marinade in glass cooking dish and cover during marinating with plastic wrap. Dish and plastic can be reused for microwaving. Refrigerate while marinating.*

*The smaller the cut of meat, the more marinade flavor it will absorb because more surface is exposed. If you prefer mild marinade flavor, use large meat pieces.*

1. Stir together marinade in 13×9×2-in. dish or 2-qt. casserole.
2. Cut steak into serving size pieces, or as desired. Arrange in marinade, turning over once. Refrigerate overnight in marinade, turning meat over after several hours.
3. Just before microwaving, turn meat over and, if desired, drain off some of marinade. Microwave at Medium 25 to 30 minutes per pound, turning over after ½ of time.

## SPICY STEAK STRIPS

*This is a variation of Greek Beef Stew, called Stifado. A good dinner dish to serve with rice, salad and hard rolls.*

POWER LEVEL: High (10) and Low (3)
MICROWAVE TIME: 75½ to 85½ min., total

| | |
|---|---|
| **3 tablespoons butter** . . . .| In 3-qt. casserole place butter. **Microwave at High ½ Minute,** until melted. Sprinkle meat with salt and pepper. Stir into melted butter until each piece is coated. Sprinkle onions over meat. |
| **2 lb. round steak, cut in strips** | |
| **½ teaspoon salt** | |
| **⅛ teaspoon pepper** | |
| **1 cup chopped onion** | |
| **1 can (6-oz.) tomato paste** . . . . .| In small bowl mix together tomato paste, wine, vinegar, brown sugar, garlic, bay leaf, cinnamon, cloves, cumin and raisins. Pour over meat and onions. Cover. **Microwave at Low 75 to 85 Minutes,** stirring after 40 minutes, until tender. Let stand 10 to 15 minutes before serving. |
| **½ cup red wine** | |
| **2 tablespoons vinegar** | |
| **1 tablespoon brown sugar** | |
| **1 clove garlic, minced** | |
| **1 bay leaf** | |
| **1 small stick cinnamon** | |
| **½ teaspoon whole cloves** | |
| **¼ teaspoon cumin** | |
| **2 tablespoons raisins** | |

Makes about 6 servings

# Beef Steaks Tender Cuts

Steaks microwaved on the browning griddle are juicy and tender. Your microwave oven can also be useful when cooking steaks conventionally. See tips below.

## HOW TO DEFROST STEAKS

POWER LEVEL: **Defrost**

**4 to 8 Minutes Per Pound**

1. Place plastic or paper wrapped package in oven. Microwave at Defrost ½ the minimum total time.
2. Turn package over and defrost second ½ of time.
3. Separate pieces with a table knife and let stand to complete defrosting, or microwave 1 to 2 minutes more.

## MICROWAVING STEAKS IN BROWN 'N SEAR DISH OR BROWNING GRIDDLE

Times are given for ¾ to 1-in. thick steaks cooked to medium (pink center). To test for doneness, cut with knife tip from edge toward center of steak. Area closest to bone is last to cook. **Preheat empty and uncovered browning utensil 8 minutes.**

POWER LEVEL: **High (10)**

| TYPE | NO. OF STEAKS | 1st SIDE MINUTES | 2nd SIDE MINUTES |
|---|---|---|---|
| **Cube Steak or Minute Steak** (4-oz. each) | 1 or 2<br>4 | 1<br>2 | 1 to 1½<br>2 to 2½ |
| **Rib Eye or Strip** | 1 or 2<br>3 | 2<br>5 | 2 to 2½<br>3 to 3½ |
| **T-Bone** | 1 | 3 | 2 |
| **Filet Mignon** | 1, 2 or 4 | 2 | 2 to 2½ |

TIP: For browner color, butter both sides of steak before cooking, using 1 tablespoon of butter per steak. When using the Brown 'N Sear Dish, drain juices after cooking the first side of steak.

## HOW TO REHEAT FROZEN PRE-COOKED STEAKS

Always undercook steaks slightly. This two-step process produces steak which is not dry or overdone.

1. Unwrap steak and place on microwave ovenproof serving plate. Cover with wax paper. **Microwave at Defrost,** allowing 4 to 8 minutes for each 1-lb. steak. Turn steak over after ½ the defrosting time. Let stand a few minutes before reheating.

2. While steak is still covered with wax paper, reheat it by **Microwaving at Medium (5),** using the following times for each 1-lb. steak:

| DONENESS | TIME MINUTES | COMMENTS |
|---|---|---|
| Rare | 5 to 7 | Turn steak over after ½ the time. Let stand a few minutes before serving. |
| Medium | 6 to 8 | |
| Well | 7 to 9 | |

Brown 'N Sear Steak

**Sear** extra 1-in. steaks while your charcoal grill is hot, but undercook them slightly. Cool, wrap in paper or plastic and freeze for future defrosting and microwaving. You'll have charcoal flavor without re-lighting the grill. This is also a good idea when you are grilling hamburgers.

# Roast Defrosting

## MICROLESSON

Defrosting is one of the major benefits of the microwave oven, but it is not miraculous. Roasts need attention dur-

## HOW TO DEFROST ROASTS

POWER LEVEL: **Defrost**

**10 to 12 Minutes Per Pound**

**Place** unopened paper or plastic wrapped package in oven. Microwave at Defrost for ½ the time.

**Remove** wrappings, which will come off easily.

**Turn** roast over onto a trivet set over a cooking dish.

## DEFROSTING ROASTS OVER 6 POUNDS

1. Place wrapped roast in oven and defrost for first ½ of time. Unwrap roast and shield any warm areas.

2. Turn roast over into baking dish. If roast is over 5-in. high, do not use trivet.

3. Defrost for second ½ of time. Let stand 30 minutes.

ing defrosting or they will start to cook. Follow directions carefully for successful defrosting of these expensive cuts of meat.

The procedure demonstrated here applies to pork, lamb and veal roasts as well as beef. Warm areas after de-frosting indicate that the meat has started to cook and should be roasted immediately. If you are defrosting a roast for later cooking, be especially careful. We recommend that you defrost for ¾ the time and allow the roast to finish defrosting in the refrigerator.

**Feel** roast for warm spots, especially on edges and thinner areas. Shield warm areas with small pieces of foil. Defrost for final ½ of time.

**Juices** begin to appear. Meat should look moist with glistening fat and should feel cool.

**Test** meat by inserting a skewer into the center. Do not insert the temperature probe until meat is completely defrosted.

**Shape of Meat** as well as size influences defrosting time.

**Thick** roasts defrost evenly and turning over is very important. Allow some standing time to be sure interior is completely defrosted.

**Flat** roasts defrost quickly. Defrost for ½ of time and turn roast over.

**Irregular** roasts need more shielding on thinner areas. Check carefully for warm spots.

# Beef Roasts
# Less Tender Cuts

In microwaving, as in conventional cooking, less tender cuts of beef call for some liquid, tight covering and Low or Medium Power setting to make them juicy and tender. Use sirloin tip, rump, arm or blade chuck for pot roasts, and brisket or corned beef for simmered beef.

If you want vegetables with your meat, you may use either of two methods. One is to cook vegetables separately, either before the roast or during standing time. Add them to the meat and heat briefly. Or you may add vegetables to the meat half way through the cooking period and microwave until meat is fork tender.

## MICROLESSON

### HOW TO MICROWAVE A POT ROAST

**Arrange** sirloin tip, rump or chuck roast weighing 3 to 5 pounds, in a roasting dish of appropriate size and shape. Brush all sides with a mixture of equal parts of brown bouquet sauce and water.

**Pour** in ½ cup water. If roast has been marinated (recipes page 100), substitute marinade for water. Cover tightly with plastic wrap, turning back corner to vent. **Microwave at Medium (5)** for ½ the cooking time.

### HOW TO MICROWAVE SIMMERED BEEF

**Combine** brisket or corned beef, weighing 3 to 3½ pounds, with 3 cups water, onion, garlic, bay leaf and peppercorns in a casserole.

**Cover** and **Microwave at High (10) for 15 to 25 Minutes.**

Chuck Roast With Vegetables

**Turn** roast over. If meat is more than 3-in. higher than liquid, shield top with foil.

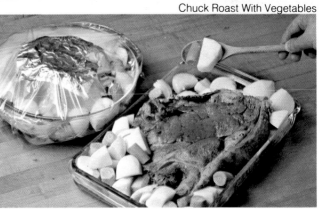

**Arrange** vegetables around roast, if desired. Cover and microwave until meat is fork tender. Thinner roasts cook faster than thick ones. Microwave time: **20 to 25 Minutes Per Pound.**

**Turn** meat over and recover. **Microwave at Medium (5) for 1 to 1½ Hours,** turning meat again after ½ of time, until fork tender.

**Carve** roast diagonally across the grain in thin slices for attractive, tender meat.

## SIRLOIN TIP ROAST

POWER LEVEL: **Medium (5)**

**11 to 16 Minutes Per Pound**

High quality sirloin tip may be cooked to medium- rare or medium at Medium. It will be juicy, tender and pink. On removal from oven, the roast will appear moist, but the surface will dry and darken attractively after standing.

Brush roast with diluted brown bouquet sauce. Place meat in cooking dish, add ½ cup water or wine and cover tightly with plastic wrap. If you are using a temperature probe, arrange plastic wrap loosely around probe to vent and set for 90°. When oven signals, turn meat over and roast to 130° or 135°. If you are cooking by time, estimate 11 to 16 minutes per pound.

To cook by time, microwave for ⅔ total cooking time. Turn meat over and microwave for remaining time. Remove meat from oven and test for doneness with a meat thermometer. *Do not use meat thermometer inside the microwave oven.*

## PEPPERED SIRLOIN TIP ROAST

POWER LEVEL: Medium (5)          TEMP: See Recipe
APPROX. MICROWAVE TIME: 11 to 16 min. per pound

**3 to 5 lb. rolled sirloin tip**
**Liquid smoke seasoning**
**Garlic powder**
**Cracked black pepper**

....Brush liquid smoke on roast to cover. Rub evenly with garlic powder. Press cracked pepper evenly over roast.

Insert temperature probe from cut side so tip rests in center of roast. Place roast in 12×8×2-in. dish. Add ½ cup red wine or water to roasting dish. Cover tightly with plastic wrap, arranging loosely around probe to vent. **Microwave at Medium. Set Temp, Set 90°.**

When oven signals, turn roast over. Recover with plastic wrap and return to microwave oven. **Reset Temp, Set 130°** for medium doneness.

VARIATION: For well done roast, cook on first side to 125°, then turn over and cook to 200°. Let stand 10 to 15 minutes before carving. Approximate microwave time is 21 to 24 minutes per pound.

Makes 6 servings

## CHUCK ROAST

*To microwave milk gravy as an accompaniment, see recipe page 189.*

POWER LEVEL: Medium (5)
MICROWAVE TIME: 21 to 24 min., per pound

**3 to 5 lb. chuck roast**
**1 teaspoon seasoned salt**
**1 tablespoon Worcestershire sauce**
**1 teaspoon bottled brown bouquet sauce**
**½ cup water**

....Rub both sides of roast with salt. Mix together Worcestershire sauce and bottled brown bouquet sauce. Brush on roast. In 13×9×2-in. dish place roast and ½ cup water. Cover tightly with plastic wrap, turning back one corner to vent. **Microwave at Medium 21 to 24 Minutes** per lb. Turn roast over after ½ of total time. Let stand about 10 minutes before serving.

Makes 5 to 8 servings

**Chuck Roast with Vegetables:** After ½ of cooking time add 2 large onions, cut in 8ths; 4 medium potatoes, cut in 6ths or 8ths; and 6 carrots, cut in large chunks. Recover and continue microwaving.

## ROLLED RUMP ROAST

*Bacon cover over roast bastes it while cooking, keeps top surface moist and gives delicious flavor to roast.*

POWER LEVEL: Medium (5)
MICROWAVE TIME: 24 to 27 min., per pound

**3 to 5 lb. rolled rump roast**
**1 teaspoon onion salt**
**1 tablespoon brown bouquet sauce**
**1 tablespoon water**

.....Rub both sides of roast with salt. Brush with brown bouquet sauce mixed with water.

**Bacon strips, uncooked**

....Cover roast, except cut sides, with bacon strips laying side by side and securing with toothpicks if necessary.

In 3-qt. casserole place roast and ½ cup water. Cover tightly with plastic wrap, turning back 2-in. at edge to vent. **Microwave at Medium 24 to 27 Minutes,** per pound, turning over after ½ of time. Let stand about 10 minutes before serving.

Makes 6 to 10 servings

**Rump Roast with Vegetables:** Add vegetables suggested under Chuck Roast after ½ of cooking time, if desired. Or, substitute peeled and cut up rutabagas for potatoes.

## SIMMERED CORNED BEEF

POWER LEVEL: High (10) and Medium (5)
MICROWAVE TIME: 1 hr. 25 min. to 1 hr. 35 min., total

**3 to 3½ lb. corned beef** . . . In 3-qt. casserole place
    **brisket**
**3 cups water**
**1 medium onion, thinly**
    **sliced**
**2 cloves garlic, minced**
**2 bay leaves**

In 3-qt. casserole place brisket with water. Slice onion over brisket and add garlic and bay leaves. Cover. **Microwave at High 25 Minutes.** Turn brisket over. Recover. **Microwave at Medium 60 to 70 Minutes,** turning brisket over after 30 minutes. To serve: diagonally slice corned beef very thin for sandwiches or for serving with boiled vegetables.

Makes 6 to 8 servings

## NEW ENGLAND BOILED DINNER

POWER LEVEL: High (10)
MICROWAVE TIME: 1 hr. 50 min. to 2 hrs. 5 min., total

**1 recipe Simmered** . . . . . . .Microwave corned beef as
    **Corned Beef (above)**

Microwave corned beef as described above. Remove meat from broth and keep warm.

**2 large potatoes, cut up**
**4 medium carrots, cut**
    **lengthwise**
**1 medium head cabbage**
    **cut in 6 wedges**

Add potatoes and carrots to broth. Arrange cabbage in a pinwheel on top.

Cover. **Microwave at High 25 to 30 Minutes,** rearranging after 15 minutes, until vegetables are tender. Discard bay leaves. To serve: diagonally slice corned beef very thin and serve with vegetables.

Makes 6 servings

## BEEF BRISKET

POWER LEVEL: High (10) and Medium (5)
MICROWAVE TIME: 1 hr. 35 min. to 1 hr. 45 min., total

**3 lb. beef brisket** . . . . . .
**3 cups water**
**1 tablespoon salt**
**¼ teaspoon**
    **peppercorns**
**1 medium onion**

In 3-qt. casserole place brisket, water, salt and peppercorns. Place onion slices on top of brisket. Cover. **Microwave at High 15 Minutes.**

**Microwave at Medium 80 to 90 Minutes,** until tender, turning brisket over after 45 minutes. For maximum juiciness, let brisket stand in juices 10 minutes before serving.

Makes 6 to 8 servings

New England Boiled Dinner

## SPICY BEEF BRISKET

POWER LEVEL: High (10) and Medium (5)
MICROWAVE TIME: 1 hr. 45 min. to 2 hrs., total

**½ cup ketchup** . . . . . . . . . .In small bowl mix together
**1 medium onion,**
    **chopped**
**3 tablespoons brown**
    **sugar**
**2 tablespoons vinegar**
**1 teaspoon basil or**
    **bouquet garnish**
**½ teaspoon garlic salt**
**¼ teaspoon thyme**
**¼ teaspoon salt**
**⅛ teaspoon pepper**
**3 lb. beef brisket**

In small bowl mix together ketchup, onion, brown sugar, vinegar, garlic salt, basil, thyme, salt and pepper. Pour half of sauce over brisket in 12×8×2-in. dish. Cover with plastic wrap turning back one corner to vent. **Microwave at High 15 Minutes.**

**Microwave at Medium 45 Minutes.** Turn brisket over and pour other half of sauce over meat. **Microwave at Medium 45 to 60 Minutes,** until meat is tender. Let stand 10 minutes, then carve into very thin slices and serve with sauce.

Makes 6 to 8 servings

**Microwave Roasted Beef.** This rolled rib was microwave roasted to an internal temperature of 130°. It has the same medium color internally as conventionally roasted beef, although the temperature is lower. Roast was brushed with browning agent before microwaving.

**Conventionally Roasted Beef.** This rolled rib was roasted conventionally to an internal temperature of 140°. Both roasts stood about 15 minutes before carving.

**Rare.** Meat microwaved to an internal temperature of 120° is red in the center, with running juices. Since microwaving is so fast, the exterior will not be browned. If you desire a brown color, brush the meat with a browning agent before roasting.

**Medium.** Meat microwaved to an internal temperature of 130° is rosy in the center, with pink juices. Some browning occurs on the outside. If you prefer a browner exterior, brush the meat with a browning agent before roasting.

**Well Done.** Meat microwaved to an internal temperature of 155° is brown in the center, with clear juices. The time needed to cook beef well done is enough to brown the exterior, so no browning agent is needed.

# Beef Roasts Tender Cuts

Tender cuts of beef, such as rolled or standing rib, tenderloin, or eye of round, are ideal for microwave roasting. Lower power settings allow carefree, no attention roasting at faster than conventional speed.

Since these roasts are expensive, and generally reserved for special occasions, you'll want to follow directions carefully. Before you purchase roasts, select meat carefully; standards for grading beef have changed recently, which may affect grain and resulting tenderness. Pay special attention to internal temperatures so you don't overcook! Since meat continues to cook while standing, rare to medium roasts are microwaved to lower internal temperatures than conventional roasts. After 10 minutes standing they reach about the same final temperature as conventionally cooked.

Small, compact and evenly shaped roasts cook best. Just as in conventional cooking, a roast which is thinner on one end will be done first in that area. Long, thin roasts cook faster than short, thick ones.

Roasts of 5 to 6 pounds may be more done in the first two slices from the top than in the center, because these slices are closer to the source of energy. This can be useful if some guests prefer more doneness than others.

If you want a large roast done uniformly, it can be turned over halfway through the estimated roasting time.

If family or guests differ in preference between rare and well-done, roast the meat to the minimum doneness. Carve it, and return some slices to the microwave oven. It takes just a short time to bring a slice from rare to well-done.

Due to the slotted design of the microwave trivet accessory shown below, bottom areas of rare or medium done roasts may not be brown when meat is done. This allows greater area of rare or medium meat for serving. Flat glass or pottery trivets such as top of refrigerator dish, flat top of casserole, or china plate hold heat to bottom of roast and bottom browning will occur; or, turn roast over and continue microwaving for a few minutes.

## HOW TO MICROWAVE TENDER BEEF ROASTS

**Tie** standing rib roasts across the meat to secure fat. Fold the thin end of a half tenderloin under and tie the roast to maintain an even, compact shape.

**Brush** half tenderloin or eye of round with equal parts of brown bouquet sauce and melted butter.

**Place** roast on a trivet in a 12×8×2 or 13×9×2-in. cooking dish. DO NOT SALT. Cover with wax paper.

## MICROWAVING BEEF BY TEMPERATURE

If your oven is equipped with a temperature probe, be sure to use it when roasting tenderloin beef. See chart below for power level and internal temperature. Note that the internal temperature is lower for microwaved beef roast than it is for conventionally roasted beef.

When microwaving tenderloin and eye of round with the temperature probe, set for 90°, turn over and reset to finished temperature.

## HOW TO INSERT THE TEMPERATURE PROBE

Measure the distance to the center of the roast by laying the temperature probe on top of the meat. If the roast is uneven in shape or contains fat or bone, select an angle which will bring the tip of the probe to the center of the

thickest meaty area without touching fat or bone. Mark with your thumb and forefinger where the edge of the meat comes on the probe. Insert the probe up to the point marked off with your finger.

**Standing Rib.** Insert probe from the front of roast so that tip is in the center of roast.

**Rolled Rib.** Insert probe into the rolled side so that tip is in the center of roast.

**Half Tenderloin.** Insert probe into the cut end so that tip is in the center of roast.

**Eye Of Round.** Insert probe through side of roast so that tip is in the center of meat.

## MICROWAVING BEEF BY TIME

Estimate the cooking time for the type, size and desired doneness of your roast. See chart below. Cook for the minimum time suggested on the chart. You may need to reset the timer to complete the minimum cycle for larger or well done roasts.

After the minimum time, remove the roast from the oven and test the temperature with a meat thermometer, fol-

lowing the directions for probe placement given with your type of roast. Remember that microwave roasted meats are cooked to a lower temperature than conventionally roasted meats. If the roast has not reached the desired doneness, remove the thermometer and return the meat to the oven for a few more minutes of cooking time. *Do not use meat thermometer in the microwave oven.*

## TENDER BEEF ROAST COOKING CHART

The estimated microwaving times are based on meat at refrigerated temperature. Rib roasts up to 6 pounds microwave well. If meat has been frozen, be sure to

thoroughly defrost before roasting, especially if you are using the temperature probe. Let roast stand about 10 to 15 minutes before carving.

| ITEM | POWER LEVEL | INTERNAL TEMP. | MIN. PER LB. |
|---|---|---|---|
| **Standing Rib** | | | |
| Rare | Med. (5) | 120-125° | 11-13 |
| Medium | Med. (5) | 130-140° | 13-15 |
| Well Done | Med. (5) | 155-165° | 15-17 |
| **Rolled Rib** | | | |
| Rare | Med. (5) | 120-125° | 11-13 |
| Medium | Med. (5) | 130-140° | 13-15 |
| Well Done | Med. (5) | 155-165° | 15-17 |

| ITEM | POWER LEVEL | INTERNAL TEMP. | MIN. PER LB. |
|---|---|---|---|
| **Half Tenderloin** | | | |
| Rare | Low (3) | 120-125° | 8-9 |
| Medium | Low (3) | 130-140° | 9-10 |
| Well Done | Low (3) | 155-165° | 10-12 |
| **Eye of Round** | | | |
| Rare | Low (3) | 120-125° | 9-10 |
| Medium | Low (3) | 130-140° | 10-11 |
| Well Done | Low (3) | 155-165° | 11-13 |

# Ham & Pork Ground

Lower power settings are ideal for ground ham, which tends to become dry and crusty at high settings due to the curing process. The addition of some ground pork or beef not only makes ham go farther, but adds enough moisture so that it remains tender and juicy.

Patties containing ground ham do not require use of the Brown 'N Sear Dish or a browning agent because ham has a naturally attractive pink color; however, a light brushing of brown bouquet sauce may be used.

**Defrosting Ground Pork.** Ground pork should be defrosted in the same way as ground beef. See page 82. Ham does not freeze well, but small quantities of leftover ground ham may be frozen for use in appetizers, casseroles or Oriental and Italian dishes which call for small amounts of ham to heighten color and flavor.

## CLASSIC HAM LOAF

POWER LEVEL: Medium (5)          TEMP: 170°
APPROX. MICROWAVE TIME: 25 to 30 min.

                              **Cook Code:** 255

| | |
|---|---|
| **1 lb. ground ham** . . . . . | Mix ground ham and pork |
| **½ lb. ground fresh pork** | thoroughly with crumbs, |
| **½ cup soft bread crumbs** | water, onion, and pepper. |
| **½ cup water** | Mold into flat oval loaf in |
| **2 tablespoons instant minced onion** | 10×6×2-in. dish, or flat loaf in 9-in. pie plate. |
| **¼ teaspoon pepper** | |

Insert temperature probe so tip is in center of food. Cover tightly with plastic wrap, arranging loosely around probe to vent. Attach cable end at receptacle. **Microwave at Medium. Set Temp, Set 170°.**

When oven signals, remove loaf from oven and let stand 5 minutes before serving.

Makes 6 servings

NOTES:

1. If a fast simple glaze is desired, spoon pineapple or apricot preserves over cooked ham loaf a few minutes before serving.

2. For best cooking results, do not exceed recommended weight of meat.

Classic Ham Loaf

**Shape** ham loaf in an oval or circle. Insert the temperature probe so the tip is in the center of the loaf. Cover tightly with plastic wrap, arranging loosely around probe to vent. Microwave to an internal temperature of 170°.

Sweet 'N' Sour Porkies

## SWEET 'N' SOUR PORKIES

POWER LEVEL: High (10)        **Cook Code:** 150
MICROWAVE TIME: 15 to 18 min., total

| | |
|---|---|
| **1 lb. ground cooked ham** <br> **½ lb. ground fresh pork** <br> **½ cup soft bread crumbs** <br> **½ cup water** <br> **1 egg** <br> **¼ cup minced celery** <br> **2 tablespoons minced green pepper** <br> **2 tablespoons instant minced onion** <br> **½ teaspoon dry mustard** <br> **¼ teaspoon pepper** | In large mixing bowl mix together ham, pork, crumbs, water, egg, celery, green pepper, onion, mustard and pepper. Shape mixture into 4 individual patties and place in 8-in. square dish. |
| **8 to 12 whole cloves** | Score tops of patties and place 2 or 3 whole cloves in top of each. |
| **⅓ cup brown sugar (packed)** <br> **1 tablespoon prepared mustard** <br> **1 tablespoon vinegar** | Stir together sugar, mustard and vinegar. Pour evenly over patties. |

Cover dish with wax paper. **Microwave at High 15 to 18 Minutes,** rotating dish ½ turn after 10 minutes.
Makes 4 generous servings

## TRIPLE MEATLOAF

POWER LEVEL: Medium (5)      TEMP: 170°
APPROX. MICROWAVE TIME: 45 to 50 min.
                      **Cook Code:** 455

| | |
|---|---|
| **1½ lb. ground cooked ham** <br> **1 lb. ground chuck beef** <br> **½ lb. ground fresh pork** <br> **3 eggs beaten** <br> **1¼ cup graham cracker crumbs, 16 squares** <br> **½ cup diced red or green pepper** <br> **1 teaspoon ground cloves** | In large bowl place ham, beef, pork, eggs, crumbs, pepper and cloves. Mix together very well. In 12×8×2-in. dish form mixture into flat oval loaf. Insert temperature probe so tip is in center of loaf. Cover tightly with plastic wrap, arranging loosely around probe to vent. |

Attach cable end at receptacle. **Microwave at Medium. Set Temp, Set 170°.** When oven signals, remove loaf and microwave Topping (below), spread over loaf. Let stand 10 minutes before slicing.
Makes 10 to 12 servings

**Raisin Topping:** In small bowl stir together ½ cup brown sugar, ½ teaspoon dry mustard, 1 tablespoon vinegar and ¼ cup raisins. **Microwave at High 3 to 5 Minutes. Cook Code: 30.**

## HOLIDAY HAM LOAF

POWER LEVEL: Medium (5)      TEMP: 170°
APPROX. MICROWAVE TIME: 40 to 50 min.
                      **Cook Code:** 405

| | |
|---|---|
| **1½ lb. ground cooked ham** <br> **1½ lb. ground fresh pork** <br> **1½ cups fine bread crumbs** <br> **2 eggs beaten** <br> **½ cup chopped onion** <br> **½ cup milk** | In large bowl mix together ham, pork, crumbs, eggs, onions and milk. In 12×8×2-in. dish form mixture into flat oval loaf. Insert temperature probe so tip is in center of loaf. Cover tightly with plastic wrap, arranging loosely around probe to vent. |

Attach cable end at receptacle. **Microwave at Medium. Set Temp, Set 170°.** When oven signals, remove loaf and microwave Topping (below); spread over loaf. Let stand 10 minutes for topping to set and to allow loaf to firm before slicing.
Makes 10 to 12 servings

**Spicy Topping:** In small bowl stir together 2 tablespoons butter, 1 cup brown sugar (packed) and 1 teaspoon allspice. **Microwave at High 3 to 5 Minutes,** until dissolved. **Cook Code: 30.**

# Pork Spareribs

Everyone agrees that the barbecued sparerib is one of America's greatest inventions. No one agrees on how it should be cooked. One side advocates the moist, fork tender rib which falls off the bone and melts in the mouth. Another side is devoted to the dry, chewy rib, and considers eating ribs with anything but the fingers a sacrilege. Ever since our first Microwave Cookbook, in 1962, we've provided recipes for both types, because the staff couldn't agree on which rib was the real rib.

Whichever rib you fancy, the microwave oven cooks it fast and flavorful. The fork tender rib takes a little longer, because you add moisture which absorbs some power, and you cook part of the time at a lower power setting. Either way, turn or rearrange ribs half way through the cooking time. Both styles may be served as a main dish or as an appetizer.

## HOW TO DEFROST SPARERIBS
POWER LEVEL: **Defrost**

### 4 to 8 Minutes Per Pound

1. Place plastic or paper wrapped package in oven. Microwave at Defrost ½ the minimum total time.

2. Turn package over and defrost second ½ of time.

3. Separate pieces with a table knife and let stand to complete defrosting, or microwave 1 to 2 minutes more.

NOTE: For a rack of ribs, let stand 15 minutes to completely defrost largest end.

## CHEWY STYLE SPARERIBS

POWER LEVEL: High (10)
MICROWAVE TIME: 30 to 35 min., total

| | |
|---|---|
| **3 lb. rack of spareribs** | In 13×9×2-in. dish place spareribs, bone side up. Cover with wax paper. **Microwave at High 15 Minutes,** turning over after 10 minutes. Drain off liquid. |
| **1 medium onion, very thinly sliced**<br>**1 lemon, very thinly sliced**<br>**1 cup barbecue sauce bottled, or page 192** | Distribute onion and lemon slices over ribs, pour sauce over top. Cover. **Microwave at High 15 to 20 Minutes,** until no pink remains in meat. Spoon sauce over ribs before serving. |

Makes about 4 servings

TO COOK RIBS IN PIECES: Cut into 2 or 3-rib pieces and microwave in 3-qt. covered casserole.

Chewy Style Spareribs          Fork Tender Spareribs

## FORK TENDER SPARERIBS

POWER LEVEL: Medium (5)
MICROWAVE TIME: 1 hr. 30 min. to 1 hr. 45 min., total

| | |
|---|---|
| **3 lb. rack of spareribs**<br>**2 cups hot tap water**<br>**1 medium onion, very thinly sliced**<br>**1 lemon, very thinly sliced** | In 13×9×2-in. dish place spareribs, bone side up. Add water. Cover tightly with plastic wrap, turning back one corner to vent. **Microwave at Medium 80 to 90 Minutes,** turning over and arranging onion and lemon over top after 40 minutes, until fork tender. |
| **1 cup barbecue sauce, bottled, or page 192** | Drain liquid from ribs and pour sauce over top. **Microwave at Medium 10 to 15 Minutes,** loosely covered with plastic wrap, until sauce has dried on top. Spoon sauce over ribs before serving. |

Makes about 4 servings

TO COOK RIBS IN PIECES: Cut into 2 or 3-rib pieces and microwave in 3-qt. covered casserole.

Sweet-Sour Spareribs

## SMOKEY PINEAPPLE SPARERIBS

POWER LEVEL: Medium (5)
MICROWAVE TIME: 80 to 90 min., total

| | |
|---|---|
| 3 lb. spareribs, cut in serving pieces<br>2 cups hot tap water | In 3-qt. casserole place ribs and water. Cover. **Microwave at Medium 40 Minutes.** Drain ribs. |
| 1 can (8½-oz.) crushed pineapple<br>1 can (8-oz.) tomato sauce<br>⅓ cup vinegar<br>1 teaspoon garlic salt<br>1 teaspoon chili powder<br>2 tablespoons light molasses<br>1 tablespoon prepared mustard<br>1 tablespoon liquid smoke | In 1-qt. glass measure mix together pineapple, tomato sauce, vinegar, garlic salt, chili powder, molasses, mustard and liquid smoke. Pour over drained ribs, stirring to coat each piece. Cover. **Microwave at Medium 40 to 50 Minutes,** until ribs are tender. |

Makes about 4 servings

## TERIYAKI RIBLETS

*Ribs may be marinated in sauce several hours or overnight before cooking, if desired.*

POWER LEVEL: Medium (5) and High (10)
MICROWAVE TIME: 73 to 84 min., total

| | |
|---|---|
| 3 lb. spareribs | Have butcher cut rack of spareribs in half crosswise. Cut ribs into 3-in. pieces and place in 3-qt. casserole. |
| ¼ cup soy sauce<br>½ cup sliced onion<br>2 tablespoons brown sugar<br>1 clove garlic, minced<br>1 teaspoon ground ginger<br>1 teaspoon salt<br>2 tablespoons sherry wine<br>3 cups apricot nectar or orange juice | In mixing bowl stir together soy sauce, onion, brown sugar, garlic, ginger, salt, sherry and nectar. Pour over ribs. Cover. **Microwave at Medium 70 to 80 Minutes,** rearranging after 40 minutes. Remove ribs to platter and keep warm. Skim fat from top of liquid remaining in dish. |
| 1½ tablespoons cornstarch<br>2 tablespoons water | In small bowl, stir together cornstarch and water. Blend into liquid in dish. **Microwave at High 3 to 4 Minutes,** stirring every minute until sauce is clear and thickened. Serve sauce over ribs. |

Makes about 8 appetizer servings, or
4 entree servings

## SWEET-SOUR SPARERIBS

POWER LEVEL: Medium (5) and High (10)
MICROWAVE TIME: 1 hr. 33 min. to 1 hr. 47 min., total

| | |
|---|---|
| 3 lb. spareribs, cut in serving pieces<br>1 large onion, chopped<br>2 cups hot tap water | In 3-qt. casserole place ribs. Add onion and water. Cover. **Microwave at Medium 80 to 90 Minutes,** rearranging after 40 minutes. Drain meat. |
| ¾ cup cider vinegar<br>¾ cup sugar<br>½ cup sherry wine<br>1 tablespoon soy sauce<br>2 teaspoons ground ginger | In small bowl stir together vinegar, sugar, wine, soy sauce and ginger. Add to drained cooked ribs. **Microwave at High 5 to 7 Minutes,** until hot. |
| 3 tablespoons cornstarch<br>2 tablespoons cold water | In small bowl stir cornstarch into cold water. Add to hot saucy ribs, mixing well. **Microwave at High 8 to 10 Minutes,** stirring after 5 minutes, until sauce is thickened. |

Makes about 4 entree servings, or
8 appetizer servings

# Pork Chops & Steaks

Just as in conventional cooking, texture of pork chops depends upon the cooking method used. Fried chops are chewy; steamed chops are more soft. Some people prefer to brown chops in a skillet on the range top, then finish them by microwaving.

## HOW TO DEFROST CHOPS & STEAKS

POWER LEVEL: **Defrost**

### 4 to 8 Minutes Per Pound

1. Place plastic or paper wrapped package in oven. Microwave at Defrost ½ the minimum total time.

2. Turn package over and defrost second ½ of time.

3. Separate pieces with a table knife and let stand to complete defrosting, or microwave 1 to 2 minutes more.

## MICROWAVING CHOPS OR STEAKS

1. Select steaks or chops about ¾-in. thick. Cut steaks into pieces about 3×4-in. Arrange in suitable dish.

2. On each chop or steak, spread 2 tablespoons of Topping. (See suggestions below.)

3. Cover tightly with plastic wrap, venting 2-in. at one side. Microwave at Medium, rotating dish ½ turn after ½ of time.

4. Add salt and pepper after microwaving, as desired.

POWER LEVEL: **Medium (5)**

| NO. | UTENSIL | TIME MIN. | COOK CODE | COMMENTS |
|---|---|---|---|---|
| 2 | Microwave-type dinner plate or 9-in. pie plate | 14-18 | 145 | Let stand covered 5 to 10 minutes before serving. |
| 3 | 8-in. square | 19-24 | 195 | |
| 4 | 8-in. square | 26-32 | 265 | |
| 6 | 12×8×2-in. | 33-37 | 335 | |

## TOPPINGS

1. Equal parts Worcestershire or steak sauce and water.

2. Barbecue sauce (bottled or see recipe, page 192).

3. Teriyaki sauce, bottled.

4. Any marinade from page 100. Marinate chops several hours, if desired, then cook in marinade.

5. Brush meat with diluted brown bouquet sauce or soy sauce. Add 2 tablespoons water or red wine per chop.

**Microwaved** pork chops or steaks need to be browned or cooked in a colorful sauce. From the top: Conventional, Plain Microwaved, Steak Sauce and Water Topping, Brown 'N Sear Dish.

Golden Breaded Pork Cutlets

## CHILI PORK CHOPS

| POWER LEVEL: Medium (5) | Cook Code: 355 |
|---|---|
| MICROWAVE TIME: 35 to 45 min., total | |

**4 pork chops, 1-in. thick**
**4 onion slices, ¼ to**
**  ½-in. thick**
**4 green pepper rings, ¼**
**  to ½-in. thick**
**1 bottle (12-oz.) chili**
**  sauce**

..Score fat on chops and arrange in 3-qt. casserole so "tails" are in center. Place onion and green pepper slices on top of chops. Pour chili sauce over top. Cover. **Microwave at Medium 35 to 45 Minutes,** rotating dish ½ turn after 20 minutes.

Makes 4 servings

## PORK CHOPS WITH SAUERKRAUT AND BEER

*When possible, assemble this dish ahead of time and allow to marinate several hours to blend flavor and tenderize meat.*

| POWER LEVEL: Medium (5) | Cook Code: 355 |
|---|---|
| MICROWAVE TIME: 35 to 40 min., total | |

**4 pork chops, 1-in. thick**
**½ cup chopped onion**
**1 can (16-oz.)**
**  sauerkraut, drained**
**1 teaspoon caraway**
**  seed (optional)**
**1 can (12-oz.) beer**

..In 8-in. square dish arrange chops with thickest meaty areas to edge and "tails" to center. Sprinkle evenly with onion. Spread sauerkraut over top. Sprinkle with caraway. Pour beer around chops.

Cover dish tightly with plastic wrap, turning back one corner to vent. **Microwave at Medium 35 to 40 Minutes,** rotating dish ½ turn after 17 minutes.

Makes 4 servings

## GOLDEN BREADED PORK CUTLETS

*Pounding the cutlets thin tenderizes them and allows for fast cooking at High.*

| POWER LEVEL: High | Cook Code: 120 |
|---|---|
| MICROWAVE TIME: 12 to 14 min. | |

**6 lean pork rib chops**
**  (8-oz. each)**

..Remove bone from each chop leaving a single solid piece of meat. Pound each chop with wooden mallet or foil-covered brick until meat is ½-in. thick.

**1¼ cups buttery**
**  cracker crumbs**
**  (about 45 crackers)**
**¾ teaspoon salt**
**2 eggs, beaten**
**¼ cup butter, melted**

..Combine crumbs and salt. Dip flattened cutlets into crumbs to coat, then in mixture of eggs and melted butter. Coat again with crumbs.

Place coated cutlets in 12×8×2-in. dish. Cover with wax paper. **Microwave at High 12 to 14 Minutes,** rotating dish ½ turn after 6 minutes. Let stand 5 to 10 minutes before serving. If desired, garnish with chutney.

Makes 6 servings

VARIATION: To crumb mixture add 1 tablespoon curry powder. Or, use a flavored snack cracker, such as onion or cheese cracker, to make crumbs for breading.

## GOLDEN BREADED PORK CHOPS

Cook Code: 553

Prepare above recipe, except use 1-in. pork chops with bone in and 13×9×2-in. dish, if necessary. **Microwave at Low 55 to 65 Minutes,** rotating dish ½ turn after 30 minutes.

## MICROWAVING PORK CHOPS IN BROWN 'N SEAR DISH OR BROWNING GRIDDLE

Preheat empty dish or griddle at High. Add chops; cover (if Brown 'N Sear Dish is used), and cook first side. Turn chops and recover dish. Cook second side.

POWER LEVEL: **High (10)**

| NO. OF CHOPS | PREHEAT MINUTES | 1st SIDE MINUTES | 2nd SIDE MINUTES |
|---|---|---|---|
| 1 | 3 | 2 | 4 to 6 |
| 2 | 4 | 4 | 4 to 6 |
| 3 | 4 | 4, then pour off juice | 5 to 6 |
| 4 (griddle) | 6 | 6 | 5 to 7 |
| 6 (griddle) | 8 | 9 | 7 to 10 |

## STUFFED 'N' TENDER PORK CHOPS

POWER LEVEL: Medium (5)  **Cook Code:** 355
MICROWAVE TIME: 35 to 40 min., total

1. Select **4 (1-in. thick) pork chops** with pocket cut in each.

2. Fill pocket with Apple Stuffing or Cornbread Stuffing (below), dividing all of stuffing among chops. Arrange chops in 12×8×2-in. dish, with thickest meaty areas to edge and "tails" in center. Brush half of glaze (below) over top of chops. Cover with wax paper.

3. **Microwave at Medium 35 to 40 Minutes,** rotating dish ½ turn after 15 minutes, until tender. Let stand 5 minutes. Brush with remaining glaze before serving.

Makes 4 servings

## APPLE STUFFING WITH SWEET GLAZE

**2 cups chopped apples**
**¼ cup raisins**
**1 egg, beaten**
**2 tablespoons butter, melted**
**½ teaspoon cinnamon**
**½ teaspoon salt**
**⅛ teaspoon pepper**

In mixing bowl combine apples, raisins, egg, butter, cinnamon, salt and pepper. Divide evenly between chops.

**Sweet Glaze:** Mix together ⅓ cup currant jelly and 2 tablespoons orange juice.

Makes about 1½ cups

## CORNBREAD STUFFING WITH SAVORY GLAZE

**2 cups crumbled cornbread**
**¼ cup chopped onion**
**¼ cup chopped green pepper**
**¼ cup butter, melted**
**1 egg, beaten**
**1 tablespoon chopped pimiento**
**½ teaspoon salt**
**⅛ teaspoon pepper**

In mixing bowl toss together cornbread, onion, green pepper, butter, egg, pimiento, salt and pepper. Divide evenly between chops.

**Savory Glaze:** Mix together ½ cup ketchup, 2 tablespoons brown sugar, 2 teaspoons prepared mustard and ¼ teaspoon chili powder.

Makes about 1½ cups

Cornbread Stuffed 'N' Tender Pork Chops

## PORK CHOPS ROSADO

*This dish is very saucy, so plan rice or noodles to serve under chops and sauce.*

POWER LEVEL: Medium (5)  **Cook Code:** 355
MICROWAVE TIME: 35 to 45 min., total

**4 center cut loin pork chops, 1-in. thick**
**1 large onion, cut in ¼-in. slices**
**1 medium lemon or lime, cut in ⅛-in. slices**

In 12×8×2-in. dish arrange pork chops with thickest meaty areas to edge and "tails" in center. Place onion and lemon slices over top of chops.

**1 cup ketchup**
**1 cup (8-oz.) dairy sour cream**

Combine ketchup and sour cream. Pour over top. Cover dish with plastic wrap, turning back one corner to vent.

**Microwave at Medium 35 to 45 Minutes,** rotating dish ½ turn after 18 minutes.

Makes 4 servings

Sweet and Sour Pork

## SWEET AND SOUR PORK

POWER LEVEL: Medium (5) and Medium High (7)
MICROWAVE TIME: 45 to 50 min., total

| | |
|---|---|
| 1½ lbs. fresh pork, cut into 1-in. cubes<br>1 tablespoon instant minced onion<br>1 tablespoon soy sauce<br>1 teaspoon brown bouquet sauce<br>1 can (8¾-oz.) pineapple chunks | In 2-qt. casserole place pork, onion, soy sauce and bouquet sauce. Reserving juice, drain pineapple. Set aside. Add reserved juice to meat, stirring well. Cover. **Microwave at Medium 30 Minutes,** stirring after 15 minutes. |
| 1 cup water<br>¼ cup cider vinegar<br>¼ cup brown sugar (packed)<br>3 tablespoons cornstarch<br>1 can (5-oz.) water chestnuts, drained and sliced<br>1 medium green pepper, sliced in ½-in. strips | In small bowl stir together water, vinegar, brown sugar and cornstarch. Add to meat along with pineapple and water chestnuts. Cover. **Microwave at Medium High 15 to 20 Minutes,** stirring and adding green pepper after 8 minutes, until thickened and clear. |
| 1 medium firm tomato cut into chunks | Fold in tomato chunks and let stand, covered, 10 minutes before serving. Serve over rice or crisp noodles. |

Makes 6 servings

## CHOW MEIN

POWER LEVEL: High (10)  Cook Code: 200
MICROWAVE TIME: 20 to 22 min., total

| | |
|---|---|
| ⅓ cup soy sauce<br>3 tablespoons cornstarch<br>2 cans (5-oz. each) water chestnuts, sliced and undrained<br>1 can (1-lb.) bean sprouts, undrained<br>1 can (7-oz.) mushroom stems and pieces, undrained<br>2 cups diced cooked pork or other meat<br>2 cups ½-in. diagonal slices celery<br>1 cup thinly sliced onion | In 3-qt. casserole stir together soy sauce and cornstarch. Stir in water chestnuts, bean sprouts and mushrooms, then meat, celery and onion. **Microwave at High 20 to 22 Minutes,** stirring well after 10 minutes. Stir thoroughly and serve over cooked rice or chow mein noodles. |

Makes 4 to 6 servings

## GOLDEN PORK CASSEROLE

POWER LEVEL: High (10)  Cook Code: 90
MICROWAVE TIME: 9 to 12 min., total

| | |
|---|---|
| 4 to 6 slices (½-in. thick) cooked pork roast (¾ to 1-lb.)<br>1 can (17-oz.) yams, drained and cut in 1-in. slices<br>1 cup coarsely shredded, unpeeled apple<br>½ cup grated sharp cheddar cheese<br>3 tablespoons brown sugar<br>1 tablespoon lemon juice<br>2 tablespoons butter | In 2-qt. casserole layer pork, yams, apple and cheese. Sprinkle on brown sugar and lemon juice. Dot with butter. Cover. **Microwave at High 9 to 12 Minutes,** until hot throughout. |

Makes 4 to 6 servings

# Ham Slices & Steaks

Slices and steaks of ready-to-eat ham are precooked, so they need only be reheated. Cooking times are short because the high sugar content attracts microwaves, but browning is not necessary, since ham has a naturally attractive color. When baking a ham slice, 1 to 2-in. thick, add some liquid to keep it juicy and cover the dish tightly with plastic wrap. Due to the salt, ham can become dry if moisture is not sealed in.

**Baked Ham Slice.** Use a slice of fully cooked ham, 1 to 2-in. thick. Slash the edges to prevent curling. Place ham in a baking dish large enough to hold it easily. Add a small amount of liquid. Cover the dish tightly.

**Fried Ham.** Thin slices and steaks of fully-cooked ham may be fried with a Brown 'N Sear Dish or griddle. Preheat the dish 3½ to 4 minutes. Cook ¼ to ½-in. thick slices 1 minute per side.

## FRUITED HAM SLICE

POWER LEVEL: High (10)
MICROWAVE TIME: 18 to 27 min., total

| | |
|---|---|
| **1 slice fully cooked ham, 1 to 2-in. thick**<br>**1 can (11-oz.) mandarin orange segments**<br>**1 can (8¼-oz.) crushed pineapple** | Score or remove fat from ham. Depending on size of slice, place in 8-in. square dish or 12×8×2-in. dish. Drain fruit, reserving juice. Arrange fruit attractively over ham slice. Cover with wax paper. **Microwave at High 10 to 15 Minutes.** |
| **Juice from fruits**<br>**2 tablespoons brown sugar**<br>**1 tablespoon cornstarch**<br>**¼ teaspoon ground cloves** | Combine juice, sugar, cornstarch and cloves. Pour carefully over ham slice to avoid disturbing the arranged fruit. Rotate dish ½ turn. Cover. **Microwave at High 8 to 12 Minutes,** until hot. Spoon juice over fruit and serve. |

Makes 4 to 6 servings

Brown 'N Sear Dish Ham and Eggs

# Pork Roasts

Pork is leaner than it used to be, giving you more meat and less fat. Roasted conventionally or microwaved, this leaner meat has a firm texture. We recommend using a cooking bag and a small amount of water to keep roast pork tender and juicy. If you prefer, you may cover the roast with wax paper. Start the roast bone side up and turn it over after ½ the time. When using the temperature probe, set it for 120°. When oven signals, turn roast over and reset for 170°.

Microwaved pork roasts develop browning, especially when the fat coating is thin. If the roast has a heavy coating of fat, you may want to add brown bouquet sauce.

Microwave pork roast to 170° to cook it thoroughly and maintain juiciness. Be sure to allow the entire standing time, which allows meat to complete cooking and makes it more tender.

Microwaved Pork Roast

## HOW TO INSERT THE TEMPERATURE PROBE

**Rib end or center cut roasts.** Identified by arch shaped bones on the edge of the roast and clearly-defined large muscle. Insert the temperature probe through the bag* slightly below center of the largest muscle, so tip is in the center of the roast.

*Roast is pictured without cooking bag for a clear view of probe placement.

**Loin end roast.** Identified by circular bone at one end of the roast and rack of bones at the bottom. Insert the temperature probe through the bag* into the end where the round bone is located, placing it ¾ to 1-in. above the bottom of the roast on the meatiest side of the round bone. Follow the bone structure, angling if necessary, so that tip of probe is in the center of the roast. Do not allow tip of probe to touch bone.
*Roast is pictured without cooking bag for a clear view of probe placement.

# HOW TO DEFROST PORK ROAST

POWER LEVEL: **Defrost**

## 10 to 12 Minutes Per Pound

1. If roast is wrapped in paper or plastic, place the unopened package in the oven and defrost for half the time. (Foil wrapping must be removed before defrosting.)

2. Unwrap roast and feel it for warm areas. Shield any warm spots with small pieces of foil. Turn roast over, place it in a roasting dish and return it to the oven.

3. Defrost for second half of time and let the roast stand for 15 to 30 minutes. For step-by-step pictures of roast defrosting, see page 102.

# MICROWAVING PORK ROAST

POWER LEVEL: **Medium (5)**

## 13 to 15 Minutes Per Pound

Do not salt roast. Cut a ½-in. strip from the open end of a cooking bag. Place roast in the bag in a 13×9×2-in. dish. Add ½ cup water to the bag.

Tie end securely with the strip of plastic. Do not use metal twist ties in the microwave oven. Make an X-shaped slash in the bag near the closure.

**Microwaving By Temperature.** Insert temperature probe through the bag, following directions for probe placement on the previous page. Correct position of the probe is extremely important. Attach cable end at receptacle. **Microwave at Medium. Set Temp, Set 170°.** When oven signals, remove roast and let stand 20 minutes.

**Microwaving By Time.** Estimate the minimum total roasting time. If your oven has a 35 minute timer you will have to reset it to complete the cooking cycle. **Microwave at Medium.** After the minimum cooking time, test the internal temperature of the roast with a meat thermometer, following instructions given for probe placement. Allow 2 minutes for thermometer to register. If roast has not reached 170°, remove the thermometer and return roast to the oven for a few more minutes. When cooking is completed remove and let stand 20 minutes.

Do not place conventional metal meat thermometer in microwave oven; remove from roast if meat needs additional microwaving.

# GLAZES FOR PORK ROASTS

*The following glazes may be spooned or poured over pork roasts just before serving.*

## WINEBERRY GLAZE

POWER LEVEL: High (10)     **Cook Code:** 50
MICROWAVE TIME: 5 to 7 min., total

| | |
|---|---|
| **1 can (8-oz.) whole cranberry sauce**<br>**½ cup vermouth**<br>**1 tablespoon cornstarch**<br>**1 tablespoon steak sauce** | In 1-qt. casserole mix together cranberry sauce, vermouth, cornstarch and steak sauce. **Microwave at High 5 to 7 Minutes,** stirring after 3 minutes, until thickened and clear. |

Makes about 1½ cups

## APRICOT PRESERVES GLAZE

POWER LEVEL: High (10)     **Cook Code:** 30
MICROWAVE TIME: 3 to 4 min., total

| | |
|---|---|
| **1 jar (12-oz.) apricot preserves**<br>**½ teaspoon ground ginger**<br>**1 tablespoon lemon juice** | In 1-qt. casserole stir together preserves, ginger and lemon juice. **Microwave at High 3 to 4 Minutes,** until warm and well blended. |

Makes about 1¼ cups

## CHERRY ALMOND GLAZE

POWER LEVEL: High (10)
MICROWAVE TIME: 8 to 12 min., total

| | |
|---|---|
| **1 teaspoon butter**<br>**¼ cup slivered almonds** | In 8 or 9-in pie plate place butter and almonds. **Microwave at High 3 to 5 Minutes,** stirring every 2 minutes, until toasted. Set aside. |
| **1 jar (12-oz.) cherry preserves**<br>**2 tablespoons white corn syrup**<br>**¼ cup red wine vinegar**<br>**¼ teaspoon salt**<br>**¼ teaspoon cinnamon**<br>**¼ teaspoon nutmeg**<br>**¼ teaspoon cloves** | In 1½-qt. casserole stir together preserves, corn syrup, vinegar, salt, cinnamon, nutmeg and cloves. Cover. **Microwave at High 5 to 7 Minutes,** stirring very well after 4 minutes. Mixture should be well blended. Stir in toasted almonds just before glazing. |

Makes about 1¾ cups

# Ham Roasts

Most hams are now precooked and can be microwaved quickly and easily on Medium Power. The meat will be juicy and tender if you take care not to overcook. If your oven is equipped with a temperature probe, use it for carefree cooking. Hams which are already cooked need only be heated to internal temperature of 115°.

## HOW TO MICROWAVE PRECOOKED OR CANNED HAMS
POWER LEVEL: **Medium (5)**

### 10 to 13 Minutes Per Pound

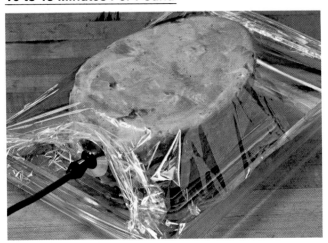

**Place** ham in a 12×8×2 or 13×9×2-in. roasting dish. Canned ham may be placed on a trivet, if desired, but precooked ham halves or pieces should be microwaved without a trivet to prevent overcooking top. Precooked ham should be arranged with fat side up and shielded on the top cut edge with a strip of foil. When roasting a ham over 5 pounds, tie butcher's string around and across it in several places to keep it from pulling apart. Cover tightly with plastic wrap, turning back corner to vent, or insert temperature probe, cover tightly and arrange plastic wrap loosely around probe to vent.

**Microwaving By Temperature.** Insert probe as close to the center as possible. **Microwave at Medium. Set Temp, Set 115°.** When oven signals, remove ham and let stand 5 to 10 minutes.

**Microwaving By Time.** Estimate the minimum roasting time. If your oven has a 35 minute timer you may need to reset the timer to complete the cooking cycle. **Microwave at Medium** for minimum time and test for an internal temperature of 115° with a meat thermometer following directions at right.

## HOW TO MICROWAVE A RAW HAM
POWER LEVEL: **Medium (5)**

### 12 to 15 Minutes Per Pound

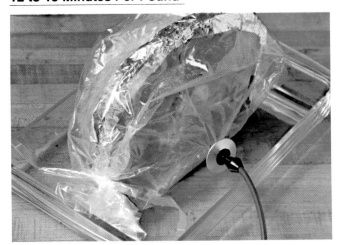

**Shield** top cut edge of ham with 1½-in. strip of foil. Place ham in cooking bag and arrange in baking dish so cut side will be to front of oven. Tie end of bag with string or strip of plastic cut from open end of bag. Make an X-shaped slash near closure.

**Microwaving By Temperature.** Insert probe through bag into the center of the lowest large muscle. **Microwave at Medium. Set Temp, Set 160°.** When oven signals, remove ham and let stand 10 minutes before carving.

**Microwaving By Time.** Estimate the minimum roasting time. **Microwave at Medium** to an internal temperature of 160°, resetting timer as needed.

Do not use meat thermometer in the microwave oven.

**To Test Time-Cooked Hams With Meat Thermometer.** Insert thermometer into ham, following directions for probe placement. Allow 2 minutes for thermometer to register. If specified temperature has not been reached, remove the thermometer and return to the oven for a few more minutes. After cooking remove ham and let stand 5 to 10 minutes before carving.

Microwaved Precooked Ham with Currant Jelly Glaze

**Glazes.** For an attractive finish, brush cooked ham with ½ cup jelly or preserves, such as pineapple, apricot or cherry; or, use bottled ham glaze. Use one of the following glazes, or the superb Kentucky Bourbon Sauce (right). Also try Raisin Sauce, page 191, or Horseradish Sauce, page 189.

**Traditional Pineapple Glaze:** Drain 1 can (8-oz.) pineapple slices, saving juice. Arrange pineapple over ham. In small bowl stir together ½ cup brown sugar, 2 tablespoons reserved pineapple syrup and 2 tablespoons prepared mustard. Pour over microwaved (finished) ham. **Microwave at High 5 Minutes,** to set.

**Currant Jelly Glaze:** In small bowl stir together 1 jar (10-oz.) currant jelly, 1 tablespoon prepared mustard and 1 tablespoon brown sugar. Brush over microwaved ham. Let stand few minutes to set.

**Honey Glaze:** In small bowl stir together ¼ cup honey, ¼ cup soy sauce and 1 teaspoon dry mustard. Brush over microwaved ham. Let stand few minutes to set.

## KENTUCKY BOURBON SAUCE FOR HAM

POWER LEVEL: High (10)          **Cook Code:**    40
MICROWAVE TIME: 4 to 5 min., total

| | |
|---|---|
| **1 jar (10-oz.) currant jelly** | In 1-qt. casserole place jelly. **Microwave at High 4 to 5 Minutes,** stirring after 2 minutes, until hot and melted. Add butter, mustards, and bourbon, stirring well. |
| **¼ cup butter** | |
| **½ teaspoon dry mustard** | |
| **2 teaspoons prepared mustard** | |
| **¼ cup Kentucky bourbon** | |

Makes 6 to 8 servings

## HAM-AGETTI CASSEROLE

POWER LEVEL: High (10)
MICROWAVE TIME: 23 to 27 min., total

**4 strips bacon** . . . . . . . . . .With scissors, snip bacon into 1-in. pieces into 2-qt. casserole. **Microwave at High 4 to 5 Minutes.** Remove approximately half the fat.

**2 cups cooked ham, cut** . . .Add ham, tomatoes, spaghetti, onion, green pepper, salt and pepper. Stir well. Cover. **Microwave at High 18 to 20 Minutes,** until spaghetti is tender, stirring after 8 minutes.
**into strips**
**1 can (1-lb. 14-oz.) tomatoes**
**1 cup spaghetti, broken into 1-in. pieces**
**½ cup chopped onion**
**¼ cup chopped green pepper**
**½ teaspoon salt**
**⅛ teaspoon pepper**

**½ cup shredded** . . . . . . . .Sprinkle with cheese. **Microwave at High 1 to 2 Minutes,** uncovered, until cheese is melted.
**cheddar cheese**

Makes 6 servings

## SWEET AND SOUR HAM

POWER LEVEL: High (10) **Cook Code:** 140
MICROWAVE TIME: 14 to 17 min., total

**⅓ cup pineapple juice** . . . .In 3-qt. casserole combine juice, broth and cornstarch.
**1 can (10½-oz.) condensed beef broth**
**3 tablespoons cornstarch**

**2 cups cooked ham, cut** . . .Add ham, pineapple, green pepper, onion, mustard, brown sugar and vinegar. Cover. **Microwave at High 14 to 17 Minutes,** stirring every 5 minutes. Serve over rice or crisp noodles.
**into 1-in. cubes**
**1 can (1-lb. 4-oz.) pineapple chunks, drained**
**1 green pepper, cut into strips**
**1 small onion, thinly sliced**
**¾ teaspoon dry mustard**
**2 tablespoons brown sugar**
**3 tablespoons vinegar**

Makes 4 servings

## PINEAPPLE HAM AND YAMS

POWER LEVEL: High (10)
MICROWAVE TIME: 5¼ to 7½ min., total

**1 tablespoon butter** . . . . . .In 1-qt. casserole place butter. **Microwave at High ¼ to ½ Minute,** to melt. Add drained yams and mash well. Stir in brown sugar. Divide mixture equally over one end of each ham slice. Roll up into firm rolls.
**1 can (8-oz.) yams or sweet potatoes, drained**
**2 tablespoons brown sugar**
**4 slices (about 4-oz.) packaged, thinly sliced cooked ham** *

**1 can (8-oz.) sliced** . . . . . .Drain pineapple, reserving juice. Place pineapple slices in 8-in. square dish. Cover each with ham roll, seam side down.
**pineapple (4 slices)**

**¼ cup coarsely** . . . . . . . . .Combine pecans, sugar and pineapple syrup. Spoon over ham rolls. Cover with wax paper.
**chopped pecans**
**¼ cup light brown sugar (packed)**
**¼ cup syrup reserved from pineapple**

**Microwave at High 5 to 7 Minutes,** rotating dish ½ turn after 4 minutes.

Makes 4 servings

*Or use thinly sliced leftover ham, about 6-in. long by 3-in. wide.

## CREAMED HAM

*If ham is salty, omit salt when preparing White Sauce.*

POWER LEVEL: High (10) **Cook Code:** 80
MICROWAVE TIME: 8 to 10 min., total

**2 cups (double recipe)** . . .In 2-qt. casserole, mix together white sauce, ham, eggs, mushrooms, green pepper, pimiento and mustard. Cover. **Microwave at High 8 to 10 Minutes,** stirring after 4 minutes, until hot. Serve as desired, over cornbread, rice or noodles.
**White Sauce, page 189**
**2 cups diced cooked ham**
**2 hard-poached eggs, diced (below)**
**1 can (2-oz.) sliced mushrooms, drained**
**1 tablespoon chopped green pepper**
**1 tablespoon chopped pimiento**
**¼ teaspoon dry mustard**

Makes 4 to 6 servings

**Hard-poached Eggs:** In 1-qt. casserole, place 2 cups water. **Microwave at High 5 to 6 Minutes,** until boiling. Break eggs onto plate, puncture membrane. Gently slip eggs into water. Cover. **Microwave at Medium 3 Minutes.** Let eggs stand in water 5 minutes before removing to dice.

# Bacon

Microwaving is a superior way to cook bacon. It is spatter-free. There is less curling and shrinkage than with conventional frying, and if you cook it on paper towels, there is no messy pan to wash.

When cooked until crisp, bacon will be evenly cooked and flat. Just as in conventional cooking, under-crisp bacon may be randomly cooked, with some spots fatty while others are crisp. Bacon varies in quality, depending upon the amount of sugar and salt used in curing and thickness of slices. The following chart is for average cure, commercially sliced, thin bacon. Cook less time for extra-sweet bacon, more for thick slices.

### HOW TO DEFROST BACON
POWER LEVEL: **Defrost**

**4 to 6 Minutes Per Pound**

Place unopened package of bacon in oven. Microwave at Defrost for ½ of time. Turn package over. Defrost second ½ of time, just until strips can be separated with a rubber spatula.

Bacon continues to brown on standing. Left, crisp-cooked bacon as it should look when removed from oven. Right, crisp-cooked bacon after standing 5 minutes.

NOTE: Brown spots on paper towel are due to sugar in the bacon. A high sugar content may also cause bacon to stick to the towel slightly.

### HOW TO MICROWAVE BACON
POWER LEVEL: **High (10)**

**¾ to 1 Minute Per Slice**

**Place** two layers of paper towels on paper or pottery plate without metal trim. Arrange bacon on towels and cover with another towel to prevent spatters. Place in oven with strips running from back to front. Microwave at **High** ¾ to 1 minute per slice.

**Layer** bacon when microwaving more than 6 slices. Place 5 slices of bacon on 2 layers of paper towels in a 13×9×2-in. dish. Cover with a paper towel. Add second layer of bacon. Cover and add more layers as desired. Microwave 4 minutes for each layer of bacon and rotate dish ½ turn after ½ the time. A pound of bacon takes about 15 minutes.

**To Save** bacon drippings for use in frying, cornbread, or microwave recipes such as wilted lettuce, cabbage or German potato salad, cook bacon on a trivet in a cooking dish. Bacon may also be cooked in a casserole or roasting dish directly in its own fat. As with conventional cooking, remove bacon to paper towel to drain and pour off drippings.

# Canadian Bacon

Like most ham, Canadian bacon is precooked and needs only heating to be ready to eat. Whether cooked conventionally or by microwave, Canadian bacon will be dry if it is allowed to cook until brown.

## MICROWAVING WHOLE PIECE OF CANADIAN BACON

POWER LEVEL: Medium High (7)  **Cook Code:** 237
MICROWAVE TIME: 23 to 26 min., total

| | |
|---|---|
| **2 to 3-lb. piece** .......... | Remove casing from bacon and arrange in 12×8× |
| **Canadian bacon** | con and arrange in 12×8× |
| **¼ cup water** | 2-in. dish. Add water. |

Cover tightly with plastic wrap, turning back one corner to vent. **Microwave at Medium High 23 to 26 Minutes,** turning over after 13 minutes. Let bacon stand 10 minutes before serving.

## MICROWAVING SLICES OF CANADIAN BACON

Place slices in single layer on dinner plate. Cover with wax paper. Timing below is for thin slices, about ¼-in. thick, such as used for Eggs Benedict, sandwiches or as a breakfast meat.

### POWER LEVEL: **High (10)**

| SLICES | TIME MIN. | COOK CODE | COMMENTS |
|---|---|---|---|
| 2 | 1-1½ | 10 | No rotation necessary. |
| 4 | 2-2½ | 20 | Rotate ½ turn after 1 min. |
| 6 to 8 | 3½-4 | 40 | Rotate ½ turn after 2 min. |

# Breakfast Sausage

Breakfast sausage comes in many forms. Each defrosts and cooks differently, but all will be tender, juicy and fully cooked in a very short time. Due to quick cooking, breakfast sausage doesn't brown and, since it is rarely served with a sauce, it will be more attractive if it is brushed with a browning agent before cooking. Use equal parts of brown bouquet sauce and water. If you cook sausage frequently, keep this mixture on hand in a small covered container.

Whole Canadian Bacon

Sliced Canadian Bacon

## BROWN 'N SEAR SAUSAGE CHART

### POWER LEVEL: **High (10)**
**Preheat dish 4½ to 5½ minutes.**

| ITEM | 1st SIDE TIME MINUTES | 2nd SIDE TIME MINUTES |
|---|---|---|
| **Pork Sausage,** 4 slices ½-in. thick | 1 covered | 1½ to 2 covered |
| **Pork Sausage Links,** 6 to 8 links, uncooked, 8-oz. | 1 covered | 2 to 2½ covered |
| **Brown 'n Serve,** 10 links 8-oz. pkg. | 1 covered | 1½ to 2 covered |

**Compare** link and patty sausage cooked with and without a browning agent. Both are juicy and flavorful, but sausages cooked with a browning agent have more appetite appeal.

# SAUSAGE DEFROSTING & MICROWAVING CHART

The following chart gives specific directions for different types and forms of sausage. Whatever type you are microwaving, a few basic rules are common to all.

Defrost sausage in package, removing any metal closures. When defrosted, sausage should still be cold.

When cooking, select a utensil which is appropriate in size for the amount of sausage you wish to cook: a saucer for 1 or 2 links, a glass pie plate for an 8-oz. package, a roasting dish for a full pound of slices. Add browning agent, if desired, before cooking. Always cover the dish with wax paper to prevent spatters.

| **DEFROSTING** POWER LEVEL: **Defrost** | | | **MICROWAVING** POWER LEVEL: **High (10)** | | |
|---|---|---|---|---|---|
| ITEM | TIME MINUTES | COMMENTS | ITEM | TIME MINUTES | COMMENTS |
| **Bulk** (1-lb. tray) | 8 to 9 | Defrost like ground beef page 82 | **4 Patties** (½-lb.) | 4 to 5 | Rotate dish ½ turn after 1½ minutes. |
| | | | **8 Patties** (1-lb.) | 7½ to 8 | Rotate dish ½ turn after 2 minutes. |
| **Bulk** (1-lb. roll) | 4 to 6 | Turn over after 1 minute | **4 Patties** (½-lb.) | 4 to 5 | Rotate dish ½ turn after 1½ minutes. |
| | | | **8 Patties** (1-lb.) | 7½ to 8 | Rotate dish ½ turn after 2 minutes. |
| **Preformed Patties** (12-oz. pkg.) | 2 to 3 | Turn over after 1 minute | **4 Patties Raw** | 2½ to 3½ | Rotate dish ½ turn after 1½ minutes. |
| | | | **8 Patties Raw** | 4 to 5 | Rotate dish ½ turn after 2 minutes. |
| **Preformed Patties Brown 'n Serve** (12-oz. pkg.) | 2 to 3 | Turn over after 1 minute. | **4 Patties Brown 'n Serve** | 1 to 1½ | No turns. |
| | | | **8 Patties Brown 'n Serve** | 2¼ to 2½ | Rotate dish ½ turn after 1½ minutes. |
| **Link Sausage Raw** (1-lb.) | 3 to 4 | Turn over after 1 minute | **4 Links** | 2 to 3 | No turns. |
| | | | **7 to 8 Links** | 4 to 5 | Rotate dish ½ turn after 2 minutes. |
| **Link Sausage Brown 'n Serve** (8-oz.) | 3 to 4 | Turn over after 1 minute | **4 Links** | 1 | No turns. |
| | | | **6 Links** | 1½ to 2 | Rotate dish ½ turn after 1 minute. |
| | | | **10 Links** | 2 to 2½ | Rotate dish ½ turn after 1 minute. |

Add sauces and condiments, such as ketchup, mustard or relish after heating. Saucy spots absorb microwave energy and may toughen the bun.

# Franks

Frankfurters are precooked so they only need heating. They react quickly to microwave energy and many beginners overheat them because they can't believe franks will be ready in such a short time.

If you are cooking franks in a main dish casserole, bury them under moist ingredients, such as beans or sauerkraut. If meat is on the bottom, the casserole won't need stirring.

**Defrosting.** For 1-lb. of franks, place unopened package in oven. **Microwave at Defrost 3 to 5 Minutes,** just until franks can be separated. For ½-lb., cut time in half.

**Microwaving.** Franks vary in size. Larger ones such as Polish or bratwurst, will take longer than times in chart below. For foot-long hot dogs add ¼ to ½ minute more time, and rotate them once or twice, because they tend to get overdone on the ends.

## FRANKS MICROWAVING CHART

When microwaving on microwave ovenproof plate, cover with wax paper. When microwaving in bun, wrap in paper towel. Watch carefully. If ends appear dry, it means they are overdone.

POWER LEVEL: **High (10)**

| NO. OF FRANKS | TIME MIN. | COOK CODE | COMMENTS |
|---|---|---|---|
| 2 | 1-2 | 10 | Do not microwave more than 4 franks in buns at once. |
| 4 | 3-4 | 30 | |
| 6 to 8 | 4-6 | 40 | Add ½ cup water; rearrange after 2 minutes. |
| 10 (1-lb. pkg.) | 7-9 | 70 | Add ¾ cup water; rearrange after 4 minutes. |

## HOW TO MICROWAVE FRANKS

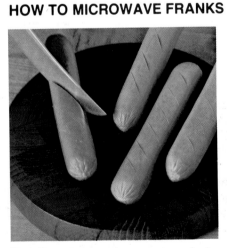

**Franks** are prone to pop or explode. You can remedy this by pricking them with a fork, but diagonal slashes are especially attractive.

**To Microwave** franks on a paper or pottery plate, cover them with wax paper. Use a casserole and additional water to heat more than 6 franks.

**To Heat** franks right in the buns, place a napkin or paper towel under the bun to absorb moisture. A bun placed directly on a plate or the oven floor gets steamy underneath. To heat more than four, do them in successive batches.

## CASSEROLE OF BEANS AND SAUSAGES
*The French name for this type of casserole is Cassoulet.*

POWER LEVEL: High (10)                        TEMP: 160°
APPROX. MICROWAVE TIME: 20 min.

**Cook Code:** 200

**1 lb. Polish sausage** . . . . .In 2-qt. casserole place
   **diagonally sliced in** both kinds of sausages.
   **1-in. pieces**
**1 pkg. (8-oz.) brown**
   **and serve sausages**

**1 can (16-oz.) kidney** . . . . .Layer beans evenly over
   **beans, drained** sausage.
**1 can (15-oz.) Northern**
   **beans, drained**
**1 can (15-oz.) pinto**
   **beans, drained**

**1 can (8-oz.) tomato** . . . . .In one of the empty cans or
   **sauce** small bowl mix together to-
**⅓ cup red cooking wine** mato sauce, wine, brown
**2 tablespoons brown** sugar, mustard, salt, garlic
   **sugar** powder and pepper. Pour
**1 tablespoon prepared** over sausages and beans.
   **mustard**
**1 teaspoon salt**
**¼ teaspoon garlic**
   **powder**
**⅛ teaspoon pepper**

Insert temperature probe so tip rests on center bottom of dish. Cover tightly with plastic wrap, arranging loosely around probe to vent. Attach cable end at receptacle. **Microwave at High. Set Temp, Set 160°.**

When oven signals, stir casserole well and let stand 10 minutes before serving to blend flavors and thicken sauce.

*Makes 6 to 8 servings*

## WIENER BEAN POT

POWER LEVEL: High (10)              **Cook Code:** 130
MICROWAVE TIME: 13 to 15 min., total

**2 cans (1-lb. each) pork** . .In 2-qt. casserole stir to-
   **and beans** gether beans, onion,
**⅓ cup chopped onion** ketchup, water, brown
**¼ cup ketchup** sugar and mustard. Add
**¼ cup water** wieners, pushing pieces
**2 tablespoons brown** below surface of beans to
   **sugar** prevent overcooking. Cov-
**1 tablespoon prepared** er. **Microwave at High 13**
   **mustard** **to 15 Minutes,** stirring af-
**1 lb. wieners (8 to 10)** ter 8 minutes, until hot.
   **cut in thirds**

*Makes 6 to 8 servings*

## SAUSAGE AND SAUERKRAUT

POWER LEVEL: High (10)              **Cook Code:** 120
MICROWAVE TIME: 12 to 14 min., total

**1 lb. franks (8 to 10)** . . . . .In 2-qt. casserole place
   **scored, or 1-lb. Polish** meat. Cover with sauer-
   **sausage (Kielbasa)** kraut mixed with onions
   **cut in ½-in. pieces** and bouillon. Cover. **Mi-**
**1 can (1-lb.) sauerkraut,** **crowave at High 12 to 14**
   **rinsed and drained** **Minutes,** rotating dish ½
**2 tablespoons instant** turn after 6 minutes, until
   **minced onion** hot.
**1 teaspoon beef**
   **bouillon granules**

*Makes 4 to 6 servings*

## BARBECUED FRANKS

POWER LEVEL: High (10)              **Cook Code:** 90
MICROWAVE TIME: 9 to 12 min., total

**¾ cup ketchup** . . . . . . . . . .In 2-qt. casserole mix to-
**1 tablespoon** gether ketchup, Worces-
   **Worcestershire** tershire sauce, chili pow-
   **sauce** der, sugar, salt, liquid pep-
**¼ to ½ teaspoon chili** per seasoning and water.
   **powder**
**1 tablespoon sugar**
**½ teaspoon salt**
   **Dash liquid pepper**
   **seasoning (tabasco)**
**½ cup water**

**1 lb. franks (8 to 10),** . . . . .Place in sauce, pushing
   **scored** pieces below surface to
     prevent overcooking. Cov-
     er.

**Microwave at High 9 to 12 Minutes,** rearranging franks after 5 minutes. Serve on buns, if desired, with generous amount of sauce over each.

*Makes 8 to 10 servings*

## TAVERN FRANKS
*For fuller flavor, prick franks and marinate in beer 3 to 4 hours or overnight before cooking.*

POWER LEVEL: High (10)              **Cook Code:** 70
MICROWAVE TIME: 7 to 9 min., total

**1 lb. franks (8 to 10)** . . . . . .In 2-qt. casserole place
**1 small onion, thinly** franks. Separate onion into
   **sliced** rings and distribute over
**1 can (12-oz.) beer** franks. Pour beer over all.
   **(1½ cups)** Cover.

**Microwave at High 7 to 9 Minutes,** redistributing franks so bottom ones are on top after 4 minutes.

*Makes 4 to 5 servings*

# Lamb & Veal

Lamb is naturally juicy and can be prepared in a variety of ways. In addition to the recipes given here, we suggest that you try some of our pork recipes with lamb or use one of the beef marinades, page 100.

Veal is dry because it has no fat marbling. Whether cooked conventionally or microwaved, chops and cutlets should be sliced thinly or pounded to tenderize them. Veal roasts may be microwaved on trivet in cooking dish at Medium with the temperature probe set to 155° (15 to 18 minutes per pound). Let roast stand about 15 minutes to complete cooking and slice thinly. Chunks and pieces of veal which need long slow cooking may be substituted in several of the stew and other main dish recipes.

## HOW TO DEFROST CHOPS AND CUTLETS
POWER LEVEL: **Defrost**

### 4 to 8 Minutes Per Pound

1. Place plastic or paper wrapped package in oven. Microwave at Defrost ½ the minimum total time.

2. Turn package over and defrost second ½ of time.

3. Separate pieces with a table knife and let stand to complete defrosting, or microwave 1 to 2 minutes more.

## HOW TO DEFROST ROASTS
POWER LEVEL: **Defrost**

### 10 to 12 Minutes Per Pound

1. If roast is wrapped in paper or plastic, place the unopened package in microwave oven. (Foil wrapping must be removed before microwaving.)

2. Defrost ½ of total time. Remove paper, place on trivet in dish.

3. Defrost last ½ of time.

4. Let stand 30 minutes before microwaving or conventional cooking.

NOTE: Feel roast for warm areas after each microwaving period. Cover these areas with foil (warmth indicates they have begun to cook).

## HOW TO INSERT THE TEMPERATURE PROBE
**Lamb Leg (shown):**
Insert probe from the side of the roast into the meaty area so tip is in the center under the joint.
**Boned Rolled Lamb or Veal Shoulder:** Insert probe same as for half tenderloin roast page 110.

## CRANBERRY-ORANGE RUBY SAUCE
*This sauce complements Microwaved Lamb Roast.*

POWER LEVEL: High (10)
MICROWAVE TIME: 4 to 6 min., total

| | |
|---|---|
| **1 can (11-oz.) mandarin oranges** | Drain oranges, saving juice. In 1-qt. measuring cup stir together cranberry sauce and 2 tablespoons liquid saved from oranges. |
| **1 can (16-oz.) cranberry sauce** | |

**Microwave at High 3 to 4 Minutes,** stirring after 1½ minutes.

Stir in drained oranges. **Microwave at High 1 to 2 Minutes** more, until hot and well blended.

Makes about 2½ cups

## HOW TO MICROWAVE LAMB ROASTS
POWER LEVEL: **Medium (5)**

**9 to 11 Minutes Per Pound for Medium**
**11 to 13 Minutes Per Pound for Well Done**

**Microwaving by Temperature:** If desired, brush roast with diluted brown bouquet sauce. Place roast fat side up on trivet in 13×9×2-in. dish. Insert temperature probe as directed below. Cover with wax paper. **Microwave at Medium. Set Temp, Set 130°** for medium and **180°** for well done. When oven signals, let stand 10 minutes before carving.

**Microwaving by Time:** Use minutes per pound, above. When oven signals, remove roast and insert conventional meat thermometer into roast in same location described for temperature probe. Check temperature after about 2 minutes; it should read 130° for medium and 180° for well done. If not, return to microwave oven a few minutes, then check again.

NOTE: Do not place conventional metal meat thermometer in microwave oven.

# MANDARIN LAMB CHOPS

POWER LEVEL: Medium High (7)
MICROWAVE TIME: 24 to 27 min., total

**4 loin lamb chops, 1 to** . . .In 8-in. square dish ar-
**1½-in. thick (1½ to** range chops so thickest
**2-lb.)** meaty areas are to edges.
Cover with wax paper. **Microwave at Medium High
12 Minutes.** Drain off fat
and turn chops over.

**1 can (11-oz.) mandarin** . .Arrange orange segments
**oranges, save syrup** over top. Mix ⅓ cup or-
**¼ cup sugar** ange syrup with sugar,
**½ cup chopped chutney** chutney and lemon juice.
**2 tablespoons lemon** Spoon over chops. Recov-
**juice** er with wax paper. **Microwave at Medium High 10
to 12 Minutes,** until tender.
Remove chops to serving
platter.

**1 tablespoon** . . . . . . . . . .Mix cornstarch with syrup.
**cornstarch** Stir into juices in dish. **Mi-
2 tablespoons** crowave at Medium High
**mandarin orange** **2 to 3 Minutes,** stirring
**syrup** once, until thick. Spoon
over chops.

Makes 4 servings

# VEAL PARMIGIANA

*For a meatier entree, substitute veal cutlets for chops.*

POWER LEVEL: Medium High (7)
MICROWAVE TIME: 25 to 28 min., total

**6 small veal loin chops,** . .Coat chops with beaten
**¾-in. thick** egg, then with mixture of
**1 egg, beaten** crumbs, salt, pepper and
**1 cup buttery flavored** cheese. In 12×8×2-in.
**cracker crumbs** dish, arrange chops so
**1 teaspoon salt** thickest meaty areas are
**¼ teaspoon pepper** close to edges and "tails"
**½ cup grated Parmesan** are in center. Cover with
**cheese** wax paper. **Microwave at
Medium High 10 Minutes.**

**1 cup (4-oz.) shredded** . . .Turn chops over. Distribute
**Mozzarella or pizza** cheese over chops, then
**cheese** mixture of tomato sauce
**2 cans (8-oz. each)** and oregano. Top with Par-
**tomato sauce.** mesan. Cover. **Microwave
1 teaspoon crushed** **at Medium High 15 to 18
oregano** **Minutes** more, until ten-
**¼ cup grated Parmesan** der. Let stand, covered, 10
**cheese** minutes before serving.

Makes 6 servings

# BROWN VEAL ROLL UPS

*An attractive main dish to serve with rice, mixed green
salad and a light dessert, such as sherbet.*

POWER LEVEL: High (10)
MICROWAVE TIME: 15½ to 17½ min., total

**4 boneless veal cutlets** . .Pound cutlets thin, using a
**(4-oz. each)** wooden mallet or foil cov-
**1 can (4½-oz.) deviled** ered brick. Mix ham with
**ham** minced onion and spread
**1 tablespoon instant** over cutlets, just to edge.
**minced onion**

**1 pkg. (3-oz.) cream** . . . . .Slice cream cheese into 12
**cheese** narrow strips. Place 3
strips on each cutlet. Roll
up firmly. Fasten each roll
with a toothpick.

**2 tablespoons butter** . . . .Place butter in small glass
**½ cup fine dry bread** bowl. **Microwave at High
crumbs** **½ Minute,** until melted. Dip
veal rolls in butter, then
coat with crumbs. Arrange
in 10×6×2-in. dish.

**¾ cup water** . . . . . . . . . . . .In 1-pt. glass measure,
**1 pkg. (1½-oz.) dry** combine water, gravy mix
**mushroom gravy** and sherry. **Microwave at
mix** **High 2 Minutes,** stirring
**¼ cup cooking sherry or** after 1 minute. Pour over
**water** veal rolls.

Cover with plastic wrap turning back one corner to vent.
**Microwave at High 13 to 15 Minutes,** rotating dish ½
turn every 5 minutes, until meat is tender and filling is set.

Makes 4 veal rolls

# MICROWAVING LAMB CHOPS IN BROWN 'N SEAR DISH OR BROWNING GRIDDLE

Preheat empty dish or griddle at High. Add chops, cover
if Brown 'N Sear Dish is used, and cook first side. Turn
chops over, recover dish, cook second side.

### POWER LEVEL: **High (10)**

| NO. OF CHOPS | PREHEAT MINUTES | 1st SIDE MINUTES | 2nd SIDE MINUTES |
|---|---|---|---|
| 2 | 5 to 6 | 3 | 3 to 4 |
| 4 | 6 to 8 | 3 to 4 | 4 to 5 |
| 6 (griddle) | 8 | 7 to 8 | 8 to 9 |

# Poultry

Chicken is one of America's most popular foods and microwaving chicken is one of the best uses of your microwave oven. Chicken microwaves well at High Power and stays juicy and tender. However, juiciness prevents browning because chicken crisps and browns only when the skin dries out enough to change color.

Whole chickens and turkeys up to 12 pounds may be microwaved at Medium High with a minimum of attention. Use the temperature probe, if you have one, for completely carefree microwaving. Standing time is important, because it allows the interior to finish cooking without toughening the delicate breast meat. Directions and recipes for microwaving Cornish hen and duck provide additional variety for this poultry section.

1. Crumb Coated Chicken, page 138
2. Barbecued Stuffed Chicken, page 143
3. Saucy Turkey and Broccoli, page 152
4. Cornish Hen Halves, page 146

# Chicken Defrosting

**MICROLESSON**

Chicken is frozen in many forms, whole or cut-up into halves, quarters or one-of-a-kind pieces, such as breasts or drum sticks. These timings are for one whole or cut-up broiler-fryer, weighing 2½ to 3½ pounds. Several cut-up chickens or a roasting chicken will take longer. Follow directions for turkey when defrosting a large roasting chicken.

## HOW TO DEFROST A CUT-UP CHICKEN

**Place** wrapped chicken, packaged in paper or plastic, directly on the oven shelf. If chicken is wrapped in foil, unwrap it and place it in a baking dish. Microwave at Defrost for ½ the time.

**Unwrap** chicken pieces and turn the block over into a baking dish. Defrost for second ½ of time, or until pieces can be separated.

## HOW TO DEFROST A WHOLE CHICKEN

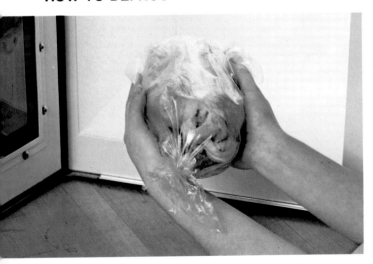

**Whole** chickens are usually frozen in a plastic bag. Remove twist tie, place package on the oven shelf and microwave at Defrost ½ the time. Unwrap chicken and turn it over into cooking dish.

**Shield** wing tips, tail, ends of legs and any other areas which feel warm or have begun to change color. Microwave for second ½ of time.

With frozen packages of one-of-a-kind pieces, you will need to use your judgement. Bony pieces, such as wings, will take less time than meaty pieces, such as thighs. The defrosting steps also apply to other poultry, such as ducks or cornish game hens. Two cornish hens take about the same amount of time as one chicken.

## DEFROST CHART
POWER LEVEL: **Defrost**

| ITEM | TIME/MINUTES |
| --- | --- |
| **Broiler-fryer,** cut up (2½ to 3½-lb.) | 14 to 16 |
| **Broiler-fryer,** whole (2½ to 3½-lb.) | 18 to 22 |

**Separate** chicken pieces and let them stand until defrosted, or if faster defrosting is desired, arrange them in the cooking dish, medium parts to the outside, and microwave 1 to 2 minutes more..

**Defrosted** chicken will be soft to the touch, very moist and cold, but not frosty. There may be a very small amount of running juice.

**Giblets** can be loosened but not removed. Chicken should be soft and cool to the touch, with a glistening surface.

**Run Cold Water** inside chicken until giblets can be freed. Interior will be cold but not icy.

# Chicken Pieces

Chicken is naturally an excellent food for microwaving and illustrates all the advantages of microwave cooking. It is tender, flavorful and juicy. It microwaves rapidly, and takes very little attention during cooking. Don't overcook chicken; it really will be done in the very short cooking periods given in the chart. Because they cook so quickly, chicken pieces do not get brown and crisp. Unless chicken is cooked in a sauce, it will be more attractive if brushed with a browning agent, coated with crumbs, or cooked in a Brown 'N Sear Dish. Plain microwaved chicken is perfect for salads and casseroles.

If you are concerned about calories or cholesterol, skin chicken before cooking, since most of the fat is located directly below the skin. If cooked in a sauce, the flavor will be absorbed by the chicken instead of the skin. Skinned chicken pieces may also be brushed with a browning agent or coated with crumbs, but cannot be cooked in the Brown 'N Sear Dish.

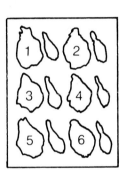

1. Plain microwaved chicken
2. Prepared coating mix
3. Brushed with melted butter, sprinkled with paprika
4. Well seasoned flour in Brown 'N Sear Dish
5. Crushed barbecue potato chips
6. Equal parts brown bouquet sauce and water

## HOW TO MICROWAVE CHICKEN PIECES

Use utensils suitable for microwave oven. For a few pieces, use a paper plate or dinner plate. For larger amounts use a suitable size utility dish, such as an 8-in. square, 12×8×2-in., or 13×9×2-in. dish.

Brush chicken pieces with browning agent or sauce before cooking, if desired. Arrange meatiest area toward outside edge of dish.

Cover with wax paper. Microwave according to times given in chart, rotating dish ½ turn where noted. Times given below are for legs, thighs and breasts.

Let stand, covered, about 5 minutes before serving.

### POWER LEVEL: **High (10)**

| AMOUNT | TIME MIN. | COOK CODE | ½ TURN |
|---|---|---|---|
| 1 piece | 2-4 | 20 | No |
| 2 pieces | 4-6 | 40 | No |
| 3 pieces | 5-7 | 50 | No |
| 4 pieces | 6½-10 | 70 | After 4 minutes |
| 5 pieces | 7½-12 | 80 | After 4 minutes |
| 6 pieces | 8-14 | 80 | After 5 minutes |
| 1 chicken, 2½ to 3½-lbs., cut up | 18-22 | 180 | After 10 minutes |

## TIPS FOR SUCCESSFUL MICROWAVING

**Arrange** chicken in baking dish so that the meatiest portions are to the outside of the dish. Brush with browning agent, if desired, or add sauce ingredients.

**Cover** with wax paper during microwaving. For dryer chicken, uncover during the second ½ of cooking time. Rotate dish ½ turn after ½ the cooking time when microwaving 4 or more pieces.

**Test** for doneness. Chicken should be fork tender, with no pinkness next to bone. For chicken baked in sauce, remove paper after cooking and let stand 5 minutes to glaze and blend flavors.

## CRUMB-COATED CHICKEN

*This has the same appearance and taste as oven fried.*

| POWER LEVEL: High (10) | **Cook Code:** 180 |
|---|---|
| MICROWAVE TIME: 18 to 22 min., total | |

**2 eggs** .............. In small bowl beat together
**⅓ cup melted butter** eggs, butter and salt.
**1 teaspoon salt**

**1½ cups buttery** ........ In shallow dish place
**flavored cracker** crumbs. Coat chicken with
**crumbs (about 50)** crumbs, then egg mixture
**1 chicken, 2½ to** and crumbs again. In 12×
**3½-lb., cut up,** 8×2-in. dish arrange
**skin removed** chicken with meatiest
pieces to outside edges of
dish. Cover with wax pa-
per. **Microwave at High
18 to 22 Minutes,** rotating
dish ½ turn after 10 min-
utes.

Makes about 4 servings

## SAVORY ONION CHICKEN

| POWER LEVEL: High (10) | **Cook Code:** 180 |
|---|---|
| MICROWAVE TIME: 18 to 22 min., total | |

**1 chicken, 2½ to 3½-lb.,** ..Dip chicken in butter. Coat
**cut up** with dry soup mix and ar-
**⅓ cup butter, melted** range in 12×8×2-in. dish,
**1 pkg. (½ of 2¾-oz. box)** skin side up, with thick
**dry onion soup mix** meaty pieces to the outside edges of dish. Cover
with wax paper. **Micro-
wave at High 18 to 22
Minutes,** until meat is tender. Let stand 5 minutes
before serving.

Makes about 4 servings

## CHICKEN PARMESAN

Substitute ½ cup bread or corn flake crumbs mixed with
¼ cup grated Parmesan cheese for dry onion soup mix.
Sprinkle with paprika before microwaving.

## CRUNCHY COATED CHICKEN

Substitute ¾ cup finely crushed cheese cracker crumbs
or potato chips (plain or barbecued) for dry onion soup
mix.

## CHICKEN 'N' DRESSING

*For richer flavor, use ¼ cup melted butter for part of
chicken broth.*

| POWER LEVEL: High (10) | **Cook Code:** 180 |
|---|---|
| MICROWAVE TIME: 18 to 22 min., total | |

**1 pkg. (8-oz.) herb** ...... In 12×8×2-in. dish toss to-
**seasoned stuffing** gether stuffing mix, celery,
**mix** onion, pimiento, egg and
**½ cup chopped celery** broth.
**¼ cup minced onion**
**2 tablespoons**
**chopped pimiento**
**1 egg**
**1¾ to 2 cups chicken**
**broth**

**1 chicken, 2½ to** ....... Dip chicken pieces into
**3½-lb., cut up** melted butter, place on top
**¼ cup butter, melted** of dressing with meaty
**Salt** pieces to the outside
**Paprika** edges of dish. Sprinkle
with salt and paprika. Cover with wax paper.

**Microwave at High 18 to 22 Minutes,** rotating dish ½
turn after 10 minutes. Let stand about 5 minutes before
serving.

Makes about 4 servings

## YOUR FAVORITE SAUCY CHICKEN

*For easy chicken creole, use condensed chicken gum-
bo soup. For "smothered" type chicken, sprinkle with 1
teaspoon instant minced onion, then cover with condensed cream of chicken soup (or use canned chicken
gravy). Use other favorite canned soup or ready-to-use
canned sauce, or barbecue sauce, if desired.*

| POWER LEVEL: High (10) | **Cook Code:** 180 |
|---|---|
| MICROWAVE TIME: 18 to 22 min., total | |

**1 chicken, 2½ to 3½-lb.,** ..In 12×8×2-in. dish ar-
**cut up** range chicken skin side up
with meatiest pieces to the
outside edges of dish.

**½ teaspoon salt** ........ .Sprinkle chicken with salt.
**1 can (about 10-oz.)** Pour soup over chicken.
**condensed soup** Cover with wax paper.

**Microwave at High 18 to 22 Minutes,** rotating dish ½
turn after 10 minutes. Let stand 5 minutes before serving.

Makes about 4 servings

## NOT THE SAME OLD CHICKEN

*This golden glazed chicken is named for the comments it elicits. It really does taste special.*

POWER LEVEL: High (10)                    **Cook Code:** 180
MICROWAVE TIME: 18 to 22 min., total

| | |
|---|---|
| **1 chicken, 2½ to 3½-lb., cut up** | ..In 12×8×2-in. dish arrange chicken with thickest, meaty pieces to outside edges of dish. |
| **¼ cup mayonnaise** ...... **1 pkg. (½ of 2¾-oz. box) dry onion soup mix** **½ cup bottled Russian dressing** **1 cup apricot-pineapple preserves** | .In small bowl stir together mayonnaise, onion soup mix, dressing and preserves. Spread over chicken, coating each piece. Cover with wax paper. |

**Microwave at High 18 to 22 Minutes,** rotating dish ½ turn after 10 minutes. Allow to stand 5 to 10 minutes before serving, so chicken absorbs flavor of sauce. Serve with rice, if desired.

Makes about 4 servings

## ITALIAN CHICKEN

*Tastes like pizza and chicken together. Our microwave oven owners have liked this for years.*

POWER LEVEL: High (10)
MICROWAVE TIME: 22 to 26 min., total

| | |
|---|---|
| **1 chicken, 2½ to 3½-lb., cut up** | .Remove skin from chicken pieces and arrange in lightly greased 12×8×2-in. dish with meatiest pieces to the outside edge of dish. |
| **1 can (10-oz.)** .......... **condensed tomato soup** **1 can (6-oz.) tomato paste** **¼ teaspoon onion salt** **¼ teaspoon garlic salt** **¼ teaspoon oregano** **1 can (4-oz.) mushroom pieces, drained** | .In mixing bowl stir together tomato soup, tomato paste, onion salt, garlic salt, oregano and mushrooms. Generously spoon sauce over chicken. **Microwave at High 20 to 22 Minutes,** rotating dish ½ turn after 10 minutes. |
| **2 cups (8-oz.) shredded Mozzarella cheese** **¼ cup grated Parmesan cheese** | .Sprinkle cheese over chicken. **Microwave at High 2 to 4 Minutes,** until cheese is melted. Let stand about 5 minutes before serving. |

Makes about 4 servings

## ORIENTAL CHICKEN

*An interesting brown raisin wine sauce gives this dish a sweet but savory flavor.*

POWER LEVEL: High (10)                    **Cook Code:** 110
MICROWAVE TIME: 11 to 13 min., total

| | |
|---|---|
| **2 chicken breasts split, skinned and boned** | ..Pierce chicken breasts with cooking fork. Arrange in 3-qt. casserole. |
| **1 tablespoon** .......... **cornstarch** **2 tablespoons brown sugar** **¼ teaspoon oregano** **1 clove garlic, crushed** **2 tablespoons cooking oil** **¼ cup soy sauce** **¾ cup rose wine** **⅓ cup seedless raisins** | .In small bowl combine cornstarch, brown sugar, oregano, garlic, oil, soy sauce, wine and raisins. Pour over chicken. Cover. **Microwave at High 11 to 13 Minutes,** rotating dish ½ turn after 6 minutes. Serve with rice if desired. |

Makes 4 servings

## FIESTA CHICKEN KIEV

*This recipe won $5,000 in a recipe contest exclusively for microwave cooking. Serve Kiev with taco sauce, garnish with lettuce, tomatoes and ripe olives.*

POWER LEVEL: High (10)                    **Cook Code:** 100
MICROWAVE TIME: 10 to 12 min., total

| | |
|---|---|
| **4 whole chicken breasts, split, skinned and boned** | .Pound each raw chicken piece with mallet or foil covered brick to flatten. |
| **3 tablespoons butter** .. **3 tablespoons old English-style sharp cheese spread** **2 teaspoons instant minced onion** **1 teaspoon salt** **1 teaspoon monosodium glutamate (accent)** **2 tablespoons chopped green chilies** | .In small bowl beat together butter and cheese spread until well blended. Mix in onion, salt, monosodium glutamate and chilies. Place a portion of mixture at one end of each chicken piece, dividing evenly. Roll up each piece, tucking in ends to completely enclose filling. Fasten rolls with toothpicks. |
| **¼ cup butter, melted** ... **1 cup crushed cheddar cheese crackers** **1½ tablespoons taco seasoning mix** | .Dip each roll in melted butter to cover, then coat with mixture of crackers and taco seasoning mix. Arrange rolls in 12×8×2-in. dish. Cover with wax paper. **Microwave at High 10 to 12 Minutes,** rotating dish ½ turn after 5 minutes, until done. Let stand about 5 minutes before serving. |

Makes 8 servings

## HOW TO MICROWAVE A STEWING CHICKEN

**Combine** in 4-qt. casserole 1 cut up stewing chicken (4 to 5-lb.), 5 cups hot tap water, 1 onion, 1 carrot and 1 celery stem, all coarsely cut up. Add 4 peppercorns, 2 cloves and cover.

**Microwave at High 15 Minutes.** Rearrange chicken, bringing bottom pieces to the top. Cover. **Microwave at Medium 2 to 2¼ Hours,** rearranging chicken after 1 hour.

**Test** for doneness. Chicken should be fork tender. For maximum tenderness, let chicken cool in its broth. Meat will then be easily removed from the bones. To stew a broiler-fryer, microwave 1 to 1½ hours.

## CHICKEN A LA KING

*The old favorite, creamed chicken, dressed up with colorful pimiento, green pepper and flavorful mushrooms. Serve over toast or in a pastry shell.*

POWER LEVEL: High (10) and Medium High (7)
MICROWAVE TIME: 16 to 21 min., total

| | |
|---|---|
| ⅓ cup butter | In 2-qt. casserole place butter. **Microwave at High 1 Minute,** until melted. Blend in flour. Gradually stir in half & half and broth; mix well. **Microwave at High 8 to 10 Minutes,** stirring with whisk after 4 minutes, until thickened and smooth. Stir well again. |
| ½ cup unsifted all-purpose flour | |
| 2 cups dairy half & half | |
| 1 cup chicken broth | |
| 2 cups cubed, cooked chicken | Mix in chicken, pimiento, mushrooms, green pepper, salt and pepper. Cover. **Microwave at Medium High 7 to 10 Minutes,** stirring after 5 minutes, until hot. Let stand 5 to 10 minutes before serving, to blend flavors. |
| 1 jar (4-oz.) sliced pimiento | |
| 1 can (4-oz.) sliced mushrooms, undrained | |
| ½ cup diced green pepper | |
| 1 teaspoon salt | |
| ¼ teaspoon pepper | |

Makes 4 servings

## MEXICAN CHICKEN CASSEROLE

POWER LEVEL: High (10)                    TEMP:  155°
APPROX. MICROWAVE TIME: 15 min.
**Cook Code:**  150

| | |
|---|---|
| 1 can (10½-oz.) condensed cream of chicken soup | In small mixing bowl place soup, chilies, onion and water. Stir until well blended. |
| 2 tablespoons green chilies, diced | |
| ¼ teaspoon instant minced onion | |
| ½ cup water | |
| 2 large, firm, ripe tomatoes | Slice tomatoes in ½-in. slices. |
| 1 pkg. (6-oz.) corn chips | In 2-qt. casserole layer ½ of corn chips. Top with 1 cup chicken, then ½ of tomato slices. Pour ½ of soup mixture over chicken; sprinkle with ¾ of cheese, reserving rest for topping after cooking. Repeat layers. |
| 2 cups diced, cooked chicken, or 2 cans (5-oz. each) boned chicken, diced | |
| 1 cup (4-oz.) shredded cheddar cheese | |

Insert temperature probe so tip is in center of casserole. Attach cable end at receptacle. **Microwave at High. Set Temp, Set 155°.** When oven signals, sprinkle with reserved cheese and let stand 5 minutes before serving.

Makes 6 to 8 servings

## CHICKEN AND DUMPLINGS

POWER LEVEL: Med. High (7)
MICROWAVE TIME: 30 to 41 min., total

| | |
|---|---|
| **1 chicken, 2½ to 3½-lb., cut up**<br>**2 cups hot tap water**<br>**½ cup chopped onion**<br>**½ cup chopped celery**<br>**4 medium carrots, sliced**<br>**2 teaspoons salt**<br>**½ teaspoon pepper** | In 3-qt. casserole place chicken, water, onion, celery, carrots, salt and pepper. Cover. **Microwave at Medium High 15 Minutes.** |
| **¼ cup cornstarch**<br>**½ cup cold water** | In small bowl stir together cornstarch and water. Stir into chicken mixture, blending well. Cover. **Microwave at Medium High 10 to 20 Minutes,** until chicken is tender. Spoon Dumplings (below) around edge of dish. **Microwave at Medium High 5 to 6 Minutes,** covered, until puffed and not doughy. |

Makes 4 servings

**Dumplings:** In mixing bowl stir together 1½ cups unsifted all-purpose flour, 1 tablespoon dried parsley flakes, 2 teaspoons baking powder and ½ teaspoon salt. Add ⅔ cup milk, 1 beaten egg and 2 tablespoons cooking oil. Stir with table fork only until flour is moistened.

## CHICKEN ENCHILADA CASSEROLE

POWER LEVEL: High (10)          **Cook Code:** 110
MICROWAVE TIME: 11 to 13 min., total

| | |
|---|---|
| **2½ cups diced, cooked chicken**<br>**1 can (15-oz.) evaporated milk**<br>**1 can (10-oz.) condensed cream of chicken soup**<br>**1 pkg. (1¼-oz.) taco seasoning mix**<br>**1 medium onion, chopped**<br>**½ cup chopped celery**<br>**1 can (4-oz.) chopped green chilies, drained**<br>**6 corn tortillas, torn into 1-in. pieces**<br>**¾ cup diced cheddar or longhorn cheese** | In 2-qt. casserole combine chicken, evaporated milk, soup, taco mix, onion, celery, chilies, tortillas and cheese. **Microwave at High 11 to 13 Minutes,** rotating dish ½ turn after 5 minutes. |

Makes 4 to 6 servings

## BRUNSWICK STEW

*If a more highly seasoned stew is desired add about 1 teaspoon Worcestershire sauce and 3 to 5 drops hot pepper (tabasco) sauce.*

POWER LEVEL: Medium High (7) and High (10)
MICROWAVE TIME: 50 to 63 min., total

| | |
|---|---|
| **1 chicken, 2½ to 3½-lb., cut up**<br>**2 cups water** | In 3-qt. casserole place chicken pieces and water. Cover. **Microwave at Medium High 25 to 30 Minutes,** depending on weight of chicken, until tender. Remove meat from bones discarding skin. Cut meat into pieces and return to broth in casserole. |
| **2 cups diced raw potatoes (2 medium)**<br>**½ cup sliced onion (1 small)**<br>**2 teaspoons salt**<br>**¼ teaspoon pepper** | Add potatoes, onion, salt and pepper to casserole. **Microwave at Medium High 15 to 18 Minutes,** stirring after 8 minutes. |
| **½ cup unsifted all-purpose flour**<br>**1 can (12-oz.) whole kernel corn, undrained**<br>**1 pkg. (10-oz.) frozen baby lima beans, defrosted**<br>**1 can (16-oz.) tomatoes, drained** | Into small bowl drain liquid from corn and stir in flour, mixing well. Blend into hot mixture. Add corn, lima beans and tomatoes. **Microwave at High 10 to 15 Minutes,** stirring after 5 minutes, until vegetables are hot and sauce is thickened. Let stand 5 to 10 minutes before serving, to blend flavors. |

Makes about 8 servings

NOTE: For stronger tomato flavor, use juice from tomatoes for part of water in which chicken is cooked.

TIP: Microwave stewing chicken and prepare any of these casseroles early in the day. Their flavor mellows while standing. Refrigerate them and reheat just before serving.

These saucy dishes make excellent foods for the freezer. Package single servings in cooking pouches and heat as you would frozen convenience entrees.

# Whole Chicken

### MICROLESSON

When microwaving a whole chicken, be sure to select a young, plump tender bird. The skin should be smooth and have a pale, creamy color tinged with pink. If you are in doubt, choose a broiler-fryer. Avoid chickens with thick, bumpy skin and large amounts of bright yellow fat.

A whole chicken may be microwaved without special attention during cooking time by placing it in a cooking bag. The meat will be tender and moist.

If you do not care to use a cooking bag, or if you prefer a drier surface, microwave chicken covered with wax paper. Turn the chicken over after ½ the time.

Microwaving chicken at Medium High rather than High eliminates excessive handling and foil for shielding.

### HOW TO MICROWAVE WHOLE CHICKEN IN A COOKING BAG

POWER LEVEL: **Medium High (7) 9 to 10 Minutes Per Pound**

**Brush** chicken with a mixture of 1 tablespoon bottled brown bouquet sauce and 1 tablespoon melted butter. Cut a ½-in. strip from open end of an oven cooking bag.

**Place** chicken in bag on a microwave ovenproof platter or baking dish. Add ⅓ cup water, chicken broth or wine. Tie end of bag with plastic strip. Slash bag next to closure.

**Insert** temperature probe, if you are using it, through the bag into meatiest part of inner thigh, from below the end of and parallel to the leg. Microwave at Medium High to an internal temperature of 190°.

### HOW TO MICROWAVE WHOLE CHICKEN WITHOUT A COOKING BAG

POWER LEVEL: **Medium High (7) 9 to 10 Minutes Per Pound**

**Brush** chicken with a mixture of 1 tablespoon bottled brown bouquet sauce and 1 tablespoon melted butter. Place breast side down on trivet in cooking dish and cover with wax paper. Microwave at Medium High for ½ the minimum time.

**Turn** chicken breast side up. Recover with wax paper. Microwave for second ½ of time.

**Test** for doneness by cutting skin between inner thigh and breast. Meat should show no trace of pink, and juices should run clear.

## BARBECUED STUFFED CHICKEN

*We have chosen to cook this recipe by time, instead of by temperature, because of the barbecue sauce coating. The time method uses a loose covering of wax paper which allows steam to escape away from the surface of the bird. As the skin cooks, the barbecue sauce dries to form a beautiful showy glaze.*

*This stuffing makes delicious use of stale bread. Or, for Southern style, try the cornbread variation. Stuffings made from top of range stuffing mix or dried herb seasoned stuffing mix may also be used.*

POWER LEVEL: Medium High (7) **Cook Code:** 307
MICROWAVE TIME: 30 to 35 min., total

| | |
|---|---|
| **4 cups day-old ½-in. bread cubes or crumbled cornbread** | In large bowl toss together bread, onion, celery, salt, poultry seasoning, pepper, butter and chicken broth to make stuffing. |
| **¼ cup minced onion** | |
| **½ cup minced celery** | |
| **1 teaspoon salt** | |
| **1 teaspoon poultry seasoning** | |
| **¼ teaspoon pepper** | |
| **⅓ cup melted butter** | |
| **⅔ cup chicken broth** | |
| **1 whole broiler-fryer, about 3-lb. Bottled barbecue sauce** | Fill body cavity of chicken with stuffing. Tie wings flat to body with string around chicken; tie legs together. Brush all areas with barbecue sauce. |

On trivet in 12×8×2-in. dish place chicken with breast side down. Cover with wax paper. **Microwave at Medium High 30 to 35 Minutes,** turning chicken breast side up and brushing with barbecue sauce after 15 minutes. Chicken is done when no trace of pink shows in meat when cut is made between inner thigh and breast. Let chicken stand 10 minutes before serving.

Makes 2 to 4 servings

TIP: Serve plain microwaved whole chicken with Cranberry Sauce, page 153, chutney, pepper relish or Apple Cider Sauce (below).

## APPLE CIDER SAUCE
*Good with ham or chicken.*

POWER LEVEL: High (10) **Cook Code:** 50
MICROWAVE TIME: 5 to 7 min., total

| | |
|---|---|
| **2 cups apple cider** | In 1-qt. measuring cup measure cider. Stir in cornstarch until thoroughly mixed. Add raisins and lemon juice. **Microwave at High 5 to 7 Minutes,** stirring every 1½ minutes, until clear and thickened. |
| **⅓ cup cornstarch** | |
| **½ cup seedless raisins** | |
| **1 tablespoon lemon juice** | |

Makes about 2¼ cups

Chicken Teriyaki

## CHICKEN TERIYAKI

POWER LEVEL: Medium High (7) TEMP: 190°
APPROX. MICROWAVE TIME: 24 to 30 min.
**Cook Code:** 247

| | |
|---|---|
| **¼ cup soy sauce** | In small cooking bag, mix soy sauce, honey and sherry. |
| **⅓ cup honey** | |
| **⅓ cup sherry** | |
| **1 whole broiler-fryer, about 3-lb.** | Add chicken to bag and tie open end securely with plastic strip cut from open end of bag. |

Turn chicken on its side and place in 12×8×2-in. dish. Marinate in refrigerator 1 to 2 hours, turning chicken over after ½ of time. To microwave, place bird breast side up in dish. Slash bag near closure. Insert temperature probe as shown at left. **Microwave at Medium High. Set Temp, Set 190°.** When oven signals, remove chicken. Prepare Teriyaki Sauce (below) and finish chicken as described in sauce recipe.

Makes about 4 servings

**Teriyaki Sauce:** In 1-pt. glass measuring cup stir together 1 tablespoon water and 2 tablespoons cornstarch. Cut off one corner of cooking bag with scissors and drain juices into cup. **Microwave at High 2 to 3 Minutes,** until thick and clear, stirring after 1 minute. After 10 minutes, remove chicken from bag to serving platter. Pour sauce over chicken just before serving.

# Chicken Livers & Giblets

Chicken Liver Pate

Chicken livers may be sauteed in the Brown 'N Sear Dish, or microwaved in liquid at Medium before they are used in other dishes.

Prick giblets with a fork before microwaving. As with conventional cooking, giblets tend to pop, but the effect is more noticeable when they are microwaved.

Poultry Giblet Gravy may be located on page 188.

### CHICKEN LIVER PATE

*Finely chopped pieces of onion add nice texture to this creamy spread. Garnish with sieved hard-poached egg, ripe olives and additional chopped onion. Serve with crackers and, if desired, butter to spread over crackers before adding the pate.*

POWER LEVEL: Medium (5)      **Cook Code:** 185
MICROWAVE TIME: 18 to 22 min., total

| | |
|---|---|
| **1 lb. chicken livers**<br>**1 cup water** | In 2-qt. casserole place livers. Prick each liver with fork. Add water. Cover. **Microwave at Medium 18 to 22 Minutes,** stirring after 10 minutes, until tender. Drain livers, place in container of electric blender. Whir until evenly blended. |
| **⅓ cup soft butter**<br>**1 tablespoon finely chopped onion**<br>**1 tablespoon lemon juice**<br>**1 tablespoon brandy**<br>**½ teaspoon salt**<br>**½ teaspoon dry mustard**<br>**¼ teaspoon thyme**<br>**3 to 4 drops liquid pepper seasoning** | In small mixing bowl stir together butter, onion, juice, brandy, salt, mustard, thyme and pepper seasoning, to blend. Mix in livers well. Pack into well greased 1½ to 2 cup mold. Chill thoroughly, then turn out onto serving plate. Garnish and serve with crackers. |

Makes about 1½ cups

### SAUTEED CHICKEN LIVERS

POWER LEVEL: High (10)
MICROWAVE TIME: 8 to 10 min., total

| | |
|---|---|
| **1 tablespoon butter**<br>**½ lb. chicken livers** | Preheat Brown 'N Sear Dish (uncovered), or griddle. **Microwave at High 3 to 4 Minutes.** Add butter, then livers. **Microwave at High 5 to 6 Minutes,** turning over after 3 minutes, until crisp and tender. |

Makes 2 servings

# Poultry Convenience Foods

Canned convenience foods, or foods frozen in metal trays, should be removed from their containers to suitable microwave plates or casseroles. Small boil-in-bag pouches (about 5 to 10-oz.) can be placed directly in the oven. Slit or pierce the top of the pouch before microwaving and open carefully after heating to avoid burns from steam. Large boil-in-bags may be placed in a serving dish. When contents are partially defrosted, open the bag, slide food into the dish and stir before continuing to microwave.

**Chicken Gravy and Main Dishes** such as barbecue chicken, chicken a la king, chicken and dumplings, creamed chicken, croquettes, escalloped chicken with noodles, fried chicken, pieces or slices in gravy, stew and turkey tetrazzini may be microwaved according to chart below.

POWER LEVEL: **High (10)**

| CANNED AMOUNT | TIME MIN. | COOK CODE | COMMENTS |
|---|---|---|---|
| 7½-10½-oz. | 2-4 | 20 | Cover. Stir after 2 minutes and before serving, or use temperature probe set for 150°. |
| 14-24-oz. | 4-6 | 40 | Cover. Stir after 2 minutes and before serving, or use temperature probe set for 150°. |

| FROZEN AMOUNT | TIME MIN. | COOK CODE | COMMENTS |
|---|---|---|---|
| 5-6½-oz. pouch | 3 to 4 | 30 | Slit pouch before microwaving. |
| 12-oz. | 7-9 | 70 | Cover. Stir after 6 minutes. |
| 16-17-oz. | 11-14 | 110 | Cover. Stir or turn over after 8 minutes. |
| Chicken Croquettes (12-oz. pkg.) | 4-6 | 40 | Pierce sauce pouch with fork. Place with food on plate. Cover with wax paper. Rotate dish ½ turn after 2 minutes. |
| Fried Chicken 2 pieces | 2-4 | 20 | Follow procedure below. Some brands of frozen fried chicken are not fully cooked. If label does not state "fully cooked", check for doneness. |
| Fried Chicken 1 lb., 6 pieces | 6-7 | 60 | |
| Fried Chicken 2 lb., 10 pieces | 8-10 | 80 | |

## HOW TO MICROWAVE FROZEN FRIED CHICKEN

**Arrange** chicken pieces in a single layer on a microwave ovenproof platter or cooking dish with meatiest parts to the outside.

**Cover** with wax paper. Microwave at High for ½ the heating time shown on chart above.

**Rotate** platter ½ turn. Microwave for second ½ of time. If package label does not state "fully cooked", check for doneness by cutting through meat to bone. Pinkness indicates more cooking is needed.

Stuffed Cornish Hens

## CORNISH HENS FAR EAST STYLE

POWER LEVEL: High (10)
MICROWAVE TIME: 18 to 20 min., total

| | |
|---|---|
| **2 cornish hens, about 1-lb. each, defrosted** | Split hens in halves, using kitchen shears or a sharp knife. Place in 12×8×2-in. dish, skin side down. |
| **¼ cup soy sauce**<br>**¼ cup sherry wine**<br>**¼ cup pineapple juice**<br>**1 clove garlic, crushed or ⅛ teaspoon garlic powder**<br>**½ teaspoon curry powder**<br>**¼ teaspoon dry mustard** | In small bowl mix together soy sauce, sherry, pineapple juice, garlic, curry powder and mustard. Stir to blend well and pour over meat in dish. Refrigerate 4 to 6 hours, or overnight. |

To cook, turn skin side up and baste with marinade. Cover dish with wax paper. **Microwave at High 8 Minutes.** Brush with marinade and rotate dish ½ turn. Recover. **Microwave at High 10 to 12 Minutes** more, until meat is tender. Serve immediately.

Makes 2 to 4 servings

# Cornish Hens

Delicate Cornish Hens need some extra attention during defrosting or they may start to cook. We recommend defrosting in 3 steps rather than 2.

Cornish Hens are naturally tender, especially when microwaved. Because they cook so quickly, the unevenness of browning is particularly noticeable.

**Plain** microwaved Cornish Hen in background contrasts with a hen brushed with teriyaki sauce before microwaving. Teriyaki sauce gives a more golden color than brown bouquet sauce.

## HOW TO DEFROST CORNISH HENS
POWER LEVEL: **Defrost**

### 10 to 14 Minutes Per Pound

1. Place unopened packages in oven. (Metal closure need not be removed.) Microwave at Defrost for ⅓ the total defrosting time.

2. Turn packages over. Microwave for ⅓ the time.

3. Unwrap and shield ends of legs with foil. Microwave for last ⅓ of time. If giblets do not move freely, run cold water into cavities.

## MICROWAVING CORNISH HENS, Halved
POWER LEVEL: **High (10)**

### 9 to 10 Minutes Per Pound

1. Brush halves with browning sauce. Place in cooking dish, skin side up. Cover with wax paper. Microwave at High for ½ the cooking time.

2. Rotate dish ½ turn. Microwave for second ½ of time. Hen is done if juices run clear when inner thigh is pierced with a fork.

## MICROWAVING CORNISH HENS, Whole
POWER LEVEL: **High (10)**

### 6 to 8 Minutes Per Pound

1. Stuff hens*, if desired. Brush with browning sauce. Place breast side down in suitable cooking dish. Cover with wax paper. Microwave for ½ the cooking time.

2. Turn breast side up. Microwave for second ½ of time. Let stand 10 minutes. Hen is done when leg moves freely and juices run clear when inner thigh is pierced with a fork.

*Rice is an excellent stuffing for Cornish Hens. For each hen, use about ½ cup cooked rice (white and/or wild), well-buttered and seasoned.

# Duckling

Duckling with Colorful Marmalade Sauce

Like other poultry, duckling microwaves juicy and tender in a very short time. Since duckling is so fatty, browning sauce is not brushed on before the first half of cooking because it will not adhere to the skin. After the duckling has rendered some of its fat, you may brush it with browning sauce or, if you prefer, after microwaving broil it under a conventional broiler to crisp and brown the thick skin. This rich meat is traditionally served with a fruit sauce or glaze.

## HOW TO DEFROST DUCKLING
POWER LEVEL: **Defrost**

### 4 to 6 Minutes Per Pound

1. Place plastic wrapped duckling in oven. (Metal closure need not be removed.) Microwave at Defrost for ½ the time.

2. Unwrap duckling and turn over into cooking dish. Shield wings, tail, ends of legs and any other warm areas with foil. Defrost for second ½ of time.

3. Run cold water into cavity until giblets can be removed. For step-by-step photographs, see *How To Defrost A Whole Chicken,* page 134.

## MICROWAVING DUCKLING
POWER LEVEL: **High (10)**

### 7 to 8 Minutes Per Pound

1. Shield wings, tail and ends of legs with foil. Place duckling breast side down on trivet in a 12×8×2-in. dish. Microwave at High for ½ the cooking time.

2. Remove foil and turn breast side up. With a kitchen fork, prick skin of breast and legs to release fat. Baste duckling with drippings, then drain fat from dish. Brush with browning or barbecue sauce, if desired.

3. Microwave for second ½ of the time. Duckling is done when the last drops of juice drained from the cavity run clear, without a trace of pink.

**Prick** skin of breast and legs with a kitchen fork after first ½ of cooking time. Brush with diluted brown bouquet sauce, if desired. For a crisp skin, omit sauce and, after microwaving, broil under a conventional broiler until crisp and brown.

# Turkey Defrosting

## MICROLESSON

Shape as well as size influences defrosting. A broad breasted, meaty turkey takes longer to defrost than a streamlined one of the same weight. The breast may also need more shielding because it is higher in the oven and closer to the source of microwave energy.

These directions are for defrosting turkeys weighing up to 12 pounds. Larger turkeys may be defrosted using the same method, but allowing turkey to stand 30 minutes after each ¼ of defrosting time. A 5-in. strip of foil is needed on the top of these large birds during each defrosting period to prevent over-defrosting.

If you wish to start defrosting a large turkey the day before you plan to roast it, defrost for ¾ the time, letting turkey stand between each ¼ period. Then place turkey in refrigerator overnight to complete defrosting.

## HOW TO DEFROST TURKEY

POWER LEVEL: **Defrost**

**10 to 12 Minutes Per Pound**

**Place** unwrapped turkey, breast side down, in oven. It is not necessary to remove the metal closure because of the great mass of food. Microwave at Defrost for ¼ the time. Rotate turkey ½ turn, so legs point to opposite side of the oven. Microwave for ¼ the time.

**Unwrap** turkey and place it in a cooking dish. Shield legs, wing tips and any warm or brown areas, with foil. Secure with wooden picks.

Microwaved Turkey

**Turn** breast side up and defrost for ¼ of time. Check breast for warm spots and shield if necessary. Rotate dish ½ turn, so legs point to opposite side of the oven. Microwave for final ¼ of time.

**Remove** metal clamp from legs. Run cold water into breast and neck cavities until giblets and neck can be removed. Turkey should feel soft and cool with a glistening surface. Interior should be cold and slightly icy.

# Turkey

## HOW TO MICROWAVE TURKEY IN A COOKING BAG

POWER LEVEL: **Medium (5)**

**11 to 13 Minutes Per Pound**

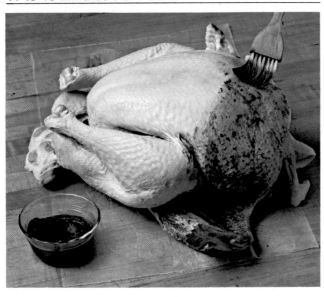

**Brush** turkey with a mixture of 2 tablespoons brown bouquet sauce and 2 tablespoons water or melted butter. When using butter mixture, dry turkey thoroughly before brushing, or sauce will not cling to bird.

## MICROLESSON

Turkeys weighing 6 to 12 pounds may be microwaved in two ways. For a moist turkey, needing no attention during cooking, use an ovenproof cooking bag.

If you do not care to use a cooking bag, or prefer turkey with a drier surface, microwave turkey in a roasting dish covered with wax paper. This method requires some attention, since you start the turkey breast side down and turn it over to finish microwaving. While dry-roasted turkeys develop some browning, you may want to use a browning sauce for even color.

If your oven is equipped with a temperature probe, be sure to use it when microwaving turkey. The oven will sig-

**Cut** ½-in. wide strip from open end of ovenproof cooking bag. Place turkey in bag and arrange in a roasting dish. Lightly oil inside of bag over breast to prevent sticking. Add ½ cup water, chicken broth or wine. Close bag by tying the open end securely with the plastic strip.
Slash bag near closure.

## HOW TO MICROWAVE TURKEY WITHOUT A COOKING BAG

**Brush** turkey with browning sauce as directed above. Place turkey in roasting dish, breast side down. Cover with wax paper. Insert temperature probe, if you are using it, as shown above. Set Temp, Set 120°, or Microwave at Medium for ½ the cooking time.

When oven signals, or after ½ the time, turn turkey, breast side up. Recover with wax paper and microwave second ½ of time to an internal temperature of 190°. Let stand 20 minutes before carving.

**Insert** meat thermometer, when not using probe, after minimum cooking time. Follow directions for probe placement and allow 2 minutes for an accurate reading. If turkey has not reached 190°, remove thermometer and return turkey to oven for a few more minutes.

Do not put conventional metal meat thermometer in microwave oven.

**Standing Time** of 20 minutes allows the interior of the turkey to finish roasting without overcooking the tender breast meat.

nal when turkey has reached 190°. Let turkey stand 20 minutes after microwaving, before serving.

When microwaving turkey by time, check for doneness after the minimum cooking time. You may have to reset your timer to complete the cooking cycle.

**Do not use a trivet** when microwaving turkey. A trivet raises turkey closer to top of oven, where microwave energy is released. Overcooking on top can result.

**TIP:** *On turkey over 6 inches high, areas next to breastbone are vulnerable to overcooking. To prevent overcooking on these high-breasted birds, shield breastbone area from neck cavity to tip of breastbone with strip of aluminum foil (5 inches long and 2 inches wide) before putting bird into cooking bag.*

**Insert** temperature probe, if you are using one, through the bag into the meatiest part of the inner thigh. Position the probe below the end of, and parallel to the leg. Microwave at Medium. Set Temp, Set 190°. If not using the probe, microwave for minimum time and check with a meat thermometer.

**Fat Free Gravy** can be made from drippings in cooking bag. Hold bag over a 1-qt. measure and strainer. Fat will rise to top of juices. Cut a small slit in bottom of bag and let only the light brown juice run into measure. Quickly remove bag with remaining yellow fat to cooking dish.

## STUFFING SUGGESTIONS FOR TURKEY

Use one of the following suggestions for stuffing, packing lightly into body cavity. Microwave as illustrated on this page.

**Savory Stuffing:** For 8 to 10-lb. bird, toss together: 8 cups day-old bread cubes, ½ cup minced onion, 1 cup minced celery, 2 teaspoons salt, 2 teaspoons poultry seasoning, ¼ teaspoon pepper, ⅔ cup melted butter and 1 cup chicken broth.

**Range Top Stuffing Mix:** Prepare as package directs.

**Prepared Seasoned Stuffing Mix:** Follow package directions.

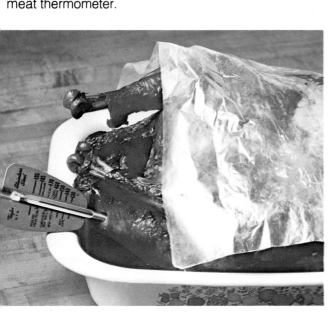

## SAVORY TURKEY SQUARES

POWER LEVEL: Medium High (7)    **Cook Code:** 267
MICROWAVE TIME: 26 to 30 min., total

| | |
|---|---|
| **3 cups cooked,** ........<br>    **chopped turkey**<br>**2 cups day-old bread**<br>    **cubes**<br>**½ cup minced celery**<br>**¼ cup minced onion**<br>**2 tablespoons chopped**<br>    **pimiento**<br>**1 tablespoon lemon**<br>    **juice**<br>**½ teaspoon salt**<br>**¼ teaspoon pepper**<br>**⅔ cup milk**<br>**½ cup chicken broth**<br>**3 eggs, slightly beaten** | In large mixing bowl mix together turkey, bread cubes, celery, onion, pimiento, lemon juice, salt, pepper, milk, broth and eggs. Pour into 12×8×2-in. dish. Cover with wax paper. **Microwave at Medium High 26 to 30 Minutes,** rotating dish ½ turn after 15 minutes, until set but still slightly soft in center. Let stand 5 to 10 minutes to firm before serving. |

Makes 6 to 8 servings

## HOT TURKEY AND CHEESE SANDWICHES

*These are known in the South as "Hot Browns", created at a once-famous hotel in Louisville.*

POWER LEVEL: Medium High (7)
MICROWAVE TIME: 9½ to 12 min., total

| | |
|---|---|
| **4 strips bacon** .......... | On paper plate lined with double thickness paper towels, arrange bacon. Cover with single thickness paper towel. **Microwave at Medium High 2½ to 3 Minutes,** until only partially cooked. |
| **4 slices toast** ...........<br>**8 to 12 large slices**<br>    **turkey breast**<br>**4 slices tomato (¼-in.**<br>    **thick)**<br>**1 recipe Cheese Sauce,**<br>    **page 189**<br>**¼ cup Parmesan cheese** | In 2 (7 to 9-in.) oval au gratin dishes, divide toast, arranging to cover bottoms of dishes. Place 4 to 6 large slices turkey in each dish and top each with 2 tomato slices. Divide cheese sauce over sandwiches. Sprinkle tops of sandwiches with Parmesan cheese. Arrange 2 slices partially-cooked bacon over each sandwich. |

Place dishes side by side in microwave oven. Cover with wax paper. **Microwave at Medium High 7 to 9 Minutes,** rearranging dishes after 4 minutes, until hot.

Makes 2 sandwiches

## SAUCY TURKEY AND BROCCOLI

*Called Turkey Divan when made with the traditional Mornay Sauce. This makes a very nice luncheon or supper dish. A salad of tomato slices is a colorful accompaniment.*

POWER LEVEL: High (10)    **Cook Code:**   60
MICROWAVE TIME: 6 to 8 min., total

| | |
|---|---|
| **1 bunch (about 1¼-lb.)**<br>    **broccoli, cut in**<br>    **spears** | ...Microwave broccoli according to directions, page 204. Drain. In 12× 8×2-in. dish or microwave ovenproof platter arrange attractively. |
| **8 large slices cooked**<br>    **turkey**<br>**1 recipe Mornay Sauce,**<br>    **or Cheese Sauce,**<br>    **both page 189** | Layer turkey slices over broccoli. Cover with sauce. **Microwave at High 6 to 8 Minutes,** rotating dish ½ turn after 5 minutes. |

Makes 4 servings

## TURKEY GOULASH

*The 2 tablespoons paprika gives a distinctive mellow flavor.*

POWER LEVEL: High (10)
MICROWAVE TIME: 12 to 15 min., total

| | |
|---|---|
| **¼ cup butter** ..........<br>**2 large onions, thinly**<br>    **sliced**<br>**1 clove garlic, minced** | In 2-qt. casserole place butter, onions and garlic. **Microwave at High 5 to 6 Minutes,** stirring after 3 minutes, until onion is limp. |
| **3 cups cooked, cubed**<br>    **turkey**<br>**1½ cups turkey or**<br>    **chicken broth**<br>**1 can (8-oz.) tomato**<br>    **sauce**<br>**2 tablespoons paprika**<br>**1½ teaspoons salt**<br>**¼ teaspoon pepper** | Add turkey, broth, tomato sauce, paprika, salt and pepper. Cover. **Microwave at High 7 to 9 Minutes,** stirring after 4 minutes, until hot. |
| **1 cup (8-oz.) dairy**<br>    **sour cream** | Stir sour cream into hot mixture just before serving. Serve over rice or noodles. |

Makes 6 servings

## TURKEY TETRAZZINI

POWER LEVEL: High (10)
MICROWAVE TIME: 24 to 28 min., total

| | |
|---|---|
| **1 pkg. (7-oz.)** ................... **spaghetti** | Cook spaghetti (see chart, page 195), except **Microwave 9 Minutes.** Drain. Place in greased 12x8x2-in. dish. |
| **¼ cup butter** .................... **1 can (4-oz.) sliced mushrooms, drained 1 small onion, chopped 1½ teaspoons lemon juice** | In 2-qt. casserole place butter, mushrooms, onion and lemon juice. **Microwave at High 2 to 3 Minutes,** stirring after 1 minute. |
| **⅓ cup flour** ....................... **1 tablespoon salt ½ teaspoon paprika ⅛ teaspoon nutmeg 2 cups turkey or chicken broth** | Stir in flour, salt, paprika and nutmeg, until smooth. **Microwave at High 1 Minute.** Stir well. Gradually stir in broth. **Microwave at High 5 to 6 Minutes,** stirring after 3 minutes, until thickened. |
| **½ cup dairy half & half 2½ cups cooked, cubed turkey ½ cup Parmesan cheese Paprika** | Mix in half & half and turkey. Pour over spaghetti. Sprinkle with cheese and paprika. **Microwave at High 7 to 9 Minutes,** rotating dish ½ turn after 4 minutes, until hot. |

Makes 4 to 6 servings

## TURKEY CONVENIENCE FOODS

Foods frozen in metal trays should be removed to suitable microwave plates or casseroles. Small boil-in-bag pouches (5 to 10-oz.) can be placed directly in the oven. Slit or pierce the top of the pouch before microwaving and open carefully after heating. Large boil-in-bags may be placed in a serving dish. When contents are partially defrosted, open the bag, slide the food into the dish and stir before continuing to microwave.

## TURKEY CONVENIENCE CHART

POWER LEVEL: **High (10)**

| ITEM | TIME MIN. | COOK CODE | COMMENTS |
|---|---|---|---|
| **Gravy & Sliced Turkey, Frozen** (5-oz. pkg.) | 3-4 | 30 | Make 1-in. slit in top of pouch with sharp knife. |
| **Turkey Tetrazzini, Frozen** (12-oz. pkg.) | 7-9 | 70 | Place food in 1-qt. casserole. Cover. Stir after 6 minutes. |

## HOW TO MICROWAVE TURKEY PARTS

POWER LEVEL: **Medium High (7)**

Turkey pieces, except whole bone-in breasts, cook best by time, rather than temperature, due to their uneven shape.

For color, brush with equal parts brown bouquet sauce and melted butter or water, or use teriyaki sauce or barbecue sauce.

To microwave by time, place turkey skin side down in appropriate size roasting dish without trivet. Add no water. Cover as indicated below. Turn over after ½ of microwaving time.

To microwave turkey breast by temperature, insert temperature probe from side into center of thickest meaty area. Set at 170°. (NOTE: Breast cooks to lower finished temperature than whole turkey.)

After microwaving, let stand 10 to 20 minutes before slicing. Special directions are given for frozen packaged turkey roasts.

| ITEM | MINUTES PER LB. | COMMENTS |
|---|---|---|
| **Frozen Packaged Turkey Roasts** (2 to 4-lb.)* | 18 to 20 | Add ½ cup water. Can be microwaved from frozen without defrosting. Cover with plastic wrap. Turn over after ½ of time. |
| **Turkey Legs Turkey Quarters Turkey Halves** | 11 to 13 | Must be defrosted before microwaving to cook evenly. Defrost like frozen whole turkey, page 148. Cover with wax paper. Turn over after ½ of time. Brush again with sauce. |
| **Whole Turkey Breast** | 9 to 11 | Microwave with temperature probe in cooking bag (see directions for whole turkey, page 150.) Do not brush with barbecue sauce when using cooking bag. Insert temperature probe as described above and microwave to 170.° |

*NOTE: When a gravy pouch is included it adds to the total package weight but should not be included in calculating total microwave time for turkey roast. For example, a two pound package frozen turkey roast may contain 6-oz. gravy pouch. Subtract weight of gravy from total package weight.

## CRANBERRY SAUCE

POWER LEVEL: High          **Cook Code:  180**
MICROWAVE TIME: 18 to 20 min., total

In 3-qt. casserole stir together 2 cups sugar, ½ cup water, and 1 lb. fresh or frozen cranberries. Cover. **Microwave at High 18 to 20 Minutes,** stirring every 6 minutes. Serve warm or cold.

Makes 3 to 4 cups

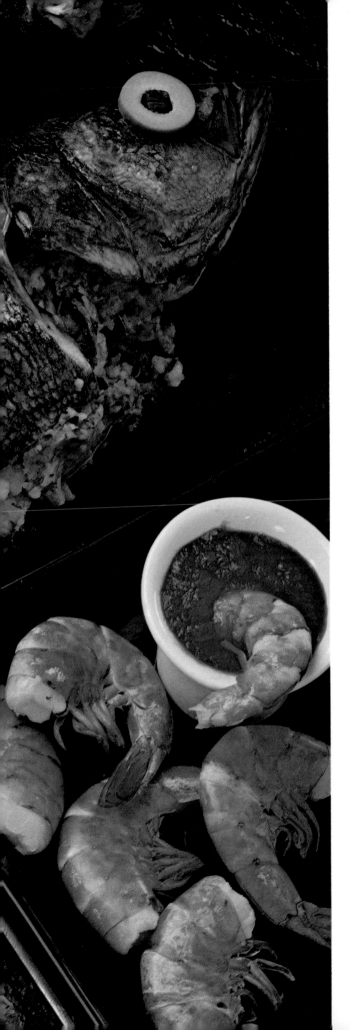

# Fish & Seafood

Fish and seafood are naturally tender and require minimal cooking to preserve their delicate flavor and texture. The speed and moisture retention of microwaving are decided advantages in cooking them.

Overcooking dries and toughens fish. We recommend that many seafoods, especially the meatier types, be cooked until the outer areas appear opaque but the centers are still slightly translucent. These areas will finish cooking as the seafood stands, while the outer areas remain tender.

1. Lobster Thermidor, page 174
2. Stuffed Whole Fish, page 164
3. Microwaved Shrimp in the Shell, page 168
4. Fillets in Lemon Butter, page 161

## MICROLESSON

Fish defrosts rapidly. It is naturally delicate and tender, so care should be taken not to toughen it by over-defrosting. Remove fish from the microwave oven while it is still slightly icy.

## HOW TO DEFROST FILLETS AND STEAKS

### DEFROSTING CHART

POWER LEVEL: **Defrost**

| ITEM | 1st SIDE TIME MINUTES | 2nd SIDE TIME MINUTES |
|---|---|---|
| Fillets, 1-lb. | 4 | 4 to 6 |
| Steaks, 6-oz. - 1 | 2 | None |
| Steaks, 6-oz. - 2 | 2 | 1 to 2 |

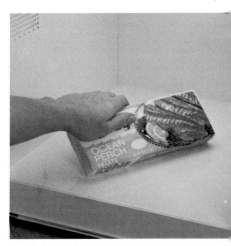

**Shape** of package, as well as its weight influences defrosting time. Thick fillets or bulky packages take longer than flat packages of the same weight.

**Place** unopened paper or plastic package directly on oven floor. Fillets frozen at home in a bag of water should be placed in a dish to avoid leakage.

## HOW TO DEFROST WHOLE FISH

### DEFROSTING CHART

POWER LEVEL: **Defrost**

| ITEM | 1st SIDE TIME MINUTES | 2nd SIDE TIME MINUTES |
|---|---|---|
| 1 - 8 to 10-oz. Fish | 2 | 2 to 4 |
| 2 - 8 to 10-oz. Fish | 4 | 6 to 8 |
| 1 - 3 to 4-lb. Fish | 8 | 12 to 14 |

**Shape** of fish, as well as weight, determines defrosting time. A short, thick fish may take longer to defrost than a long, thin one of the same weight.

**Arrange** fish in a cooking dish large enough to hold it easily. Microwave at Defrost for first part of time.

If you or a family member like to fish, freeze your catch for fresh-tasting fish all year 'round. Seal fillets or steaks in a plastic bag with a small amount of water and freeze. Clean whole fish, then dip them in water and freeze on a baking dish. The icy coating will protect fish from freezer burn. Package for freezing after icy coating forms.

When defrosting home frozen fish, use a cooking dish to collect water as it melts.

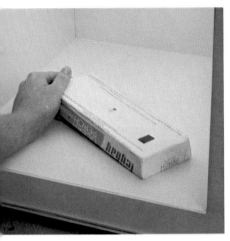

**Turn** package over so that the side which was closest to the back of the oven is brought to the front. Rotate ¼ turn.

**Check** after minimum defrosting time. Corners should not feel warm, although outer pieces may have started to loosen.

**Hold** fillets under cold running water until they can be separated.

**Turn** fish over. Microwave for second part of minimum time.

**Test** fish. It should feel cold and pliable and may still be slightly icy in the cavity.

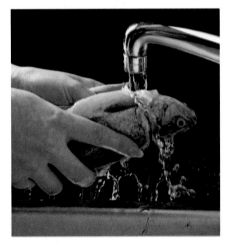

**Rinse** cavity with cold running water to complete defrosting.

# Fish Fillets & Steaks

Salmon Steaks

## MICROLESSON

Fillets of steak may be microwaved in several ways to produce a variety of dishes. Microwave them in a sauce for rich flavor. Steam or poach them for a delicate, but simple dish. Smother partially cooked fillet in crumbs and cream for scalloped fish. Whether cooked conventionally or microwaved, juices of salmon or halibut steaks coagulate on the surface of the fish. To eliminate this, before microwaving, line the dish with a paper towel to absorb excess juices, then turn over to serve. Flounder, which is extremely moist, should be microwaved on a trivet.

**Fish** is done when flesh flakes easily with a fork. Center should still be slightly translucent.

## HOW TO MICROWAVE FILLETS IN SAUCE

**Arrange** fillets in a cooking dish, thickest parts to outside of dish.

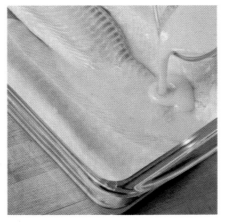

**Pour** sauce on fillets. Cover with wax paper. Microwave for ½ of time.

**Rotate** dish ½ turn and microwave until fish flakes easily.

## HOW TO MICROWAVE STEAMED FISH

**Dampen** a paper towel with water. No additional moisture is needed. Arrange fish in dish with meatiest parts to the outside.

**Cover** with dampened towel. Microwave for ½ of time. Rotate dish ½ turn and finish steaming, or remove towel and scallop fish if desired.

**Scallop** fish by spreading crumbs over fillets and pouring in cream. Return to oven and microwave second ½ of time.

## HOW TO MICROWAVE FISH STEAKS

**Brush** steaks with lemon-butter mixture. (If desired, line dish with paper towel before placing fish in it.)

**Cover** tightly with plastic wrap, turning back corner to vent. Microwave for ½ the time.

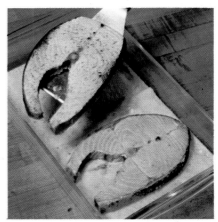

**Turn** steaks over and recover, or, if paper towel was not used, rotate dish ½ turn. Complete cooking.

## FROZEN FISH FILLETS WITH SEASONED COATING MIX

*Very moist result. Cook these on a microwave trivet for drier, firmer fish.*

POWER LEVEL: High (10)  **Cook Code:** 60
MICROWAVE TIME: 6 to 8 min., total

**1 lb. fish fillets,** .......... Separate fish fillets and
**defrosted** coat with seasoned coat-
**1 pkg. (2-oz.) seasoned** ing mix. Arrange in 12×8×
**coating mix for fish** 2-in. dish with thickest
meaty areas to outside
edges of dish. Cover with
wax paper. **Microwave at
High 6 to 8 Minutes,** rotating dish ½ turn after 4 minutes, until fish flakes with
fork.

Makes about 4 servings

## FILLETS IN CREAMY WINE SAUCE

*A dinner party dish. This French wine and cream sauce is sometimes called Bercy Sauce.*

POWER LEVEL: High (10)
MICROWAVE TIME: 11 to 14 min., total

**1 tablespoon butter** ..... In 12×8×2-in. dish place
**2 tablespoons minced** butter. **Microwave at High
green onions** **½ Minute,** until melted.
**1 lb. sole or flounder** Spread butter over bottom
**fillets, defrosted** of dish and sprinkle with
**and cut into** onions. Arrange fillets over
**serving pieces** onions and cover with
**1½ cups sliced fresh** mushrooms. Pour wine
**mushrooms** over top. **Microwave at
¾ cup dry white wine,** **High 7 to 9 Minutes,** rotat-
**such as Sauterne** ing dish ¼ turn every 3
minutes, or until fish flakes
with a fork. Remove fish to
microwave ovenproof plat-
ter and cover to keep warm
while cooking sauce.

**2 tablespoons flour** ..... In 1-qt. casserole combine
**¼ cup heavy cream** flour, cream, salt and pep-
**1 teaspoon salt** per, until smooth. Carefully
**⅛ teaspoon pepper** drain hot liquid from fish into cream mixture and stir
well. **Microwave at High 2
to 3 Minutes,** stirring
sauce every minute.

**½ teaspoon lemon** ...... Stir lemon juice into sauce.
**juice** Pour sauce over fish and
**¾ cup shredded Swiss** sprinkle cheese on top. **Mi-
cheese** **crowave at High 2 Min-
utes** more, until cheese
has melted. Garnish with
parsley sprigs.

Makes about 4 servings

## SCALLOPED FISH OR SCALLOPS

POWER LEVEL: High (10)
MICROWAVE TIME: 7 to 9 min., total

**1 lb. white fish fillets** .... On microwave ovenproof
**(flounder or sole) or** platter or 9-in. pie plate
**scallops** place fish fillets or scallops
with thickest, meaty areas
to outside edges of dish.
Cover with paper towel
which has been complete-
ly dampened, with most of
water squeezed out. **Mi-
crowave at High 4 Min-
utes.**

**½ cup (¼-lb.) butter** ..... Remove platter from oven
**1 cup soft bread** and let stand covered with
**crumbs** paper towel while prepar-
**1 cup saltine cracker** ing buttered crumbs. In
**crumbs** 1-qt. glass measure place
butter. **Microwave at High
1 Minute,** or until melted.
Add bread and cracker
crumbs. Mix with fork.

**1 teaspoon salt** ........ Remove paper towel from
**⅛ teaspoon freshly** fish and sprinkle evenly
**ground pepper** with salt and pepper, then
**⅓ cup milk or cream** buttered crumbs. Pour
milk evenly over top. **Mi-
crowave at High 2 to 4
Minutes** more, until fish
flakes easily with a fork or
scallops are tender but not
overcooked.

Makes 4 servings

NOTE: Leftover scalloped seafood may be used as a good omelet filling.

Complimentary sauces for fish and seafood include Dill Butter, or Herbed Butter, page 191, Hollandaise Sauce, page 190; or, use the microwave oven to prepare Clari-fied Butter.

**Clarified Butter:** In 1-pt. measuring cup place ½ cup (¼-lb.) butter. **Microwave at High 2 Minutes,** until boil-ing. The clear layer which floats to top is clarified butter and may be poured off into a serving container. **Cook Code:** 20.

Fish Creole

## FILLETS IN LEMON BUTTER

POWER LEVEL: High (10)
MICROWAVE TIME: 10 to 13 min., total

| | |
|---|---|
| **1 lb. firm fish fillets such as sole or haddock** | In 12×8×2-in. dish, arrange fillets with thickest, meaty areas to outside edges of dish. Sprinkle with salt and pepper. |
| **½ to 1 teaspoon salt** | |
| **⅛ teaspoon pepper** | |
| **½ cup (¼-lb.) butter** | In 1-qt. casserole place butter. **Microwave at High 1 to 2 Minutes,** until melted. Blend in parsley and lemon juice and pour over fish. Top with crumbs, then sprinkle on paprika. |
| **½ cup chopped fresh parsley** | |
| **1 tablespoon lemon juice** | |
| **½ cup buttery flavored cracker crumbs** | |
| **½ teaspoon paprika** | |

**Microwave at High 9 to 11 Minutes,** rotating dish ½ turn after 5 minutes, until fish flakes easily with fork.

Makes 4 servings

## FISH CREOLE (A Low Calorie Recipe)

POWER LEVEL: High (10)  **Cook Code:** 80
MICROWAVE TIME: 8 to 9 min., total

| | |
|---|---|
| **1 lb. sole or haddock fillets, defrosted** | Rinse fish and pat dry with paper towels. In 12×8×2-in. dish arrange fish with thickest pieces to outside edges of dish. |
| **1 can (8-oz.) tomato sauce** | In 1-qt. glass measure stir together tomato sauce, mushrooms, green pepper, celery, water, minced onion and bouillon. Pour evenly over fish. Cover tightly with plastic wrap, turning back one corner to vent. **Microwave at High 8 to 10 Minutes,** rotating dish ½ turn after 4 minutes, until fish flakes easily with fork. Let stand about 5 minutes before serving, to blend flavors. |
| **1 can (2-oz.) sliced mushrooms, drained** | |
| **½ green pepper, diced** | |
| **1 stalk celery, diagonally sliced** | |
| **3 tablespoons water** | |
| **1½ tablespoons instant minced onion** | |
| **1 teaspoon chicken bouillon granules** | |

Makes about 4 servings

## SALMON STEAKS

POWER LEVEL: High (10)          **Cook Code:** 80
MICROWAVE TIME: 8 to 10 min., total

| | |
|---|---|
| **4 (½-in. thick) salmon** . . . . | In paper towel lined 12× |
| **steaks (1-lb.)** | 8×2-in. dish place steaks. |
| **2 tablespoons melted** | Brush with melted butter |
| **butter** | mixed with lemon juice. |
| **2 teaspoons lemon** | Sprinkle with dill if desired. |
| **juice** | Cover dish with wax paper. |
| **½ teaspoon dill weed** | |

**Microwave at High 8 to 9 Minutes,** rotating dish ½ turn after 3 minutes. When done, fish will flake easily with fork. Turn fish over onto serving plate. (Paper towel absorbs juices for best appearance of fish.) Garnish top of steaks with sprinkling of paprika or parsley and additional melted butter, if desired.

*Makes 4 servings*

FOR 2 SALMON STEAKS: Use half of all ingredients and place fish in 8-in. square dish. Cover with wax paper. **Microwave at High 4 to 5 Minutes;** no turns necessary. **Cook Code:** 40.

**Salmon With Cucumber Sauce:** Cook 4 salmon steaks as directed above, but omit dill weed. Cook to minimum time, then spread over the tops a mixture of: ½ cup dairy sour cream, ⅓ to ½ cup shredded or chopped cucumber (¼ medium cucumber), 1 teaspoon chopped parsley, ½ teaspoon chopped chives, 1 teaspoon lemon juice and ¼ teaspoon salt. **Microwave at High 1 to 2 Minutes** more before serving. **Cook Code:** 10.

## ROUND SALMON LOAF

*Round shape is best for fish loaves, just as it is for meat loaves.*

POWER LEVEL: High (10)          **Cook Code:** 90
MICROWAVE TIME: 9 to 11 min., total

| | |
|---|---|
| **1 egg** . . . . . . . . . . . . . . . . . | In large mixing bowl beat |
| **1 cup milk** | egg slightly and mix with |
| **¼ cup melted butter** | milk, butter, bread cubes, |
| **3 slices soft bread,** | salt and salmon, blending |
| **cubed** | well. Pack firmly in greas- |
| **½ teaspoon salt** | ed 9-in. pie plate. Cover |
| **2 cans (1-lb. each) red** | with wax paper. **Micro-** |
| **salmon, bone and** | **wave at High 9 to 11 Min-** |
| **skin removed, if** | **utes,** rotating dish ½ turn |
| **necessary** | after 5 minutes. Let stand |
| | 10 minutes before slicing. |
| | Serve with Dill Butter, page |
| | 190, if desired. |

*Makes 6 to 8 servings*

## COLORFUL CREAMED TUNA

POWER LEVEL: High (10)
MICROWAVE TIME: 11 to 15 min., total

| | |
|---|---|
| **2 tablespoons butter** . . . . | In 2-qt. casserole place |
| **¼ cup chopped onion** | butter, onion and green |
| **¼ cup chopped green** | pepper. **Microwave at** |
| **pepper** | **High 2 to 3 Minutes,** stir- |
| | ring every minute. |
| **1 can (2-oz.)** . . . . . . . . . . | Drain mushrooms, reserv- |
| **mushrooms** | ing 2 tablespoons juice. |
| **1 can (10-oz.) cream of** | Add mushrooms and re- |
| **celery soup** | served juice to casserole |
| **1 can (6½-oz.) tuna,** | along with soup, tuna, salt |
| **drained** | and pepper. Cover. **Micro-** |
| **½ teaspoon salt** | **wave at High 7 to 9 Min-** |
| **⅛ teaspoon pepper** | **utes,** stirring after 4 min- |
| | utes. |
| **2 tomatoes, cut in** . . . . . . | Add tomatoes. Cover. **Mi-** |
| **wedges** | **crowave at High 2 to 3** |
| | **Minutes** more, until hot. |
| | Serve over rice. |

*Makes 3 to 4 servings*

## HOT TUNA SALAD

*A good dish for entertaining. Can be made ahead of time and reheated before serving. Shrimp or crab might also be used in place of tuna. Try this in a hot patty shell for a treat.*

POWER LEVEL: Medium High (7)
MICROWAVE TIME: 10 to 13 min., total

| | |
|---|---|
| **2 cans (7-oz. each)** . . . . . . | In 1½-qt. casserole mix to- |
| **tuna, drained** | gether tuna, celery, 1 cup |
| **2 cups chopped celery** | croutons, mayonnaise, al- |
| **2 cups croutons,** | monds, onion, lemon juice |
| **divided** | and salt. Cover. **Micro-** |
| **1 cup mayonnaise** | **wave at Medium High 9 to** |
| **½ cup whole almonds** | **11 Minutes,** stirring after 5 |
| **or cashews** | minutes, until hot. |
| **1 tablespoon finely** | |
| **chopped onion** | |
| **1 tablespoon lemon** | |
| **juice** | |
| **½ teaspoon salt** | |
| **½ cup shredded** . . . . . . . . | Sprinkle with cheese and |
| **cheddar or Swiss** | remaining 1 cup croutons, |
| **cheese** | **Microwave at Medium** |
| | **High 1 to 2 Minutes,** until |
| | cheese melts. |

*Makes 6 servings*

## TUNA NOODLE CASSEROLE

POWER LEVEL: High (10)
MICROWAVE TIME: 31 to 36 min., total

| | |
|---|---|
| **1 pkg. (8-oz.) fine egg noodles** | Microwave noodles (see chart, page 195), except cook 10 minutes. |
| **3 tablespoons butter**<br>**1 clove garlic, minced**<br>**½ cup finely chopped green onions**<br>**½ teaspoon salt**<br>**⅛ teaspoon pepper** | In 3-qt. casserole place butter, garlic, onion, salt and pepper. **Microwave at High 2 to 3 Minutes,** stirring after 1 minute, until onion is softened. |
| **¼ cup unsifted all-purpose flour**<br>**1½ cups milk** | Stir in flour until smooth. Gradually stir in milk. **Microwave at High 4 to 6 Minutes,** stirring every 2 minutes, until smooth and thickened. |
| **2 cans (7-oz. each) tuna, drained** | Gently stir tuna and noodles into sauce. Cover. **Microwave at High 15 to 17 Minutes,** stirring after 8 minutes, until hot. |
| **⅓ cup cracker crumbs**<br>**2 tablespoons minced parsley**<br>**2 tablespoons melted butter** | In small bowl, mix together crumbs, parsley and butter. Sprinkle over casserole before serving. |

Makes 6 to 8 servings

Tuna Wedges

## SCALLOPED TUNA AND CHIPS

*Cook by time, or use the temperature probe set at 150°.*

POWER LEVEL: High (10)     **Cook Code:** 150
MICROWAVE TIME: 15 to 17 min., total

| | |
|---|---|
| **1 can (10½-oz.) condensed cream of celery soup**<br>**1 can (7 to 8-oz.) mushrooms, stems and pieces**<br>**1 teaspoon instant minced onion**<br>**1 tablespoon chopped parsley**<br>**1 cup milk**<br>**1 tablespoon lemon juice** | Mix soup, undrained mushrooms, onion, parsley, milk and lemon juice. |
| **1 pkg. (5-oz.) potato chips, crushed (3 cups)**<br>**2 cans (7-oz. each) tuna, drained and flaked** | In 2-qt. greased casserole layer 1 cup crushed chips, ½ of tuna, ½ of soup mixture. Repeat layers and top with potato chips. **Microwave at High 15 to 17 Minutes,** until bubbly. |

Makes 6 servings

## TUNA WEDGES

*A tuna loaf, microwaved in a round shape. Garnish with tomato slices and sprinkle with grated cheese if desired.*

POWER LEVEL: High (10)
MICROWAVE TIME: 10 to 12 min., total

| | |
|---|---|
| **2 eggs**<br>**1½ cups cooked rice**<br>**6 green onions, finely chopped**<br>**2 cans (7-oz.) solid pack tuna** | In large mixing bowl beat eggs with fork. Add rice, onions and undrained tuna. Mix well. |
| **½ cup (¼-lb.) butter**<br>**¼ teaspoon thyme**<br>**1 cup fine dry bread crumbs** | In small glass bowl place butter. **Microwave at High 1 Minute,** until melted. Add to tuna along with thyme and crumbs. Mix well. |

Spread mixture evenly in lightly greased 9-in. pie plate. Cover with wax paper. **Microwave at High 9 to 11 Minutes,** rotating dish ½ turn after 5 minutes. Serve in wedges.

Makes about 6 servings

# Whole Fish

Whole fish makes a dramatic presentation. Microwaving is a superior way of preparing them. With a tight cover fish steam in their own natural moisture and are delicate and juicy.

For a baked appearance, brush with browning sauce and butter. For poached color, use lemon-butter sauce.

Although the head is not eaten, it should be shielded with foil to maintain its appearance for serving. The eye, which turns white during cooking, can be covered with an olive slice.

## HOW TO INSERT THE TEMPERATURE PROBE

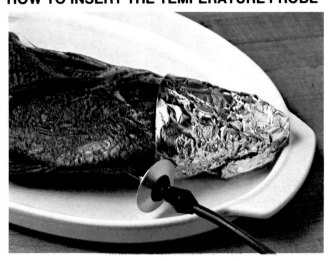

**Insert Probe** from just above the gill into the meatiest area, parallel to the backbone. Probe should be on the side of the fish closest to the dish.

## HOW TO MICROWAVE A WHOLE FISH BY TIME

## HOW TO MICROWAVE A WHOLE FISH BY TEMPERATURE (Striped Bass, Snapper, etc. 2½ to 4 pounds)

Brush entire fish with a mixture of 1 tablespoon bottled bouquet sauce and 1 tablespoon water, then with melted butter; or brush with lemon-butter sauce. Add stuffing, such as Vegetable Stuffing (below, right) if desired.

Insert temperature probe; place the fish in a baking dish with the probe on the side of the fish closest to the dish.

Shield the head and thin tail area with foil, making sure that the foil on the head is no closer than ¾-in. from the probe disc.

Cover the dish tightly with plastic wrap, arranging loosely around probe to vent. Attach cable end at receptacle. **Microwave at High. Set Temp, Set 170°.**

## STUFFED RED SNAPPER

| POWER LEVEL: High (10) | **Cook Code:** 90 |
| --- | --- |
| MICROWAVE TIME: 9 to 11 min., total | |

| | |
| --- | --- |
| **1 red snapper (1½ to 2½-lb.), cleaned and gutted**<br>**Vegetable Stuffing (right)**<br>**2 tablespoons bottled brown bouquet sauce**<br>**¼ cup butter, melted** | Place fish on microwave-type platter or in 12×8×2-in. dish. Stuff cavity with Vegetable Stuffing. Brush all areas with mixture of brown bouquet sauce and butter. |

Cover head and thin tail end with strips of aluminum foil. Cover platter or dish with plastic wrap, turning back one corner to vent. **Microwave at High 9 to 11 Minutes,** until fish flakes easily with fork. While letting stand 5 minutes, brush again with butter, if desired. Place cross-cut slice of pimiento-stuffed olive in eye cavity.

POWER LEVEL: **High (10)**                    Makes about 2 servings

5 to 7 Minutes Per Pound

**Brush** fish with sauce as directed in the recipe.

**Shield** head and thin tail area with foil

**Cover** tightly with plastic wrap, turning back one corner to vent.

## VEGETABLE STUFFING

| | |
|---|---|
| ½ cup (¼-lb.) butter, melted | In 2-qt. casserole place butter, onion, carrots, mushrooms, parsley, bread crumbs, egg, lemon juice, salt and pepper. Toss to mix well. Pack lightly into fish. |
| ½ cup finely chopped onion | |
| ½ cup finely grated carrots | |
| ½ cup chopped raw mushrooms | |
| ¼ cup finely minced parsley | |
| ½ cup fine dry bread crumbs | |
| 1 egg, beaten | |
| 1 tablespoon lemon juice | |
| 1 teaspoon salt | |
| ⅛ teaspoon pepper | |

Makes about 2 cups

## RAINBOW TROUT

POWER LEVEL: High (10)
MICROWAVE TIME: See Recipe

| | |
|---|---|
| Trout (8 to 10-oz. each) | In 12×8×2-in. dish arrange 1 to 2 trout which have been cleaned and gutted. |
| For each fish: | Brush fish with mixture of lemon juice and butter. |
| 2 tablespoons lemon juice | |
| ¼ cup butter, melted | |

Cover head and tail areas with strips of aluminum foil. Cover cooking dish with plastic wrap, turning back one corner to vent. **Microwave at High** according to times below. When done, fish flakes easily with fork. Let stand 5 minutes and serve with rest of lemon butter.

| NO. OF TROUT | TIME/MIN. | COOK CODE |
|---|---|---|
| 1 | 5 to 6 | 50 |
| 2 | 8 to 9 | 80 |

Place cross-cut slice of pimiento-stuffed olive in eye cavity.

# Defrosting Shellfish

**Small** pieces of loose-packed shellfish, such as shrimp, scallops or crab fingers, are easiest to defrost, since they can be spread out in a single layer and absorb microwave energy evenly. Check at minimum time because they defrost rapidly.

## MICROLESSON

### POWER LEVEL: **Defrost**
### HOW TO DEFROST SMALL LOOSE PIECES OF SHELLFISH

| TYPE | TIME MINUTES |
|---|---|
| **Crab Fingers** (1-lb.) | 7 to 8 |
| **Scallops** (1-lb.) | 7 to 8 |
| **Shrimp** (1-lb.) | 7 to 8 |

### HOW TO DEFROST SHELLFISH FROZEN IN BLOCKS

| TYPE | TIME MINUTES |
|---|---|
| **Crab Meat** (6-oz. pkg.) | 4 to 5 |
| **Crab Meat** (2 6-oz. pkgs.) | 6 to 7 |
| **Crab Meat** (1-lb. can) | 14 to 16 |
| **Oysters** (12-oz. can) | 8 to 10 |
| **Oysters** (3 12-oz. cans) | 18 to 20 |
| **Scallops** (1-lb. pkg.) | 8 to 10 |

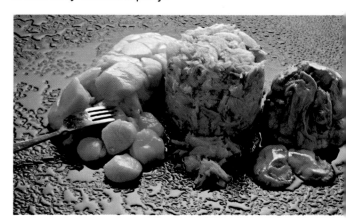

**Blocks** of shellfish, such as crab meat and scallops, frozen in paper packages, can be defrosted in the package. Turn over after ½ of time. Oysters and crab meat frozen in cans must be removed to a casserole. Break up these dense blocks as soon as possible.

### HOW TO DEFROST LARGE SHELLFISH

| TYPE | TIME MINUTES |
|---|---|
| **Crab Legs** (8 to 10-oz.) 1 to 2 | 5 to 7 |
| **Crab Legs** (8 to 10-oz.) 3 to 4 | 10 to 12 |
| **Lobster Tails** (6 to 9-oz.) 1 to 2 | 5 to 7 |
| **Lobster Tails** (6 to 9-oz.) 3 to 4 | 10 to 12 |
| **Lobster Tails** (12 to 16-oz.) 1 to 2 | 8 to 10 |
| **Whole Lobster or Crab** (1½-lb.) | 16 to 18 (approx. 12 min. per pound) |

**Large** pieces such as lobster, lobster tails, whole crab or large crab legs should be turned over after ½ of time. If thinner areas feel warm, shield them with foil. Remove large shellfish from the oven while still slightly icy and allow them to stand a few minutes.

**Spread** shellfish loosely in a baking dish so they are in a single layer. Microwave at **Defrost** for half the time.

**Rearrange** pieces and defrost for second half of time.

**Test** after minimum defrosting time. Shellfish should feel cool and soft, and still be translucent.

**Place** block in a casserole and cover. Microwave at **Defrost** for half the time.

**Turn** block over and break it up with a fork. Center may still be firm. Microwave for second half of time, breaking off pieces as they loosen.

**Pieces** should be loose and still feel icy. Let stand to complete defrosting.

**Arrange** shellfish in a baking dish with the light underside up. Paper towels hold tails upright. Microwave at **Defrost** for half the time.

**Turn** over, so that the back or darker side is up. Defrost for second half of time.

**Defrosted** shellfish should be flexible and transparent and feel cool.

# Small Shellfish

Steaming is the classic method for cooking shellfish. In the microwave oven most shellfish steam without water in a cooking dish covered tightly with plastic wrap. A dampened paper towel provides sufficient steam for scallops. Clams steam in their shells. Whole lobster needs some water because of its size. We recommend cooking unpeeled shrimp in water with bay leaf and vinegar to reduce cooking odors.

**When Done** most shellfish turns from translucent to opaque. Remove clams from oven as soon as shells open partially.

## TIPS FOR MICROWAVING SMALL SHELLFISH

**Small Shellfish** such as scallops, shrimp, oysters or clams, are cooked on a pie plate or shallow dish. Cover tightly with plastic wrap.

**Arrange** cleaned and deveined shrimp in a ring. Cover tightly with plastic wrap, turning back 2-in. to vent. Cook clams in a ring with hinged side out. Rotate dish ½ turn after ½ time.

**A Damp** paper towel helps steam scallops. The ring arrangement is not necessary for even cooking. Rotate dish ½ turn after ½ time.

## SMALL SHELLFISH CHART

POWER LEVEL: **High (10)**

| TYPE | TIME MINUTES | COOK CODE |
|---|---|---|
| **Clams** (3 to 5-oz.) 6 | 3 to 5 | 30 |
| **Scallops** (1-lb.) | 5 to 7 | 50 |
| **Shrimp,** peeled (1-lb.) | 5 | 50 |
| **Shrimp,** unpeeled (1 to 2-lb.) with 2½ cups water, 1 bay leaf, 1 tablespoon vinegar, in 2-qt. casserole. | 6 to 10 | 60 |

Cook scallops and peeled shrimp as directed under the photographs above. When cooking clams, follow the directions given under shrimp. Clams will be partially opened when done. (Tightly closed shells contain bad clams and should be discarded.)

## JIFFY SHRIMP CURRY

POWER LEVEL: High (10)
MICROWAVE TIME: 7 to 8 min., total

**1 can (10½-oz.)** . . . . . . . . . In 1½-qt. casserole com-
    **condensed cream of** bine soup, butter, onion,
    **shrimp soup** curry powder and sour
**1 tablespoon butter** cream. **Microwave at**
**2 tablespoons instant** **High 5 Minutes,** uncover-
    **minced onion** ed, or until sauce bubbles
**1 teaspoon curry** around edges.
    **powder**
**1 cup (8-oz.) dairy sour**
    **cream**

**2 cans (4½-oz. each)** . . . . . Stir in shrimp. **Microwave**
    **shrimp, drained and** **at High 2 or 3 Minutes,** un-
    **rinsed** til hot. Garnish with egg or
    **Chopped egg or** bacon, if desired.
    **crumbled bacon**
    **(optional)**

Makes 4 to 6 servings

## SHRIMP GUMBO

*For spicy flavor, tie 1 to 2 teaspoons crab boil (found in condiment section of supermarket) in a cheesecloth bag and add along with shrimp. For bright color accent, save out about ¼ of green pepper to stir into finished gumbo.*

POWER LEVEL: High (10) and Medium High (7)
MICROWAVE TIME: 32 to 34 min., total

| | |
|---|---|
| **1 medium onion, sliced (about ½ cup)**<br>**¼ cup butter (use bacon fat, if desired)** | In 3-qt. casserole place onion and butter. **Microwave at High 3 Minutes,** stirring after 2 minutes, until onion is limp. |
| **2 tablespoons cornstarch**<br>**1 cup water**<br>**2 cans (16-oz. each) stewed tomatoes**<br>**1 cup diced green pepper (2 medium)**<br>**2 cloves garlic, crushed**<br>**2 teaspoons salt**<br>**1 teaspoon ground nutmeg**<br>**¼ teaspoon pepper**<br>**1 pound raw shrimp, shelled, deveined**<br>**2 pkgs. (10-oz. each) frozen okra, defrosted, cut into 1-in. pieces** | In small bowl stir together cornstarch and water. Add to onion along with tomatoes, green pepper, garlic, salt, nutmeg, pepper, shrimp and okra. Stir well. Cover. **Microwave at Medium High 29 to 31 Minutes,** stirring and recovering after ½ of time. |

Makes 6 to 8 servings

Shrimp Gumbo

## CREAMY SHRIMP AND RICE

POWER LEVEL: High (10)
MICROWAVE TIME: 31 to 33 min., total

| | |
|---|---|
| **1½ cups uncooked long grain rice**<br>**3½ cups water** | In 3-qt. casserole place rice and water. Cover. **Microwave at High 20 Minutes,** stirring and recovering after 10 minutes. |
| **½ cup chopped onion**<br>**½ cup chopped green pepper**<br>**2 cups (16-oz.) dairy sour cream**<br>**1 cup milk**<br>**½ teaspoon salt**<br>**⅛ teaspoon pepper**<br>**2 cups cooked shrimp** | Add onion, green pepper, sour cream, milk, salt, pepper and shrimp. Stir well; then smooth top. **Microwave at High 10 to 12 Minutes,** stirring after 6 minutes, until hot. |
| **1 cup (4-oz.) shredded cheddar cheese** | Sprinkle cheese over top. **Microwave at High 1 Minute,** until melted. |

Makes 6 to 8 servings

## SHRIMP IN PARMESAN BUTTER

POWER LEVEL: High (10)
MICROWAVE TIME: 7¼ to 8¼ min., total

| | |
|---|---|
| **36 large raw shrimp, peeled and deveined** | "Butterfly" shrimp by cutting each piece lengthwise halfway through and separating the 2 sides to form thin, flat piece of shrimp. |
| **1 cup (½-lb.) butter**<br>**3 tablespoons capers, including liquid**<br>**2 cloves garlic, minced**<br>**2 tablespoons lemon juice** | In 1-qt. measure place butter. **Microwave at High 1¼ Minutes,** until melted. Stir in capers, garlic and lemon juice. Pour ⅔ of butter in 12×8×2-in. dish. Arrange shrimp in sauce. |
| **1 cup (4-oz.) grated Parmesan cheese** | Top with cheese, then remaining butter. Cover with wax paper. |

**Microwave at High 6 to 7 Minutes,** rotating dish ½ turn after 3 minutes, until shrimp is opaque and firm.

Makes 3 to 4 servings

## SHERRIED SHRIMP ROCKEFELLER

*This won $5,000 in a recent microwave recipe contest.*

POWER LEVEL: Defrost and High (10)
MICROWAVE TIME: 30 to 33 min., total

**2 pkgs. (10-oz. each)** . . . . .In 10-in. square casserole
**frozen chopped** or 12×8×2-in. dish place
**spinach** unwrapped, frozen blocks
**1 lb. medium to large** of spinach. **Microwave at**
**raw shrimp, peeled,** **Defrost 10 Minutes.** Break
**deveined** up blocks. **Microwave at**
**High 3 to 4 Minutes** more,
until just completely thawed. With hands, squeeze
out as much juice as pos-
sible. Spread over bottom
of casserole. Distribute
shrimp evenly over
spinach.

**1 can (10½-oz.)** . . . . . . . .In 1-qt. glass measure stir
**condensed cream of** together undiluted soup,
**shrimp soup** cheese and sherry. **Micro-**
**1 cup (4-oz.) shredded** **wave at High 4 Minutes,**
**sharp cheddar** stirring after 2 minutes, un-
**cheese** til cheese is melted. Set
**3 tablespoons cooking** aside while preparing
**sherry** crumb topping.

**2 medium slices fresh** . . . .Break bread in tiny bits or
**bread** coarsely crumb in blender.
**3 tablespoons butter** Place in small glass bowl
and add butter.

**Microwave at High 1 Minute,** stirring after ½ minute, until butter is distributed among crumbs. Pour hot sauce
over casserole and distribute crumbs over top. Sprinkle
with paprika, if desired.

**Microwave at High 12 to 14 Minutes,** uncovered, rotating dish ½ turn after 5 minutes. Let stand, covered, 5
minutes before serving.

Makes 4 servings

## SWEET AND SOUR SHRIMP

*Garnish with chopped bacon and green onion slices.*

POWER LEVEL: High (10)          **Cook Code:    60**
MICROWAVE TIME: 6 to 8 min., total

**1 recipe Sweet and Sour** . .Stir together Sweet and
**Sauce, page 190** Sour Sauce, shrimp and
**1 lb. cleaned and** drained pineapple slices.
**cooked shrimp** **Microwave at High 6 to 8**
**1 can (8-oz.) pineapple** **Minutes,** stirring gently
**slices** after 3 minutes.

Makes 4 to 5 servings

## SHRIMP NEWBURG

POWER LEVEL: High (10) and Medium (5)
MICROWAVE TIME: 14 to 19 min., total

**¼ cup butter** . . . . . . . . . .In 2-qt. casserole place
**¼ cup chopped green** butter, onion and mush-
**onion** rooms. **Microwave at**
**1 jar (4-oz.) sliced** **High 2 to 3 Minutes,** until
**mushrooms,** bubbly.
**drained**

**2 tablespoons flour** . . . .Stir in flour and salt. **Micro-**
**½ teaspoon salt** **wave at High 1 Minute,** to
blend.

**1¼ cup milk** . . . . . . . . . . .Stir in milk. **Microwave at**
**High 5 to 6 Minutes,** stir-
ring after 3 minutes.

**¼ cup sherry** . . . . . . . . .Stir in sherry. Stir small
**2 egg yolks** amount of sauce into yolks.
Add yolk mixture to sauce;
stir well. **Microwave at Me-**
**dium 2 to 3 Minutes,** stirring after 1 minute.

**12 oz. frozen cooked** . . . .Stir in shrimp. **Microwave**
**shrimp, defrosted** **at Medium 4 to 6 Minutes,**
stirring after 2 minutes, un-
til heated through.

Makes about 4 servings

## JAMBALAYA

POWER LEVEL: High (10)
MICROWAVE TIME: 14 to 17 min., total

**2 cups diced cooked** . . . . .In 2-qt. casserole place
**ham** ham, green pepper, onion,
**½ cup chopped green** garlic and butter. **Micro-**
**pepper** **wave at High 6 to 7 Min-**
**½ cup chopped onion** **utes** or until vegetables
**1 garlic clove, minced** are tender.
**2 tablespoons butter**

**1 can (10¾-oz.)** . . . . . . . .Stir in soup, water, shrimp,
**condensed tomato** bay leaf, oregano, salt and
**soup** pepper. **Microwave at**
**⅓ cup water** **High 4 Minutes.**
**½ cup shrimp, or 1 can**
**(4½-oz.), drained**
**1 medium bay leaf,**
**crushed**
**¼ teaspoon crushed**
**oregano**
**⅛ teaspoon salt**
**Dash pepper**

**1½ cups cooked rice** . . . . .Stir in rice. **Microwave at**
**High 4 to 6 Minutes** more,
or until bubbly.

Makes 4 servings

## SCALLOPED OYSTERS

POWER LEVEL: High (10)
MICROWAVE TIME: 13 to 15 min., total

**3 cans (12-oz. each) frozen oysters, thawed (about 4 cups)** . . . . . Drain oysters, reserving ¼ cup liquid.

**¾ cup butter, melted**
**2 cups fine soda cracker crumbs (about 40 small squares)**
**1 teaspoon salt**
**⅛ teaspoon pepper**
**⅛ teaspoon nutmeg** . . . . In small mixing bowl mix together butter and crumbs. In 10×6×2-in. dish layer ⅓ of crumb mixture, ½ of drained oysters, ½ of seasonings, then ⅓ of remaining crumbs, rest of oysters, seasonings and crumbs.

**¼ cup milk** . . . . . . . . . . . . . Mix milk with oyster liquid and pour evenly over top.

With knife, poke 3 to 4 holes through layers so liquid goes to bottom. **Microwave at High 7 Minutes.** Sprinkle with ¼ cup parsley. Rotate dish ½ turn. **Microwave 6 to 8 Minutes,** until oysters are firm when pierced with fork.

*Makes about 6 servings*

## CRAB IMPERIAL

POWER LEVEL: High (10) and Medium High (7)
MICROWAVE TIME: 12½ to 15 min., total

**2 tablespoons butter**
**2 tablespoons flour**
**1 teaspoon salt**
**¾ teaspoon pepper**
**1 teaspoon dry mustard** . . . . In 1½-qt. casserole place butter. **Microwave at High ½ Minute,** until melted. Stir in flour, salt, pepper and mustard until smooth. **Microwave at High 1 Minute.**

**1 cup dairy half & half**
**1 teaspoon lemon juice**
**2 teaspoons Worcestershire sauce**
**2 tablespoons minced green pepper**
**2 tablespoons minced pimiento** . . . Very slowly stir in half & half until mixture is smooth. Add lemon juice, Worcestershire sauce, green pepper and pimiento. **Microwave at High 3 to 3½ Minutes,** until thickened, stirring every minute.

**1 egg, beaten** . . . . . . . . . . Stir a little hot mixture into egg, then add egg to rest of sauce. **Microwave at Medium High 2 Minutes.**

**1 lb. lump crabmeat**
**½ cup fine dry bread crumbs**
**¼ cup melted butter** . . . Drain crab. Remove shells or cartilage. Stir sauce into crab. Divide mixture into 6 to 8 shells or ramekins. Combine crumbs and butter. Divide over top. **Microwave at Medium High 6 to 8 Minutes,** rearrange after 3 minutes, until heated.

*Makes 6 to 8 servings*

## COQUILLE ST. JACQUES

*The classic creamed scallop dish. Large scallop shells are natural microwave utensils for this.*

POWER LEVEL: High (10), Med. (5) and Med. High (7)
MICROWAVE TIME: 17 to 22 min., total

**3 tablespoons butter**
**1 jar (4-oz.) sliced mushrooms**
**2 green onions, sliced**
**¼ cup chopped celery** . . . . In 2-qt. casserole place butter, mushrooms, onions and celery. **Microwave at High 2 to 3 Minutes,** stirring after 1 minute.

**2 tablespoons flour**
**½ teaspoon salt**
**¼ teaspoon thyme**
**1 tablespoon pimiento, chopped**
**⅓ cup white wine**
**1 lb. raw scallops** . . . . . Stir in flour, salt, thyme and pimiento well, then wine and scallops, stirring again. **Microwave at High 5 to 6 Minutes,** stirring after 3 minutes, until thickened.

**¼ cup dairy half & half**
**1 egg yolk, beaten** . . . Stir in half & half and egg yolk. **Microwave at Medium 3 to 4 Minutes,** stirring after 2 minutes.

Divide mixture among 4 scallop shells. Top with Crumb Mixture (below). Cover with wax paper. **Microwave at Medium High 7 to 9 Minutes,** rearranging after 4 minutes, until hot.

*Makes 4 servings*

**Crumb Mixture:** In small bowl, place 2 tablespoons butter. **Microwave at High ¼ to ½ Minute,** until melted. Stir in ¼ cup fine dry bread crumbs and 2 tablespoons Parmesan cheese.

Crab Imperial

# Large Shellfish

## MICROLESSON

Arrange large shellfish in the cooking dish so that the light colored underside is up during the first half of the cooking period. Because of its size, a whole lobster needs a small amount of water for added steam. Lobster tails and crab legs steam in their own natural moisture. When done, lobster and lobster tails should still be slightly translucent in the center. Cooking will be completed during standing time.

### LARGE SHELLFISH CHART

| TYPE | TIME MIN. | COOK CODE | TYPE | TIME MIN. | COOK CODE |
|---|---|---|---|---|---|
| **Crab Legs** | | | **Lobster Tails** | | |
| (8-10-oz.) | 1-3 to 4 | 30 | (8-10-oz.) | 2-5½ to 6 | 60 |
| (8-10-oz.) | 2-5 to 6 | 50 | (8-10-oz.) | 4-9 to 11 | 90 |
| (8-10-oz.) | 4-9 to 11 | 90 | (12-16-oz.) | 1-5 to 6 | 50 |
| **Lobster Tails** | | | **Whole Lobster** | | |
| (8-10-oz.) | 1-3 to 4 | 30 | (1½-lb.) | 9 to 11 | 90 |

## HOW TO MICROWAVE LOBSTER TAILS AND CRAB LEGS

**Arrange** lobster tails in baking dish with under side up. (No water added.) Cover tightly with plastic wrap, turning back corner to vent. Microwave at High for half the time.

**Remove** tails from dish. Cut through back of shell and meat, leaving undershell intact.

**Spread** to expose meat. Loosen meat from shell with fingers.

**Brush** lobster meat with mixture of 1 tablespoon melted butter and 1 tablespoon lemon juice. Cover and microwave second half of time. Meat should still be slightly translucent in the center. Let stand 5 minutes.

**Arrange** crab legs in baking dish with light colored side up. (No water added.) Cover tightly with plastic wrap, turning back corner to vent. Microwave at High for half the time.

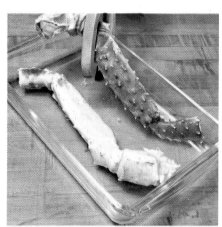

**Turn** over, so that dark side is up. Cover and continue microwaving until flesh at ends of legs is opaque. Let stand 5 minutes.

Microwaved Whole Lobster

## HOW TO MICROWAVE A WHOLE LOBSTER Cook Code: 90

**Plunge** the tip of a heavy knife into live lobster between the head and first segment to sever the spinal cord, which kills lobster. Lobster may show signs of movement for few minutes.

**Peg** the tail to prevent curling by inserting a wooden skewer lengthwise through the meat. At this time, or after lobster is cooked, cut through the undershell of the body and remove the intestinal vein and small sack below the head, if desired.

**Arrange** lobster in a baking dish with the back down and add ½ cup hot water. Cover tightly with plastic wrap, turning back a corner to vent. **Microwave at High 9 to 11 Minutes,** turning over after 6 minutes.

## LOBSTER THERMIDOR

*An enriched version of creamed lobster. It is often served in the shells of the lobster tails from which the meat was removed.*

POWER LEVEL: High (10) and Medium (5)
MICROWAVE TIME: 15¼ to 19½ min., total

| 2 tablespoons butter<br>1 can (3-oz.) mushroom slices, drained<br>2 tablespoons chopped onion | In 1½-qt. casserole place butter, mushrooms and onions. **Microwave at High 3 Minutes,** stirring after 2 minutes. |
| 2 tablespoons flour<br>¼ teaspoon salt<br>⅛ teaspoon pepper<br>⅛ teaspoon paprika | Stir in flour, salt, pepper and paprika until smooth. **Microwave at High 1 Minute.** |
| ¼ cup chicken broth<br>½ cup dairy half & half | Slowly stir in broth and half & half. **Microwave at High 3 to 4 Minutes,** stirring after 2 minutes, until thickened. |
| 1 egg yolk, beaten<br>2 tablespoons sherry<br>2 cups cooked lobster | Stir part of hot mixture into egg yolk, then add egg to rest of hot mixture. Stir in sherry. **Microwave at Medium 3 to 4 Minutes,** stirring after 2 minutes. Stir in lobster. |

Refill 4 tail shells of lobster with creamed mixture, or use 4 large scallop shells or au gratin dishes if desired. Cover with Crumb Mixture (below). Cover with wax paper. **Microwave at High 5 to 7 Minutes,** rearranging after 3 minutes, until heated through.

Makes 4 servings

**Crumb Mixture:** In small bowl, place 2 tablespoons butter. **Microwave at High ¼ to ½ Minute,** until melted. Stir in ¼ cup fine dry bread crumbs and 2 tablespoons Parmesan cheese.

## FISH AND SHELLFISH CONVENIENCE CHART

POWER LEVEL: **High (10)**

| ITEM | TIME MIN. | COOK CODE | COMMENTS |
|---|---|---|---|
| **Alaska King Crab Newburg** (6½-oz. pouch) | 3-5 | 30 | Puncture pouch with fork to vent. |
| **Deviled Crabs** (6-oz. pkg.) | 3-4 | 30 | Will not be crisp. |
| **Fish 'N' Chips** (14-oz. pkg.) | 7-9 | 70 | Distribute evenly in large dish. Will not be crisp. |
| **Fish Fillets With Crumb Coating** (8-oz. pkg.) | 4½-6 | 50 | Distribute evenly in dish and rotate ½ turn after 3 minutes. Will not be crisp. |

## MIXED SEAFOOD CASSEROLE

POWER LEVEL: High (10) and Medium High (7)
MICROWAVE TIME: 33 to 39 min., total

| 3 cups fresh bread cubes (3 medium slices bread) | In 12×8×2-in. dish place bread cubes. **Microwave at High 4 to 5 Minutes,** stirring every 2 minutes, until crisp. Remove about half of cubes and save for top layer. |
| 2 cups mixed seafood or 2 cans (7-oz.) tuna, shrimp or crab*<br>1 cup chopped onion<br>1 cup chopped celery<br>½ cup mayonnaise | In large mixing bowl mix together seafood, onion, celery and mayonnaise. Spread over bread cubes in dish. Cover seafood mixture with remaining half of bread cubes. |
| 2 eggs<br>1 cup milk<br>1 can (10-oz.) condensed cream of mushroom soup | In small bowl beat eggs well and mix in milk and soup. Pour over casserole. **Microwave at Medium High 28 to 32 Minutes,** rotating dish ½ turn after 15 minutes, until set but still slightly soft in center. |
| 1 cup (4-oz.) shredded cheddar cheese<br>Paprika | Sprinkle top with cheese, then paprika. **Microwave at Medium High 1 to 2 Minutes,** until cheese is melted. Let stand 5 to 10 minutes before serving. |

Makes 6 to 8 servings

*Canned tuna can be undrained, but canned shrimp or crab should be drained.

All these frozen seafood entrees can be heated to serving temperature at High.

| ITEM | TIME MIN. | COOK CODE | COMMENTS |
|---|---|---|---|
| **Fish Sticks** (9-oz. pkg.) | 4½-6 | 50 | Distribute evenly in dish and rotate ½ turn after 3 minutes. Will not be crisp. |
| **Shrimp Croquettes** (12-oz. pkg.) | 4-6 | 40 | Pierce sauce pouch with fork and place with food on plate. Cover with wax paper. Rotate dish ½ turn after 2 minutes. |
| **Shrimp Newburg** (6½-oz. pkg.) | 4-6 | 40 | Puncture top with fork to vent. |
| **Tuna Noodle Casserole** (11½-oz. pkg.) | 7-9 | 70 | Place in 1-qt. casserole with cover. Stir after 5 minutes and before serving. |

# Eggs & Cheese

# Eggs

## MICROLESSON

Eggs are versatile; they can be prepared in a variety of ways, each with its own character. Although omelets and poached eggs are both eggs, they are completely different. Here we present the basic ways of cooking eggs. All but one microwave well. Do not try to hard boil eggs in the microwave oven. They expand during cooking and burst the shell.

## HOW TO MICROWAVE SCRAMBLED EGGS

**Place** 1 teaspoon butter per egg in a glass measure or casserole. Microwave at High until melted.

**Scramble** eggs with the melted butter and 1 tablespoon milk per egg.

**Place** in oven. Estimate ¾ minute per egg and microwave at High for ½ of total time.

## HOW TO MICROWAVE BASIC EGGS

**Puncture** membrane of yolk to prevent bursting when microwaving shirred or poached eggs.

**Microwave** shirred eggs in buttered custard cups. Puncture membrane and cover with plastic wrap. Microwave 1 minute per egg at Medium Power, rotating ½ turn after ½ minute.

**Poach** eggs by microwaving 2 cups hot tap water 5 to 6 minutes at High, until boiling. Break eggs onto plate; puncture membrane. Swirl boiling water with spoon; slip in eggs gently. Cover. Microwave at Medium 1 minute per egg; ¾ minute per egg for more than 1 egg. Let stand in water a few minutes.

Eggs microwave rapidly, and since they are a delicate food, toughen when overcooked. The yolks, which have a higher fat content, cook faster than the whites. Poach eggs at Medium Power to allow the whites time to set without toughening the edges or overcooking the yolks.

When yolks and whites are mixed together, eggs may be cooked at higher power settings. Omelets, which need time to set, are cooked at Medium, while scrambled eggs, which are stirred, are microwaved at High. Scrambled eggs are one of the foods which microwave better than they cook conventionally. Not only do they take less time and need less stirring, but they are fluffier and greater in volume. For easy clean up, scrambled eggs may be microwaved in plastic-coated paper bowl.

**Stir** set portions from the outside to the center. Repeat 1 or 2 times during remaining cooking period.

**When Done,** eggs should be just past the runny stage.

**After Standing** 1 or 2 minutes, eggs will be set.

**Fry** eggs in the Brown 'N Sear Dish. Preheat dish at High 1 minute per egg. Add ½ tablespoon butter per egg. Break eggs into dish, cover and microwave ¾ minute per egg, or to desired doneness.

**Puffy Omelets** are microwaved in a pie plate and folded over a filling. See recipes on next page.

**Never** attempt to hard-cook eggs or reheat eggs in shells.

## JELLY OMELET

POWER LEVEL: High (10) and Medium (5)
MICROWAVE TIME: 6 to 7 min., total

| | |
|---|---|
| **¼ to ⅓ cup strawberry or currant jelly** | In custard cup place jelly. **Microwave at High 1 Minute,** until jelly is soft and can be stirred smooth. Set aside. |
| **3 eggs, separated**<br>**2 tablespoons water** | In largest mixer bowl beat egg whites at highest speed of mixer, until soft peaks form. Then, in smaller bowl, using same beaters, beat yolks and water. Gently pour yolk mixture over beaten whites. Fold together carefully. |
| **1 tablespoon butter** | In 9-in. pie plate place butter. **Microwave at High 1 Minute,** swirl to coat dish. |

Carefully pour egg mixture into pie plate. **Microwave at Medium 4 to 5 Minutes,** rotating dish ¼ turn every minute, until set but still glossy on top. Spoon jelly over half of omelet. Quickly run spatula or turner around sides and bottom of dish. Fold plain half of omelet over jelly half. Gently slide onto serving plate. If desired, sprinkle cinnamon-sugar over omelet before serving.

Makes 1 to 2 servings

## FRENCH OMELET

*French omelets need a hot pan surface to cook properly. This one, made in the Brown 'N Sear Dish, looks best when rolled to form a cylinder; it does not fold easily. Do not use a browning griddle because egg mixture runs into the grease well. This recipe serves 1 to 2 people. For more than 2 omelets we recommend the range top.*

POWER LEVEL: High (10)
MICROWAVE TIME: 5 to 5½ min., total

| | |
|---|---|
| **2 tablespoons butter**<br>**3 eggs, well beaten**<br>**Salt**<br>**Pepper** | Preheat empty, uncovered Brown 'N Sear Dish. **Microwave at High 3 Minutes.** Immediately add butter and tip dish to melt. Stir in eggs. **Microwave at High 2 to 2½ Minutes,** stirring well every ½ minute, until almost set. Do not stir last ½ minute to allow eggs to set into solid layer. Remove from oven. Immediately tip dish and roll up into cylindrical-shape omelet. |

Makes 1 to 2 servings

## PUFFY CHEESE OMELET

POWER LEVEL: High (10) and Medium (5)
MICROWAVE TIME: 7½ to 10 min., total

| | |
|---|---|
| **3 eggs, separated**<br>**⅓ cup mayonnaise**<br>**2 tablespoons water** | In largest mixer bowl beat egg whites at highest speed of mixer, until soft peaks form. Then in smaller bowl, using same beaters, beat yolks, mayonnaise and water. Gently pour yolk mixture over beaten whites. Fold together carefully. |
| **2 tablespoons butter** | In 9-in. pie plate place butter. **Microwave at High 1 Minute,** swirl to coat dish. Carefully pour egg mixture into pie plate. **Microwave at Medium 6 to 8 Minutes,** rotating dish ½ turn after 3 minutes, until set but still glossy on top. |
| **½ cup finely shredded cheddar cheese** | Sprinkle cheese over omelet. |

**Microwave at Medium ½ to 1 Minute,** until cheese is slightly melted. Quickly run spatula or turner around sides and bottom of dish. Fold half of omelet over the other half. Gently slide onto serving plate. Sprinkle with chives, if desired.

Makes 1 to 2 servings

## EGGS AND COTTAGE CHEESE SCRAMBLE

*This brunch dish has a rich but delicate flavor. Add the cottage cheese at the last minute to melt it slightly.*

POWER LEVEL: High (10)
MICROWAVE TIME: 9½ to 12 min., total

| | |
|---|---|
| **3 tablespoons butter**<br>**¼ cup finely chopped green onions** | In 3-qt. casserole place butter and onions. **Microwave at High 2 Minutes.** Stir. |
| **9 eggs**<br>**1½ cups diced, cooked ham or other firm pre-cooked meat such as salami or dried beef** | Add eggs to casserole and beat well. Stir in meat. **Microwave at High 7 to 9 Minutes,** stirring every ½ minute. |
| **½ cup creamed cottage cheese** | Stir in cottage cheese. **Microwave at High ½ to 1 Minute,** just until cottage cheese is slightly melted. Do not overmelt, or cheese becomes runny. |

Makes 6 servings

## EGGS BENEDICT

POWER LEVEL: High (10) and Medium (5)
MICROWAVE TIME: 13 to 14 min., total

| | |
|---|---|
| **4 poached eggs (page 176)** | Poach eggs and allow to stand as directed. |
| **2 egg yolks**<br>**1 tablespoon lemon juice**<br>**½ teaspoon dry mustard**<br>**⅛ teaspoon salt**<br>**½ cup (¼-lb.) butter** | While eggs are standing, make Hollandaise sauce. In container of electric blender measure egg yolks, lemon juice, mustard and salt. In 1-qt. glass measure place butter. **Microwave at High 1 Minute** until hot and bubbly. Turn electric blender to highest speed and gradually add butter, blending until creamy and thickened. |
| **8 thin slices (¼-in. thick) Canadian bacon** | Just before serving, microwave Canadian bacon which has been arranged in single layer on microwave ovenproof plate. **Microwave at High 4 Minutes,** rotating dish ½ turn after 2 minutes. |
| **4 English muffins, split and toasted\*** | Assemble Eggs Benedict by arranging 2 slices of Canadian bacon, then a poached egg over each of 4 English muffin halves. Top eggs with Hollandaise Sauce. Butter remaining muffin halves and serve as accompaniment. Decorate with parsley if desired. |

Makes 4 servings

\*Or, if desired, use only 2 English muffins and divide eggs and sauce among the 4 halves. Serve 2 halves per serving.

## EGGS BENEDICT VARIATIONS FOR BRUNCH

**Sausage and Eggs:** Substitute thin sausage patties (see Sausage Chart, page 127) for Canadian bacon. Substitute Cheese Sauce (see recipe page 189), if desired, for Hollandaise.

**Ham and Eggs:** Substitute thin slices cooked ham for Canadian bacon. Substitute Bearnaise Sauce (see recipe page 190), if desired, for Hollandaise.

**Poultry and Eggs:** Substitute thin slices cooked chicken or poultry for Canadian bacon. Substitute Curry Sauce (see recipe page 189), if desired, for Hollandaise.

Eggs Benedict

## POACHED EGGS WITH SPANISH SAUCE

*These are known as Huevos Rancheros in the Southwestern United States.*

POWER LEVEL: High (10) and Medium (5)
MICROWAVE TIME: 16 to 19 min., total

| | |
|---|---|
| **⅓ cup finely chopped onions**<br>**⅓ cup finely chopped green pepper**<br>**1 clove garlic, crushed**<br>**2 tablespoons cooking oil** | In 1-qt. casserole stir together onion, green pepper, garlic and oil. **Microwave at High 3 to 4 Minutes,** until onion is tender. |
| **1 can (16-oz.) tomatoes, drained**<br>**1 to 2 teaspoons chili powder**<br>**¼ teaspoon salt**<br>**⅛ teaspoon pepper**<br>**⅛ teaspoon oregano** | Add tomatoes, chili powder, salt, pepper and oregano. **Microwave at High 5 to 7 Minutes,** stirring after 3 minutes, until thickened and hot. |
| **4 poached eggs (page 176)**<br>**¼ to ½ cup shredded cheddar cheese** | Place poached eggs on serving plates. Spoon sauce over eggs. Sprinkle with cheese. |

Makes 2 to 4 servings

# Quiche

Quiche is simple farm-style food which has earned a gourmet reputation because it tastes so good. A quiche is a pie shell filled with chopped cooked meat, cheese and a creamy custard. Substitute about ½ cup seafood for the bacon, and any firm cheese for the Swiss, if desired. In the province of Lorraine, French farmers use bacon, cheese and onions. Quiche is so versatile that wedges make a hearty supper, while small pieces provide a distinctive appetizer.

Microwaved quiche differs from conventionally baked because the milk or cream is heated before the custard is prepared. The warm filling microwaves more evenly, allowing the center to set without overcooking the edges. With microwaving, you have tender custard in about half the time.

## HOW TO MICROWAVE QUICHE LORRAINE

**Brush** pastry with a mixture of 1 egg yolk and 1 teaspoon Worcestershire sauce. Microwave at High, rotating dish ½ turn after about ½ time.

**Fill** pastry with crumbled cooked bacon, grated cheese and green onions. Pour in hot custard mixture. Microwave at Medium High, rotating dish ½ turn after about ½ of time.

**Metal Knife** inserted in the center will come out coated with partially cooked custard when quiche is done. Center will set during the 5 minutes of standing time.

## CLASSIC QUICHE LORRAINE

POWER LEVEL: Medium High (7)
MICROWAVE TIME: 14 to 18 min., total

| | |
|---|---|
| **6 strips crisp cooked bacon, crumbled**<br>**½ cup grated Swiss cheese**<br>**3 green onions, chopped**<br>**1 Quiche Pastry** | Reserve 2 tablespoons each of bacon and cheese and 1 tablespoon onion. Sprinkle remaining bacon, cheese and onion over bottom of microwaved Quiche Pastry (right). |
| **1½ tablespoons flour**<br>**¼ teaspoon salt**<br>**¼ teaspoon nutmeg**<br>**Dash cayenne**<br>**1 cup milk**<br>**1 cup whipping cream** | In 1-qt. measure mix flour, salt, nutmeg and cayenne. Gradually stir in milk and cream. **Microwave at Medium High 7 to 8 Minutes.** Stir every 2 minutes. |
| **4 eggs** | In 1-qt. casserole beat eggs. Stir in hot liquid. |

**Microwave at Medium High 1 to 2 Minutes,** stirring every ½ minute, until thick. Pour into pastry. Top with bacon, cheese, onion and, if desired, paprika. **Microwave at Medium High 6 to 8 Minutes,** rotating dish ¼ turn every 2 minutes, until almost set. Let stand 5 minutes.

Makes 1 (9-in.) quiche, about 6 servings

## QUICHE PASTRY

POWER LEVEL: High (10)                **Cook Code:**   40
MICROWAVE TIME: 4 to 6 min., total

| | |
|---|---|
| **1 cup unsifted all-purpose flour**<br>**½ teaspoon salt**<br>**3 tablespoons shortening**<br>**3 tablespoons cold butter** | In small mixing bowl stir together flour and salt. With pastry blender, cut in shortening until it has the appearance of cornmeal. Cut in butter until particles form the size of peas. |
| **2½ tablespoons cold water** | Sprinkle mixture with cold water. Blend lightly with fingers until dough holds together and can be formed into ball. Roll out to fit 9-in. quiche dish. |
| **1 egg yolk**<br>**1 teaspoon Worcestershire sauce** | Brush pastry with mixture of egg yolk and Worcestershire sauce. |

**Microwave at High 4 to 6 Minutes,** rotating dish ½ turn after 2½ minutes.

Makes 1 (9-in.) quiche pastry

# GOLDEN ONION QUICHE

POWER LEVEL: High (10) and Medium (5)
MICROWAVE TIME: 16 to 18 min., total

| | |
|---|---|
| **1 commercially frozen pie crust**<br>**Worcestershire sauce (about 2 teaspoons)** | Remove pastry from foil pan to glass 8-in. pie plate. **Microwave at High 1 Minute,** until softened. With fingers, press firmly in pie plate. Brush inside with Worcestershire sauce. Prick pastry. **Microwave at High 4 Minutes,** rotating plate ½ turn after 2 minutes. |
| **1 cup (4-oz.) shredded Mozzarella or pizza cheese** | Sprinkle cheese over bottom of pie shell. |
| **3 eggs**<br>**½ cup whipping cream**<br>**3 drops hot pepper sauce (tabasco)** | With fork, beat together eggs, cream and hot pepper sauce. Pour over cheese in pie shell. |
| **1 can (3-oz.) French fried onions** | With sharp knife, cut through onions in can to chop medium fine. Pour over top and lightly press down. |
| **1 tablespoon dried or frozen chives** | Sprinkle chives over top. |

**Microwave at Medium 11 to 13 Minutes,** rotating pie ½ turn after 6 minutes. Let stand about 5 minutes to firm slightly before serving.

Makes 1 (8-in.) pie, about 6 servings

*Golden Onion Quiche and its variations have been favorites with our customers ever since Medium Power was available. It is easy to make because it starts with convenience ingredients.*

VARIATIONS:

## BACON AND CHEESE QUICHE

Follow recipe for Golden Onion Quiche (left) except sprinkle 4 slices crisp-microwaved bacon, crumbled over cheese before adding custard mixture. Substitute shredded Swiss cheese for Mozzarella, if desired.

## HAM AND CHEESE QUICHE

Follow recipe for Golden Onion Quiche (left), except substitute sharp cheddar cheese for Mozzarella. Before adding filling, spread 1 can (4-oz.) deviled ham over bottom of microwaved pastry crust. Then add cheese and rest of filling ingredients. **Microwave at Medium 12 to 15 Minutes.**

## GREEN CHILIES QUICHE

*Especially appropriate cut in small wedges and served as an appetizer.*

Follow recipe for Golden Onion Quiche (left) except sprinkle 2 tablespoons chopped green chilies over cheese before adding custard mixture.

Golden Onion Quiche

# Souffles

Souffles must be specially formulated for microwaving, so you cannot adapt conventional recipes. Because it cooks so quickly, a microwaved souffle needs to be stabilized. For this reason we use evaporated milk in making the cream sauce base.

A microwaved souffle rises very high because it does not form a crust. It requires a larger dish than conventionally baked. A 2½-qt. souffle dish is the minimum size for a 6-egg souffle. Souffles can be microwaved only with a combination of Low and Medium Power and should be rotated frequently.

When done, the souffle will be dry on top with a creamy meringue in the center. Traditionally, this creamy center is served as a "sauce". See page 217 for Spinach Souffle, a vegetable variation of Cheese Souffle.

## CHEESE SOUFFLE

POWER LEVEL: High (10), Low (3) and Medium (5)
MICROWAVE TIME: 27 to 32 min., total

| | |
|---|---|
| ¼ **cup flour** . . . . . . . . . . . . . | In 1½-qt. casserole blend |
| ¾ **teaspoon salt** | together flour, salt, mustard and paprika. Stir in |
| ½ **teaspoon dry mustard** | tard and paprika. Stir in |
| ⅛ **teaspoon paprika** | evaporated milk. **Micro-** |
| 1 **can (13-oz.)** | **wave at High 4 to 6 Min-** |
| **evaporated milk** | **utes,** stirring every 2 minutes, until thickened. |
| 2 **cups (8-oz.) sharp** . . . . . | Stir cheese into hot sauce. |
| **cheddar cheese** | **Microwave at High 1 to 2 Minutes,** until smooth. |
| 6 **eggs, separated** . . . . . . | In large mixer bowl beat |
| 1 **teaspoon cream of** | egg whites with cream of |
| **tartar** | tartar until stiff but not dry. Set aside and, using same beaters, beat yolks in medium mixer bowl until thick and lemon colored. |

Slowly pour cheese mixture over beaten yolks, beating until well combined. Gently pour over beaten egg whites, fold together gently just until blended. Pour into ungreased 2½-qt. souffle dish. **Microwave at Low 10 Minutes,** rotating dish ¼ turn every 5 minutes. **Microwave at Medium 12 to 14 Minutes** more, rotating dish ¼ turn every 5 minutes, until puffed top edges are beginning to appear dry and souffle has "set" appearance. Serve immediately.

Makes 6 to 8 servings

## PARMESAN AND CHEDDAR CHEESE SOUFFLE

*This combination gives a distinctive sharp cheese flavor to the souffle.*

Prepare Cheese Souffle (above), except substitute 1 cup Parmesan cheese for 1 cup of the sharp cheddar.

## CHOCOLATE SOUFFLE

*This tastes like fluffy chocolate pudding. A crack may appear on top, and is normal with this souffle.*

POWER LEVEL: High (10), Low (3) and Medium (5)
MICROWAVE TIME: 28 to 30 min., total

| | |
|---|---|
| ¼ **cup cocoa** . . . . . . . . . . . . | In 1-qt. measure mix |
| ¼ **cup flour** | cocoa, flour, sugar and |
| ½ **cup sugar** | salt to blend. Add milk and |
| 1 **teaspoon salt** | stir smooth. **Microwave at** |
| 2 **cans (5-oz. each)** | **High 6 Minutes,** stirring |
| **evaporated milk** | after 2 minutes, then after each additional minute. |
| ¼ **cup butter** . . . . . . . . . . . . | Stir butter into hot mixture. |
| 6 **eggs, separated** . . . . . . | In large mixer bowl beat |
| ¾ **teaspoon cream of** | egg whites with cream of |
| **tartar** | tartar until foamy. Gradually add sugar, beating to |
| ½ **cup sugar** | a stiff, glossy meringue. |

With same beaters, beat egg yolks in medium mixer bowl until thick and lemon colored. Add chocolate mixture, beat smooth. Gently pour chocolate mixture over meringue, fold together gently, just until blended. Pour into ungreased 3 qt. souffle dish. **Microwave at Low 10 Minutes,** rotating dish ¼ turn every 5 minutes. **Microwave at Medium 12 to 14 Minutes** more, rotating dish ¼ turn every 5 minutes, until puffed top edges begin to appear dry and souffle has "set" appearance. Serve immediately.

Makes 6 to 8 servings

## CHOCOLATE CREAM CHEESE SOUFFLE

Prepare Chocolate Souffle (above), except add 1 pkg. (8-oz.) softened cream cheese along with butter. Stir smooth; continue as in recipe. Instead of time given in recipe above, **Microwave at Low 10 Minutes** and **at Medium 16 to 18 Minutes.** This souffle has a less airy, but firm and stable consistency.

## TIPS FOR MICROWAVING A SOUFFLE

**Beat** egg whites until stiff but not dry. Set aside, and with the same beaters, beat egg yolks until thick and lemon colored. Mix yolks with prepared cheese sauce.

**Fold** egg-cheese mixture into whites, using a rubber spatula to cut down to bottom of dish, move across the bottom, and lift the egg whites up over top of sauce.

**Pour** into souffle dish. Rotate dish every 5 minutes. Microwave at Low 10 minutes, then Microwave at Medium 12 to 14 minutes, until top appears dry.

Cheese Souffle

Melted Cheese Sandwich

# Cheese

Natural cheese reacts to microwaving much as it does to conventional cooking, but faster. Because of its high fat content it melts quickly and tends to become stringy when overcooked. Where cheese must be cooked for more than a few moments, layer it between other ingredients and use Medium Power, or use process cheese, which is less apt to become stringy. Many cheese dishes make good appetizers. Try our selection of cheese fondues next time you entertain.

### MELTED CHEESE SANDWICH

POWER LEVEL: Medium High (7)
MICROWAVE TIME: 4 min., total

| | |
|---|---|
| **2 slices bread** . . . . . . . . . . . | In conventional toaster, toast bread. At the same time, preheat empty and uncovered Brown 'N Sear Dish at **Medium High 3 Minutes.** |
| **Butter** . . . . . . . . . . . . . . .<br>**2 slices processed cheese** | When toasted, assemble sandwich and butter outside surfaces. Place in Brown 'N Sear Dish. **Microwave at Medium High ½ Minute** per side. |

Makes 1 sandwich

## TIPS FOR MICROWAVING CHEESE

**Cubed** process cheese combines with cooked macaroni and evaporated milk for a quick and easy casserole. To use natural cheese, fold cooked macaroni into homemade cheese sauce.

**Add** cheese toppings to vegetables, casseroles and hamburgers after cooking. Heat from the food melts the cheese. Shredded cheese on pizza and nachos is microwaved a few seconds to melt it.

## CHEESE FONDUE WITH NATURAL CHEESE

*It is important to whisk or stir the fondue every minute after the cheese is added, and to cook only until melted. The kirsch, while a classic ingredient, is optional.*

POWER LEVEL: High (10) and Medium (5)
MICROWAVE TIME: 7 to 8 min., total

| | |
|---|---|
| **1 cup dry white wine** . . . . <br> **2 tablespoons kirsch** | In 2-qt. microwave oven-proof fondue pot or casserole place wine and kirsch. **Microwave at High 4 Minutes,** until very hot. |
| **2½ cups (10-oz.)** . . . . . . . . <br>    **shredded natural** <br>    **gruyere cheese** <br> **2½ cups (10-oz.)** <br>    **shredded natural** <br>    **baby Swiss cheese** <br> **3 tablespoons flour** <br> **⅛ teaspoon pepper** <br>    **Dash nutmeg** <br>    **(optional)** | Toss cheeses with flour, pepper and nutmeg, until cheese is well coated. When wine is very hot, whisk or stir in cheese quickly. Cover. **Microwave at Medium 3 to 4 Minutes,** stir briskly every minute, until cheese is just melted. Serve immediately with cubes of crusty French bread for dipping. |

Makes about 4 servings

## CHEESE FONDUE WITH PROCESSED CHEESE

*Processed cheese gives the fondue a very smooth, even texture.*

Follow recipe above, except substitute processed gruyere and Swiss cheeses for the natural cheeses. Or, as an alternate, use 5 cups (20-oz.) shredded Swiss cheese and omit gruyere.

## QUICK AND EASY FONDUE

*This recipe can easily be doubled or tripled to use as a party dip for crackers or the traditional bread cubes. Increase time about 2 minutes.*

POWER LEVEL: High (10)                **Cook Code:**   30
MICROWAVE TIME: 3 to 4 min., total

| | |
|---|---|
| **1 can (10-oz.)** . . . . . . . . . . <br>    **condensed cream of** <br>    **shrimp soup** <br> **1 roll (6-oz.) process** <br>    **garlic cheese, cubed** | In 1-qt. casserole stir together soup and cheese cubes. **Microwave at High 3 to 4 Minutes,** stirring after 2 minutes, until cheese is melted. |

Makes about 2 to 3 servings

Cheese Fondue

## CHEESE SANDWICH CASSEROLE

POWER LEVEL: Medium (5)          **Cook Code:**   95
MICROWAVE TIME: 9 to 12 min., total

| | |
|---|---|
| **4 slices bread** . . . . . . . . . <br>    **Butter** <br> **2 cups (8-oz.) shredded** <br>    **cheddar cheese** | Spread each bread slice with butter. In 10×6×2-in. dish place 2 slices bread, butter side up. Top with 1 cup cheese. Repeat layers. |
| **2 eggs** . . . . . . . . . . . . . . . . <br> **1 cup dairy half & half** <br> **2 tablespoons butter,** <br>    **melted** <br> **½ teaspoon salt** <br> **½ teaspoon dry mustard** <br> **¼ teaspoon paprika** <br>    **Dash cayenne pepper** | In mixing bowl beat eggs. Blend in half & half, butter, salt, mustard, paprika and cayenne pepper. Pour over sandwiches. Cover with wax paper. **Microwave at Medium 9 to 12 Minutes,** rotate dish ¼ turn every 3 minutes. Let stand 5 minutes before serving. |

Makes 2 or 4 servings

Cheese Rarebit

## CHEESE RAREBIT

*Rarebit is a rich cheese sauce traditionally served over toast points or other types of toasted bread.*

POWER LEVEL: High (10) and Medium (5)
MICROWAVE TIME: 7 to 10 min., total

| | |
|---|---|
| **8 oz. pasturized** . . . . . . . .<br>    **processed cheese,**<br>    **diced**<br>**1 tablespoon butter** | In 1-qt. casserole place cheese and butter. **Microwave at High 2 to 3 Minutes,** stirring every minute, until melted and cheese can be stirred smooth. |
| **¼ teaspoon salt** . . . . . . . . .<br>**¼ teaspoon dry mustard**<br>**½ teaspoon**<br>    **Worcestershire**<br>    **sauce**<br>    **Dash cayenne pepper**<br>**¼ cup dairy half & half**<br>**1 egg yolk, beaten** | Add salt, mustard, Worcestershire sauce and cayenne pepper. Quickly stir in half & half and egg yolk. **Microwave at Medium 5 to 7 Minutes,** stirring every minute, until hot. |

Makes 3 to 4 servings

## CHEESE ENCHILADAS

POWER LEVEL: High (10)
MICROWAVE TIME: 12½ to 15¾ min., total

| | |
|---|---|
| **1 lb. ricotta cheese** . . . . . .<br>    **(2 cups)**<br>**1 egg**<br>**1 cup chopped green**<br>    **onions**<br>**2 tablespoons chopped**<br>    **green chilies**<br>**1 teaspoon cumin**<br>**1 cup (4-oz.) shredded**<br>    **Jack cheese** | In mixing bowl stir together ricotta, egg, onions, chillies, cumin and Jack cheese. |
| **8 fresh corn or flour** . . . . .<br>    **tortillas, (about 6-in**<br>    **diameter) or, 10 to 12**<br>    **canned tortillas (5-in.**<br>    **diameter)** | Wrap tortillas in towel. **Microwave at High ½ to ¾ Minute,** until pliable. Divide filling among tortillas. Roll up each one tightly. |
| **1 can (10-oz.) enchilada**<br>    **sauce** | In lightly greased 12×8× 2-in. dish place rolls, seam side down. Pour sauce over rolls. **Microwave at High 11 to 13 Minutes,** until filling begins to bubble. |
| **2 cups (8-oz.) shredded** . . .<br>    **cheddar cheese** | Cover with cheddar cheese. **Microwave at High 1 to 2 Minutes,** until cheese is almost melted. |
| **Sour cream and** . . . . . . .<br>    **chopped green**<br>    **onions** | Garnish with sour cream and green onions. |

Makes 4 generous servings

There are many references to cheese and cheese recipes in other sections of this book; including:

Cream Cheese Dips, page 68
Cheese Crock, page 70
Crab Swiss Crisps, page 70
Soft Smokey Cheese Ball, page 70
Mushroom Stuffings, page 74
Cheese Souffle, page 182
Spaghetti and Cheese Casserole, page 194
Macaroni and Cheese, page 194
Lasagna, page 196
Grits and Cheese Casserole, page 199
Cheezy Broccoli, page 210
Zippy Zucchini, page 219
Cheesecake, page 266

## CHEESE PIE WITH HAMBURGER CRUST

POWER LEVEL: High (10) and Medium (5)
MICROWAVE TIME: 14 to 16 min., total

| | |
|---|---|
| **1 egg** . . . . . . . . . . . . . . .<br>**½ cup milk**<br>**2 cups fresh bread,<br>cubed (3 slices)** | In large mixing bowl beat egg slightly. Add milk and bread. Toss lightly, then let stand few minutes, until most of liquid is absorbed. |
| **½ lb. ground chuck** . . . . .<br>**beef**<br>**1 teaspoon<br>Worcestershire<br>sauce**<br>**1 teaspoon salt**<br>**¼ teaspoon thyme**<br>**¼ teaspoon dried<br>parsley**<br>**1¼ cups sliced green<br>onions, including<br>tops, divided** | To bread mixture add beef, Worcestershire sauce, salt, thyme, parsley and ¼ cup onions. Mix lightly until combined. Spoon into 9-in. pie plate and spread to line bottom and sides of plate. Sprinkle remaining green onions over crust. |
| **3 eggs** . . . . . . . . . . . . . .<br>**1 cup (4-oz.) shredded<br>Swiss cheese**<br>**3 to 4 drops liquid<br>pepper seasoning<br>(tabasco)**<br>**½ teaspoon salt**<br>**⅓ cup milk**<br>**Paprika** | In same bowl beat eggs until foamy. Stir in cheese, liquid pepper seasoning, salt and milk. Pour over green onions in meat crust. Sprinkle lightly with paprika. |

**Microwave at High 5 Minutes,** then rotate dish ¼ turn. **Microwave at Medium 9 to 11 Minutes,** rotating dish ¼ turn after 5 minutes. Center will be soft but set when done.

Makes 6 to 8 servings

## MICROWAVE CHEESE TOPPINGS

*The following toppings may be prepared to garnish favorite vegetables or casseroles.*

**Cheese Topping for Vegetables:** In small mixing bowl place 1 jar or pkg. (8-oz.) processed cheddar cheese food. **Microwave at Medium High 3 to 4 Minutes,** stirring after 2 minutes, until cheese is melted and can be stirred smooth. For thinner topping, add 1 to 2 tablespoons milk, beer or tomato juice. Add chopped parsley and/or garlic salt for more color or flavor.

**Cheese Topping for Casseroles:** In small mixing bowl place ¼ cup butter. **Microwave at High ½ to 1 Minute,** until melted. Stir in ½ cup fine dry bread or cracker crumbs, ¼ cup Parmesan cheese and ¼ teaspoon paprika. **Microwave at Medium High 2 to 3 Minutes,** stirring after 1 minute.

## CHEESE PUDDING

*This interesting casserole is a good substitute for potatoes, rice or pasta in a full course menu. Or serve it as a luncheon or supper dish, along with a salad.*

POWER LEVEL: High (10), Med. (5) and Med. High (7)
MICROWAVE TIME: 21¼ to 26½ min., total

| | |
|---|---|
| **2 cups water** . . . . . . . . . . .<br>**4 eggs** | Poach eggs hard; into 1½-qt. casserole pour water. **Microwave at High 5 to 6 Minutes,** until boiling. Break eggs into saucer and puncture membrane around yolk with toothpick. **Microwave at Medium 5 to 6 Minutes,** until yolks begin to harden. Let stand several minutes in water. Remove and grate or chop finely. |
| **1 cup buttery flavored<br>cracker crumbs**<br>**2 cups (double recipe)<br>thick White Sauce,<br>page 189**<br>**2 cups (8-oz.) shredded<br>cheddar cheese**<br>**2 jars (4-oz.) sliced<br>pimiento, drained** | Into 8-in. square dish place ½ of cracker crumbs. Cover with ½ of white sauce, ½ of cheese, ½ of pimiento and ½ of eggs. Repeat layers. Cover with Buttered Crumbs (below). **Microwave at Medium High 10 to 12 Minutes,** rotating dish ½ turn after 5 minutes, until heated through. |

Makes about 8 servings

**Buttered Crumbs:** In 1 cup measure place 2 tablespoons butter. **Microwave at High ¼ to ½ Minute,** until melted. Add ½ cup fine dry bread crumbs. **Microwave at Medium High 1 to 2 Minutes,** until browned.

## EGGS & CHEESE CONVENIENCE CHART

| ITEM | POWER LEVEL | TIME MINUTES | COMMENTS |
|---|---|---|---|
| **Egg Substitute (egg beaters)** (8-oz. carton) | Defrost | 4 to 4½ | Time 3 minutes, turn over after 1½ minutes. Open carton and stir every ½ minute until smooth. |
| **Cheese Souffle** (12-oz. pkg.) | Defrost<br><br>Medium High | 10 to 14<br><br>9 to 11 | To Defrost: Place in 8-in. pie plate. Stir. To Cook: Divide between 3 or 4 buttered custard cups; 6 or 7-oz. Rearrange after 4 minutes. Souffles are done when center is set. |
| **Welsh Rarebit** (10-oz. pkg.) | High | 5 to 6<br>**Cook Code:** 50 | Stir every 2 minutes. |

# Gravies & Main Dish Sauces

Gravies and sauces microwave easily because there is no scorching or lumping or constant stirring. They save time in cooking and clean-up, too. Make them right in the cup you use for measuring or in the microwave oven-proof sauce boat you use for serving.

Main Dish Sauces found in other sections include:

Kentucky Bourbon Sauce, page 123
Cranberry Orange Ruby Sauce, page 130
Apple Cider Sauce, page 143
Cranberry Sauce, page 153
Clarified Butter, page 160

## POULTRY GIBLET GRAVY

POWER LEVEL: Medium (5) and High (10)
MICROWAVE TIME: 21 to 29 min., total

| | |
|---|---|
| **Giblets from a 3-lb. chicken**<br>**1 cup water** | In 1-qt. casserole place giblets. Prick each giblet several times with fork. Add water. Cover. **Microwave at Medium 16 to 20 Minutes,** stirring after 10 minutes, until tender. Chop medium fine. |
| **¼ cup poultry drippings**<br>**¼ cup flour**<br>**½ teaspoon salt**<br>**¼ teaspoon celery salt**<br>**Dash pepper** | In separate 1-qt. casserole place drippings. **Microwave at High 1 to 2 Minutes,** until hot. Stir in flour, salt, celery salt and pepper until smooth. |
| **Broth from giblets plus water to make 1¼ cups** | Gradually stir in broth until well blended. **Microwave at High 2 to 4 Minutes,** stirring every minute. Add chopped giblets. **Microwave at High 2 to 3 Minutes** more, stirring every minute, until thickened. |

Makes about 1½ cups

Poultry Giblet Gravy

## TIPS FOR MICROWAVING GRAVIES AND SAUCES

  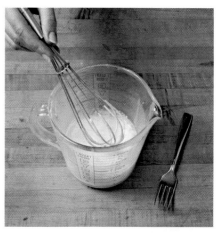

**Use More** flour or cornstarch to thicken microwaved gravies and sauces, since they will not reduce by evaporation.

**Combine** flour, butter and salt in a glass measure when making White Sauce. Microwave until butter melts and bubbles. Stir and microwave 1 minute more to cook flour.

**Stir** occasionally to bring cooked portions from the outside of the measure to the center. Use a wire whisk or table fork for a smooth sauce with minimum stirring.

## MILK GRAVY

*Be sure to use a 1-qt. utensil to prevent boilover. These proportions are for gravy which runs easily from spoon. For thicker gravy, which mounds from spoon, use ⅓ cup flour.*

POWER LEVEL: High (10)
MICROWAVE TIME: 7 to 10 min., total

| | |
|---|---|
| **¼ cup chicken or beef drippings**<br>**¼ cup flour**<br>**¼ teaspoon salt**<br>**1¼ cups milk** | In 1-qt. glass measure, measure drippings. **Microwave at High 1 to 2 Minutes,** until hot. Add flour and salt. Stir well. Stir in milk slowly. **Microwave at High 6 to 8 Minutes,** stirring every minute. |

Makes about 1½ cups

VARIATIONS:

**Cream Gravy:** Prepare Milk Gravy as above, except, instead of 1¼ cups milk, use ⅔ cup milk and ⅔ cup whipping cream.

**Brown Gravy:** Prepare Milk Gravy or Cream Gravy as above, using beef or lamb drippings and adding ½ teaspoon brown bouquet sauce.

## BASIC WHITE SAUCE

POWER LEVEL: High (10)
MICROWAVE TIME: 5½ to 6½ min., total

| | |
|---|---|
| **2 tablespoons butter**<br>**2 tablespoons flour**<br>**½ teaspoon salt** | In 1-qt. glass measure place butter, flour and salt. **Microwave at High 2 Minutes** stirring after 1 minute. |
| **1 cup milk** | Gradually stir in milk. **Microwave at High 3½ to 4½ Minutes,** stirring every minute until thick and bubbly. |

Makes 1 cup

VARIATIONS:

**Cheese Sauce:** To finished sauce, add 1 cup (4-oz.) shredded sharp cheese and a dash of cayenne pepper. **Microwave at High 1 to 2 Minutes,** to melt cheese.

**Mornay Sauce:** To finished sauce, add ½ cup shredded Swiss, gruyere or Parmesan cheese, 1 teaspoon lemon juice and a dash of cayenne pepper.

**Curry Sauce:** Add 2 to 3 teaspoons curry powder along with flour. Microwave as above.

**Dill Sauce:** To finished sauce, add 2 teaspoons dill weed and 1 teaspoon lemon juice.

**Horseradish Sauce:** To finished sauce, add 1 to 2 teaspoons cream style horseradish.

**Thick White Sauce:** Use 3 tablespoons flour instead of 2 tablespoons.

Asparagus with White Sauce

## HOLLANDAISE SAUCE FOR MICROWAVERS

*We have tried many recipes for microwaving Hollandaise Sauce, even the "never-fail" ones, and our recommendation is to use the blender method. The microwave oven helps you by rapidly melting the butter.*

*You can reheat leftover Hollandaise successfully at Low Power for ¼ to ½ minute. Stir and let the sauce stand before continuing to reheat; it is so delicate that it can curdle easily even upon reheating if you set the timer for too long.*

| POWER LEVEL: High (10) | **Cook Code:** 10 |
|---|---|
| MICROWAVE TIME: 1 to 2 min., total | |

**2 egg yolks** . . . . . . . . . . . . . Into container of electric
**1 tablespoon lemon**     blender place yolks, juice,
   **juice**     mustard and salt.
**½ teaspoon dry mustard**
**⅛ teaspoon salt**

**½ cup (¼-lb.) butter** . . . . . . In glass measuring cup place butter. **Microwave at High 1 to 2 Minutes,** until hot and bubbly. Turn electric blender to highest speed and gradually add butter, mixing well until Hollandaise is creamy and thickened.

Makes about ½ cup

## SWEET AND SOUR SAUCE

*This piquant sauce is so versatile that it goes with just about every type of meat, poultry and seafood. It's very good with hamburgers, especially if you increase garlic to 1 clove. The 10 drops liquid pepper seasoning gives it zip.*

| POWER LEVEL: High (10) | **Cook Code:** 50 |
|---|---|
| MICROWAVE TIME: 5 to 7 min., total | |

**½ cup sugar** . . . . . . . . . . . . In 1½-qt. casserole stir to-
**2 tablespoons**     gether sugar, cornstarch
   **cornstarch**     and water, until well blend-
**¼ cup cold water**     ed.

**1 can (8-oz.) crushed** . . . . Stir in pineapple, pepper,
   **pineapple**     pimiento, garlic, vinegar,
**½ cup chopped green**     soy sauce and pepper
   **pepper**     seasoning. **Microwave at**
**¼ cup (4-oz. can)**     **High 5 to 7 Minutes,** stir-
   **chopped pimiento**     ring every 2 minutes, until
**½ clove garlic, mashed**     clear and thickened. Let
**½ cup cider vinegar**     sauce stand 5 to 10 min-
**2 tablespoons soy**     utes, to develop flavor, be-
   **sauce**     fore serving.
**10 drops liquid pepper**
   **seasoning (tabasco)**

Makes about 1¾ cups

## BEARNAISE SAUCE

*Serve this sauce over steaks, poached eggs on toast, or microwaved green vegetables.*

| POWER LEVEL: High (10) | **Cook Code:** 10 |
|---|---|
| MICROWAVE TIME: 1 to 2 min., total | |

**4 egg yolks** . . . . . . . . . . . . In blender container place
**1 teaspoon instant**     yolks, onion, vinegar and
   **minced onion**     wine.
**1 teaspoon tarragon**
   **vinegar**
**1 teaspoon white wine**

**½ cup (¼-lb.) butter** . . . . . . In glass measure place butter. **Microwave at High 1 to 2 Minutes,** until hot and bubbly. Turn electric blender to highest speed and gradually add butter, mixing until sauce is creamy and thickened.

Makes about ½ cup

## WHIPPED BUTTERS

*Savory garnishes for sliced, roasted meats or plain vegetables.*

POWER LEVEL: Low (3)
MICROWAVE TIME: ½ to ¾ min., total

1. In small glass mixer bowl place ½ cup butter. **Microwave at Low ½ to ¾ Minute,** until softened.

2. Add ingredients from one of the variations.

3. Whip with electric mixer at high speed, until fluffy.

Makes ½ cup

VARIATIONS:

**Herbed Butter:** Add 2 teaspoons minced parsley, 2 teaspoons lemon juice, ¼ teaspoon thyme, ¼ teaspoon salt and ¼ teaspoon pepper.

**Parsley Garlic Butter:** Add ½ cup minced parsley, 2 cloves minced garlic, 2 teaspoons minced onion, 2 teaspoons lemon juice and 1 teaspoon dry mustard.

**Dill Butter:** Add 4 teaspoons dill weed, ½ teaspoon salt, ⅛ teaspoon pepper and 2 hard cooked egg yolks, sieved. To hard cook egg yolks: Place yolks in 6-oz. custard cup. Add 1 tablespoon water. Cover with plastic wrap. **Microwave at Medium 1 Minute.** Let stand a few minutes, then remove from water to cool.

## COLORFUL MARMALADE SAUCE

*This bright sauce looks and tastes good over duck, chicken, turkey and ham. It serves as a glaze as well as a sauce. Use sweet, not bitter, orange marmalade.*

POWER LEVEL: High (10)      **Cook Code:** 50
MICROWAVE TIME: 5 to 7 min., total

| | |
|---|---|
| **1 cup sweet orange marmalade**<br>**1 can (8-oz.) tomato sauce**<br>**2 tablespoons chopped onion**<br>**1½ teaspoons soy sauce**<br>**1 teaspoon ground ginger**<br>**½ cup sliced almonds** | In 1½-qt. casserole combine marmalade, tomato sauce, onion, soy sauce, ginger and almonds. **Microwave at High 5 to 7 Minutes,** stirring every 2 minutes, until hot and well combined. |

Makes about 2 cups

## LEMON BUTTER SAUCE

*A favorite sauce for fish and fish loaves, and for some vegetables, such as asparagus and broccoli.*

POWER LEVEL: High (10)
MICROWAVE TIME: ½ to 1 min., total

| | |
|---|---|
| **¼ cup butter** | In 1-cup glass measure place butter. **Microwave at High ½ to 1 Minute,** until melted. |
| **1 tablespoon fresh lemon juice**<br>**1 tablespoon snipped parsley**<br>**Dash pepper** | Stir lemon juice, parsley and pepper into melted butter. Keep warm. |

Makes about ¼ cup

## ALMOND BUTTER SAUCE

POWER LEVEL: High (10)
MICROWAVE TIME: 6 to 7 min., total

| | |
|---|---|
| **¼ cup slivered almonds**<br>**½ cup (¼-lb.) butter, divided** | In 9-in. pie plate place almonds and 1 teaspoon butter. **Microwave at High 5 to 6 Minutes,** stirring every 2 minutes, until toasted. Add remaining butter. **Microwave at High 1 Minute,** until melted. |
| **½ teaspoon seasoned salt** | Stir in seasoned salt. Serve warm. |

Makes ½ cup

## RAISIN SAUCE

*Traditionally served with ham or pork.*

POWER LEVEL: High (10)      **Cook Code:** 40
MICROWAVE TIME: 4 to 6 min., total

| | |
|---|---|
| **½ cup brown sugar (packed)**<br>**2 tablespoons cornstarch**<br>**1½ teaspoons mustard**<br>**⅛ teaspoon cloves** | In 1-qt. measuring cup or casserole blend together brown sugar, cornstarch, mustard and cloves, until well combined. |
| **1 cup water or apple cider**<br>**2 tablespoons lemon juice**<br>**¼ cup raisins**<br>**2 tablespoons butter** | Stir in water and lemon juice until smooth. Add raisins and butter. **Microwave at High 4 to 6 Minutes,** stirring every 2 minutes, until clear and thickened. |

Makes about 1¼ cups

## CLAM SAUCE

*This is a popular sauce for spaghetti or other pasta. If possible, buy a green (spinach) pasta to serve with this clear sauce.*

POWER LEVEL: High (10)
MICROWAVE TIME: 7 to 8 min., total

**2 tablespoons olive oil** . . .In 1-qt. casserole place oil,
**3 cloves garlic, minced**    garlic and salt. **Microwave**
**¼ teaspoon salt**            **at High 3 Minutes,** until
                               softened.

**2 cans (6.5-oz. each)** . . . .Drain clams, reserving
**minced clams**        juice. Set aside. Stir to-
**¼ cup water**         gether water and corn-
**1 tablespoon**        starch. Add to garlic along
**cornstarch**          with clam juice and pars-
**¼ cup minced parsley** ley. **Microwave at High 3**
                        **Minutes,** stirring after 2
                        minutes, until thickened.
                        Stir in clams. **Microwave**
                        **at High 1 to 2 Minutes,** un-
                        til hot.

Makes about 2 cups

## BARBECUE SAUCE

*The traditional sauce to use when cooking ribs and chicken. Or, slice leftover beef or pork into barbecue sauce and serve warm as an entree or sandwich filling.*

POWER LEVEL: High (10)          **Cook Code:    50**
MICROWAVE·TIME: 5 to 6 min., total

**1 cup chili sauce** . . . . . . .In 1-qt. casserole thor-
**½ cup water**           oughly combine chili
**¼ cup lemon juice**     sauce, water, lemon juice,
**1 tablespoon cooking**  cooking oil, brown sugar,
**oil**                   salt, paprika, pepper sea-
**2 tablespoons brown**   soning and Worcester-
**sugar (packed)**        shire sauce. Cover. **Micro-**
**½ teaspoon salt**       **wave at High 5 to 7 Min-**
**¼ teaspoon paprika**    **utes,** stirring after 3 min-
**¼ teaspoon liquid**     utes, until hot. Use as de-
**pepper seasoning**      sired.
**(tabasco)**
**1 tablespoon**
**Worcestershire**
**sauce**

Makes 2 cups

## CLASSIC ITALIAN SAUCE

*Complements pasta, meatballs, meat slices and cooked chicken pieces.*

POWER LEVEL: High (10)
MICROWAVE TIME: 15 to 18 min., total

**1 large onion, chopped**  . .In 3-qt. casserole place
**3 tablespoons olive or**  onion, oil and garlic. **Mi-**
**cooking oil**             **crowave at High 3 to 4**
**3 cloves garlic, minced** **Minutes,** stirring after 2
                            minutes, until onion is limp.

**2 cans (15-oz. each)** . . . . .Add tomato sauce, tomato
**tomato sauce**           paste, wine, broth or juice,
**2 cans (6-oz. each)**    brown sugar, Worcester-
**tomato paste**          shire sauce, oregano,
**⅔ cup burgundy, beef**   basil, salt and pepper. Mix
**broth or tomato juice**  together well. Cover. **Mi-**
**2 tablespoons brown**    **crowave at High 12 to 14**
**sugar**                  **Minutes,** stirring after 6
**2 teaspoons**            minutes, until very hot.
**Worcestershire**
**sauce**
**1 teaspoon oregano**
**1 teaspoon basil**
**1 teaspoon salt**
**½ teaspoon pepper**

Makes about 2 quarts

**Italian Sauce With Meat:** Add 2-lb. ground chuck beef, crumbled, seasoned and cooked.

**Italian Sauce With Mushrooms:** Add 2-lb. fresh mushrooms, sliced and sauteed.

## MUSHROOM SAUCE

*This is elegant for steaks or chops.*

POWER LEVEL: Medium High (7)
MICROWAVE TIME: 6 to 7 min., total

**2 cups sliced fresh** . . . . . .In 1-qt. casserole place
**mushrooms**           mushrooms and butter.
**¼ cup butter**        Cover. **Microwave at Me-**
                        **dium High 3 Minutes.**

**¼ cup water** . . . . . . . . . . .Mix together water, sherry,
**¼ cup sherry wine or**  cornstarch and salt. Grad-
**additional water**     ually stir into mushrooms.
**1 tablespoon**         Cover. **Microwave at Me-**
**cornstarch**          **dium High 3 to 4 Minutes,**
**⅛ teaspoon salt**      stirring after 2 minutes, un-
                        til thickened.

Makes about 2 cups

# Pasta, Rice & Cereal

Among microwave cooks and microwave cookbooks, pasta and rice are a controversial subject. They take about the same time to soften, whether you cook them by microwave or conventionally. Advocates of microwaved pasta insist that they have a better flavor and firm, "al dente" texture. Other people prefer to cook them conventionally because this leaves the microwave oven free to cook the sauce or main dish.

Both sides agree that microwaving is a perfect way to reheat pasta and rice. Reheated conventionally, pasta and rice will dry out unless you add more water, which overcooks them. Tightly covered with plastic wrap, pasta and rice reheat to "fresh cooked" flavor and texture. Undercook pasta and rice 3 to 5 minutes if you are using it in a casserole which requires further cooking.

Many of our recipes in the main dish sections call for quick-cooking rice, because regular rice will not be cooked in the short times needed for the other ingredients. Make this same substitution in adapting your own recipes.

For sauces try Italian Sauce and variations, page 192, with spaghetti; Clam Sauce, page 192, with linguine; Flavored Butters, page 191, with noodles or rice.

## SPAGHETTI-CHEESE CASSEROLE

*As a garnish, save out a few olive slices from sauce to decorate top.*

POWER LEVEL: High (10)
MICROWAVE TIME: 21 to 26 min., total

| | |
|---|---|
| **1 pkg. (7-oz.) spaghetti** | Cook spaghetti (see chart at right), except **Microwave 9 Minutes.** |
| **1 can (10½-oz.) condensed cream of mushroom soup** <br> **½ cup milk** <br> **1 teaspoon instant minced onion** <br> **⅛ teaspoon pepper** <br> **½ cup sliced stuffed olives** | In small bowl mix soup, milk, onion, pepper and olives. |
| **2 cups (8-oz.) cheddar cheese, cubed** | In greased 1½-qt. casserole alternate layers of spaghetti, cheese and soup mixture. **Microwave at High 9 to 12 Minutes,** rotating dish ½ turn after 4 minutes. |

Makes 4 to 6 servings

NOTE: This casserole is a good meat accompaniment or makes a nice luncheon dish, served with sliced tomato salad.

## CREAMY MACARONI AND CHEESE

POWER LEVEL: High (10) and Medium High (7)
MICROWAVE TIME: 23 to 27 min., total

| | |
|---|---|
| **1 pkg. (7-oz.) elbow macaroni** | Cook macaroni (see chart at right), except **Microwave 10 Minutes.** Drain well and return to same casserole. |
| **¼ cup butter** | In 1-qt. measure place butter. **Microwave at High ½ to 1 Minute,** to melt. |
| **6 tablespoons flour** <br> **1 teaspoon salt** <br> **2 cups milk** | Blend in flour and salt. Stir in milk until smooth. **Microwave at High 5½ to 6 Minutes,** stirring with table fork every minute, until thickened. |
| **2 cups (8-oz.) grated sharp cheddar cheese** | Stir in cheese until completely melted. |

Stir sauce into drained macaroni, mixing well. **Microwave at Medium High 7 to 10 Minutes,** stirring every 3 minutes. If desired, sprinkle top with paprika or buttered crumbs before serving.

Makes 6 to 8 servings

## QUICK AND EASY MACARONI AND CHEESE

*A family-type favorite. For added zip, stir in a few drops Worcestershire sauce.*

POWER LEVEL: High (10)
MICROWAVE TIME: 16 to 18 min., total

| | |
|---|---|
| **1 pkg. (7-oz.) elbow macaroni** | Cook macaroni (see chart at right), except **Microwave 10 Minutes.** |
| **1 block pkg. (1-lb.) pasteurized process cheese spread** <br> **1 can (5⅓-oz.) evaporated milk** | Cut cheese into cubes. Into 3-qt. casserole place cheese with macaroni and milk. Toss together until cheese is distributed. |

**Microwave at High 6 to 8 Minutes,** stirring after 3 minutes, until cheese is melted and mixture bubbles. Stir to blend.

Makes 6 to 8 servings

# HOW TO MICROWAVE PASTA & RICE

**Combine** pasta or rice with very hot tap water and salt in the recommended cooking dish. Add oil if needed.

**Cover** tightly with casserole cover or plastic wrap, turned back at edge 2-in. to vent. Microwave at High Power.

**Stir** or rearrange after ½ the time. Recover and continue microwaving. Drain immediately.

## PASTA & RICE MICROWAVING CHART          POWER LEVEL: **High (10)**

| FOOD TYPE | AMOUNT | UTENSIL | WATER SALT & OIL | TIME MIN. | COOK CODE | GENERAL DIRECTIONS |
|---|---|---|---|---|---|---|
| **Macaroni** | 6 to 8-oz. pkg. | 2-qt. casserole | 3 cups water 2 teaspoons salt | 15 to 18 | 150 | Stir after 10 minutes. |
| **Rotini** | 16-oz. pkg. | 3-qt. casserole | 6 cups water 1 teaspoon salt | 13 to 16 | 130 | Stir after 10 minutes. Check rotini after 10 minutes as this cooks faster than other types. |
| **Spaghetti or Linguine** | 16-oz. pkg. | 13×9×2-in. dish | 6 to 7 cups water 1 tablespoon salt 1 tablespoon oil | 16 to 19 | 160 | Rearrange after 10 minutes. |
| **Spaghetti or Linguine** | 7-oz. pkg. | 13×9×2-in. dish | 6 to 7 cups water ½ teaspoon salt 1 tablespoon oil | 12 to 14 | 120 | Rearrange after 8 minutes. |
| **Egg Noodles, Narrow** | 3 cups or 6 oz. | 8-in. square dish | 3 cups water 1 teaspoon salt | 13 to 16 | 130 | Time is the same for spinach or regular. |
| **Egg Noodles, Wide** | 8-oz. | 3-qt. casserole | 8 cups water 1 teaspoon salt 1 teaspoon oil | 23 to 25 | 230 | Stir after 10 minutes. |
| **Lasagna** | 16-oz. pkg. | 13×9×2-in. dish | Cover with water placing ½ teaspoon salt in bottom of dish 1 tablespoon oil | 14 to 16 | 140 | Rearrange after 7 minutes. |
| **Lasagna** | ½ pkg. | 13×9×2-in. dish | Cover with water placing ½ teaspoon salt in bottom of dish 1 tablespoon oil | 11 to 13 | 110 | Rearrange after 6 minutes. |
| **Manicotti** | 10 to 12 pieces, about 5-oz. pkg. | 12×8×2-in. dish | Brush with oil first then cover with water | 22 to 25 | 220 | Using fork turn over every 5 minutes to prevent sticking. |
| **Long Grain Rice** | 1 cup | 3-qt. casserole | 2¼ cups water 1 teaspoon salt | 18 to 21 | 180 | Stir after 10 minutes. |
| **Minute Rice** | 1½ cups | 2-qt. casserole | 1½ cups water ½ teaspoon salt | 4 to 6 | 40 | Stir after 2 minutes. |
| **Rice-Vermicelli Mixes** | 8-oz. pkg. | 2-qt. casserole | Follow package directions | 18 to 22 | 180 | Stir every 6 minutes. Let stand 5 minutes before serving. |

## CHEESE STUFFED MANICOTTI

*Add cooked meatballs or sausages for an even heartier dish.*

POWER LEVEL: High (10)
MICROWAVE TIME: 35 to 38 min., total

| | |
|---|---|
| **10 manicotti** . . . . . . . . . . | Cook manicotti (see chart, page 195), except **Microwave 20 Minutes.** |
| **1 pkg. (6-oz.) sliced Mozzarella cheese** . . . . | Dice cheese into ½-in. cubes before separating slices. Reserve about ⅓ cup for topping. Combine rest of Mozzarella with ricotta, romano, spinach, garlic, salt and pepper. Stuff cooked manicotti with cheese filling. Rearrange in 12×8×2-in. dish. |
| **2 cups (1-pt.) ricotta cheese** | |
| **½ cup romano cheese** | |
| **1 can (7¾-oz.) spinach, drained** | |
| **½ teaspoon garlic powder** | |
| **½ teaspoon salt** | |
| **¼ teaspoon pepper** | |
| **1 can (15-oz.) tomato sauce** . . . . | Pour tomato sauce over top. Sprinkle with cheese and marjoram. Cover with wax paper. |
| **Marjoram** | |

**Microwave at High 15 to 18 Minutes,** rotating dish ½ turn after 8 minutes.

Makes 4 servings

## NOODLES ROMANOFF

*A traditional combination of noodles, cheese and sour cream.*

POWER LEVEL: High (10)
MICROWAVE TIME: 19 to 21 min., total

| | |
|---|---|
| **1 pkg. (7 to 8-oz.) narrow noodles** . . . . . . . | Cook noodles (see chart, page 195), except **Microwave 9 Minutes.** Place cooked noodles in 3-qt. casserole. |
| **1 cup cottage cheese** . . . . | Add cheese, sour cream, olives, onion, salt, Worcestershire sauce and liquid pepper. Mix well. Cover. **Microwave at High 8 Minutes,** stirring after 4 minutes, until hot. |
| **1 cup (8-oz.) dairy sour cream** | |
| **¼ cup chopped stuffed olives** | |
| **1 teaspoon instant minced onion** | |
| **½ teaspoon salt** | |
| **½ teaspoon Worcestershire sauce** | |
| **Dash liquid pepper seasoning (tabasco)** | |
| **1 cup (4-oz.) shredded sharp cheese** . . . | Sprinkle cheese on top. **Microwave at High 2 to 4 Minutes** more, uncovered. |

Makes 6 servings

## LASAGNA

POWER LEVEL: High (10)
MICROWAVE TIME: 28 to 34 min., total

| | |
|---|---|
| **½ pkg. (½-lb.) lasagna noodles** | Cook noodles (see chart, page 195), except **Microwave 8 Minutes.** |
| **2 cans (8-oz. each) tomato sauce** . . . . . | In large bowl mix together tomato sauce, tomato paste, oregano, basil, salt and garlic. Spread ½ cup sauce over bottom of 12× 8×2-in. dish. |
| **1 can (6-oz.) tomato paste** | |
| **1 tablespoon leaf oregano** | |
| **2 teaspoons basil** | |
| **½ teaspoon salt** | |
| **¼ teaspoon garlic powder or 1 garlic clove, minced** | |
| **1 lb. ground chuck beef cooked, drained** . . . . . | Mix beef with remaining sauce. |
| **2 cups (1-pt.) small curd cottage cheese** . . . . . | In small bowl mix together cottage cheese, egg, parsley and salt. Layer 3 noodles, half of cottage cheese mixture, half of Mozzarella cheese, half of tomato sauce in dish. Repeat layers. |
| **1 egg** | |
| **1 tablespoon dried parsley flakes** | |
| **½ teaspoon salt** | |
| **1 pkg. (6-oz.) sliced Mozzarella cheese** | |
| **½ cup grated Parmesan cheese** | . . Sprinkle Parmesan cheese over top. Cover with wax paper. |

**Microwave at High 20 to 26 Minutes,** rotating dish ¼ turn every 8 minutes. Letting lasagna stand about 10 minutes helps it hold shape when cutting.

Makes 6 to 8 servings

NOTE: Lasagna may be made and refrigerated. Add about 4 to 6 minutes to total cooking time.

VARIATIONS:

**Meat:** Substitute bulk pork sausage, cooked and drained, for ground chuck; or instead of bulk sausage use 2 pkg. (8-oz. each) brown and serve sausages, diced. (When brown and serve sausages are substituted no precooking is needed. Sausages heat as assembled casserole microwaves.) Or substitute Italian sausages, diced in same way as brown and serve sausages.

**Cheese:** Substitute ricotta cheese for cottage cheese and provolone cheese for Mozzarella, and, if desired, romano cheese for Parmesan.

**Lasagna With Hard Cooked Eggs:** Hard cook eggs in shell on range top, not in microwave oven. Layer slices of 3 or 4 hard cooked eggs over first layer of cottage cheese mixture. Eggs give an especially rich flavor to lasagna.

## PASTA & RICE CONVENIENCE CHART

Canned or frozen pasta and rice should be removed from metal containers, placed in a casserole or dish of appropriate size and covered. Check at minimum time.

POWER LEVEL: **High (10)**

| ITEM | TIME MIN. | COOK CODE | COMMENTS |
|---|---|---|---|
| CANNED Or use temperature probe and dial 150°. | | | |
| **Macaroni & Cheese, Ravioli, Spaghetti, Spanish Rice, (12 to 15-oz.)** | 3 to 5 | 30 | Stir after ½ time and before serving. |
| **Lasagna (40-oz.)** | 9 to 11 | 90 | Stir after ½ time and before serving. |
| FROZEN **Rice Dishes (10-oz. pouch)** | 6 to 8 | 60 | Puncture pouch and flex after ½ time. |
| **Macaroni & Cheese, Macaroni & Beef, (8-oz. pkg.)** | 5 to 6 | 50 | Stir after 3 minutes. |
| **Macaroni & Cheese Stuffed Shells, Spaghetti & Meatballs (11 to 14-oz.)** | 8 to 12 | 80 | Stir after ½ time and before serving. |
| **Macaroni & Cheese (2-lb.)** | 15 to 22 | 150 | Stir after ½ time and before serving. |
| **Lasagna (3-lb. 8-oz.)** | 33 to 37 | 330 | Rotate dish ½ turn every 10 minutes. Let stand 5 to 10 minutes before serving. |

## JIFFY SPANISH RICE

POWER LEVEL: High (10)
MICROWAVE TIME: 13 to 17 min., total

1 lb. ground chuck beef
1 cup packaged precooked (minute) rice
1 can (1-lb. 12-oz.) tomatoes, undrained, cut up
1 tablespoon instant minced onion
1 to 2 tablespoons chili powder
2 teaspoons salt
⅛ teaspoon pepper

.In 3-qt. casserole crumble beef. **Microwave at High 5 to 6 Minutes,** stirring after 3 minutes. Drain. Add rice, tomatoes, onion, chili powder, salt and pepper. Cover. **Microwave at High 8 to 11 Minutes,** stirring after 4 minutes. Stir well. Let stand, covered, about 5 to 10 minutes before serving.

Makes 4 to 6 servings

## RIPE OLIVE RISOTTO

*Risotto means rice casserole. This combination is colorful with olives and pimiento.*

POWER LEVEL: High (10)
MICROWAVE TIME: 22 to 24 min., total

¼ cup butter or cooking oil
1 cup finely chopped onion
⅓ cup chopped celery
1 cup uncooked long grain rice
2 cups chicken bouillon
1 teaspoon salt
¼ teaspoon pepper

.In 2-qt. casserole combine butter, onion, celery, rice, bouillon, salt and pepper. Cover. **Microwave at High 20 Minutes,** stirring after 10 minutes.

½ cup chopped ripe olives
1 can (4-oz.) mushroom stems and pieces, drained
1 jar (2-oz.) pimiento strips
¼ cup grated Parmesan cheese

.Add olives, mushrooms, pimiento and cheese. Stir to mix well. **Microwave at High 2 to 4 Minutes.** Stir before serving.

Makes 6 to 8 servings

## SAVORY TOMATO RICE

*This casserole is very juicy immediately after microwaving. Stir and let stand uncovered a few minutes before serving. Very good with pork or chicken.*

POWER LEVEL: High (10)        **Cook Code** 230
MICROWAVE TIME: 23 to 25 min., total

4 strips bacon, cooked and crumbled
1 can (1-lb.) tomatoes, undrained, cut up
½ cup uncooked long grain rice
½ cup chili sauce
¼ cup finely chopped green pepper
2 tablespoons instant minced onion
1 teaspoon brown sugar
1 teaspoon salt
⅛ teaspoon pepper
½ teaspoon Worcestershire sauce
2 cups hot tap water

.In 2-qt. casserole place bacon, tomatoes, rice, chili sauce, green pepper, onion, brown sugar, salt, pepper, Worcestershire sauce and water. Mix well. Cover. **Microwave at High 23 to 25 Minutes,** stirring every 8 minutes, until hot and rice is done.

Makes 4 to 6 servings

Cereals microwave in a simple, 1-step process. You don't have to boil the water first, or stir frequently during cooking. Microwaved cereals are easy to clean up since the cereal does not stick to the cooking dish. Family members can microwave single servings of instant cereal in paper bowls. There'll be no dirty dishes in the sink after breakfast.

## HOW TO MICROWAVE CEREALS

**Mix** cereal and hottest tap water in a bowl large enough to prevent boilover. Microwave at High, uncovered.

**Stir** half way through the cooking time. For softer cereal, let stand a few minutes after microwaving.

## CEREAL MICROWAVING CHART          POWER LEVEL: **High (10)**

| TYPE CEREAL | NO. OF SERVINGS | WATER | SALT | CEREAL | CONTAINER | TIME MIN. | COOK CODE |
|---|---|---|---|---|---|---|---|
| | | | | INGREDIENTS | | | |
| **Oatmeal, Quick*** | 1 | ¾ cup | ¼ teaspoon | ⅓ cup | 16-oz. cereal bowl | 1 to 2 | 10 |
| | 2 | 1½ cups | ½ teaspoon | ⅔ cup | 1½-qt. casserole | 2 to 3 | 20 |
| | 4 | 3 cups | ¾ teaspoon | 1⅓ cups | 2-qt. casserole | 5 to 6 | 50 |
| | 6 | 4 cups | 1 teaspoon | 2 cups | 3-qt. casserole | 7 to 8 | 70 |
| **Oatmeal, Old-fashioned** | 1 | ¾ cup | ¼ teaspoon | ⅓ cup | 1-qt. casserole | 3 to 5 | 30 |
| | 2 | 1½ cups | ½ teaspoon | ⅔ cup | 2-qt. casserole | 6 to 7 | 60 |
| | 4 | 3 cups | ¾ teaspoon | 1⅓ cups | 3-qt. casserole | 8 to 9 | 80 |
| | 6 | 4 cups | 1 teaspoon | 2 cups | 3-qt. casserole | 10 to 11 | 100 |
| **Cornmeal** | 1 | ⅔ cup | ¼ teaspoon | 3 tbsp. | 16-oz. cereal bowl | 1½ to 2 | 20 |
| | 2 | 1⅓ cups | ½ teaspoon | ⅓ cup | 1½-qt. casserole | 2½ to 3 | 30 |
| | 4 | 2⅔ cups | ¾ teaspoon | ⅔ cup | 2-qt. casserole | 3½ to 4 | 40 |
| | 6 | 4 cups | 1 teaspoon | 1 cup | 2-qt. casserole | 4½ to 5 | 50 |
| **Grits, Quick*** | 1 | ¾ cup | Dash | 3 tbsp. | 16-oz. cereal bowl | 3 to 4 | 30 |
| | 2 | 1⅓ cups | ¼ teaspoon | ⅓ cup | 1½-qt. casserole | 6 to 7 | 60 |
| | 4 | 2⅔ cups | ¾ teaspoon | ⅔ cup | 2-qt. casserole | 8 to 9 | 80 |
| | 6 | 4 cups | 1 teaspoon | 1 cup | 2-qt. casserole | 10 to 11 | 100 |
| **Cream of Wheat** | 1 | 1 cup | ⅛ teaspoon | 2½ tbsp. | 1-qt. casserole | 3 to 4 | 30 |
| | 2 | 1¾ cups | ¼ teaspoon | ⅓ cup | 2-qt. casserole | 5 to 6 | 50 |
| | 4 | 3½ cups | ½ teaspoon | ⅔ cup | 3-qt. casserole | 7 to 8 | 70 |
| | 6 | 5 cups | 1 teaspoon | 1 cup | 3-qt. casserole | 9 to 10 | 90 |
| **Cream of Rice** | 1 | ¾ cup | Dash | 3 tbsp. | 16-oz. cereal bowl | 1½ to 2 | 20 |
| | 2 | 1⅓ cups | ¼ teaspoon | ⅓ cup | 1½-qt. casserole | 2 to 3 | 20 |
| | 4 | 2⅔ cups | ½ teaspoon | ⅔ cup | 2-qt. casserole | 3½ to 4½ | 40 |
| | 6 | 4 cups | 1 teaspoon | 1 cup | 2-qt. casserole | 6 to 7 | 60 |

*Single servings of instant oatmeal or grits (about 1-oz. pkg.): Follow package directions for amount of water. **Microwave at High ½ to 1 Minute.**

Old-Fashioned Oatmeal

## GRITS AND CHEESE CASSEROLE

POWER LEVEL: High (10)
MICROWAVE TIME: 28 to 33 min., total

| | |
|---|---|
| **4 cups hot tap water** ..... | .In 3-qt. casserole place |
| **1 cup quick grits** | water, grits and salt. **Mi-** |
| **1 teaspoon salt** | **crowave at High 10 to 12 Minutes,** stirring after 5 minutes. |
| **6 tablespoons butter,** .... | .Add butter and cheese to |
| **sliced** | grits. Mix well. **Microwave** |
| **8 oz. pasteurized processed cheese*** **cut into cubes** | **at High 1 to 2 Minutes,** until melted, stirring well. |
| **2 eggs, beaten** ......... | .In 1-cup measure beat |
| **Milk** | eggs and fill to 1 cup line |
| **½ teaspoon garlic powder** | with milk. Add garlic powder and pepper sauce. |
| **Dash hot pepper sauce (tabasco)** | Quickly stir into grits. Pour into well greased 12×8× 2-in. dish. |
| **1 cup coarsely crushed corn flakes** | .Sprinkle corn flakes over top. Dot with butter. |
| **2 tablespoons butter** | Sprinkle with paprika. |
| **Paprika** | **Microwave at High 17 to 19 Minutes,** rotating dish ½ turn after 9 minutes, until set. Serve in squares. Especially good with ham. |

Makes 8 to 10 servings

*1 roll (5-oz.) garlic cheese may be substituted for processed cheese and garlic powder. Reduce final cooking time by about 2 minutes.

## MOLASSES CORNMEAL PUDDING

*Known as Indian Pudding in the New England states. Serve with vanilla ice cream, cream or hard sauce.*

POWER LEVEL: High (10) and Medium High (7)
MICROWAVE TIME: 33 to 35 min., total

| | |
|---|---|
| **3 cups milk** ............ | .In 2-qt. casserole stir together milk and molasses. |
| **⅔ cup dark molasses** | **Microwave at High 5 Minutes.** |
| **⅔ cup yellow cornmeal** ... | .In small bowl mix together |
| **⅓ cup sugar** | cornmeal, sugar, salt, cin- |
| **1 teaspoon salt** | namon and nutmeg. Grad- |
| **¾ teaspoon cinnamon** | ually stir into hot milk mix- |
| **¾ teaspoon nutmeg** | ture. Add butter. Cover. |
| **¼ cup butter** | **Microwave at High 14 Minutes,** stirring every 2 to 3 minutes, until smooth and thickened. (If a softer consistency is preferred add 1 cup milk at this time.) **Microwave at Medium High 12 to 14 Minutes** more until consistency of cornmeal mush. Let stand about 10 minutes before serving. |

Makes about 8 servings

# Vegetables

With microwaving, vegetables are not only an essential part of the meal, they're one of the best parts. Fresh, frozen or canned, microwaved vegetables retain their attractive color, fresh taste and natural texture. Since you add only a small amount of water, just enough to produce steam, you don't drain off flavor and nutrients before serving.

Vegetables with a high natural moisture content will taste more like themselves than you've ever experienced before. Until you taste microwaved corn on the cob, you'll never realize how much good corn taste you discarded with the cooking water.

1. Fresh Broccoli, page 204
2. Twice Baked Potatoes, page 216
3. Squash Combo, page 217
4. Tomato Halves Au Gratin, page 218

## MICROLESSON:

Vegetables should be tightly covered. Vegetables cooked in their skins, such as potatoes, are already so tightly covered, that they should be pricked with a fork before cooking to release excess steam.

Salt vegetables after cooking, or put salt in the casserole with the water before adding vegetables. Salting the tops of vegetables before microwaving causes darkened, dried-out spots.

Vegetables continue to cook after they are removed from the microwave oven, even in the time it takes to serve them. Many of our instructions include standing time to finish cooking and develop flavors. Our recipes are timed for tender texture. If you prefer crisper vegetables, reduce cooking time a minute or two. For very soft texture, increase the time.

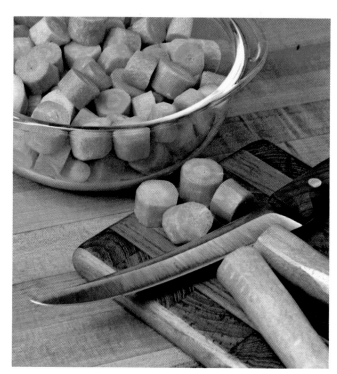

**Small Pieces** cook faster than large ones. Cut vegetables, such as carrots, to uniform size. Unless otherwise directed, vegetables should be tightly covered.

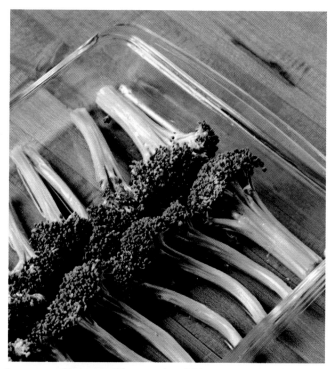

**Large or Uneven Pieces** should be arranged with thinner or more tender portions toward the center of the dish. Rotate dish ½ turn half way through cooking time.

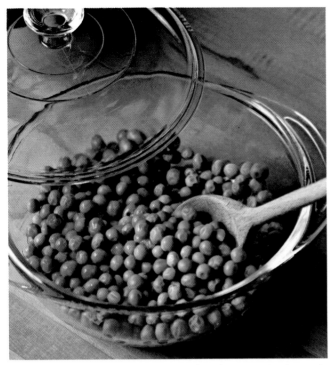

**Stir Vegetables,** either fresh or frozen, ½ to ⅓ through the cooking time. This helps distribute heat. Rotate dish or turn over vegetables too large to stir.

**Frozen Vegetables** may be heated in pouch, package or freezer container. Puncture pouch before heating, and flex half way through cooking to distribute heat.

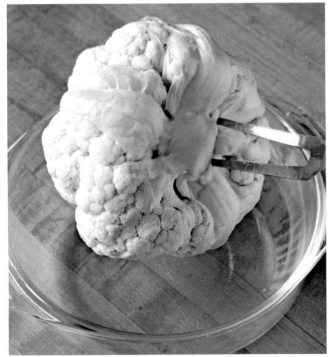

**Whole or Chunky** vegetables should be turned over half way through cooking time. Pierce vegetables cooked in skins, such as potatoes or squash, with fork.

**Canned or Cooked** vegetables reheat without flavor loss. With temperature probe, include small amount of liquid. Place probe tip in center of dish and heat to 150°.

## VEGETABLE MICROWAVING CHART   ■ FRESH   ■ FROZEN

| VEGETABLE | AMOUNT | PROCEDURE | POWER LEVEL | TIME MINUTES | COMMENTS |
|---|---|---|---|---|---|
| **Artichokes** Fresh | 4 medium | Prepare by discarding tough outer leaves. Snip tips with scissors and cut off stems. In 3-qt. casserole place 1 cup water and ½ teaspoon salt. Add artichokes. Cover. Rotate dish ½ turn after 7 minutes. Test for doneness: At minimum time, try to pull a leaf from whole artichoke. If it comes away freely, artichoke is done. | High **Cook Code:** 140 | 14 to 15 | Drain artichokes upside down before serving. Curry mayonnaise is easy accompaniment; mix 1 cup mayonnaise with 1 to 2 teaspoons curry powder. Artichokes are eaten by pulling off leaves and, with teeth, scraping tender green inner leaf; cut heart into chunks and eat. |
| **Asparagus** Fresh Cuts | 1 lb. (3 cups, cut into 1 to 2-in. pieces) | In 2-qt. casserole place ¼ cup water and ½ teaspoon salt; add asparagus. Cover. Stir asparagus every 3 minutes. | High **Cook Code:** 90 | 9 to 11 | If pieces are longer than 4-in. lengths microwave at Medium following technique below. |
| **Asparagus** Fresh Spears | 1 lb. | In 10×6×2-in. dish place ¼ cup water and ¼ teaspoon salt. Add asparagus, arranging thicker pieces to outside of dish with tender tops to center. Cover dish with plastic wrap turning back corner to vent. Rotate dish ½ turn after 5 min. | Medium High **Cook Code:** 157 | 15 to 17 | Larger, more mature stem ends should be peeled. |
| **Asparagus** Frozen Spears | 10-oz. pkg. | In 1-qt. casserole place ½ teaspoon salt and asparagus spears. Cover. Rearrange asparagus after 4 minutes. | High **Cook Code:** 80 | 8 to 10 | No water is needed with this frozen vegetable. |
| **Beans** Fresh Green & Wax | 1 lb. cut in half | In 1½-qt. casserole place ½ cup water and ½ teaspoon salt. Add beans. Cover. Stir beans after 7 minutes. | High **Cook Code:** 150 | 15 to 17 | Tenderness in beans varies. Test beans after 15 minutes to determine if more cooking is needed. |
| **Beans** Frozen French Cut Green & Wax | 10-oz. pkg. (about 2 cups) | In 1-qt. casserole place 2 tablespoons water and ½ teaspoon salt. Add beans. Stir beans after 5 minutes. | High **Cook Code:** 100 | 10 to 12 | For 2 packages or about 4 cups frozen beans microwave 15 to 18 minutes. |
| **Beans** Frozen Lima | 10-oz. pkg. (about 2 cups) | In 1-qt. casserole place ¼ cup water and ½ teaspoon salt. Add limas. Stir beans after 4 minutes. | High **Cook Code:** 70 | 7 to 8 | For 2 packages or about 4 cups frozen limas microwave 10 to 12 minutes. |
| **Beets** Fresh Whole | 1 bunch (5 medium) | In 2-qt. casserole place ½ cup water and ½ teaspoon salt; add beets. Cover. Stir beets after 11 minutes. | High **Cook Code:** 220 | 22 to 25 | After cooking, skins peel easily. Slice or dice and season. |
| **Broccoli** Fresh Spears | 1 bunch (1¼ to 1½ lb.) | In 13×9×2-in. dish place ¼ cup water and ½ teaspoon salt. Arrange broccoli spears with stalks to outside of dish and flowerets in center. Cover with plastic wrap, turning back one corner to vent. Rotate dish ½ turn after 6 minutes. | Medium High **Cook Code:** 157 | 15 to 17 | Larger, more mature stalks should be peeled. As an alternate arrangement place in circular dish, flowers to center, stalks to edges. |
| **Broccoli** Fresh Cut | 1 bunch (1¼ to 1½ lb.) cut into 1-in. pieces | In 2-qt. casserole place ½ cup water and ½ teaspoon salt. Add broccoli. Cover. Stir broccoli after 6 minutes. | High **Cook Code:** 120 | 12 to 14 | Broccoli cooks most evenly cut in 1-in. pieces. |
| **Broccoli** Frozen Chopped | 10-oz. pkg. (about 2 cups) | In 1-qt. casserole place 2 tablespoons water and ½ teaspoon salt. Add broccoli. Cover. Break up and stir broccoli after 7 minutes. | High **Cook Code:** 80 | 8 to 10 | For 2 packages or about 4 cups frozen broccoli microwave 12 to 15 minutes. |

| VEGETABLE | AMOUNT | PROCEDURE | POWER LEVEL | TIME MINUTES | COMMENTS |
|---|---|---|---|---|---|
| **Broccoli** Frozen Spears | 10-oz. pkg. | In 1-qt. casserole place 3 table-spoons water and ½ teaspoon salt. Add broccoli. Cover. Rearrange broccoli after 4 minutes. | High **Cook Code:** 80 | 8 to 10 | Broccoli should be rearranged carefully to avoid breaking tender flower tips. |
| **Brussels Sprouts** Fresh | 1 lb. | In 1½-qt. casserole, place ¼ cup water and ½ teaspoon salt. Add brussels sprouts. Cover. Stir brussels sprouts after 4 minutes. | High **Cook Code:** 70 | 7 to 9 | Trim dry or old outer leaves and cut extra-large sprouts in half before cooking. |
| **Brussels Sprouts** Frozen | 10-oz. pkg. (1½ to 2 cups) | In 1-qt. casserole place 2 table-spoons water and ½ teaspoon salt. Add brussels sprouts. Cover. Stir brussels sprouts after 4 minutes. | High **Cook Code:** 80 | 8 to 10 | For 2 packages or about 3 to 4 cups frozen brussels sprouts microwave 12 to 15 minutes. |
| **Cabbage** Fresh Chopped | 1 medium head (about 2 lbs.) | In 1½ or 2-qt. casserole place ¼ cup water and ½ teaspoon salt. Add cabbage. Stir cabbage after 5 minutes. | High **Cook Code:** 90 | 9 to 11 | Use large enough casserole so cabbage fits loosely. |
| **Cabbage** Fresh Wedges | 1 medium head (about 2 lbs.) | In 2 or 3-qt. casserole place ¼ cup water and ½ teaspoon salt. Add cabbage. Cover. Rearrange cabbage after 7 minutes. | High **Cook Code:** 130 | 13 to 15 | Use large enough casserole so cabbage fits loosely. |
| **Carrots** Fresh Whole | 1 to 2 lb. (see time column) | In 1½-qt. casserole place ½ cup water and ¼ teaspoon salt; add carrots. Cover. Rearrange carrots after half of time. | High **Cook Code:** 120 **Cook Code:** 180 | 1 lb.-12 to 14 2 lb.-18 to 20 | Size of carrots affects cooking time; larger carrots take longer time. |
| **Carrots** Fresh Sliced | 1 lb. (6 to 8 carrots) | In 1½-qt. casserole place ¼ cup water and ½ teaspoon salt; add slices. Cover. Stir carrots after 7 minutes. | High **Cook Code:** 120 | 12 to 14 | Cut slices about ½-in. thick. Old carrots take longer to cook. Diagonally sliced carrots reduce cooking time by about 2 minutes. |
| **Carrots** Frozen Sliced | 10-oz. pkg. (about 2 cups) | In 1-qt. casserole place 2 table-spoons water and ½ teaspoon salt. Add carrots. Stir carrots after 4 minutes. | High **Cook Code:** 80 | 8 to 10 | |
| **Carrots & Peas** Frozen | 10-oz. pkg. (about 2 cups) | In 1-qt. casserole place 2 table-spoons water and ½ teaspoon salt. Add vegetables. Cover. Stir carrots and peas after 3 minutes. | High **Cook Code:** 50 | 5 to 7 | For 2 packages or about 4 cups microwave about 8 to 11 minutes. |
| **Cauliflower** Fresh Whole | 1 medium head (about 1½ lb.) | In 1½-qt. casserole place ½ cup water and ¼ teaspoon salt. Place cauliflower stem side down. Cover. Turn cauliflower over after 7 minutes. | Medium High **Cook Code:** 137 | 13 to 17 | Let stand about 5 minutes before serving. If desired, surround on platter with French style green beans. |
| **Cauliflower** Fresh Flowerets | 1 medium head (about 1½ lb.) cut into flowerets | In 1½-qt. casserole place ½ cup water and ¼ teaspoon salt; add flowerets. Cover. Stir cauliflower after 6 minutes. | High **Cook Code:** 120 | 12 to 14 | |
| **Cauliflower** Frozen Flowerets | 10-oz. pkg. (about 1½ cups) | In 1-qt. casserole place 2 table-spoons water and ½ teaspoon salt. Add flowerets. Stir cauliflower after 4 minutes. | High **Cook Code:** 80 | 8 to 9 | For 2 packages or about 3 cups flowerets microwave 12 to 14 minutes. |
| **Celery** Fresh | 4 cups ½-in. slices | In 2-qt. casserole place ¼ cup water and ¼ teaspoon salt; add celery. Cover. Stir celery after 6 minutes. | High **Cook Code:** 110 | 11 to 13 | Celery is crisp-tender when cooked. |

| VEGETABLE | AMOUNT | PROCEDURE | POWER LEVEL | TIME MINUTES | COMMENTS |
|---|---|---|---|---|---|
| **Corn** Frozen Kernel | 10-oz. pkg. (about 2 cups) | In 1-qt. casserole place 2 tablespoons water and ½ teaspoon salt; add corn. Stir corn after 3 minutes. | High **Cook Code:** 50 | 5 to 7 | For 2 packages or about 4 cups microwave 9 to 11 minutes. |
| **Corn on the Cob** Fresh | 1 to 5 ears (see time column) | In 2 or 3-qt. casserole place corn. If corn is in husk, use no water; if corn has been husked, add ¼ cup water. Cover. If ears are stacked in casserole rearrange after half of time. | High | 3 to 4 per ear | For convenience and freshest flavor, microwave corn in husk. |
| **Corn on the Cob** Frozen | 1 to 6 ears (see time column) | In 2 or 3-qt. casserole place corn. (No additional water needed.) Cover tightly with lid or plastic wrap. Turn over after half of time. Let stand 5 minutes after microwaving. | High | 1 ear 5 to 6 min., over 1 ear 3 to 4 min. per ear | Corn should lay flat in dish. Use oblong glass casserole if necessary. |
| **Eggplant** Fresh | 1 medium (about 1 lb.) 4 cups cubed | In 2-qt. casserole place 2 tablespoons water and ¼ teaspoon salt; add peeled, diced eggplant. Cover. Stir eggplant after 3 minutes. | High **Cook Code:** 50 | 5 to 6 | If peeled, cubed vegetable is prepared ahead of cooking; cover with salted water to retain color and flavor. |
| **Mushrooms** Fresh Sliced | ½ to 1 lb. (see time column) | In 1½-qt. casserole place 2 tablespoons butter or water for each ½ lb. mushrooms. Add mushrooms. Cover. Stir mushrooms after half of time. | High **Cook Code:** 20 **Cook Code:** 40 | ½ lb.-2 to 4 1 lb-4 to 6 | Don't overcook. As soon as color begins to darken remove from oven and let stand a few minutes before serving. If mushrooms are thinly sliced they will take minimum time. |
| **Onions** Fresh | 4 to 8 medium quartered | In 1 or 2-qt. casserole place ½ cup water and ½ teaspoon salt; add onions. Cover. Stir onions after half of time. | High **Cook Code:** 100 **Cook Code:** 140 | 4-10 to 12 8-14 to 16 | Timing gives tender but not mushy onions. |
| **Okra** Frozen Whole | 10-oz. pkg. | In 1-qt. casserole place 2 tablespoons water and ½ teaspoon salt; add okra. Cover. Rearrange after 4 minutes. | High **Cook Code:** 70 | 7 to 9 | |
| **Parsnips** Fresh | 1 lb. (2 to 3 cups cubed) | In 1½-qt. casserole place ¼ cup water and ¼ teaspoon salt; add peeled, cubed parsnips. Cover. Stir parsnips after 4 minutes. | High **Cook Code:** 80 | 8 to 10 | Age of parsnips affects microwaving time. |
| **Peas** Fresh Shelled | 2 lb. | In 1-qt. casserole place ¼ cup water and ½ teaspoon salt; add peas. Cover. Stir peas after 6 minutes. After microwaving, add 1 tablespoon butter and let stand 5 minutes. | High* **Cook Code:** 120 | 12 to 14 | *Fresh young peas microwave best at High. Mature peas (yellow color, some sprouts) should be microwaved at Low Power for longer time. |
| **Peas** Frozen Shelled | 10-oz. pkg. (about 2 cups) | In 1-qt. casserole place 2 tablespoons water and ½ teaspoon salt; add peas. Cover. Stir peas after 3 minutes. | High **Cook Code:** 50 | 5 to 6 | For 2 packages or about 4 cups microwave 8 to 10 minutes. |
| **Peas & Onions** Frozen | 10-oz. pkg. (about 2 cups) | In 1-qt. casserole place 2 tablespoons water and ½ teaspoon salt; add peas and onions. Cover. Stir peas and onions after 3 minutes. | High **Cook Code:** 60 | 6 to 8 | For 2 packages or about 4 cups microwave 9 to 12 minutes. |
| **Potatoes** Fresh Whole Sweet or White | 6 to 8-oz. each (see time column) | Pierce with cooking fork. Place on paper towel on shelf of microwave oven, 1-in. apart. Turn potatoes over and rearrange after half of time. | High **Cook Code:** 40 **Cook Code:** 60 **Cook Code:** 80 **Cook Code:** 120 **Cook Code:** 160 | 1-4 to 6 2-6 to 8 3-8 to 12 4-12 to 16 5-16 to 20 | Potatoes may still feel firm when done; let stand to soften. Dry or old potatoes do not microwave well whole. Peel and dice them before microwaving. |

See page 11 for step-by-step picture directions.

NOTE: When microwaving more than 2 potatoes, moisture can collect in oven. This does not harm food or oven and will evaporate (or may be wiped with cloth) when door is opened. Cook potatoes just until done. Excessive cooking dehydrates them.

| VEGETABLE | AMOUNT | PROCEDURE | POWER LEVEL | TIME MINUTES | COMMENTS |
|---|---|---|---|---|---|
| **Potatoes** Fresh Cubed White | 4 potatoes (6 to 8-oz. each) | Peel potatoes and cut into small pieces (1-in. cubes). Place in 2-qt. casserole with ½ cup water. Cover. Stir potatoes after 6 minutes. | High **Cook Code:** 120 | 12 to 14 | Drain potatoes and mash with electric mixer, adding 1 teaspoon salt, ¾ cup milk and 2 tablespoons butter. |
| **Spinach** Fresh | 10 to 16-oz. washed | In 2-qt. casserole place ¼ teaspoon salt; add washed spinach (no extra water needed). Cover. Stir spinach after 4 minutes. | High **Cook Code:** 70 | 7 to 9 | Water which clings to leaves is enough moisture to create steam for cooking. |
| **Spinach** Frozen Chopped & Leaf | 10-oz. pkg. | In 1-qt. casserole place 3 tablespoons water and ½ teaspoon salt. Add spinach. Break up and stir well after 5 minutes. | High **Cook Code:** 70 | 7 to 8 | |
| **Squash** Fresh Summer & Yellow | 1 lb. sliced or cubed | In 1½-qt. casserole place ¼ cup water and ½ teaspoon salt; add squash. Cover. Stir squash after 5 minutes. | High **Cook Code:** 100 | 10 to 12 | If desired, add 2 tablespoons butter to water before microwaving. |
| **Squash** Fresh Winter (Acorn or Butternut) | 1 to 2 squash (about 1 lb. each) | Cut in half and remove fibrous membranes. In 8-in. square dish or 12×8×2-in. oblong dish, place squash cut side down. Cover with wax paper. Turn cut side up and brush with butter (sprinkle with brown sugar if desired) after 8 minutes. | High **Cook Code:** 100 | 10 to 15 | Wax paper cover is best to hold right amount of steam. |
| **Squash** Frozen Summer | 10-oz. pkg. (about 1½ cups) | In 1-qt. casserole place ½ teaspoon salt and squash (no extra water needed). Cover. Stir squash after 3 minutes. | High **Cook Code:** 50 | 5 to 7 | Ice crystals in frozen squash provide enough moisture for microwaving. For 2 packages or about 3 cups microwave 8 to 11 minutes. |
| **Succotash** Frozen | 10-oz. pkg. (about 2 cups) | In 1-qt. casserole place 2 tablespoons water and ½ teaspoon salt; add succotash. Cover. Stir succotash after 4 minutes. | High **Cook Code:** 80 | 8 to 9 | For 2 packages or 4 cups frozen succotash microwave 12 to 14 minutes. |
| **Turnips** Fresh | 1 lb. cubed (2 to 3 medium) | In 1½-qt. casserole place 3 tablespoons water and ¼ teaspoon salt; add peeled cubed turnips. Cover. Stir turnips after 5 minutes. | High **Cook Code:** 100 | 10 to 12 | If desired, turnips can be mashed with added butter after microwaving. |
| **Vegetables, Mixed** Frozen | 10-oz. pkg. (about 2 cups) | In 1-qt. casserole place 2 tablespoons water and ½ teaspoon salt; add vegetables. Cover. Stir vegetables after 5 minutes. | High **Cook Code:** 90 | 9 to 10 | Lima beans are last vegetable to cook; check them for tenderness. Stir and let stand 5 minutes before serving. For 2 packages or 4 cups frozen mixed vegetables microwave 14 to 16 minutes. |
| **Zucchini** Fresh | 1 lb. sliced or cubed | In 1½-qt. casserole place ¼ cup water and ½ teaspoon salt; add zucchini. Cover. Stir zucchini after 5 minutes. | High **Cook Code:** 100 | 10 to 12 | If desired, add 2 tablespoons butter to water before microwaving. |

**VEGETABLE SUMMARY:** Always add salt to water before adding vegetable. Times here are for just-tender texture. Reduce time a minute or two for crisp-tender; increase time for very soft texture. Remember to allow standing time of 3 to 5 minutes after cooking, if possible. If you cook more, or less, vegetables than described in the chart, be sure to adjust the time accordingly.

## VEGETABLE CONVENIENCE FOODS

| VEGETABLE | PROCEDURE | POWER LEVEL | TIME MIN. | COOK CODE |
|---|---|---|---|---|
| **Breaded Vegetables** 7-oz. pkg., Frozen | Place on plate suitable for microwaving. Cook uncovered. Rotate dish ½ turn after 2 minutes. Breading will not be crisp. Cook conventionally for crispness. | High | 3 to 4 | 30 |
| **Canned Vegetables** | Place vegetables in serving dish suitable for microwave oven. Use about ½ cup liquid. Cover dish with plastic wrap. As a general rule, when heating more than 2 cups of vegetables, check at about half of cooking time. Stir or rearrange to shorten total cooking time Or use temperature probe set to 150°. | High | 8 to 9-oz. - 1½ to 2½ 15 to 17-oz. - 3½ to 4½ 28 to 32-oz. - 5 to 7 | 20 40 50 |
| **Casserole, Vegetable** 8 to 10-oz. pkg., Frozen | Place in 1-qt. casserole. Cover. Stir after 4 minutes. | High | 5 to 7 | 50 |
| **Casserole, Vegetable** 11 to 12-oz. pkg., Frozen | Place in 1-qt. casserole. Cover. Stir after 4 minutes. | High | 7 to 9 | 70 |
| **Potatoes** Baked, Stuffed, Frozen | Examine potatoes to see that mashed filling is encased in potato skin, NOT FOIL. Place potato(es) on plate suitable for microwave oven. Cover with wax paper. Rotate dish ½ turn after half of cooking time. | High | 1-3 to 4 2-5 to 6 3-7 to 8 4-8 to 9 | 30 50 70 80 |
| **Potatoes** Canned German Potato Salad 15½-oz. can | Place food in 1-qt. casserole. Cover. Stir after 2 minutes. Stir before serving. At minimum time food is warm; at maximum time, hot. | High | 2 to 4 | 20 |
| **Potatoes** Instant Mashed | Use utensil size and amounts of water, milk, butter and salt on package. Cover. After heating, briskly stir in potatoes, adding extra 1 to 2 tablespoons dry mix. (Or heat liquid with temperature probe set to 200°.) | High | 5 | Cook Code: 50 |
| **Souffle** 11-oz. pkg., Frozen | To Defrost: Place food in 8-in. pie plate. Stir. | Low | 9 to 11 | 93 |
| | To Cook: Divide equally between 3 or 4 buttered custard cups (6 or 7-oz.). Rearrange after 4 minutes. Souffles are done when center is set. Invert on serving plate. | Medium High | 9 to 11 | 97 |

## COOKING DRIED BEANS AND PEAS

POWER LEVEL: High (10) and Medium (5)
MICROWAVE TIME: See Recipe

1. Place specified amount of beans and water in casserole. Cover.
2. **Microwave at High** to bring to boil, then **Microwave at Medium** until tender. Cooking time depends on variety and amounts. See recommendations below.

## GREAT NORTHERN BEANS

1 pkg. (12-oz.) rinsed beans (2 cups) . . . .In 3-qt. casserole place
6 cups water
1 small onion
½ carrot
½ stalk celery
4 strips cooked bacon, crumbled
2 teaspoons salt
¼ teaspoon pepper

beans, water, onion, carrot, celery, bacon, salt and pepper. Cover. **Microwave at High 20 Minutes.** Stir. Recover. **Microwave at Medium 1 Hour 30 Minutes to 1 Hour 40 Minutes,** until tender. Stir every 45 minutes.

**For Ranch Style Beans:** Remove celery and carrot. Stir in 2 tablespoons brown sugar, 1 tablespoon dark molasses and ½ teaspoon dry mustard. Cover. **Microwave at Medium High 20 to 30 Minutes.** Stir after 10 minutes.

Makes 8 to 10 servings

## PINTO BEANS

1 pkg. (1-lb.) beans, . . . . . .In 3-qt. casserole place
    rinsed
4 cups water
1 ham hock
1 small onion, sliced

beans, water, ham hock and onion. Cover. **Microwave at High 30 Minutes,** stirring after ½ time. **Microwave at Medium 1 Hour 40 Minutes to 1 Hour 50 Minutes,** until tender. Stir every 45 minutes..

**For "Let's Eat" Bean Soup:** Remove ham hock. Cut meat into small pieces and return to casserole. Add water to thin soup as desired. Cover. Microwave to heat.

Makes 6 to 8 servings

## SPLIT PEAS

1 cup split peas . . . . . . . . .In 3-qt. casserole place
4 cups water
1 ham hock
1 rib celery, cut in half
1 small onion, sliced
1 tablespoon lemon
    juice

peas, water, ham hock, celery, onion and lemon juice. Cover. **Microwave at High 15 Minutes.** Stir well. **Microwave at Medium 60 to 70 Minutes,** until tender, stirring every ½ hour.

**For Split Pea Soup:** Dice meat from ham hock. Slice celery. Return to dish. Stir in 1 cup water. Cover. **Microwave at Medium 5 to 10 Minutes,** until hot.

Makes 6 to 8 servings

Golden Stuffed Artichokes

## GOLDEN STUFFED ARTICHOKES

POWER LEVEL: High (10)
MICROWAVE TIME: 27 to 31 min., total

**4 medium artichokes** . . .Prepare artichokes by dis-
**1 cup water** carding the tough outer
**½ teaspoon salt** leaves. Snip tips off. with
scissors and cut off stems.
In 3-qt. casserole place
artichokes with salted water. Cover. **Microwave at
High 14 to 15 Minutes,** rotating dish ½ turn after 7
minutes. Remove and
place artichokes upside
down to partially cool.

**1 pkg. (6-oz.) chicken** . . .In 1½-qt. casserole, com-
**flavor top-of-range** bine vegetable seasoning
**type stuffing mix** packet from stuffing mix,
**with crumbs** water and butter. Cover.
**1½ cups water** **Microwave at High 4 to 5**
**¼ cup butter** **Minutes.** Stir crumbs into
mixture just to moisten.
Cover and let stand.

**2 small carrots, grated** . .In 1-qt. casserole combine
**1 small onion, diced** carrots, onion and oil. Cov-
**1 tablespoon olive oil** er. **Microwave at High 5**
**1 pkg. (3¼-oz.)** **Minutes,** until vegetables
**cashews, salted** are soft. Add these vegetables to bread stuffing
along with cashews.

Force the center of each artichoke open to form a well.
Remove the center leaves and the choke (the choke is
the fuzzy, purple-tinged area covering the heart, or base
of the artichoke) with a spoon. Stuff artichokes with
cashew-carrot stuffing. Rearrange in 3-qt. casserole. **Microwave at High 4 to 6 Minutes,** uncovered, until
heated.

Makes 4 stuffed artichokes

## POPULAR GREEN BEAN CASSEROLE

POWER LEVEL: Low (3) and High (10)    TEMP: 170°
APPROX. MICROWAVE TIME: 12 to 15 min.

**3 pkgs. (10-oz. each)** . . . . .Defrost beans by placing
**frozen French-style** packages in single layer in
**green beans** microwave oven. **Microwave at Low 10 to 12 Min-
utes,** turning over and rearranging packages every
2 to 3 minutes.

**1 can (10-oz.) cream of** . . .Separate beans into 1½-
**mushroom soup** qt. casserole. Mix with can-
**½ cup milk** ned soup, milk and pimien-
**1 jar (2-oz.) pimiento,** to to blend well.
**sliced and drained**

**1 can (3-oz.) French** . . . . .Arrange onions in a ring
**fried onions** around edge of dish.

Insert temperature probe so tip rests on center bottom of
dish. Cover with plastic wrap, arranging loosely around
probe to vent. Attach cable end at receptacle. **Microwave at High. Set Temp, Set 170°.** When oven signals
let stand, covered, about 10 minutes before serving.
Toss to mix, if desired. Makes about 8 servings

Popular Green Bean Casserole

Hot Bean Salad

## HOT BEAN SALAD

*This sweet-sour bean salad tastes even better when made in advance. Reheat before serving.*

POWER LEVEL: High (10)
MICROWAVE TIME: 12 to 14 min., total

**4 strips bacon** . . . . . . . . . .Using scissors, snip bacon strips into small pieces into 2-qt. casserole. **Microwave at High 3 to 4 Minutes,** stirring after 2 minutes. With slotted spoon, remove cooked bacon pieces to paper towels to drain.

**½ cup sugar** . . . . . . . . . . . .To bacon drippings in casserole, add sugar and cornstarch, blending well. Stir in salt, pepper and vinegar. **Microwave at High 3 to 4 Minutes,** until thick.
**1 tablespoon cornstarch**
**1 teaspoon salt**
**¼ teaspoon pepper**
**⅔ cup vinegar**

**1 can (1-lb.) cut green beans, drained** . . . .Add drained beans and onion slices to sauce in casserole, stirring well. Cover. **Microwave at High 6 Minutes,** stirring after 3 minutes. Let compote stand 10 minutes before serving to blend flavors. Sprinkle cooked bacon pieces over top and serve.
**1 can (1-lb.) cut wax beans, drained**
**1 can (15-oz.) red kidney beans, drained**
**1 onion, sliced**

Makes 8 to 10 first course servings or 4 to 5 servings as vegetable

## CHEEZY BROCCOLI

POWER LEVEL: High (10)
MICROWAVE TIME: See Recipe

**2 pkgs. (10-oz. each) frozen chopped broccoli** . . . . .Place unopened packages of broccoli on end in microwave oven. **Microwave at High 4 to 5 Minutes,** turning over after 2 minutes. Set aside.

**2 cups packaged precooked (minute) rice** . . . . . . .In 3-qt. casserole combine rice, soup, milk, cheese, salt, pepper. **Microwave at High 2 to 4 Minutes,** until cheese melts and can be blended easily.
**2 cans (10¾-oz. each) cream of chicken soup**
**1 cup milk**
**1 jar (16-oz.) pasteurized processed cheese food**
**1 tablespoon salt**
**½ teaspoon pepper**

**½ cup chopped onion** . . . .To cheese mixture, add onion, celery, water chestnuts and broccoli. Stir thoroughly. Divide evenly between 2 lightly greased 10×6×2-in. dishes. Microwave one dish at a time. **Microwave at High 12 to 14 Minutes,** rotating dish ½ turn after 5 minutes. Let stand 5 minutes before serving.
**1 cup chopped celery**
**1 can (6-oz.) water chestnuts, drained and sliced**

Makes 12 servings

NOTE: For convenience, freeze one dish of broccoli. When cooking from the frozen state, unwrap, **Microwave at High 18 to 21 Minutes,** rotating dish ½ turn every 5 minutes.

## SWEET-SOUR BEETS

POWER LEVEL: High (10)
MICROWAVE TIME: 18 to 22 min., total

**1 medium bunch beets (about 1-lb.)**
**1 cup warm tap water**
...Wash and remove tops from beets. Place in 1½-qt. casserole with water. Cover. **Microwave at High 10 to 12 Minutes,** until fork tender. Place beets in cold water. Peel and quarter.

**2 tablespoons butter**
**2 tablespoons cider vinegar**
**2 tablespoons sugar**
....Return beets to casserole. Add butter, vinegar and sugar. Cover. **Microwave at High 8 to 10 Minutes,** stirring after 5 minutes.

Makes 3 to 4 servings

## CABBAGE PATCH CASSEROLE

*If you prefer, you may substitute 2 cups homemade Cheese Sauce, page 189, for the diluted cheese soup in this recipe.*

POWER LEVEL: High (10)
MICROWAVE TIME: 20 to 24 min., total

**1 medium head cabbage**
**2 tablespoons water**
**½ teaspoon salt**
...Chop cabbage into small pieces. Place in 2-qt. casserole along with water and salt. **Microwave at High 10 to 12 Minutes,** rearranging cabbage after 5 minutes. Drain off liquid.

**4 strips bacon**
...Separate and place strips of bacon on a double thickness of paper towels which have been placed on a paper or pottery plate. Cover with single layer of paper towel. **Microwave at High 4 Minutes.** Crumble.

**1 can (10¾-oz.) condensed cheddar cheese soup**
**½ cup milk**
...Mix together crumbled bacon, soup and milk until well blended. Pour over cooked cabbage and mix thoroughly. Cover. **Microwave at High 5 to 6 Minutes.** Stir.

**1 can (3-oz.) French fried onions**
...Sprinkle onions over top of casserole. **Microwave at High 1 to 2 Minutes** more, uncovered, until lightly bubbling around edges.

Makes 6 servings

## HARVARD BEETS

POWER LEVEL: High (10)
MICROWAVE TIME: 18 to 24 min., total

**1 medium bunch beets (about 1-lb.)**
**1 cup warm tap water**
...Wash and remove tops from beets. Place beets and water in 1½-qt. casserole. Cover. **Microwave at High 10 to 12 Minutes,** until fork tender. Remove beets from oven and place in cool water. Peel and slice or cube as desired.

**1 tablespoon cornstarch**
**1 tablespoon sugar**
**¾ teaspoon salt**
**Dash pepper**
**⅔ cup water**
**¼ cup vinegar**
...In same 1½-qt. casserole stir together cornstarch, sugar, salt, pepper, water and vinegar. **Microwave at High 3 to 4 Minutes,** until thickened, stirring after 2 minutes. Add beets and **Microwave at High 5 to 8 Minutes,** until hot, or, if desired, serve cold.

Makes 4 servings

## COLORFUL CARROT RING

POWER LEVEL: High (10) and Medium High (7)
MICROWAVE TIME: 26 to 32 min., total

**½ cup water***
**½ teaspoon salt**
**2 lbs. carrots, peeled**
...In 3-qt. casserole place water, salt and carrots. Cover. **Microwave at High 18 to 20 Minutes,** rearranging after 9 minutes, until tender. Drain. Press carrots through coarse sieve with back of wooden spoon, or for more coarse texture run through meat grinder.

**¼ cup softened butter**
**2 egg yolks**
**2 tablespoons brown sugar (packed)**
**1 teaspoon salt**
**½ teaspoon pepper**
...To the sieved carrots add butter, egg yolks, brown sugar, salt and pepper. Generously butter 1-qt. casserole. Place small drinking glass (3-in. or less diameter, 4 to 5-in. high) in center of dish. Pack carrot mixture evenly around glass. Cover with plastic wrap, turning one edge back slightly to vent.

**Microwave at Medium High 8 to 12 Minutes,** until hot. Let stand 5 minutes to set, then invert on serving plate. Garnish with chopped parsley and cooked, crumbled bacon if deisred.
*½ teaspoon chicken bouillon granules may be added for additional flavor.

Makes 4 to 6 servings

## SUNDAY GLAZED CARROTS

POWER LEVEL: High (10)
MICROWAVE TIME: 11 to 15 min., total

| | |
|---|---|
| **1 lb., about 6 to 8 medium carrots**<br>**2 tablespoons butter**<br>**¼ cup brown sugar (packed)** | Wash and cut carrots into ½-in. diagonal slices. Place in 1-qt. casserole with butter and brown sugar. Cover. **Microwave at High 9 to 11 Minutes,** stirring after 5 minutes. |
| **2 tablespoons cold water**<br>**1½ teaspoons cornstarch**<br>**¼ cup pecans, coarsely chopped (optional)** | Mix water and cornstarch until smooth. Stir into carrot mixture. Add pecans. Cover. **Microwave at High 2 to 4 Minutes,** until thickened. Stir before serving. |

Makes 3 to 4 servings

TO DOUBLE THIS RECIPE: Use 2-qt. casserole and double the ingredients. Microwave the carrots 15 minutes, stirring after 7 minutes. Add thickening and microwave 4 to 6 minutes more.

Sunday Glazed Carrots

## CREAMY CAULIFLOWER

POWER LEVEL: High (10)
MICROWAVE TIME: 16 to 19 min., total

| | |
|---|---|
| **½ teaspoon salt**<br>**2 tablespoons water**<br>**2 pkgs. (10-oz. each) frozen cauliflower** | In 2-qt. casserole place salt and water. Add cauliflower. **Microwave at High 5 to 7 Minutes,** until just done. Place in strainer or colander to drain. |
| **1 tablespoon butter, softened**<br>**1 tablespoon flour**<br>**½ cup milk**<br>**1 cup small curd cottage cheese**<br>**½ cup shredded cheddar cheese**<br>**1 tablespoon chopped pimiento**<br>**½ teaspoon salt**<br>**⅛ teaspoon pepper** | In same 2-qt. casserole, stir to mix butter and flour. Stir in milk, cheeses, pimiento and seasonings. **Microwave at High 6 Minutes,** stirring after 3 minutes, until cheese melts and mixture thickens. |
| **½ cup crushed corn flakes**<br>**½ teaspoon paprika**<br>**½ teaspoon dill weed** | Mix cauliflower gently into sauce and sprinkle top with corn flakes mixed with paprika and dill weed. **Microwave at High 5 to 6 Minutes,** until hot. |

Makes 6 servings

## CAULIFLOWER AU GRATIN

*For convenience, this recipe uses herb-seasoned stuffing mix, but you may substitute coarse bread crumbs dried in the microwave oven.*

POWER LEVEL: High (10)
MICROWAVE TIME: 9 to 11 min., total

| | |
|---|---|
| **1 pkg. (10-oz.) frozen cauliflower**<br>**2 tablespoons water**<br>**½ teaspoon salt** | In 1½-qt. casserole place cauliflower in water and salt. **Microwave at High 8 to 9 Minutes,** stirring after 4 minutes. Drain off liquid from dish. |
| **¼ cup herb-seasoned stuffing mix**<br>**½ cup shredded mild cheese** | Sprinkle stuffing mix, then cheese, over cauliflower. **Microwave at High 1 to 2 Minutes,** uncovered, until cheese melts. |

Makes 2 to 3 servings

Corn on the cob is a microwave specialty, see page 206.

## CELERY AND PEAS, BRAISED

POWER LEVEL: High (10)
MICROWAVE TIME: 12 to 14 min., total

| | |
|---|---|
| **2 cups celery slices,** ..... | In 2-qt. casserole combine |
| **¼-in. thick** | vegetables, butter, water |
| **⅓ cup chopped onion** | and salt. Cover. **Micro-** |
| **2 tablespoons butter** | **wave at High 6 Minutes.** |
| **2 tablespoons water** | Stir. |
| **½ teaspoon salt** | |
| **1 package (10-oz.)** ...... | Add peas. Cover. **Micro-** |
| **frozen peas** | **wave at High 6 to 8 Min-** |
| | **utes,** stirring after 4 min- |
| | utes. |

Makes 6 servings

## CORN PUDDING

POWER LEVEL: Medium High (7)
MICROWAVE TIME: 18 to 21 min., total

| | |
|---|---|
| **1 egg** ................ | Place egg in 1½-qt. casse- |
| **½ cup milk** | role and beat well with fork. |
| **1 tablespoon sugar** | Stir in milk, sugar, corn, |
| **1 can (16-oz.) cream-** | crackers and butter. **Mi-** |
| **style corn** | **crowave at Medium High** |
| **¾ cup crushed crackers** | **7 Minutes** and stir well. |
| **2 tablespoons butter,** | |
| **cut in pieces** | |
| **Paprika** ............ | Sprinkle with paprika. **Mi-** |
| | **crowave at Medium High** |
| | **11 to 14 Minutes,** rotating |
| | dish ¼ turn after 5 minutes. |
| | When done, center will be |
| | just barely set. |

Makes 4 servings

## SOUTHERN STUFFED EGGPLANT

POWER LEVEL: High (10)
MICROWAVE TIME: 13 to 18 min., total

| | |
|---|---|
| **1 medium eggplant** ..... | Cut eggplant in half. Scoop |
| **2 tablespoons water** | out insides leaving outer |
| | shell intact. Dice the |
| | scooped-out eggplant into |
| | 2-qt. casserole. Add water. |
| | Cover. **Microwave at High** |
| | **5 to 6 Minutes,** stirring |
| | after 3 minutes. |
| **¼ cup chopped onion** .... | In 1½-qt. casserole, place |
| **2 tablespoons butter** | onion, butter and parsley. |
| **2 teaspoons chopped** | **Microwave at High 2 to 3** |
| **parsley** | **Minutes,** until onion is soft- |
| **1 can (10½-oz.)** | ened. Add to eggplant with |
| **condensed cream of** | soup, salt, pepper, Wor- |
| **mushroom soup** | cestershire sauce, crumbs |
| **¼ teaspoon salt** | and peanuts; blend well. |
| **⅛ teaspoon pepper** | Evenly divide filling be- |
| **1 teaspoon** | tween the 2 shells. Place in |
| **Worcestershire** | 12×8×2-in. dish. |
| **sauce** | |
| **½ cup butter-cracker** | |
| **crumbs** | |
| **½ cup coarsely chopped** | |
| **salted peanuts, if** | |
| **desired** | |
| **½ cup water** ............ | Add water to dish. Cover |
| | with plastic wrap, turning |
| | back one corner to vent. |
| | **Microwave at High 5 to 7** |
| | **Minutes,** rotating dish ½ |
| | turn after 3 minutes, until |
| | hot. |
| **¼ cup butter-cracker** ..... | Sprinkle crumbs and pap- |
| **crumbs** | rika over top. **Microwave** |
| **Paprika** | **at High 1 to 2 Minutes,** un- |
| | til bubbly. |

Makes 4 servings

## EGGPLANT ITALIANO

*This hearty vegetable casserole goes well with plain meats such as roasts, lamb, ham or chicken.*

POWER LEVEL: High (10)
MICROWAVE TIME: 15 to 18 min., total

**1 medium eggplant** . . . . . .Pare eggplant; slice ⅛-in. thick.

**2 cans (8-oz. each)** . . . . .Spread 2 tablespoons to-
**tomato sauce** mato sauce in bottom of
**1 to 2 teaspoons** 2-qt. casserole. Layer half
**oregano** of eggplant, 1 can tomato
**½ cup shredded sharp** sauce, half of oregano and
**cheese, optional** half of sharp cheese. Repeat layers. Cover. **Micro-
wave at High 14 to 16
Minutes,** rotating dish ¼
turn after 8 minutes.

**1 pkg. (6-oz.)** . . . . . . . . . . .Add mozzarella cheese.
**mozzarella cheese,** **Microwave at High 1 to 2**
**sliced** **Minutes,** until cheese has
melted.

Makes 4 to 6 servings

## WILTED LETTUCE SALAD

POWER LEVEL: High (10)
MICROWAVE TIME: 5 to 6 min., total

**3 strips bacon** . . . . . . . . . .With scissors, snip bacon
into 1-in. pieces into 3-qt.
casserole. **Microwave at
High 3 Minutes,** until
crisp. With slotted spoon,
remove bacon to paper
towels to drain.

**¼ cup vinegar** . . . . . . . . . .To drippings in casserole
**2 teaspoons sugar** add vinegar, sugar, salt,
**¼ teaspoon salt** pepper and tarragon. **Mi-**
**⅛ teaspoon pepper** **crowave at High 2 to 3**
**⅛ teaspoon crushed** **Minutes** to boil. Stir in cel-
**dried tarragon** ery and onion.
**¼ cup chopped celery**
**1 tablespoon sliced**
**green onion**

**1 medium head of** . . . . . .Gradually add lettuce to
**lettuce, torn (about** hot dressing, tossing to
**8 cups total)** coat each piece, just until
**2 medium oranges,** slightly wilted. Add orange
**sectioned, each** segments and crisp bacon
**section seeded and** pieces and toss again
**cut in half\*** lightly. Serve immediately.

Makes 8 to 10 servings

*\*Or substitute 1 can (11-oz.) Mandarin oranges, drained.*

## LIMA BEAN SPECIAL

POWER LEVEL: High (10)
MICROWAVE TIME: 14 to 15 min., total

**4 strips bacon** . . . . . . . . . .Place bacon on 2 thick-
nesses of paper towels in
2-qt. casserole. Cover with
paper towel. **Microwave
at High about 4 Minutes**
until crisp. Drain off fat;
crumble bacon and re-
serve.

**1 pkg. (10-oz.) frozen** . . . .In same 2-qt. casserole,
**lima beans** combine beans, apple,
**½ cup chopped unpared** green pepper, water, salt
**red apple** and rosemary. Cover. **Mi-**
**¼ cup green pepper** **crowave at High 10 to 11**
**½ cup water** **Minutes** stirring after 5
**¼ teaspoon salt** minutes. Stir in reserved
**¼ teaspoon crushed** bacon before serving.
**rosemary**

Makes 4 servings

## ZESTY SEASONED ONIONS

*Using this recipe as a guide, try garnishing onions with different herb and cheese combinations, bacon crumbles, crushed crackers or potato chips.*

POWER LEVEL: High (10)
MICROWAVE TIME: See Recipe

**Large whole onions** . . . .Wash and halve onions.
Arrange in dish suggested
below, depending on num-
ber of onions.

**For each onion** . . . . . . . . .Sprinkle seasonings over
**1 tablespoon steak** onion halves. **Microwave**
**sauce** **at High** according to chart
**1 tablespoon** below.
**Worcestershire**
**sauce**
**1 to 2 drops tabasco**
**sauce**
**1 tablespoon butter**
**¼ teaspoon garlic salt**
**1 teaspoon Parmesan**
**cheese**

| AMOUNT | DISH | TIME MIN. | COOK CODE |
|---|---|---|---|
| 1 (2 halves) | 1-qt. casserole (covered) | 4 to 5 | 40 |
| 2 (4 halves) | 1½-qt. casserole (covered) | 8 to 9 | 80 |
| 3 (6 halves) | 2-qt. casserole (covered) | 11 to 13 | 110 |

NOTE: A good side dish with roasted or broiled meats.

## HOT GERMAN POTATO SALAD

POWER LEVEL: High (10)
MICROWAVE TIME: 19 to 22 min., total

| | |
|---|---|
| **4 medium potatoes** | Wash and pierce potatoes through with fork. Place on paper towel in microwave oven. **Microwave at High 10 to 12 Minutes,** turning over and rearranging after 4 minutes, or until tender. Remove from oven, cool slightly, peel potatoes and cut in ⅛-in. slices to make about 4 cups. |
| **6 strips bacon** | In 2-qt. casserole cut bacon in small pieces. Cover with paper towel. **Microwave at High about 6 Minutes,** stirring after 3 minutes, until crisp. With slotted spoon remove bacon to paper towels to drain. Set aside. |
| **2 tablespoons flour**<br>**¼ cup sugar**<br>**1½ teaspoons salt**<br>**½ teaspoon celery seed**<br>**⅛ teaspoon pepper** | Stir flour, sugar and seasonings into bacon fat until smooth. **Microwave at High 1 to 2 Minutes,** until bubbly, stirring after 1 minute. |
| **1 cup water**<br>**½ cup vinegar** | Add water and vinegar to flour mixture. **Microwave at High 4 Minutes,** until mixture boils and thickens, stirring after 1 minute. Remove from oven and stir smooth. Add potatoes and bacon; stir gently so potatoes hold their shape. Cover casserole and let stand until ready to serve. |

Makes 4 to 6 servings

TIP: Not all potatoes are suitable for baking. Dry or old potatoes do not bake well, either conventionally or by microwaving, and are best peeled, cubed and cooked with water.

Hot German Potato Salad

## GREEN AND GOLD POTATO CASSEROLE

POWER LEVEL: High (10)
MICROWAVE TIME: 17½ to 21 min., total

| | |
|---|---|
| **3 or 4 large potatoes**<br>**2 large onions** | Peel potatoes and onions. Slice in ¼-in. slices. Layer in 2-qt. casserole. |
| **3 tablespoons butter**<br>**1½ cups hot tap water**<br>**2 teaspoons instant chicken bouillon seasoning or 2 chicken bouillon cubes** | Dot butter over top. Then pour over the hot water mixed with the chicken bouillon. Cover. **Microwave at High 17 to 20 Minutes,** until potatoes are tender, stirring after 10 minutes. |
| **¼ cup shredded sharp cheese**<br>**1 teaspoon minced parsley** | Uncover casserole and sprinkle with cheese and parsley. **Microwave at High ½ to 1 Minute,** uncovered, or until cheese melts. |

Makes 6 to 8 servings

## SCALLOPED POTATOES

*If desired, sprinkle top with paprika and/or ½ cup shredded sharp cheese after cooking. Cheese melts as casserole stands.*

POWER LEVEL: High (10)
MICROWAVE TIME: 25½ to 29½ min., total

| | |
|---|---|
| 3 tablespoons butter<br>2 tablespoons flour *cornstarch*<br>1 teaspoon salt<br>¼ teaspoon pepper<br>3 cups milk<br><br>*cheese* | Place butter in 1-qt. measuring cup. **Microwave at High ½ Minute,** or until melted. Blend in flour and seasonings. Gradually stir in milk. **Microwave at High 8 to 10 Minutes,** stirring every 3 minutes. |
| 3½ to 4 cups thinly<br>  sliced white<br>  potatoes (about<br>  3 medium)<br>2 tablespoons minced<br>  onion | Layer half of potatoes, onion and sauce in greased 2-qt. casserole. Repeat layers. Cover. |

**Microwave at High 17 to 19 Minutes,** stirring after 10 minutes. Remove from oven and let stand 5 minutes before serving.

Makes 4 to 6 servings

## TWICE BAKED POTATOES

POWER LEVEL: High (10)
MICROWAVE TIME: See Recipe

| | |
|---|---|
| Potatoes | Microwave desired number of potatoes according to chart, page 206. Slice the top from each potato. With teaspoon, remove center of potatoes to mixing bowl, leaving shells intact. |
| For each potato<br>2 tablespoons butter<br>2 tablespoons sour<br>  cream<br>¼ teaspoon salt<br>  Dash pepper | Add to mixing bowl butter, sour cream, salt and pepper. Mix with electric mixer until smooth. Divide potato mixture evenly among shells, mounding, if necessary. Sprinkle with chives if desired. Place potatoes on plate suitable for microwave oven. Potatoes may be refrigerated at this point if desired. |

If potatoes are microwaved immediately, **Microwave at High 1 Minute** per potato. If more than 2 potatoes are microwaved at one time, arrange in a circle and rotate dish ½ turn after half of time.

If potatoes are microwaved from refrigerator temperature, increase time for each potato by ½ minute.

## POTATO-CHEESE HURRY UP

POWER LEVEL: High (10)       **Cook Code:**   90
MICROWAVE TIME: 9 to 11 min., total

| | |
|---|---|
| 1 can (10½-oz.)<br>  condensed cream of<br>  celery soup<br>½ cup chopped onions<br>½ cup shredded<br>  cheddar cheese<br>¼ teaspoon dill weed<br>1 teaspoon salt<br>¼ teaspoon pepper | Mix together soup, onions, cheese, dill weed, salt and pepper in 1½-qt. casserole. |
| 2 cans (1-lb. each)<br>  sliced white<br>  potatoes, drained | Add potatoes and mix thoroughly. **Microwave at High 9 to 11 Minutes,** stirring after 5 minutes. |
| 2 tablespoons grated<br>  Parmesan cheese | Sprinkle cheese on top before serving. |

Makes 4 to 6 servings

## EGGPLANT-VEGETABLE CASSEROLE

*This casserole, known as Ratatouille in Southern France, combines eggplant, green pepper, onion, zucchini and tomato in the classic seasonings of Provence.*

POWER LEVEL: High (10) and Medium (5)
MICROWAVE TIME: 18 to 22 min., total

| | |
|---|---|
| 1 medium eggplant,<br>  peeled and cut into<br>  ½-in. cubes<br>1 large green pepper,<br>  cut into strips<br>1 large onion, thickly<br>  sliced<br>3 tablespoons olive or<br>  cooking oil<br>1 clove garlic, finely<br>  chopped | In 3-qt. casserole, mix together eggplant, green pepper, onion, oil and garlic. Cover. **Microwave at High 5 to 6 Minutes,** or until onions are transparent. |
| 2 medium zucchini<br>  sliced ¼-in. thick | Stir in zucchini and cover. **Microwave at High 5 to 6 Minutes.** |
| 2 to 3 large tomatoes,<br>  peeled (if desired)<br>  and cut in wedges<br>  or 1 can (16-oz.)<br>  tomato wedges,<br>  drained<br>2 teaspoons minced<br>  parsley<br>1 teaspoon basil<br>1 teaspoon salt<br>⅛ teaspoon pepper<br>1 bay leaf | Gently stir in tomatoes, parsley, basil, salt, pepper and bay leaf. **Microwave at Medium 8 to 10 Minutes,** or until vegetables are barely tender. |

Makes 6 to 8 servings

## SPINACH-CHEESE SOUFFLE

*Souffles designed for conventional baking cannot be adapted to microwaving without changing the recipe. One of the "success ingredients" in this recipe is the evaporated milk.*

POWER LEVEL: Defrost, High (10) and Medium (5)
MICROWAVE TIME: 33 to 41 min., total

| | |
|---|---|
| **1 pkg. (10-oz.) frozen chopped spinach** | Microwave spinach in package. **Microwave at Defrost 8 to 10 Minutes,** turning over after 4 minutes, until no ice remains. Remove spinach from package. With hands, squeeze out all juice and set aside. |
| **¼ cup flour**<br>**¾ teaspoon salt**<br>**½ teaspoon dry mustard**<br>**⅛ teaspoon paprika**<br>**1 can (13-oz.) evaporated milk (1⅔ cups)** | In 1½-qt. casserole, blend together flour, salt, mustard and paprika. Stir in evaporated milk. **Microwave at High 4 to 6 Minutes,** until thickened, stirring every 2 minutes. |
| **1 cup (4-oz.) sharp cheddar cheese** | Stir cheese and squeezed-out spinach into hot sauce. **Microwave at High 1 to 2 Minutes,** until cheese melts. |
| **6 eggs, separated**<br>**1 teaspoon cream of tartar** | Beat egg whites with cream of tartar until stiff but not dry. Set aside and, using same beater, beat yolks until thick and lemon colored. Slowly pour spinach-cheese mixture over beaten egg yolks, beating constantly until well combined. Gently pour over beaten egg whites and fold together gently just until blended. Pour into ungreased 2½-qt. souffle dish. **Microwave at Medium 20 to 23 Minutes,** rotating dish ¼ turn every 5 minutes, until puffed top edges are beginning to appear dry and souffle has "set" appearance. |

Makes 6 to 8 servings

NOTE: Center of souffle will remain creamy.

## SQUASH COMBO

POWER LEVEL: High (10)                          TEMP: 200°
APPROX. MICROWAVE TIME: 12 to 15 min.

**Cook Code:** 120

| | |
|---|---|
| **1 lb. zucchini squash (4 medium)**<br>**1 lb. yellow squash (4 medium)**<br>**1 jar (2-oz.) pimiento**<br>**2 tablespoons water**<br>**2 tablespoons butter** | Wash squash and cut into chunks, alternating yellow and zucchini into 2-qt. casserole. Arrange undrained pimiento strips over top. Add water and dot with butter. |

Insert temperature probe so tip rests on center bottom of dish. Cover with plastic wrap, arranging loosely around probe to vent. Attach cable end at receptacle. **Microwave at High. Set Temp, Set 200°.** When oven signals, let squash stand, covered, about 10 minutes before serving. Toss to mix, if desired.

Makes 6 to 8 servings

## PECAN CRISP SQUASH

*Squash is easy to cut into halves if microwaved 1 to 2 minutes at High. Let stand a few minutes before cutting.*

POWER LEVEL: High (10)
MICROWAVE TIME: 12 to 14 min., total

| | |
|---|---|
| **2 acorn squash (about 1 lb. each)** | Cut squash in half lengthwise. Remove seeds and fibrous membranes. Place cut side down in 12×8×2-in. dish. Cover with plastic wrap turning back one corner to vent. **Microwave at High 6 Minutes,** rotating dish ¼ turn after 3 minutes. |
| **⅔ cup butter-cracker crumbs**<br>**⅓ cup coarsely chopped pecans**<br>**⅓ cup butter, melted**<br>**3 tablespoons brown sugar (packed)**<br>**½ teaspoon salt**<br>**¼ teaspoon nutmeg** | While squash is cooking, toss together crumbs, pecans, butter, brown sugar, salt and nutmeg. |

After squash has cooked 6 minutes, turn cut-side-up and divide filling among the 4 halves. Recover with plastic wrap and **Microwave at High 6 to 8 Minutes,** until squash is tender. Remove plastic wrap and let stand 5 minutes until serving.

Makes 4 servings

NOTE: Recipe may be doubled for a party. Microwave squash in 13×9×2-in. dish, cut side down, about 10 minutes; turn over and fill. Recover. Finish microwaving 9 to 12 minutes more.

## YELLOW SQUASHEROLE

POWER LEVEL: High (10) and Medium (5)
MICROWAVE TIME: 16½ to 21 min., total

| | |
|---|---|
| **2 tablespoons butter**<br>**¼ cup buttery flavored<br>cracker crumbs**<br>**¼ cup chopped pecans** | In 1-qt. casserole place butter. **Microwave at High ½ to 1 Minute** until melted. Add crumbs and pecans. **Microwave at High 2 Minutes,** stirring after 1 minute. Pour crumbs onto wax paper and set aside. |
| **¼ cup water**<br>**½ teaspoon salt**<br>**1 lb. yellow squash,<br>sliced** | In same casserole, place water, salt and squash. Cover. **Microwave at High 8 to 10 Minutes,** stirring after 4 minutes, until tender. Drain. |
| **¼ cup mayonnaise**<br>**1 egg, beaten**<br>**½ cup shredded<br>cheddar cheese**<br>**2 tablespoons butter,<br>melted**<br>**1½ teaspoons sugar**<br>**¼ to ½ teaspoon<br>instant minced<br>onion** | Mix together mayonnaise, egg, cheese, butter, sugar and onion. Pour over squash, mixing well. **Microwave at Medium 4 Minutes.** Stir, then add crumb topping. **Microwave at Medium 2 to 4 Minutes** more until center is set. Let Stand 5 Minutes before serving. |

Makes about 4 servings

## TOMATO PEPPER QUICKIE

POWER LEVEL: High (10)
MICROWAVE TIME: 8 to 9 min., total

| | |
|---|---|
| **2 medium green<br>peppers, cut into<br>chunks**<br>**1 medium onion**<br>**½ teaspoon basil**<br>**1 teaspoon salt**<br>**2 tablespoons water** | In 1-qt. casserole place green pepper. Cut onion into ¼-in. slices, separate into rings and lay on top of green pepper. Sprinkle on seasonings. Add water. Cover. **Microwave at High 6 Minutes,** stirring after 3 minutes. |
| **2 medium ripe<br>tomatoes or 1 can<br>(1-lb.) tomato<br>wedges, drained** | Cut tomatoes into ¾-in. wedges and arrange over casserole. Cover. **Microwave at High 2 to 3 Minutes** more, until tomatoes are just heated. |

Makes 4 servings

## TOMATO HALVES AU GRATIN

*For a simple version of this recipe, sprinkle tomato halves with Butter Crumb Topping (right), and microwave as directed below.*

POWER LEVEL: High (10)
MICROWAVE TIME: See Recipe

| | |
|---|---|
| **Tomatoes** | Wash and halve tomatoes. Arrange in dish suggested below, or in microwave ovenproof pottery plate of suitable size. |
| **For each tomato half:**<br>**½ teaspoon instant<br>minced onion**<br>**½ teaspoon sugar**<br>**½ teaspoon sweet basil**<br>**¼ teaspoon salt**<br>**Dash pepper**<br>**1 tablespoon crushed<br>potato or corn chips**<br>**1 tablespoon shredded<br>cheddar cheese** | Sprinkle each tomato half with seasonings. **Microwave at High** according to times below. Time may vary due to size and variety of tomato. |

| NUMBER OF<br>TOMATOES | DISH | TIME<br>MIN. | COOK<br>CODE |
|---|---|---|---|
| 2 halves | 1-qt. casserole | 2 to 2½ | 20 |
| 4 halves* | 2-qt. casserole | 3 to 4 | 30 |
| 6 or 8 halves* | 12×8×2-in. dish | 5 to 6 | 50 |

*Rotate dish ½ turn after half of cooking time.

## YAMS HAWAIIAN STYLE

POWER LEVEL: High (10)
MICROWAVE TIME: 6 to 8 min., total

| | |
|---|---|
| **2 cans (1-lb. 2-oz. each)<br>yams or sweet<br>potatoes, drained**<br>**1 can (8½-oz.) crushed<br>pineapple**<br>**½ cup (¼-lb.) melted<br>butter**<br>**¼ cup granulated sugar**<br>**1 teaspoon cinnamon** | Slice yams into ½-in. thick pieces. Combine with pineapple, butter, sugar and cinnamon in 2-qt. casserole. **Microwave at High 4 Minutes.** Stir. |
| **½ cup coarsely<br>chopped pecans**<br>**¼ cup light brown sugar<br>(packed)** | Sprinkle top with pecans and brown sugar. **Microwave at High 2 to 4 Minutes.** If dish is not hot and topping not melted after 2 minutes, rotate dish ¼ turn, continue to microwave. |

Makes 6 to 8 servings

NOTE: If desired, yams may be mashed with the next 4 ingredients, then cooked. Finish with brown sugar-nut topping and continue to microwave as above.

## BUTTER CRUMB TOPPING FOR VEGETABLES

POWER LEVEL: Medium High (7)
MICROWAVE TIME: 3 to 4½ min., total

| | |
|---|---|
| ¼ cup butter ........... | In small mixing bowl place butter. **Microwave at Medium High 1 to 1½ Minutes,** until melted. Add crumbs and dill weed, mixing well with butter. **Microwave at Medium High 2 to 3 Minutes** more, stirring after 1 minute. |
| 1 cup fine dry bread crumbs | |
| ¼ to ½ teaspoon dill weed or other desired seasoning | |
| | Makes 1 cup topping |

NOTE: Butter Crumb Topping is good with cauliflower, asparagus, broccoli and tomatoes.

## TOSSED VEGETABLE DRESSING

*This unusual tossed vegetable dressing combines crunchy, quick cooked vegetables tossed with savory croutons. As a bonus, each serving is only about 87 calories. Toss just before serving.*

POWER LEVEL: High (10)
MICROWAVE TIME: 8½ to 10½ min., total

| | |
|---|---|
| 2 chicken bouillon cubes ...... | In 3-qt. casserole, place bouillon cubes and water. **Microwave at High ¼ Minute.** Stir to blend. |
| 1 tablespoon water | |
| 2 tablespoons butter ... | Add butter, salt and pepper. **Microwave at High ¼ Minute** more to melt and blend. |
| 1 teaspoon salt | |
| ¼ teaspoon pepper | |
| 2 eggs, well beaten .... | Quickly whisk eggs into hot mixture. Then toss in vegetables to mix well. Cover dish tightly with plastic wrap turning one edge back slightly to vent. **Microwave at High 8 to 10 Minutes** stirring mixture after 4 minutes. Vegetables should be just crisp-tender. |
| 1½ cups finely grated carrots | |
| 1 cup finely chopped onions | |
| 2½ cups (8-oz.) sliced fresh mushrooms | |
| ¾ cup finely chopped parsley, slightly packed down in cup | |
| 1 pkg. (6-oz.) ......... seasoned croutons | Remove vegetables from oven and toss in croutons. To retain best crispy texture of dressing, serve immediately. |

Makes 12 (½-cup) servings

## ZIPPY ZUCCHINI

*Covering the custard mixture during the first 4 to 5 minutes of microwaving helps it to cook evenly and shortens the total time.*

POWER LEVEL: High (10) and Medium High (7)
MICROWAVE TIME: 15 to 17 min., total

| | |
|---|---|
| 4 cups zucchini, cut .... into chunks (2 medium) | Place zucchini and onion in 10×6×2-in. dish. Cover with plastic wrap, turning one edge back slightly to vent. **Microwave at High 7 Minutes.** Drain. |
| ½ medium onion, thinly sliced | |
| 4 eggs, beaten ........ | In large bowl mix together eggs, cheese, pimiento, salt and pepper. Add zucchini and onions, stirring well. Grease dish in which vegetables were cooked. Pour mixture into dish and cover with paper towel. **Microwave at Medium High 8 to 10 Minutes,** stirring and removing paper towel after 4 minutes, until center is set. |
| 1½ cups (6-oz.) shredded cheddar cheese | |
| 1 jar (2-oz.) pimiento, drained | |
| ½ teaspoon salt | |
| ⅛ teaspoon pepper | |

Makes 4 servings

Zippy Zucchini

# Blanching Vegetables

For those who like to freeze fresh vegetables while they are in season, highest in quality and lowest in price, the microwave oven is a great help. It's especially useful to home gardeners, since vegetable crops do not ripen uniformly. You can pick vegetables as they reach the peak of flavor, even if you have only a few servings. Minutes after the vegetables are picked, you'll have them blanched and ready-to-freeze, without spending all day in a steamy kitchen, handling heavy pots of boiling water.

## HOW TO BLANCH AND FREEZE VEGETABLES

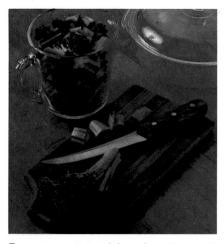

**Prepare vegetables** (wash, peel, slice or dice) as you would for regular cooking. Measure 1 quart or 1 pound of vegetables into the recommended casserole. Add water, as given in the chart. DO NOT ADD SALT. Cover the casserole.

**Set Power at High.** Microwave for half the minimum time and stir. Recover the casserole and microwave for second half of minimum time. Stir again.

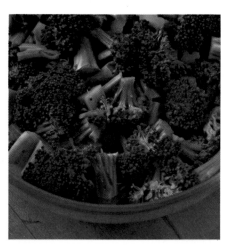

**Check for Doneness.** Vegetables should have an evenly bright color throughout. If all the vegetables are not evenly bright, recover the casserole and cook to maximum time. Drain vegetables.

POWER LEVEL: **High (10)**

| VEGETABLE | AMOUNT | CASSEROLE SIZE | WATER | MIN. | COOK CODE |
|---|---|---|---|---|---|
| **Asparagus** | 1-lb. cut into 1 to 2-in pieces | 2-qt. | ¼ cup | 3 to 4 | 30 |
| **Beans,** Green or Wax | 1-lb. | 1½-qt. | ½ cup | 4 to 6 | 40 |
| **Broccoli** (1-in. cuts) | 1 bunch 1¼ to 1½ lb. | 2-qt. | ½ cup | 4 to 5½ | 40 |
| **Carrots** | 1-lb. sliced | 1½-qt. | ¼ cup | 4 to 6 | 40 |
| **Cauliflower** | 1 head, cut into flowerets | 2-qt. | ½ cup | 4 to 5½ | 40 |
| **Corn on the Cob*** | | | | | |

## *Special Directions for Corn On The Cob

For most even blanching, cut corn off the cob before blanching. Blanch corn cut from 4 ears at a time. Place cut corn in 1-qt. casserole. Add ¼ cup water. Cover. Cook 4 to 5 minutes, stirring after 2 minutes. Cool by setting casserole in ice water, stirring occasionally until cool.

## Cooking Frozen Blanched Vegetables

A 1-pint container holds about the same amount of vegetables as a 10-ounce package of commercially frozen vegetables. To cook this amount, follow directions on the Vegetable Cooking Chart, page 204. If you package vegetables in smaller or larger amounts, adjust the casserole size, amount of water and cooking time proportionately.

DO NOT OVER-COOK. Home-frozen vegetables taste best when cooked to crisp-tender. Cook for a minimum time, then let stand, covered, an additional 5 to 10 minutes to finish softening and develop flavor.

**Plunge** vegetables into ice water immediately, to prevent further cooking. Spread them on paper towels and blot with additional towels to absorb excess moisture.

**Package** in freezing containers or boil-in-bag pouches. Label packages with type of vegetable, amount and date. Freeze.

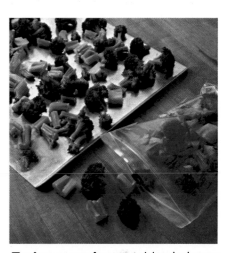

**To loose-pack** vegetables in larger containers or bags, spread individual pieces on a cookie sheet. Place in freezer until vegetables are frozen; then place loose pieces in containers. Seal, label and freeze.

POWER LEVEL: **High (10)**

| VEGETABLE | AMOUNT | CASSEROLE SIZE | WATER | MIN. | COOK CODE |
|---|---|---|---|---|---|
| **Onions** | 4 medium quartered | 1-qt. | ½ cup | 3 to 4½ | 30 |
| **Parsnips** | 1-lb. cubed | 1½-qt. | ¼ cup | 2½ to 4 | 30 |
| **Peas** | 2-lb. shelled | 1-qt. | ¼ cup | 3½ to 5 | 40 |
| **Spinach** | 1-lb. washed | 2-qt. | None | 2½ to 3½ | 30 |
| **Squash,** Summer, Yellow | 1-lb. sliced or cubed | 1½-qt. | ¼ cup | 3 to 4½ | 30 |
| **Turnips** | 1-lb. cubed | 1½-qt. | ¼ cup | 3 to 4½ | 30 |
| **Zucchini** | 1-lb. sliced or cubed | 1½-qt. | ¼ cup | 3 to 4½ | 30 |

For vegetables not given on the chart, refer to the Vegetable Cooking Chart, page 204. Follow directions for fresh vegetables, but DO NOT ADD SALT. Blanching time will be ¼ to ⅓ the regular cooking time. Stir, test and cool as directed in blanching steps.

# Breads

Quick breads really are quick with microwaving. Whether you start from scratch or use a mix, you'll have fresh, hot muffins, breads or coffee cakes in minutes. Microwaved quick breads have an even texture and greater volume than conventionally baked, but they do not brown. Use batters with color, such as corn, bran or spice bread, or a topping. For "up-side-down" breads, butter the baking dish and coat the bottom and sides with topping. Savory or sweet toppings add eye appeal as well.

1. Cornbread Ring, page 226
2. Savory Cheese Bread, page 231
3. Bran Nut Muffins, page 225
4. Stacked Maple Nut Rings, page 228

**Savory Toppings** on microwaved quick breads are shown below in comparison with conventional and microwaved breads without toppings. See Quick Bread Toppings, next page.

Conventional    Microwaved    Crushed French    Crumbled Bacon    Sauteed Onions    Taco Seasoning
                              Fried Onions       & Shredded        & Green Pepper    Mix
                                                 Cheddar Cheese    With Paprika

**Sweet Toppings** on microwaved quick breads are shown below in comparison with conventional and microwaved breads without toppings. See Quick Bread Toppings, next page.

Conventional    Microwaved    Nut-Crunch    Microwaved         Cinnamon &    Chopped Nuts
                              Topping       Toasted Coconut    Sugar

## HOW TO MICROWAVE MUFFINS

**Cupcaker,** especially designed for microwaving, assures good shape and even cooking for muffins and cupcakes; or, make your own muffin cups.

**Cut The Tops** from paper hot drink cups, leaving 1-in. sides. Line each with a fluted paper baking cup. Arrange in a ring on a flat plate.

**Fill Cups** half full. Microwaved muffins rise higher than conventionally baked. Rotate ½ turn half way through the cooking time.

**Test** after minimum time. A wooden pick inserted in center comes out clean. Muffins will appear barely set; there may be moist spots on the surface.

## FLUFFY MUFFINS

*Select a topping (at right) to add color to top of muffins. This versatile quick bread batter is also used for Simple Coffee Cake, page 227.*

POWER LEVEL: Medium High (7)
MICROWAVE TIME: See Recipe

| | |
|---|---|
| **2 cups unsifted** . . . . . . . . .<br>   **all-purpose flour**<br>**½ cup sugar**<br>**3 teaspoons baking<br>   powder**<br>**½ teaspoon salt** | In mixing bowl stir flour with sugar, baking powder and salt. Make a well in center of dry mixture. |
| **2 eggs, beaten** . . . . . . . . .<br>**½ cup cooking oil**<br>**½ cup milk** | Combine eggs, oil and milk. Add all at once to dry ingredients and stir just to moisten. Fill paper lined microwave containers ½ full; see comments. Cook according to chart below. Muffins are done when toothpick stuck in center comes out clean. |

| NO. | TIME<br>MIN. | COOK<br>CODE | COMMENTS |
|---|---|---|---|
| 1 | ½-1 | | For best shape use microwave cupcaker or make reusable "homemade muffin supports" by cutting down paper hot drink cups. Check for doneness at minimum time. Redistribute after ½ of cooking time. If using cupcaker, rotate ½ turn. Rich, thick batters may take longest time. |
| 2 | 1-1¾ | 17 | |
| 3 | 1½-2¼ | 17 | |
| 4 | 2-3 | 27 | |
| 5 | 2½-3½ | 37 | |
| 6 | 3-5 | 37 | |

Makes about 14 muffins

## FLUFFY MUFFINS VARIATIONS

Fold ½ cup raisins or rinsed, drained blueberries into batter (top with cinnamon sugar); or add ½ cup shredded cheese (top with bacon-cheese topping); or add ½ cup chopped nuts (top with toasted coconut).

## SAVORY OR SWEET TOPPINGS FOR MICROWAVED MUFFINS & BREADS

Before microwaving, sprinkle suggested toppings over 12 muffins or a bread ring made with muffin or cornbread batter. Microwave as for Cornbread (page 226) or Muffins (left).

### SAVORY TOPPINGS:

**Onion:** Crush ½ can (3-oz.) French fried onions.

**Bacon-Cheese:** Microwave 3 slices bacon until very crisp; crumble finely. Mix with ⅓ cup grated sharp cheddar cheese.

**Onion-Green Pepper:** Saute ¼ cup each of chopped vegetables in 1 teaspoon butter 3 to 4 minutes at High. Sprinkle with paprika.

**Taco Seasoning Mix:** Use ½ pkg. (1¼-oz.)

### SWEET TOPPINGS:

**Nut Crunch:** Cut together with pastry blender: ¼ cup flour, 2 tablespoons brown sugar, 2 tablespoons butter and ¼ cup chopped nuts.

**Microwaved Coconut:** Spread 1 pkg. (4-oz.) shredded coconut in 9-in. pie plate. Microwave 5 to 6 minutes stirring after 2 minutes and then every minute.

**Cinnamon, Sugar or Chopped Nuts:** Use about ⅓ cup.

## BRAN NUT MUFFINS

POWER LEVEL: Medium High (7)
MICROWAVE TIME: See Recipe

| | |
|---|---|
| **2 cups unsifted all-purpose flour**<br>**1 cup sugar**<br>**5 teaspoons baking powder**<br>**1½ teaspoons salt**<br>**2 cups whole bran cereal**<br>**1 cup chopped nuts (or raisins)** | In large mixing bowl stir together flour, sugar, baking powder, salt, bran and nuts or raisins. |
| **2 eggs**<br>**1½ cups milk**<br>**½ cup cooking oil** | Combine eggs, milk and oil. Stir into dry mixture just until all flour is dampened. Fill paper lined muffin cups ½ full. |
| **¼ cup crushed bran cereal or chopped nuts** | Sprinkle muffins with cereal or nuts. **Microwave at Medium High,** using same directions as Fluffy Muffins. |

Makes about 24 muffins

### BRAN NUT BREAD VARIATION

Prepare batter for Bran Nut Muffins. Pour into well greased 10-in. microwave fluted ring mold. **Microwave at Medium High 14 to 16 Minutes,** rotating dish ½ turn after 6 minutes, until toothpick stuck into center comes out clean. Let stand 5 minutes, then turn out onto cooling rack. Serve warm or cool.

Makes 1 (10-in.) fluted ring

## APPLESAUCE GINGER GEMS

POWER LEVEL: Medium High (7)
MICROWAVE TIME: See Recipe

| | |
|---|---|
| **1 pkg. (about 14-oz.) gingerbread mix**<br>**Applesauce**<br>**Egg, if package directs** | In mixing bowl prepare gingerbread batter as package directs, except substitute applesauce for amount of water called for on package. Add egg if package directs. |

**Microwave at Medium High,** using same directions as Fluffy Muffins. Because this is a very moist batter, maximum time will probably be required. If desired, sprinkle tops of muffins with cinnamon and drizzle with Simple Glaze before serving.

Makes about 2 dozen

### APPLESAUCE GINGER BREAD VARIATION

Prepare batter for Ginger Gems. Divide evenly between 2 greased 8×4×3-in. dishes. Microwave one loaf at a time. **Microwave at Medium High 5 to 6 Minutes,** rotating dish ½ turn after 3 minutes, until toothpick stuck in center comes out clean.

Makes 2 (8×4×3-in.) loaves

Blueberry Fluffy Muffins

## PUMPKIN GEMS

*Gems is an old-fashioned word for small muffins or cupcakes. These muffins keep very well if tightly covered.*

POWER LEVEL: Medium High (7)
MICROWAVE TIME: See Recipe

| | |
|---|---|
| **1⅓ cups sugar**<br>**⅓ cup shortening**<br>**2 eggs**<br>**1 cup mashed pumpkin** | In large mixing bowl beat together sugar, shortening and eggs. Stir in pumpkin. |
| **1⅓ cups unsifted all-purpose flour**<br>**1 teaspoon baking soda**<br>**¼ teaspoon baking powder**<br>**¾ teaspoon salt**<br>**½ teaspoon cinnamon**<br>**½ teaspoon nutmeg** | Stir together flour, soda, baking powder, salt, cinnamon and nutmeg. Add to pumpkin mixture, stirring well. |
| **½ teaspoon vanilla**<br>**⅓ cup water**<br>**½ cup chopped nuts** | Mix in vanilla, water and nuts. |

**Microwave at Medium High,** using same directions as Fluffy Muffins. Because this is a very moist batter, maximum time will probably be required. If desired, sprinkle tops of muffins with cinnamon and drizzle with Simple Glaze before serving.

Makes about 25 gems

**Simple Glaze:** Stir together ½ cup sifted confectioners sugar, 1 to 2 tablespoons milk or hot water, ¼ teaspoon vanilla extract and ⅛ teaspoon salt.

## BASIC NUT BREAD

*To vary this recipe, add 1 cup chopped dates or cran-berries. Best shape is attained when baked in micro-wave fluted ring mold.*

POWER LEVEL: Medium High (7)     **Cook Code:  117**
MICROWAVE TIME: See Recipe

**2½ cups unsifted** . . . . . . . In large mixing bowl stir to-
**all-purpose flour**         gether flour, sugar, baking
**1 cup sugar**              powder and salt.
**3 teaspoons baking**
**powder**
**1 teaspoon salt**

**1¼ cups milk** . . . . . . . . . . .Measure milk into 1-pt.
**1 egg**                   glass measure. Add egg
**3 tablespoons**           and oil. Beat well. Add to
**cooking oil**             flour mixture along with 1
**1¼ cups finely chopped**  cup nuts. Stir until flour is
**nuts, divided**           moistened. Generously
                            grease 10-in. microwave
                            fluted ring mold. Dust with
                            ¼ cup nuts. Pour batter in-
                            to prepared mold.

**Microwave at Medium High 11 to 13 Minutes,** rotating
dish ¼ turn every 4 minutes, until toothpick stuck into
center comes out clean. Let stand 5 minutes; then turn
out onto cooling rack. Serve warm or cool.

Makes 1 (10-in.) fluted ring

To microwave 2 (8×4×3-in.) loaves, divide batter evenly
between 2 greased 8×4×3-in. dishes. Sprinkle remaining ¼ cup nuts over breads. Microwave one loaf at a
time. **Microwave at Medium High 6 to 8 Minutes,** rotating dish ¼ turn every 2 minutes, until toothpick stuck into
center comes out clean. **Cook Code:** 67.

## NUT BREAD FROM A MIX

POWER LEVEL: Medium High (7)     **Cook Code:    97**
MICROWAVE TIME: 9 to 12 min., total

1. Make batter as directed on package, using greased
   9×5×3-in. dish.

2. Sprinkle batter with ¼ cup finely chopped nuts.

3. **Microwave at Medium High 9 to 12 Minutes,** rotating
   dish ½ turn after 5 minutes. Bread is done when toothpick inserted in center comes out clean. Top surface
   appears different from conventionally baked.

Makes 1 (9×5×3-in.) loaf.

## CORNBREAD RING

POWER LEVEL: High (10) and Medium (5)
MICROWAVE TIME: 8 to 10 min., total

**1 cup yellow corn meal** . . In large mixing bowl, stir
**1 cup unsifted**            together cornmeal, flour,
**all-purpose flour**        sugar, baking powder and
**2 tablespoons sugar**      salt.
**4 teaspoons baking**
**powder**
**½ teaspoon salt**

**1 egg** . . . . . . . . . . . . . . . .Add egg, milk and cooking
**1 cup milk**               oil. Beat until smooth,
**½ cup cooking oil**        about 1 minute.

**½ cup finely crushed** . . . .Place onions and cheese
**French fried onions**      in well-greased 8-in. round
**(about ½ of 3-oz.**        dish. Tilt to coat all sides,
**can)**                     reserving excess crumbs.
**1 tablespoon Parmesan**    Place a small drinking
**cheese**                   glass (3-in. or less diame-
                             ter, 4 to 5-in. high) in center
                             of dish. Pour batter around
                             glass and sprinkle with re-
                             served crumbs.

**Microwave at Medium 5 Minutes.** Rotate dish ½ turn.
**Microwave at High 3 to 5 Minutes** more, until toothpick
stuck in center comes out clean. Turn out on cooling rack
or serving plate. Serve warm.

Makes 1 (8-in.) ring

## TRADITIONAL STEAMED BROWN BREAD

POWER LEVEL: Medium (5)          **Cook Code:  195**
MICROWAVE TIME: 19 to 21 min., per loaf

**1¼ cups cornmeal** . . . . . .Stir together cornmeal,
**1¼ cups whole wheat**      whole wheat flour, rye
**flour**                    flour, baking soda and salt.
**1¼ cups rye flour**
**1 tablespoon baking**
**soda**
**1 teaspoon salt**

**1 cup dark molasses** . . .Stir in molasses, buttermilk
**2½ cups buttermilk**       and raisins thoroughly.
**1¼ cups raisins**          Pour into 2 greased
                             9×5×3-in. loaf dishes.

Cover each dish tightly with plastic wrap so bread
steams as it cooks. Microwave one dish at a time. **Microwave at Medium 19 to 21 Minutes,** rotating dish ¼ turn
every 6 minutes. Unmold and let stand 10 minutes before
slicing.

Makes 2 (9×5×3-in.) loaves

# Coffee Cakes

Coffee cakes may be microwaved in a round dish, rather than a ring. The richer, sweeter batter cooks evenly, so there will be no depression in the center. Like other quick breads, coffee cakes do not brown, and need a colorful topping or simple icing to give them a finished appearance.

## EVERYDAY COFFEE CAKE

*Biscuit mix recipe.*

POWER LEVEL: High (10)      **Cook Code:**    50
MICROWAVE TIME: 5 to 7 min., total

| Ingredients | Instructions |
|---|---|
| **1½ cups buttermilk biscuit mix** <br> **¼ cup sugar** | In mixing bowl stir together biscuit mix and sugar. |
| **½ cup milk** <br> **'1 egg** <br> **2 tablespoons cooking oil** | Add milk, egg and oil. Beat by hand, mixing well. Pour into greased 8-in. round dish. |
| **⅓ cup buttermilk biscuit mix** <br> **⅓ cup brown sugar (packed)** <br> **2 tablespoons butter** <br> **1 teaspoon cinnamon** <br> **¼ cup chopped nuts** | Blend biscuit mix, brown sugar, butter and cinnamon until crumbly. Sprinkle over batter and sprinkle with nuts. **Microwave at High 5 to 7 Minutes,** rotating dish ½ turn after 3 minutes. Cool 15 minutes; drizzle with Fine Glaze. Serve warm. |

**Fine Glaze:** Stir together ¾ cup confectioners sugar and 1 tablespoon milk. From tip of spoon, drizzle glaze over cake in spoke fashion.

Makes 1 (8-in. round) cake

**Coffee Cakes** microwave very quickly, and should be checked for doneness after the minimum cooking time. The cake is done when a wooden pick inserted in the center comes out clean. There may be some doughiness on the outside, which will disappear on standing. Drizzle icing or glaze over the cake to finish.

Stacked Maple Nut Rings, page 228

## SIMPLE COFFEE CAKE

*Scratch recipe.*

POWER LEVEL: High (10)      **Cook Code:**    50
MICROWAVE TIME: 5 to 7 min., total

| Ingredients | Instructions |
|---|---|
| **2 cups unsifted all-purpose flour** <br> **½ cup sugar** <br> **3 teaspoons baking powder** <br> **½ teaspoon salt** | In mixing bowl stir flour with sugar, baking powder and salt. Make a well in center of dry mixture. |
| **2 eggs, beaten** <br> **½ cup cooking oil** <br> **½ cup milk** | Combine eggs, oil and milk. Add all at once to dry ingredients and stir just to moisten. |

Pour into greased 8-in. round dish and sprinkle with Topping (below). **Microwave at High 5 to 7 Minutes,** rotating dish ½ turn after 3 minutes. Cool 15 minutes; if desired, drizzle with Fine Glaze (left).

Makes 1 (8-in. round) coffee cake

**Topping:** Blend 2 tablespoons flour, 1 tablespoon cinnamon, 1 tablespoon cocoa, ⅓ cup sugar and ¼ cup cold butter until crumbly.

## MAPLE-NUT RING

POWER LEVEL: Medium (5)          **Cook Code:**    85
MICROWAVE TIME: 8 to 10 min., total

**⅓ cup finely chopped** . . . .Invert 6-oz. custard cup in
   **walnuts** center of lightly greased
**2 tablespoons brown** 8-in. round dish. In small
   **sugar (packed)** bowl, mix together wal-
**2 tablespoons sugar** nuts, brown sugar, sugar
**1 teaspoon cinnamon** and cinnamon.

**¼ cup maple syrup** . . . . . .Place maple syrup in small
**1 roll (10-oz.)** bowl. Coat each biscuit
   **refrigerated** with syrup, then sugar-nut
   **buttermilk biscuits** mixture. Arrange in circle
in prepared dish, overlap-
ping edges.

**Microwave at Medium 8 to 10 Minutes,** rotating dish ½
turn after 4 minutes. Let cool 5 minutes. Remove custard
cup and invert onto serving plate. Sprinkle with any remaining sugar-nut mixture. Serve warm.

Makes 1 (8-in.) ring

## STACKED MAPLE-NUT RINGS

Make two rings, inverting one over the other. Drizzle with
confectioners sugar glaze made by mixing 1 cup confectioners sugar and 1 to 2 tablespoons milk.

## CHERRY CARAMEL RING

POWER LEVEL: High (10) and Medium (5)
MICROWAVE TIME: 8½ to 10¾ min., total

**¼ cup butter** . . . . . . . . . . . .Place butter in 8-in. round
dish. **Microwave at High
½ to ¾ Minute,** until melted.

**½ cup brown sugar** . . . . .Sprinkle sugar over butter
   **(packed)** and add corn syrup. Stir
**2 tablespoons light** well with fork. Place drink-
   **corn syrup** ing glass in center of dish.
**½ cup pecan halves** Sprinkle with pecans and
**¼ cup maraschino** cherries.
   **cherries, quartered**

**1 roll (10-oz.)** . . . . . . . . . .Arrange biscuits over mix-
   **refrigerated** ture in dish in petal shape,
   **buttermilk biscuits** squeezing to fit, if necessary. **Microwave at
Medium 6 to 8 Minutes,**
rotating dish ½ turn after 3
minutes. Remove glass
and invert onto serving
plate. Let dish stand over
rolls a few minutes so remaining syrup in dish may
drizzle over rolls. Serve
warm.

Makes 1 (8-in.) ring

## HOW TO MICROWAVE A CARAMEL BISCUIT RING

**Prepare** topping in bottom of improvised tube pan made
by placing a drinking glass about 4-in. high or inverted 6-
oz. custard cup, in an 8-in. dish.

**Arrange** biscuits over topping and around glass center.

**Inverted** onto a serving plate, the ring has a rich cara-
mel-colored syrup over the top and sides, although the
bottoms of the biscuits are not brown.

# CONVENIENCE BREADS

One of the best uses for the microwave oven is defrosting frozen convenience breads and warming bakery products. The Defrost setting provides rapid defrosting and warming, yet keeps breads tender.

Coffeecakes packaged in foil should be removed from the container. If the cardboard cover is not foil-lined it may be used as a plate under cake. Other breads may be placed on pottery or paper plates before heating.

**Metal Twist Ties** must be removed before package of rolls or bread is placed in oven. Under some conditions, metal twist ties can cause package to catch fire.

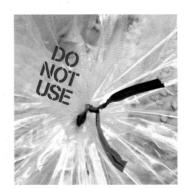

## CONVENIENCE BREADS DEFROSTING AND WARMING CHART
### POWER LEVEL: **Defrost**

| ITEM | TIME MINUTES | COMMENTS | ITEM | TIME MINUTES | COMMENTS |
|---|---|---|---|---|---|
| **DEFROSTING** | | | **Doughnuts** (1 to 3) | ½ to 1 | No turn needed. |
| **Bread or Buns** (1-lb. pkg.) | 3 to 4 | Turn over after 2 minutes. | **Doughnuts** (4 to 6) | 1 to 2 | No turn needed. |
| **Heat & Serve Rolls** (7-oz. pkg.) | 2 to 3 | Rotate ½ turn after 1 minute. | **Doughnuts** (1 box of 12 glazed) | 2 to 3 | Rotate ½ turn after 1 minute. |
| **Coffee Cake** (11 to 13-oz. pkg.) | 5½ to 6 | Rotate ½ turn after 3 minutes. | **French Toast** (2 slices) | 5½ to 6½ | Rotate ½ turn after 3 minutes. |
| **Coffee Cake** (6½-oz. pkg.) | 2 to 3 | No turn needed. | **French Toast** (4 slices) | 9 to 10 | Rotate ½ turn after 5 minutes. |
| **Coffee Ring** (10-oz. pkg.) | 3½ to 4 | Rotate ½ turn after 2 minutes. | WARMING (room temperature) | | |
| **Sweet Rolls, Crumb Cakes, Pull-aparts** (8¾ to 12-oz. pkg.) | 2½ to 3½ | Rotate ½ turn after 1½ minutes. | **Dinner Rolls** (1 to 3) | ½ to 1½ | No turn needed. |
| | | | **Dinner Rolls** (4 to 6) | 1½ to 2½ | No turn needed. |
| | | | **Doughnuts** | 1 to 2 | Rotate more than 6. |

Cherry Caramel Ring

# Breads/Yeast

The microwave oven can be used to defrost frozen yeast bread and, if you wish, to cook the dough. However, its appearance will not be the same as if it were conventionally baked.

Breads cooked in the microwave oven do not brown or develop a crust as they do conventionally because there is no hot air in the oven to dry out the surfaces. Microwaved bread raises higher during cooking than conventionally baked bread, because it does not have a firm crust to prevent it from rising too much. For this reason bread must be microwaved in a larger loaf dish and carefully cooked to avoid forming large air pockets which collapse and cause uneven shape. When properly microwaved, breads look set and dry on top and, when touched, the surface springs back. Toppings provide a colorful finished appearance.

**Toppings** on microwaved breads made from frozen dough are shown at the left in comparison with conventional and microwaved breads without toppings. From the top: Conventional, Microwaved, Taco Seasoning Mix with Cornmeal, Toasted Sesame Seeds, Cinnamon Sugar, Crushed Canned Onion Rings.

**Toast Sesame Seeds** in a small bowl or 10-oz. custard cup, using 1 teaspoon of butter and 1 jar (2¾-oz.) seeds. **Microwave at High 4 to 5 Minutes,** stirring every minute, until toasted. **Cook Code:** 40.

## HOW TO DEFROST FROZEN BREAD DOUGH

**Place** frozen bread in 9×5×3-in. loaf dish containing 1 tablespoon softened butter. Turn loaf to coat dish and bread with butter. (For conventional baking use 8×4×3-in. dish.)

**Defrost** for a total time of 4 minutes, turning loaf over and rotating dish ¼ turn every ¾ minute. Let rise 2 hours in a warm place until double. Top of loaf should be about 1-in. below top of dish.

After defrosting and proofing frozen bread dough **Microwave at Medium 10 to 12 Minutes,** rotating loaf ½ turn after 5 minutes. **Cook Code:** 105.

**Savory Cheese Bread,** created especially for microwaving contains butter and cheese for richness. A topping adds color and flavor. Low shape provides maximum exposure to microwave energy for even cooking.

## SAVORY CHEESE BREAD

POWER LEVEL: Medium (5)     **Cook Code:** 105
MICROWAVE TIME: 10 to 12 min. per loaf

| | |
|---|---|
| **2¾ cups unsifted all-purpose flour**<br>**2 tablespoons sugar**<br>**½ teaspoon salt**<br>**½ cup (¼-lb.) butter** | In large mixing bowl place flour, sugar, salt and butter. Cut through mixture with pastry blender until mixture resembles coarse meal. |
| **1 pkg. (¼-oz.) active dry yeast**<br>**¼ cup warm water**<br>**1 cup milk**<br>**1 egg, beaten** | Dissolve yeast in warm water. Add to crumbly mixture along with milk and egg. Beat with spoon until well blended. |
| **1 pkg. (½ of 2¾-oz. box) dry onion soup mix**<br>**1 cup (4-oz. pkg.) shredded cheddar cheese** | Mix together 2 tablespoons onion soup mix and ¼ cup shredded cheese. Set aside. Add remaining soup mix and cheese to batter. Stir well. |

Divide batter evenly between 2 well greased 8×4×3-in. dishes. Sprinkle loaves with reserved cheese mixture. Cover lightly and let rise in warm place 1½ to 2 hours, just until dough is slightly puffy.

Microwave one loaf at a time. **Microwave at Medium 10 to 12 Minutes,** rotating dish ½ turn after 5 minutes. Let stand in dish 5 minutes.

Carefully remove breads to cooling rack. Serve warm or cool.

Makes 2 (8×4×3-in.) loaves

## NO-KNEAD OATMEAL BREAD

POWER LEVEL: Medium (5)     **Cook Code:** 105
MICROWAVE TIME: 10 to 12 min. per loaf

| | |
|---|---|
| **2 pkg. (¼-oz. each) active dry yeast**<br>**½ cup warm water** | Dissolve yeast in warm water. Set aside. |
| **1½ cups boiling water**<br>**⅓ cup shortening**<br>**1 cup quick oatmeal**<br>**½ cup light molasses**<br>**1 tablespoon salt** | In large bowl, combine boiling water, shortening, oatmeal, molasses and salt. Cool to lukewarm. |
| **6 cups unsifted all-purpose flour**<br>**2 eggs, slightly beaten** | Stir in well 2 cups flour and eggs. Add yeast and beat well. Add flour, 2 cups at a time, mixing well after each addition. Beat smooth, about 10 minutes. Grease top lightly. Cover tightly with plastic wrap. Refrigerate 2 hours or overnight. |
| **2 tablespoons wheat germ or ¼ cup quick oatmeal** | Shape 2 loaves. Place in greased 9×5×3-in. dishes. Sprinkle with wheat germ or oatmeal. |

Cover with plastic wrap. Let rise in warm place until double, about 2 hours. Microwave one loaf at a time. **Microwave at Medium 10 to 12 Minutes,** rotating dish ½ turn after 5 minutes. Let stand 5 minutes. Turn out of dish. Cool on wire racks.

Makes 2 (9×5×3-in.) loaves

233

# Desserts

Your microwave oven can help you prepare almost any dessert, both those you have baked in your conventional oven and those you have cooked on the range top. Candies, custards, puddings, fruits and frosting are usually easier to microwave than they are to cook on your range top. Microwave energy is absorbed from all surfaces, the top and sides as well as the bottom, so less stirring is needed to heat them evenly.

Baked desserts are likely to appear different when microwaved. Brownies, bars and dark batters such as gingerbread or chocolate cake are the exceptions.

Pastries and cakes do not brown, but because they are served with fillings or toppings, the difference will not be apparent when they are served. What will impress you is the time saved by microwaving them.

1. Pecan Sponge Roll, page 265
2. Layered Fudge, page 235
3. Rainbow Pretzels, page 238
4. Floating Islands, page 246
5. White Chocolate Nut Bark, page 237
6. Black Forest Trifle, page 248

## HOW TO MICROWAVE PEANUT BRITTLE

**Stir well** to combine sugar and corn syrup. Stirring this mixture helps it to microwave evenly. Add peanuts, stirring well. Stir again when adding butter and vanilla.

**Stir in** baking soda until mixture is light and foamy. Spread out quickly on greased cookie sheet. When cool, flex sheet to remove.

Munching Peanut Brittle

# Candies

Candies demonstrate many of the advantages of microwaving. Chocolate and caramelized mixtures which require careful attention and constant stirring by old-fashioned methods, microwave with occasional stirring.

## MUNCHING PEANUT BRITTLE

*This is the same old-fashioned recipe which required constant stirring in a black iron skillet. Stir only 4 times when microwaving.*

POWER LEVEL: High (10)
MICROWAVE TIME: 8 to 11 min., total

| | |
|---|---|
| **1 cup sugar**<br>**½ cup white corn syrup** | In 1½-qt. casserole stir together sugar and syrup. **Microwave at High 4 Minutes.** |
| **1 cup roasted, salted peanuts** | Stir in peanuts. **Microwave at High 3 to 5 Minutes,** until light brown. |
| **1 teaspoon butter**<br>**1 teaspoon vanilla extract** | Add butter and vanilla to syrup, blending well. **Microwave at High 1 to 2 Minutes** more. Peanuts will be lightly browned and syrup very hot. |
| **1 teaspoon baking soda** | Add baking soda and gently stir until light and foamy. |

Pour mixture onto lightly greased cookie sheet, or unbuttered non-stick coated cookie sheet. Let cool ½ to 1 hour. When cool, break into small pieces and store in airtight container.

Makes about 1 pound

NOTE: If raw peanuts are used add, before microwaving, to the sugar-syrup mixture, along with ⅛ teaspoon salt.

## ALMOND BRITTLE

Substitute 1 jar (7-oz.) dry roasted almonds for peanuts and 1 teaspoon almond extract for vanilla. Omit butter and add 1 cup (4-oz.) shredded coconut with 1 teaspoon almond extract.

## PECAN OR CASHEW BRITTLE

Omit peanuts and add 1 cup pecan halves or 1 jar (7-oz.) dry-roasted cashews.

# REAL CHOCOLATE FUDGE

POWER LEVEL: High (10) and Medium High (7)
MICROWAVE TIME: 20 to 22 min., total

**2 cups sugar** . . . . . . . . . . .In 3-qt. casserole stir to-
**⅛ teaspoon salt**                gether sugar, salt and milk,
**¾ cup milk**                     mixing well. Add chocolate
**2 squares (2-oz.)**              and butter. Cover. **Micro-**
  **unsweetened**                  **wave at High 6 Minutes,**
  **chocolate**                    until hot and bubbly. Stir
**¼ cup butter**                   very well. **Microwave at**
                                   **Medium High 14 to 16**
                                   **Minutes,** uncovered. Stir
                                   well every 5 minutes. When
                                   sufficiently cooked, a few
                                   drops of mixture will form
                                   a soft ball in cup of cold
                                   water. (Candy thermome-
                                   ter reads 235°.)

**2 teaspoons vanilla** . . . . . .Let candy stand without
                                   stirring, at room tempera-
                                   ture, until lukewarm.* Add
                                   vanilla, beat with spoon or
                                   mixer until it begins to
                                   thicken and loses its gloss.

**½ cup chopped nuts** . . . . .Quickly stir in nuts and
  **(optional)**                   pour into 8×4×3-in. loaf
                                   dish which has been lined
                                   with wax paper (or use but-
                                   tered plate). Cut when set.

Makes about 1 pound

*Or place bowl in a pan of cool water or place in refriger-
ator until lukewarm.

## REAL PEANUT BUTTER FUDGE

Make Real Chocolate Fudge as above, except substitute
⅓ cup crunchy peanut butter for chocolate and butter. If
desired, use coarsely chopped salted peanuts for nuts
in recipe, or omit nuts altogether.

## LAYERED FUDGE

Prepare 2 (8-in.) loaf dishes by lining with wax paper.
Prepare Real Chocolate Fudge and divide between the 2
dishes. Let set in refrigerator while preparing Real Peanut Butter Fudge. Divide evenly over chocolate fudge.
Refrigerate until firm. Cut into squares. (Wiping knife with
damp cloth between cuts best shows layered effect.)

**For Shapely Square Pieces** line loaf dish with wax paper. Use a 14×12-in. strip of wax paper (wax paper is 12-
in. wide so cut 14-in. off roll); fold in half. Fit the 7-in. side
on longest sides and bottom of loaf dish, leaving about 1-
in. "handles" at each edge. When fudge is hardened,
loosen fudge at narrow edges of loaf dish and lift out
fudge in one piece using wax paper "handles". Pull off
wax paper and, with sharp knife, cut into squares.

## HOW TO MICROWAVE FUDGE

**Combine** first 5 ingredients in large bowl to prevent
overboiling. Stir very well when mixture is hot and chocolate melted. Then stir every 5 minutes.

**Soft ball** will form from a small amount of mixture drop-
ped into very cold water when fudge is sufficiently cooked. Line dish with 14×12-in folded strip of wax paper.
Use long ends to lift out fudge when set.

Real Chocolate Fudge

## 2-MINUTE FUDGE

POWER LEVEL: High (10)  **Cook Code:** 20
MICROWAVE TIME: 2 min., total

**1 box (1-lb.)** . . . . . . . . . . . . In 1½-qt. casserole stir
    **confectioners sugar** sugar, cocoa, salt, milk
**½ cup cocoa** and vanilla together until
**¼ teaspoon salt** partially blended (mixture
**¼ cup milk** is too stiff to thoroughly
**1 tablespoon vanilla** blend in all of dry ingredi-
    **extract** ents). Put butter over top in
**½ cup (¼-lb.) butter** center of dish. **Microwave**
**at High 2 Minutes,** or until
milk feels warm on bottom
of dish. Stir vigorously until
smooth. If all butter has not
melted in cooking, it will as
mixture is stirred.

**1 cup chopped nuts** . . . . . Blend in nuts. Pour into
wax paper lined (see page
219) 8×4×3-in. dish. Chill
1 hour in refrigerator or 20
to 30 minutes in freezer.
Cut into squares.

Makes about 36 squares

## COFFEE FONDANT

Prepare 2-Minute Fudge as above, except, omit cocoa
and substitute 1 tablespoon instant coffee granules dissolved in 2 tablespoons milk. Before fondant sets, press
"chocolate shot" decors into top.

## TOFFEE HEATH SQUARES

POWER LEVEL: High (10)  **Cook Code:** 50
MICROWAVE TIME: 5 to 6 min., total

**1 cup chopped nuts** . . . . . Sprinkle nuts over bottom
of buttered 8-in. square
dish.

**1 cup brown sugar** . . . . . . In 1½-qt. casserole place
    **(packed)** brown sugar, butter and
**⅓ cup butter** water. **Microwave at High**
**3 tablespoons water** **5 to 6 Minutes,** stirring after 2 minutes, until thick.
Stir well; quickly spread
over chopped nuts.

**½ cup semi-sweet** . . . . . . . Sprinkle chocolate pieces
    **chocolate pieces** over toffee. Cover dish so
heat melts chocolate. Let
stand 5 minutes. Spread
chocolate evenly over top.
Refrigerate to set. Turn out
of dish and break into
pieces to serve.

Makes about 1 pound

## BROWN SUGAR FUDGE

*Its old-fashioned name is Penuche. When done just
right, it is soft and creamy. Overcooked, it can be dry and
crumbly. It has same soft ball test as fudge, page 235.*

POWER LEVEL: High (10)  **Cook Code:** 170
MICROWAVE TIME: 17 to 19 min., total

**2 cups light brown** . . . . . . In 3-qt. casserole stir to-
    **sugar (packed)** gether brown sugar,
**1 cup whipping cream** cream and syrup. **Micro-**
**1 cup maple syrup** **wave at High 17 to 19**
**Minutes,** stirring well after
7 minutes. When cooked, a
few drops of the syrup will
form a soft ball when drop-
ped into a cup of cold
water.

**2 cups chopped walnuts** . . Let stand until lukewarm,
then beat with electric mix-
er 10 to 12 minutes, until
mixture becomes creamy.
Add nuts and stir well. Pour
into buttered 8-in. square
dish. Refrigerate until set.

Makes about 36 squares

## MARSHMALLOW CRISP

POWER LEVEL: High (10)
MICROWAVE TIME: 2½ to 3 min., total

**¼ cup butter** . . . . . . . . . . . In 3-qt. casserole place
**1 pkg. (10-oz.) large** butter. **Microwave at High**
    **marshmallows*** **1 Minute** to melt. Add
    **(about 40)** marshmallows. Cover. **Mi-**
**5 cups crispy rice** **crowave at High 2½ to 3**
    **cereal** **Minutes.** Remove from
oven and stir until butter is
melted and marshmallows
are well blended. Add ce-
real. Stir until well coated.

Press warm mixture evenly and firmly into lightly buttered
12×8×2-in. dish. Use wax paper or buttered spatula to
press firmly into an even layer. Cut into squares when
cool.

Makes 24 (2-in.) squares

*Or use 4 cups miniature marshmallows or 1 jar (9-oz.)
marshmallow cream (about 2 cups).

VARIATIONS:

**Peanut:** Add 1 cup whole or chopped peanuts, or stir ¼
cup peanut butter into marshmallow mixture just before
adding cereal.

**Chocolate Dot:** After cereal has been stirred into marshmallow mixture, quickly stir in 1 pkg. (6-oz.) semi-sweet
chocolate pieces.

# HOW TO MELT CHOCOLATE

**Chocolate Bits** may be melted in a paper bowl. Cover with plastic wrap and Microwave at Medium or Low. For 6-oz. pkg. (1 cup) microwave 3 to 4 minutes, until bits are glossy but hold their shape. They smooth out when stirred. Chocolate burns easily, so check at minimum time.

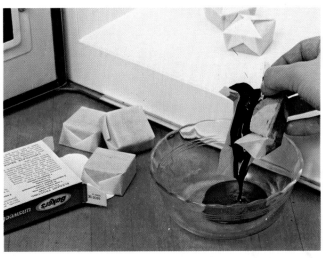

**Chocolate Squares** can be melted in paper wrappers, seam side up. Microwave up to 3 squares at Medium or Low about 2 to 3 minutes per square (1-oz.). For 4 to 6 squares, allow ¾ to 1¼ minute per square. Melt until square feels soft. Beyond this point, chocolate will scorch or burn.

## CHOCOLATE NUT BARK

POWER LEVEL: Medium (5) or Low (3)
MICROWAVE TIME: 5 to 7 min., total
**Cook Code:**     55 or     53

**1 pkg. (12-oz.) semi-** . . . . . .In 1-qt. casserole place
**sweet or milk** chocolate. Cover. **Micro-**
**chocolate, broken or** **wave at Medium or Low 5**
**in squares** **to 7 Minutes.** Stir well.

**1 cup whole toasted** . . . . .Stir nuts into chocolate.
**almonds or coarsely** Place a piece of wax paper
**chopped Brazil nuts** on small cookie sheet.
Spread chocolate mixture
in a thin layer over wax paper. Refrigerate until firm,
about 1 hour. Break into
pieces.

Makes about ¾ pound

VARIATIONS:

1. Use 16-oz. white chocolate and melt in 1½-qt. casserole 5 to 6 minutes. Good with whole almonds in above recipe.

2. Any number of variations of chocolate and other ingredients are good: Cashews and semi-sweet chocolate, raisins and milk chocolate, even other dried fruits such as apricots and white chocolate. Candied cherries with white or milk chocolate are colorful for Christmas. Milk chocolate and peanuts is an all-time favorite combination.

## ROCKY ROAD CANDY

POWER LEVEL: Medium (5) or Low (3)
MICROWAVE TIME: 5 to 7 min., total
**Cook Code:**     55 or     53

**1 pkg. (12-oz.) semi-** . . . . . .In 2-qt. casserole place
**sweet chocolate** chocolate and butter. Cov-
**pieces** er. **Microwave at Medium**
**¼ cup butter** **or Low 5 to 7 Minutes,** until chocolate and butter
can be stirred smooth.

**1 pkg. (10-oz.)** . . . . . . . . . .Add marshmallows and
**miniature** nuts blending well. Spread
**marshmallows** evenly in greased 8-in.
**½ cup chopped nuts** square dish or pan. Refrigerate until firm. Cut in
squares.

Makes about 25 squares

## CHOCOLATE RAISIN NUT CLUSTERS

POWER LEVEL: Low (3)                    **Cook Code:**     43
MICROWAVE TIME: 4 to 5 min., total

**1 pkg. (6-oz.) semi-** . . . . . . .In 1½-qt. casserole place
**sweet chocolate bits** chocolate, peanuts and
**1 cup salted jumbo** raisins. Cover. **Microwave**
**peanuts** **at Low 4 to 5 Minutes,** or
**1 cup seedless raisins** until chocolate is melted.

Stir mixture until chocolate covers peanuts and raisins. Drop by teaspoonfuls onto wax paper. Chill until firm.

Makes about 24 pieces

## S'MORES

POWER LEVEL: High (10)
MICROWAVE TIME: ¼ min., per S'More

| | |
|---|---|
| **2 graham cracker squares** | On paper napkin place 1 graham cracker square. Top with chocolate and marshmallow. **Microwave at High ¼ Minute,** or until marshmallow puffs. Place remaining cracker over top and eat like a sandwich. |
| **½ plain chocolate bar (1.15-oz.)** | |
| **1 large marshmallow** | |

Makes 1 S'More

## RAINBOW PRETZELS

POWER LEVEL: Medium (5)      **Cook Code:**   35
MICROWAVE TIME: 3 to 4 min., total

| | |
|---|---|
| **½ lb. white chocolate** | In 1-qt. casserole place chocolate, syrup, butter and water. Cover. **Microwave at Medium 3 to 4 Minutes,** until melted. Stir well, until smooth. |
| **2 tablespoons white corn syrup** | |
| **2 tablespoons butter** | |
| **1 tablespoon water** | |
| **Food coloring** | Prepare up to 2 colors of Rainbow Pretzels per batch. Tint with food coloring as desired. |
| **Miniature pretzel twists** | Dip "mini-size" pretzels into mixture, removing excess. Place on cooling rack over wax paper to dry. |

Makes about 1 cup, or enough to cover about 50 to 60 miniature pretzels

NOTE: If mixture becomes firm, **Microwave at Medium ½ to 1 Minute,** stirring smooth and adding a few drops of water if necessary.

## CHOCOLATE CHOW MEIN "HAYSTACKS"

POWER LEVEL: Medium (5) or Low (3)
MICROWAVE TIME: 4 to 5½ min., total
                                **Cook Code:**   45 or 43

| | |
|---|---|
| **1 pkg. (6-oz.) semi-sweet chocolate pieces** | In 3-qt. casserole or large bowl place chocolate pieces. Cover with lid or plastic wrap. **Microwave at Medium or Low 4 to 5½ Minutes,** until melted. |
| **1 can (3-oz.) chow mein noodles** | Stir chocolate smooth. Add noodles and, using 2 forks, toss to coat well. On strips of foil or wax paper form into 1½-in. clusters. Cool to set. |

Makes about 24 1½-in. "Haystacks"

## CHOCOLATE COVERED RUM BALLS

*Some people call these "rumbles". Stale, unfrosted cake, finely crumbled, is even better than wafer crumbs.*

POWER LEVEL: Low (3)            **Cook Code:**   53
MICROWAVE TIME: 5 to 6 min., total

| | |
|---|---|
| **2 cups fine vanilla wafer crumbs** | In mixing bowl place crumbs, nuts, butter and rum. Stir together well. Shape mixture into 1-in. balls. Refrigerate while melting chocolate. |
| **1 cup finely chopped nuts** | |
| **¼ cup butter, melted** | |
| **¼ cup rum** | |
| **6 squares semi-sweet chocolate** | In 1-qt. casserole place chocolate. Cover. **Microwave at Low 5 to 6 Minutes,** until melted. Stir. |

Dip balls into chocolate, coating well but removing excess chocolate. Excess chocolate can be removed by holding dipped ball on a fork and tapping on side of dish so excess chocolate drops into dish. Place on wax paper lined cookie sheet and refrigerate until set.

Makes about 36 rum balls

## CHOCOLATE FONDUE

POWER LEVEL: Medium (5)
MICROWAVE TIME: 8 to 10 min., total

| | |
|---|---|
| **4 squares (1-oz. each) unsweetened or semi-sweet chocolate (see note)** | In 1-qt. casserole place chocolate and half & half. **Microwave at Medium 5 to 6 Minutes,** or until chocolate melts. Stir well. |
| **1 cup (8-oz.) dairy half & half** | |
| **1 cup sugar** | Add sugar and vanilla. **Microwave at Medium 3 to 4 Minutes,** or until sugar is dissolved. |
| **½ teaspoon vanilla extract** | |

Serve immediately or transfer mixture to fondue pot. Serve with marshmallows, apple, pear, banana or pineapple chunks, strawberries, cherries, ladyfingers, cubes of firm pound cake or angel food cake, or cookies.

Makes 2 cups of fondue

NOTE: If you plan to use sweet dippers such as marshmallows or cookies, use unsweetened chocolate in fondue. If you plan to use fruits, use semi-sweet chocolate in fondue. To eat, spear the "dipper" on a fork and dip into fondue. Let excess drip off into pot, then eat. Kids will enjoy dipping firm cookies into fondue with their fingers.

# Fruit Desserts

Pound Cake

Fruits microwave tender but still crisp, retain their fresh flavor, texture, color and shape. One reason for the flavor retention of microwaved fruit is the shorter cooking time. Another is that fruit is microwaved with little or no water, which intensifies the flavor of both fruit and juice.

## DEFROSTING CHART

Properly defrosted fruit should be cold, firm and slightly icy for best flavor and texture. Remove any metal or foil from package and, if necessary, place fruit in a casserole. Be sure to check at minimum time and break up with a fork. Flex package to speed defrosting of fruit frozen in plastic pouches.

| TYPE | POWER LEVEL | TIME MIN. | COOK CODE |
|---|---|---|---|
| **Fruit** (10 to 16-oz. pkg.) | Defrost | 5-10 | 53 |
| **Fruit,** plastic pouch (1 or 2 10-oz. pkgs.) | Defrost | 5-8 | 53 |
| **Escalloped Apples** (12-oz. pkg.) | High | 6-8, covered | 60 |

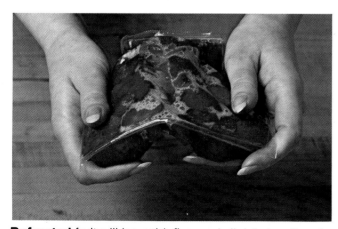

**Defrosted** fruit will be cold, firm and slightly icy. Pouch will be flexible and juices liquid.

## QUICK STRAWBERRIES AND POUND CAKE DESSERT

*Three separate defrostings make one good and easy assembled dessert.*

POWER LEVEL: Defrost
MICROWAVE TIME: 9 to 12 min., total

**1 frozen, baked, pound cake (about 12-oz.), unfrosted** . . . Place cake on microwave ovenproof plate or board. **Microwave at Defrost 2 Minutes.** Let stand while defrosting berries.

**2 pkg. (10-oz. each) frozen strawberries in plastic pouch** . . . . . Place unopened packages on microwave oven shelf. **Microwave at Defrost 5 to 8 Minutes,** removing from boxes and flexing packages after 3 minutes.

**1 pkg. (9-oz.) commercially frozen whipped topping** . . . . . . . . . . . Place topping container on microwave oven shelf. **Microwave at Defrost 2 Minutes,** turning over after 1 minute.

To serve, slice cake and serve slices topped with strawberries and whipped topping.

Makes 6 to 8 servings

Baked Apple

## BAKED APPLES OR PEARS

*The chart below is a good guide to time but because fruit varies, time may vary too. Small, juicy apples and pears cook faster than larger, drier ones.*

POWER LEVEL: High (10)
MICROWAVE TIME: See Recipe

**Large whole apples or** . . . . Core apples or pears. Slit
    **pears\*** through skin around center of each fruit to prevent bursting. Arrange in casserole, see chart below.

**For each fruit:** . . . . . . . . . Fill each fruit core with
**2 tablespoons brown** brown sugar, cinnamon
    **sugar** and butter. Pour total
**⅛ teaspoon cinnamon** amount of water around
**1 teaspoon butter** fruit. Cover casserole. **Mi-**
**2 tablespoons water** **crowave at High** according to chart below.

\*Peel pears before microwaving.

| NO. OF FRUIT | CASSEROLE SIZE | TIME MIN. | COOK CODE |
|---|---|---|---|
| 1 | 1-qt. | 2 to 4 | 20 |
| 2 | 1½-qt. | 4 to 5½ | 40 |
| 3 | 2-qt. | 6 to 8 | 60 |
| 4 | 2-qt. | 9 to 10 | 90 |

## APPLESAUCE

POWER LEVEL: High (10)      **Cook Code:**   70
MICROWAVE TIME: 7 to 8 min., total

**6 apples, pared, cored** . . .In 2-qt. casserole place
    **and quartered** apples with water. Cover.
**¼ cup water** **Microwave at High 7 to 8 Minutes,** until fork-tender.

**⅓ cup sugar** . . . . . . . . . . .Into blender container,
**⅛ teaspoon salt** place apple mixture, sug-
**⅛ teaspoon cinnamon,** ar, salt and spices, if desir-
    **nutmeg or cloves** ed.Blend until smooth.
    **(optional)**

Makes 3 to 4 cups

If blender is unavailable, mash with potato masher or put apples through ricer.

## STREUSELED APPLES

*Known conventionally as Apple Crisp. Vary this recipe by substituting other fresh or canned fruits for apples.*

POWER LEVEL: High (10)      **Cook Code:**   90
MICROWAVE TIME: 9 to 12 min., total

**6 cups sliced, peeled** . . . .In 8-in. square dish place
    **apples** apples and sugar.
**¾ cup brown sugar**
    **(packed)**

**½ cup unsifted** . . . . . . . . . .With pastry blender mix
    **all-purpose flour** flour, sugar, oats, butter
**⅓ cup brown sugar** and cinnamon until crumb-
    **(packed)** ly. Sprinkle over top of
**⅓ cup quick-cooking** apples.
    **oats**
**¼ cup butter**
**½ teaspoon cinnamon**

**Microwave at High 9 to 12 Minutes,** rotating dish ½ turn after 5 minutes. Let stand few minutes before serving.

Makes 6 to 8 servings

## STEWED PEARS OR APPLES

*Juice bubbles up high. Be sure to use large casserole.*

POWER LEVEL: High (10)      **Cook Code:**   90
MICROWAVE TIME: 9 to 10 min., total

**¾ cup sugar** . . . . . . . . . . . .In 3-qt. casserole mix to-
**¼ cup light corn syrup** gether sugar and syrup.
**6 pears or apples,** Gently mix in fruit.
    **pared, cored, halved**

Cover. **Microwave at High 9 to 10 Minutes,** stirring gently after 5 minutes.

Makes 3 to 6 servings

# BUTTERSCOTCH BANANAS

POWER LEVEL: High (10)
MICROWAVE TIME: 5 to 7 min., total

| | |
|---|---|
| **½ cup brown sugar (packed)**<br>**¼ cup rum**<br>**¼ cup butter** | In 1½-qt. casserole stir together brown sugar and rum. Add butter. Cover. **Microwave at High 4 to 5 Minutes,** stirring after 2 minutes, until sugar is dissolved. |
| **2 large ripe, firm bananas** | Cut bananas lengthwise, then crosswise so there are 8 pieces. Add to syrup, stirring to coat each piece. **Microwave at High 1 to 2 Minutes,** until hot. Serve over ice cream. |

Makes 4 servings

# CHERRIES JUBILEE

POWER LEVEL: High (10)
MICROWAVE TIME: 5½ to 6½ min., total

| | |
|---|---|
| **2 cans (16-oz. each) dark sweet cherries**<br>**3 tablespoons cornstarch**<br>**1 tablespoon lemon juice**<br>**1 teaspoon grated lemon rind**<br>**¾ cup sugar** | Into 2-qt. casserole drain cherry syrup. Stir in cornstarch, lemon juice, rind and sugar. **Microwave at High 5 to 6 Minutes,** stirring after 3 minutes, until sauce begins to thicken. Add cherries, stirring well. |
| **½ cup brandy** | Measure brandy into glass measure. **Microwave at High ½ Minute.** |

Pour 1 tablespoon heated brandy into metal tablespoon and remaining brandy over top of cherries. Ignite brandy in the tablespoon and pour over cherries. When flame has subsided, serve over ice cream.

Makes 8 to 10 servings

# STEWED DRIED FRUIT

POWER LEVEL: High (10)          **Cook Code:**    80
MICROWAVE TIME: 8 to 11 min., total

| | |
|---|---|
| **1 pkg. (12 to 16-oz.) dried apricots or prunes**<br>**¼ cup sugar (optional)**<br>**2 cups water** | In 1½-qt. casserole place fruit, sugar (if desired), and water. Cover. **Microwave at High 8 to 11 Minutes,** until tender. Serve warm or cold. |

Makes about 6 to 8 servings

# EASY FRUIT PUDDING

POWER LEVEL: High (10)
MICROWAVE TIME: 15 to 17 min., total

| | |
|---|---|
| **1 can (20 to 22-oz.) cherry, blueberry, apple or other prepared fruit pie filling** | Spread pie filling in 8-in. square dish. **Microwave at High 4 Minutes,** stirring after 2 minutes, until heated through. |
| **1 box (about 9-oz.) 1-layer cake mix (white, yellow or spice)**<br>**¼ cup cold butter, thinly sliced** | Sprinkle dry cake mix evenly over fruit. Distribute butter slices over top. |
| **2 tablespoons sugar mixed with 1 teaspoon cinnamon, or, ¼ cup finely chopped nuts** | Sprinkle cinnamon sugar or chopped nuts evenly over top. |

**Microwave at High 11 to 13 Minutes,** rotating dish ½ turn after 6 minutes. Serve warm with ice cream, if desired.

Makes 6 servings

# ALL SEASONS FRUIT COMPOTE

*This is a tangy, rather than sweet, fruit compote. It may also be served as a meat accompaniment.*

POWER LEVEL: High (10)                        TEMP:  160°
APPROX. MICROWAVE TIME: 14 to 16 min.
                                          **Cook Code:**   140

| | |
|---|---|
| **1 pkg. (12-oz.) dried apricots**<br>**1 can (1-lb.) sliced peaches, drained**<br>**1 can (16-oz.) pitted bing cherries, undrained**<br>**¾ cup brown sugar (packed)**<br>**½ cup orange juice**<br>**1 tablespoon grated orange peel**<br>**¼ cup lemon juice**<br>**1 tablespoon grated lemon peel** | In 2-qt. casserole place apricots and peaches. Drain cherry juice into small bowl. Add cherries to other fruit. To cherry juice add brown sugar, orange juice and peel, lemon juice and peel. Stir well. Pour over fruit. Insert temperature probe so tip is in center of food. Cover with plastic wrap, arranging loosely around probe to vent. |

Attach cable end at receptable. **Microwave at High. Set Temp, Set 160°.**

When oven signals, remove from oven and stir. Recover compote and chill overnight. Serve with garnish of sour cream, or omit garnish and serve with meat.

Makes 8 to 10 servings

## FLAMING PEACHES

POWER LEVEL: High (10)
MICROWAVE TIME: 4¼ to 5¾ min., total

| | |
|---|---|
| **4 large fresh peaches, or 1 can (29-oz.) peach halves** | Peel and halve peaches and remove pits. In 10× 6×2-in. dish place peaches cut side up. For canned fruit, drain syrup, reserving 1 tablespoon. |
| **¼ cup apricot jam** **3 tablespoons sugar** **1 tablespoon peach syrup or water** **2 teaspoons lemon juice** | In 1-cup glass measure place jam, sugar, syrup and juice. **Microwave at High 1 to 1½ Minutes,** or until sugar dissolves. Mix well. Pour over peaches. |
| **8 teaspoons currant jelly** **8 tablespoons macaroon crumbs** | Place 1 teaspoon currant jelly and 1 tablespoon macaroon crumbs on each peach half. **Microwave at High 3 to 4 Minutes.** |
| **¼ cup brandy** | Measure brandy into 1-cup glass measuring cup and **Microwave at High ¼ Minute.** Remove 1 metal tablespoonful. Pour rest of brandy over peaches. Ignite brandy in spoon and pour over peaches to flame. Serve peaches hot with ice cream if desired. |

*Makes 8 servings*

## STRAWBERRIES HAWAIIAN

*Serve as a sauce for ice cream and pineapple chunks.*

POWER LEVEL: High (10)
MICROWAVE TIME: 8½ to 9½ min., total

| | |
|---|---|
| **1 pkg. (10-oz.) frozen sliced strawberries** **½ cup red currant jelly** | In 1½-qt. casserole place berries. **Microwave at High 2½ to 3½ Minutes,** until defrosted. Mash with spoon. Add jelly. Cover. **Microwave at High 4 Minutes,** or until boiling. |
| **2 tablespoons cornstarch** **2 tablespoons rum or syrup from canned pineapple** | Mix cornstarch with rum or syrup. Add to hot strawberries. Stir well. Cover. **Microwave at High 2 Minutes** more, until thick. |

*Makes about 1½ cups*

## COLD LIME SOUFFLE

*To prepare limes, first grate the rind, then squeeze out the juice. This souffle mixture also makes an excellent chiffon pie filling and the lime version here is often known as Key Lime Pie when piled into a 9-in. shell.*

POWER LEVEL: Medium High (7)    **Cook Code:** 67
MICROWAVE TIME: 6 to 8 min., total

| | |
|---|---|
| **1½ tablespoons gelatin** **½ cup sugar** **4 egg yolks** **½ cup fresh lime juice (5 limes)** | In 1-qt. measure stir together gelatin and sugar. Beat in egg yolks and lime juice. **Microwave at Medium High 6 to 8 Minutes,** until hot and well blended, stirring every 2 minutes. |
| **2 tablespoons grated lime peel** **5 drops green food coloring** | To hot mixture, add lime peel and food coloring. Stir well. Cool mixture. While mixture is cooling, prepare souffle dish (see below). |
| **6 egg whites** **½ cup sugar** **1¼ cups whipping cream** | When mixture is cool, beat egg whites, adding sugar gradually, to make soft meringue. Also beat whipping cream to soft peaks. |

Fold cool lime mixture gently into soft meringue. Then lightly fold in whipped cream. Pile mixture into prepared souffle dish and chill until set, at least 3 hours. Remove wax paper collar. Garnish sides with chopped pistachio nuts (¼ to ½ cup needed).

*Makes about 8 servings*

To prepare souffle dish: Place a strip of double thick (folded) wax paper around edge of 1-qt. souffle dish so wax paper collar rises about 3-in. above edge of dish. Secure wax paper with tape. This technique allows mixture to be piled into dish above the rim. When souffle is set, paper collar is easily removed and souffle appears to have "risen" above edge of dish.

## CARAMEL APPLES

POWER LEVEL: High (10)    **Cook Code:** 20
MICROWAVE TIME: 2 to 3 min., total

| | |
|---|---|
| **½ of 14-oz. pkg. caramels (about 25)** **1 tablespoon water** | In 1-pt. glass measure place unwrapped caramels and water. **Microwave at High 2 to 3 Minutes,** until mixture can be stirred smooth. |
| **4 apples** **4 wooden sticks (usually come with caramels)** | Insert sticks into stem ends of apples. Dip one apple at a time into caramel, coating evenly. Repeat. Place apples on buttered wax paper, stick side up, to set. |

*Makes 4 apples*

# FRUIT-FILLED PINEAPPLE

POWER LEVEL: High (10)  TEMP: 120°
APPROX. MICROWAVE TIME: 10 to 12 min.

**Cook Code:** 100

**1 medium fresh pineapple** . . . . . . . . Cut pineapple, including leafy crown, in half lengthwise. Cut out fruit, leaving outside shell intact. Remove woody core; cut remaining fruit in chunks.

**1 cup (3 to 4-oz.) shredded coconut**
**½ cup toasted sliced almonds**
**1 can (11-oz.) mandarin orange sections, drained**
**½ cup maraschino cherries without stems, drained**
**½ cup sweet orange marmalade** . . . . . . . Toss pineapple chunks with coconut, almonds, oranges, cherries and marmalade. Place pineapple shells in 13×9×2-in. dish or on serving plate suitable for microwave oven. Fill shells with fruit mixture. Insert temperature probe so tip is in center of one of pineapple halves. Cover with wax paper. Attach cable end at receptacle. **Microwave at High. Set Temp, Set 120°.**

**¼ cup light rum** . . . . . . . . . Measure rum into glass measure. **Microwave at High ¼ Minute.** Remove 1 metal tablespoonful. Pour rest of rum over pineapple. Ignite rum in spoon and pour over pineapple to flame.

Makes 6 servings

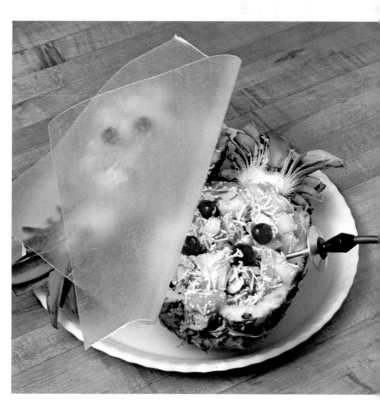

**The Temperature Probe,** dialed to 120°, will signal when the pineapple is warm enough to develop flavor and be flamed.

# Custards & Puddings

Custards and puddings are a microwave specialty. Conventionally baked custard must be set in a pan of water, which provides moisture to prevent drying and browning. On the range top you must stir custard or pudding constantly to keep it free from lumps. Delicate custard microwaves smooth and creamy with a minimum of stirring and the microwave oven does not dry or brown it. The variety of custards and puddings extends from simple desserts to dramatic looking presentations.

1. Caramel Flan, right
2. Bavarian Cream, page 247
3. Cup Custard, below
4. English Trifle, page 248

## BASIC CASSEROLE CUSTARD

POWER LEVEL: High (10) and Low (3)
MICROWAVE TIME: 14 to 17 min., total

| | |
|---|---|
| **3 eggs** | In 1½ qt. casserole beat eggs, sugar, vanilla, and salt with table fork, until very well blended and sugar is dissolved. |
| **¼ cup sugar** | |
| **1 teaspoon vanilla** | |
| **⅛ teaspoon salt** | |
| | |
| **1½ cups milk** | Place milk in glass measure. **Microwave at High 4 Minutes,** until scalded. Gradually add to egg mixture, stirring well. |

Cover with casserole lid. **Microwave at Low 10 to 13 Minutes,** rotating dish ¼ turn every 3 minutes, until set. Sprinkle top with nutmeg before serving, if desired.

NOTE: Covering with casserole lid is important for success. Cool before serving.

Makes 4 to 6 servings.

**Cup Custards:** Prepare custard mixture as above except pour into 4 (6-oz.) custard cups. Place in circle on shelf in microwave oven. **Microwave at Low 11 to 13 Minutes,** rearranging every 3 minutes. If some custards are done before others, remove those and continue cooking until all custards are cooked.

## CARAMEL FLAN

POWER LEVEL: High (10) and Low (3)
MICROWAVE TIME: 20 to 25 min., total

| | |
|---|---|
| **½ cup water** | In 1-pt. glass measure place water and sugar, stirring well. **Microwave at High 10 to 12 Minutes,** until light but rich brown. (Do not let syrup get too dark before taking from oven; it continues to cook after it has been microwaved.) Pour ¾ of caramel syrup into 1½-qt. casserole and quickly rotate casserole to coat bottom and about half way up sides with caramel. Let cool to harden before adding custard. Drizzle remaining ¼ of syrup in fine ribbons onto ungreased cookie sheet to harden. |
| **½ cup sugar** | |
| | |
| **1 recipe Basic Casserole Custard** | Prepare custard in small mixing bowl. Pour or strain mixture into caramel lined casserole. Cover with casserole lid. |

**Microwave at Low 10 to 13 Minutes,** rotating dish ¼ turn every 3 minutes, until set. Chill thoroughly. Unmold onto serving plate which has shallow rim. Crush the syrup which has hardened into a brittle and sprinkle in a wreath shape over top of flan.

NOTE: Covering with casserole lid is important for success.

Makes 4 to 6 servings.

**Dramatic** Caramel Flan is Basic Custard strained into a caramel-lined casserole. After microwaving, garnish it with crushed caramel brittle, on the right.

## FLOATING ISLANDS

POWER LEVEL: High (10), Med. High (7) and Med. (5)
MICROWAVE TIME: 11 to 16 min., total

**⅓ cup sugar** . . . . . . . . . . .In 2-qt. casserole blend
**3 tablespoons** together sugar, cornstarch
**cornstarch** and salt until well mixed.
**¼ teaspoon salt** Add milk and food color-
**2¾ cups milk** ing, stirring until well
**2 drops yellow food** blended. **Microwave at**
**color (optional)** **High 8 to 10 Minutes,** stirring every 3 minutes until
smooth and slightly thickened.

**2 egg yolks, well** . . . . . . .Stir a small amount of hot
**beaten** pudding quickly into yolks.
Return egg mixture to hot
pudding, mixing well. **Mic-**
**rowave at Medium High**
**2 to 4 Minutes,** stirring
after 1 minute, until slightly
thickened.

**2 egg whites** . . . . . . . . . . .Beat egg whites until
**¼ cup sugar** foamy, on high speed of
mixer.
Gradually add sugar, beating to a stiff glossy meringue.
Drop meringue immediately in 8 to 10 mounds over hot
pudding. **Microwave at Medium 1 to 2 Minutes** to set
meringues slightly. Chill before serving.

Makes 6 to 8 servings

## BASIC BREAD PUDDING

POWER LEVEL: High (10) and Medium High (7)
MICROWAVE TIME: 13 to 16 min., total

**4 cups bread cubes** . . . . .Spread bread cubes even-
**lightly packed into** ly in 8-in. round dish. Sprin-
**cup (4 to 5 slices)** kle evenly with brown sug-
**½ cup brown sugar** ar and salt, then raisins.
**(packed)**
**¼ teaspoon salt**
**½ cup raisins (optional)**

**2 cups milk** . . . . . . . . . . . .Measure milk into 1-qt.
**¼ cup butter** measuring cup. Add butter.
**2 eggs, beaten** **Microwave at High 4 Min-**
**utes,** until butter is melted
and milk is warm. Rapidly
stir in eggs with a fork and
mix well. Pour over bread
cubes in dish.

**Microwave at Medium High 9 to 12 Minutes,** rotating
dish ½ turn after 6 minutes. When cooked, center may still
be slightly soft but it will set up as pudding cools. Serve
warm or chilled.

Makes about 6 servings

## TWO WAYS TO MICROWAVE INDIVIDUAL MERINGUES

**On Pudding.** The traditional way to serve Floating Islands is to drop mounds of meringue over hot pudding.
**Microwave at Medium 1 to 2 Minutes.** Serve with small,
crisp cookies, if desired.

**On Brown Paper.** For best shape cook pudding for
maximum time and microwave meringues separately.
Place sheet of brown wrapping paper on a flat cookie
sheet and drop 6 to 8 mounds of meringue in a circle on
paper. Slide paper from cookie sheet into oven. **Micro-**
**wave at Medium 1 to 2 Minutes.** Slide back onto cookie
sheet and remove from oven to cool.

# VANILLA PUDDING

POWER LEVEL: High (10) and Medium High (7)
MICROWAVE TIME: 6 to 10 min., total

| | |
|---|---|
| **¾ cup sugar** . . . . . . . . . . . . | In 1-qt. casserole blend together sugar, cornstarch and salt.. Gradually stir in milk, mixing well. **Microwave at High 5 to 7 Minutes,** stir every 3 minutes, until mixture is smooth, thickened and clear. |
| **2 tablespoons cornstarch** | |
| **¼ teaspoon salt** | |
| **2 cups milk** | |
| **2 egg yolks, slightly beaten, or 1 egg, well beaten** . . . . . | Stir a small amount of hot pudding quickly into egg yolks. Return egg mixture to hot pudding, mixing well. **Microwave at Medium High 1 to 3 Minutes,** stirring after 1 minute, until smooth and thickened. |
| **2 tablespoons butter** . . . . . | Add butter and vanilla. Stir until butter is melted. Pour into serving dishes. |
| **1 teaspoon vanilla extract** | |

Makes 4 servings

# CHOCOLATE PUDDING

Prepare Vanilla Pudding except, increase sugar to 1 cup. Add 2 squares (1-oz. each) unsweetened chocolate along with milk.

# BUTTERSCOTCH PUDDING

Prepare Vanilla Pudding except, use brown sugar and increase butter to 3 tablespoons.

# CREAM CHEESE PUDDING

Prepare Vanilla Pudding and cool until lukewarm. With high speed of mixer, whip 1 pkg. (8-oz.) softened cream cheese until light and fluffy. Gradually beat in pudding until smooth. Serve as pudding or pie filling.

# CREAMY RICE PUDDING

Prepare Vanilla Pudding except, increase milk to 2½ cups. Into warm pudding, stir 2 cups cooked rice.

# PUDDING SAUCE

*Nice to serve over plain cake or gingerbread. Vanilla pudding sauce is good with fruit cake or steamed holiday pudding.*

Prepare Vanilla, Chocolate or Butterscotch pudding as above, except increase milk to 2¾ cups.

# BAVARIAN CREAM

*This is basic custard sauce to which gelatin is added so it can be molded. It is lightened with meringue and whipped cream.*

POWER LEVEL: High (10) and Medium High (7)
MICROWAVE TIME: 10 to 14 min., total

| | |
|---|---|
| **⅓ cup sugar** . . . . . . . . . . . | In 2-qt. casserole blend together sugar, cornstarch, gelatin and salt, until well mixed. Gradually add milk, stirring until well blended. **Microwave at High 8 to 10 Minutes,** stirring every 3 minutes, until smooth and slightly thickened. |
| **3 tablespoons cornstarch** | |
| **2 tablespoons unflavored gelatin** | |
| **¼ teaspoon salt** | |
| **2¾ cups milk** | |
| **2 egg yolks, well beaten** . . . . . . | Stir a small amount of hot pudding quickly into egg yolks. Return egg mixture to hot pudding, mixing well. **Microwave at Medium High 2 to 4 Minutes,** stirring after 1 minute. Cool in refrigerator until mixture mounds slightly, about 1½ hours. Stir in vanilla. |
| **1 teaspoon vanilla extract** | |
| **2 egg whites** . . . . . . . . . | When gelatin mixture has cooled, beat egg whites until foamy. |
| **¼ cup sugar** | |
| **1 cup whipping cream, whipped** | |

Gradually add sugar, beating to a soft meringue. Fold cooled gelatin mixture into meringue; fold in whipped cream. Pile mixture into 4½ to 5-cup mold. Chill until set. Unmold and serve with fruit garnish, such as sliced strawberries or peaches.

Makes 6 to 8 servings

# NESSELRODE BAVARIAN

*Definitely a holiday dessert.*

| | |
|---|---|
| **1 recipe Bavarian Cream (above)** | Into 2-qt. fluted mold, distribute about ¼ of Bavarian cream, ⅓ of nesselrode, ¼ of cream, ⅓ of nesselrode, ¼ of cream, last of nesselrode and last ¼ of cream on top. |
| **1 jar (10-oz.) nesselrode fruit mixture** | |

(Layering technique best distributes fruit and cream.) Chill until set. Unmold onto plate which has a fairly high rim (about 1-in.). Some of nesselrode syrup will separate from bavarian upon unmolding and high rim is needed to contain syrup. Spoon syrup over nesselrode bavarian as it is served.

Makes about 8 servings

## ENGLISH TRIFLE

POWER LEVEL: High (10) and Medium High (7)
MICROWAVE TIME: 12 to 13 min., total

| | |
|---|---|
| ½ cup sugar<br>½ teaspoon salt<br>2 tablespoons cornstarch<br>2½ cups milk | In 1½-qt. casserole mix together sugar, salt and cornstarch. Gradually stir in milk. **Microwave at High 7 Minutes,** stirring every 3 minutes, until slightly thickened. |
| 4 egg yolks, beaten<br>2 teaspoons vanilla extract | Stir in a little over half thickened mixture into beater egg yolks. Return mixture to casserole blending well. **Microwave at Medium High 5 to 6 Minutes** more, stirring after 2 minutes Cool; then stir in vanilla. |
| 1 (8-in.) microwaved yellow or white layer cake<br>½ cup raspberry preserves<br>¼ to ½ cup sherry | Split cake and fill with preserves. Cut preserve-filled cake into 12 pieces and place half in 2 to 3-qt. serving dish. Sprinkle with half of sherry and cover with half of custard. Repeat. |
| 1 cup whipping cream<br>3 tablespoons confectioners sugar<br>¼ cup toasted, sliced almonds | Whip cream with confectioners sugar until peaks form. Spread over custard. Sprinkle with almonds. Chill 4 hours or more before serving. |

Makes 9 to 12 servings

## COOKING COMMERCIAL DRY PUDDING MIX

*Since there is less evaporation in microwaving, microwaved pudding is often creamier in texture, lighter in color and greater in volume than it is conventionally.*

POWER LEVEL: High (10)          **Cook Code:**   60
MICROWAVE TIME: 6 to 8 min., total

| | |
|---|---|
| 1 pkg. (3¾-oz.) pudding or pie filling mix, not instant<br>½ cup milk | Empty pudding mix into 1-qt. glass measure. Add ½ cup milk and stir until all mix is moistened and blended. |
| 1½ cups milk | Add 1½ cups more milk and blend well. |

**Microwave at High 6 to 8 Minutes,** stirring thoroughly every 3 minutes.

Pour into 4 or 5 serving dishes. Cover top of pudding with wax paper or plastic wrap to prevent "skin" from forming on top, if desired. Serve cool.

Makes 4 to 5 servings

## PUDDING TRIFLE

POWER LEVEL: High (10) and Medium High (7)
MICROWAVE TIME: 10 to 14 min., total

| | |
|---|---|
| 1 pkg. (3¾-oz.) vanilla pudding mix, not instant<br>2½ cups milk | In 1½-qt. casserole place pudding. Gradually add milk, stirring to blend well. **Microwave at High 6 to 8 Minutes,** stirring every 3 minutes, until thickened. |
| 2 egg yolks, beaten | Gradually stir half of pudding into beaten yolks. Return egg mixture to casserole, stirring well. **Microwave at Medium High 4 to 6 Minutes** more, stirring every 2 minutes, until thickened. Cool. |
| 1 (8-in.) microwaved yellow or white cake layer<br>½ cup cherry preserves<br>¼ to ½ cup sherry, rum or pineapple juice | Split cake layer and fill with preserves. Cut into pieces and arrange half in 2-qt. casserole. Sprinkle with half of sherry and cover with half of cooled pudding. Repeat. |
| 1 cup whipping cream<br>3 tablespoons confectioners sugar | Whip cream with confectioners sugar until soft peaks form. Spread over pudding. Chill 4 hours or more before serving. |

Makes 8 to 12 servings

## BLACK FOREST TRIFLE

*This trifle combines the principle flavors of the famous Black Forest Torte; chocolate, cherries and cream.*

Make Pudding Trifle above, except substitute chocolate pudding mix for vanilla and chocolate cake layer for yellow or white. Instead of cherry preserves, fill the split cake layer with 1 can (22-oz.) cherry pie filling.

Arrange filled cake in 12×8×2-in. dish and sprinkle with ½ cup rum or brandy. Pour cooled chocolate pudding over all. Top with sweetened whipped cream as in above recipe and garnish with maraschino cherries, if desired.

# Pies

Because microwaved pie shells set and cook rapidly, plain pastry does not brown. Flavored pastry and toppings brushed on before microwaving have appealing color.

**Plain** microwaved pastry looks different from conventionally baked. From top to bottom: Conventional, Microwaved, Molasses, Maple Syrup, Chocolate Pastry, Dark Corn Syrup, Vanilla, Egg Yolk Toppings.

**Check For Doneness** on the bottom of the crust, which is critical. It should look opaque and dry. Top will be dry and blistered. A clear glass utensil is best because you can see the bottom.

## BASIC PASTRY SHELL

POWER LEVEL: High (10)     **Cook Code:**  60
MICROWAVE TIME: 6 to 7 min., total

| | |
|---|---|
| **1 cup unsifted** . . . . . . . . . .<br>   **all-purpose flour**<br>**1 teaspoon salt**<br>**6 tablespoons**<br>   **shortening\***<br>**2 tablespoons ice water** | In small bowl place flour and salt. With pastry blender cut in shortening, until mixture resembles the size of small peas.<br>Sprinkle water over flour-shortening mixture. Stir with fork to form ball. |

Roll out on floured pastry cloth with rolling pin to ⅛-in. thickness. Let stand a few minutes before shaping. Use to line 9-in. pie plate shaping pastry to the edge of pie plate. Prick pastry with fork. **Microwave at High 6 to 7 Minutes,** rotating dish ½ turn after 3 minutes. Pastry is done when it looks dry and blistered and is not doughy.

Makes 1 (9-in.) pastry shell

\*If desired, 3 tablespoons cold butter and 3 tablespoons shortening may be used for more flavor and color.

## CHOCOLATE PASTRY SHELL

To flour add only ½ teaspoon salt along with 2 tablespoons cocoa and ⅓ cup sugar.

**Crumb Crusts** are perfect pie partners. Their crunchy texture complements light and airy or smooth and creamy fillings. They are also faster to make than pastry crusts. Reserve 2 tablespoons crumbs to garnish top of pie, if desired. For easy removal, set pie plate on towel dampened with hot water for a few minutes. Vary the character of pies by using different crumbs. To make 1¼ cups of fine crumbs, use 15 to 18 squares of graham crackers, 18 to 22 medium gingersnaps, 18 to 20 chocolate (not cream filled) wafers, 30 to 36 vanilla wafers. When using pecan sandies 1½ to 1¾ cups crumbs are needed, about 18 to 20 cookies.

## NUT CRUNCH PASTRY SHELL

POWER LEVEL: High (10)
MICROWAVE TIME: 6 to 8 min., total

| | |
|---|---|
| **1 cup flour** . . . . . . . . . . . . . | .In small mixing bowl place |
| **½ cup light brown sugar (packed)** | flour and brown sugar. With pastry blender, cut in |
| **½ cup (¼-lb.) butter** | butter until mixture is crum- |
| **1 cup chopped pecans or walnuts** | bly. Mix in nuts. |

Place crumbly mixture loosely in 9-in. pie plate. **Microwave at High 4 to 5 Minutes,** stirring every 1 or 2 minutes. Stir again after cooking and, if desired, reserve about 2 tablespoons crumbly mixture to garnish top of pie. Press remainder of hot crumbs into pie plate. **Microwave at High 2 to 3 Minutes,** until set, rotating dish ¼ turn every minute. Cool before filling.

Makes 1 (9-in.) pie shell

## TOASTED COCONUT PIE SHELL

*This shell is a good one to use for ice cream pies. Use recipe to make 8-in. pie shell, then fill with 1-qt. vanilla or favorite flavor ice cream. Freeze. Drizzle sundae sauce over top and garnish with additional coconut, nuts or fruit as desired.*

POWER LEVEL: High (10)
MICROWAVE TIME: 6½ to 7½ min., total

| | |
|---|---|
| **3 tablespoons butter** . . . . . | .In 8 or 9-in. pie plate place |
| **1 cup (3 to 4-oz.) flaked coconut** | butter. **Microwave at High ½ Minutes,** until melted. Add coconut. |

**Microwave at High 6 to 7 Minutes,** stirring every 2 minutes, then every minute after 4 minutes, until coconut is evenly browned. Spread coconut in pie plate. Cool before filling.

Makes 1 (8 or 9-in.) pie shell

## CRUMB PIE SHELL

*A pretty scalloped pie shell such as the one used in the Grasshopper Pie, page 253, can easily be made by lining the bottom of a pie plate with ½ of this recipe, then standing small whole cookies around the sides of plate.*

POWER LEVEL: High (10)
MICROWAVE TIME: 2½ to 3 min., total

| Ingredients | Instructions |
|---|---|
| **¼ cup butter** . . . . . . . . . . | . .In 9-in. pie plate place butter. **Microwave at High ½ Minute,** until melted. Blend in crumbs and sugar. If desired, reserve 2 tablespoons crumb mixture for garnish. Press firmly and evenly into 9-in. pie plate. **Microwave at High 2 to 2½ Minutes,** rotating dish ½ turn after 1 minute. |
| **1¼ cups fine cookie crumbs (vanilla wafer, graham cracker, chocolate wafer, gingersnaps, etc.)** | |
| **2 tablespoons sugar** | |

Makes 1 (9-in.) crumb shell

## FROZEN CHOCOLATE ALMOND PIE

*This pie cuts well straight from the freezer. No thawing is necessary. Use a wet knife for sharpest cut.*

POWER LEVEL: High (10)          Cook Code:    30
MICROWAVE TIME: 3 to 4 min., total

| | |
|---|---|
| **1 crumb pie shell made with vanilla wafers or Chocolate Pastry Shell, page 249** | . .Microwave pie shell. Cool. |
| **4 milk chocolate candy bars with almonds (1.15-oz. each)** **½ of 10-oz. pkg. large marshmallows (about 20)** **½ cup milk** | . .In 2-qt. casserole place candy, marshmallows and milk. **Microwave at High 3 to 4 Minutes,** stirring after 2 minutes, until mixture can be stirred smooth. Chill in refrigerator about 30 to 40 minutes, or in pan of ice water until thickened, stirring occasionally. |
| **1 cup whipping cream whipped** | .Fold whipped cream into cooled chocolate mixture. Pile into pie shell and freeze until firm. |

To serve, garnish pie wedges with whipped cream, chocolate curls and/or additional almonds, if desired.

Makes 1 (9-in.) pie

## ROCKY ROAD CHOCOLATE ALMOND PIE

Microwave chocolate and milk, then stir in 2 cups miniature marshmallows. Stir well, but do not melt marshmallows.

Rocky Road Chocolate Almond Pie

## PECAN PIE

POWER LEVEL: High (10) and Medium (5)
MICROWAVE TIME: 19 to 24 min., total

| | |
|---|---|
| **1 Basic Pastry Shell, uncooked, page 249** **1 egg yolk** **2 tablespoons dark corn syrup** | .Roll out pastry and fit into 9-in. pie plate. Brush inside of shell with mixture of egg yolk and corn syrup. **Microwave at High 6 to 7 Minutes,** rotating dish ½ turn after 3 minutes. |
| **¼ cup butter** . . . . . . . . . . | .In large glass mixing bowl place butter. **Microwave at High ½ to 1 Minute,** until melted. |
| **3 whole eggs, plus extra egg white** **1 cup dark corn syrup** **⅓ cup brown sugar (packed)** **1 tablespoon flour** **1 teaspoon vanilla** **1½ cups pecan halves** | . Add eggs to melted butter. Beat with fork to mix eggs well. Blend in syrup, sugar, flour and vanilla. Then, mix in pecan halves. Pour into crust. **Microwave at Medium 12 to 15 Minutes,** rotating ½ turn after 5 minutes. When done, top surface is dry and puffed, and filling is set. |

Makes 1 (9-in.) pie

## HOW TO MICROWAVE MARSHMALLOW PIE FILLING

**Combine** milk or other liquid with marshmallows. Microwave at High 2 to 3 minutes.

**Air** heats and expands inside marshmallows, causing them to puff up before they melt.

**Stir** mixture until smooth. Chill until cool and thickened before adding flavoring and whipped cream.

### FLUFFY MARSHMALLOW PIES

POWER LEVEL: High (10)      **Cook Code:**   20
MICROWAVE TIME: 2 to 3 min., total

| | |
|---|---|
| **Crumb Pie Shell, page 251** | Microwave Crumb Pie Shell using the flavor of cookie that best complements filling. Cool. |
| **1 pkg. (10-oz.) large marshmallows** **½ cup milk** | In 3-qt. casserole place marshmallows and milk. Cover. **Microwave at High 2 to 3 Minutes,** until mixture can be stirred smooth. Chill in refrigerator (about 30 to 40 minutes) or in pan of ice water, until thickened, stirring occasionally. |
| **1 cup whipping cream, whipped** **Special pie ingredient (see right)** | Fold in whipped cream and special pie ingredient. Pour into crust and decorate with reserved crumbs or additional whipped cream, if desired. Refrigerate several hours or overnight. |

Makes 1 (9-in.) pie

FRUIT PIE VARIATIONS:

### PEACH OR BERRY PIE

Fold in 1¾ to 2 cups peeled and sliced fresh peaches, sliced fresh strawberries or fresh whole raspberries.

LIQUEUR PIE VARIATIONS:

*These pies are soft and creamy when served from refrigerator; for firm pieces which hold sharp cut, serve frozen. Frozen pie releases easily from bottom of pie plate if set a few minutes on towel dampened with hot water.*

### GRASSHOPPER PIE

Into cooled marshmallow mixture, stir ¼ cup green creme de menthe and 2 tablespoons white creme de cocoa. Garnish with mounds of additional whipped cream and chocolate curls.

### BRANDY ALEXANDER PIE

Into cooled marshmallow mixture, stir ¼ cup dark creme de cocoa and 2 tablespoons brandy.

### KAHLUA PIE

Add 1 teaspoon instant coffee powder to marshmallows and milk. Into cooled marshmallow mixture, stir ½ cup kahlua.

Grasshopper Pie

## LEMON MERINGUE PIE

*Meringue will set in a microwave oven but top will not be brown. The lemon filling, often done in a double boiler on range top, is easier to microwave.*

POWER LEVEL: High (10), Med. High (7) and Med. (5)
MICROWAVE TIME: 12 to 17 min., total

| | |
|---|---|
| **1 microwaved pastry shell, page 249**<br>**1 cup sugar**<br>**⅓ cup cornstarch**<br>**⅛ teaspoon salt**<br>**2 cups cold water**<br>**1 to 2 drops yellow food color** | .In 2-qt. casserole mix together sugar, cornstarch and salt. Blend in water and food color; stir smooth. **Microwave at High 6 to 8 Minutes,** stirring after 3 minutes, until slightly thickened. |
| **3 egg yolks** . . . . . . . . . . . . | .In medium bowl beat yolks well. Add sauce; mix well. **Microwave at Medium High 3 to 5 Minutes,** stir after 2 minutes, until thick. |
| **3 tablespoons butter** . . . .<br>**¼ cup fresh lemon juice**<br>**2 teaspoons grated lemon rind** | .Stir butter, juice and rind into mixture. Pour into pastry. Finish with meringue or, if desired, cool and decorate pie with whipped cream. |

Makes 1 (9-in.) pie

**Meringue:** Beat 3 egg whites with ½ teaspoon cream of tartar until stiff peaks form. Gradually beat in 6 tablespoons sugar to make glossy meringue. Spread over pie. **Microwave at Medium 3 to 4 Minutes,** until meringue is set (top won't brown).

## APPLE GRAHAM PIE

POWER LEVEL: High (10)          TEMP: 200°
APPROX. MICROWAVE TIME: 10 to 12 min.

| | |
|---|---|
| **½ cup (¼-lb.) butter** . . . . .<br>**¼ cup sugar**<br>**2 cups graham cracker crumbs** | .In large glass mixing bowl place butter. **Microwave at High 1 Minute,** until melted. Add sugar and crumbs. Mix well. Press half of mixture firmly and evenly into 9-in. pie plate. |
| **5 cups thinly sliced apples (4 to 6 medium)**<br>**½ cup sugar**<br>**1 teaspoon cinnamon** | .In large mixing bowl place apple slices; they should be ⅛ to ¼-in. thick. Add sugar and cinnamon, mixing well. Mound and press down into crumb crust. |

Cover apples with remaining crumbs to make top crust. Press crumbs down firmly, especially at edges, to prevent boilover.

Insert temperature probe so tip is in center of pie. Cover with wax paper. Attach cable end at receptacle. **Microwave at High. Set Temp, Set 200°.** When oven signals, remove pie and let stand 10 minutes covered with wax paper. Remove wax paper so crumb topping is allowed to dry and crisp. Serve warm or cold.

Makes 1 (9-in.) pie

## BRANDIED CRANBERRY PIE

POWER LEVEL: High (10)              TEMP: 200°
APPROX. MICROWAVE TIME: 13 to 16 min.

**Cook Code:** 130

| | |
|---|---|
| **2 cups prepared** . . . . . . .<br>    **graham cracker**<br>    **crumbs**<br>**¼ cup sugar**<br>**½ cup (¼-lb.) butter,**<br>    **melted** | In small bowl mix together crumbs, sugar and butter. Pat half of mixture firmly into 9-in. pie plate. |
| **1 can (16-oz.) whole** . . . .<br>    **cranberry sauce**<br>**1¼ cup prepared**<br>    **mincemeat**<br>**1 cup coarsely**<br>    **chopped pecans**<br>**2 tablespoons sugar**<br>**2 tablespoons butter,**<br>    **melted**<br>**¼ cup brandy**<br>**2 tablespoons**<br>    **cornstarch** | In mixing bowl stir together cranberry sauce, mincemeat, pecans, sugar, butter, brandy and cornstarch. Spread mixture over crust. Pat remaining crumbs firmly in wreath around outside edge of pie forming a firm unbroken crust about 2-in. wide. (Center of pie remains open for attractive finished appearance.) |

Insert temperature probe so tip is in center of pie. Cover with wax paper. Attach cable end at receptacle. **Microwave at High. Set Temp, Set 200°.**

When oven signals, remove pie and let stand 10 minutes covered with wax paper. Then remove wax paper so crumb topping is allowed to dry and crisp. Serve warm or cold.

TO FLAME PIE: Measure ¼ cup brandy into glass measuring cup. **Microwave at High ¼ Minute.** Remove 1 metal tablespoonful and pour the rest over the pie. Using lighter or long match, warm and ignite brandy in tablespoon. Pour over pie to ignite brandy on top of pie.

## DEFROSTING FROZEN PRE-BAKED PIES

Remove whole pie from foil pan to an 8 or 9-in. glass pie plate. Or cut in wedges and place on serving plates.

## HEATING FRUIT AND NUT PIES FROM THE REFRIGERATOR

Defrosted fruit and nut pies may be heated with the temperature probe set at 120°. For a single slice, set High Power. For a whole pie (in glass pie plate), set Medium Power.

Time per slice is about ½ to 1 minute. For whole pie, allow about 2 minutes. Let stand a few minutes before serving.

TIP: Soften too-hard ice cream by placing in microwave oven briefly at Medium or Low. Allow about ¼ minute. It's easier to scoop into servings and over pie.

## PUMPKIN PIE

POWER LEVEL: High (10) and Medium (5)
MICROWAVE TIME: 37 to 42 min., total

| | |
|---|---|
| **½ cup (¼-lb.) butter** . . . . . . | In 10-in. pie plate place butter. **Microwave at High 1 Minute,** until melted. |
| **2 cups vanilla wafer** . . . .<br>    **crumbs**<br>**2 tablespoons sugar** | Add crumbs and sugar; mix well. Firmly press on bottom and up sides of dish. **Microwave at High 2 Minutes,** rotating dish ½ turn after 1 minute. |
| **1 can (16-oz.) mashed** . . .<br>    **pumpkin**<br>**1 cup brown sugar**<br>    **(packed)**<br>**1 tablespoon pumpkin**<br>    **pie spice**<br>**1 tablespoon flour**<br>**½ teaspoon salt**<br>**1 can (13-oz.)**<br>    **evaporated milk**<br>**2 eggs, beaten** | In 2-qt. casserole blend together pumpkin, brown sugar, pumpkin pie spice, flour, salt, evaporated milk and eggs. **Microwave at Medium 12 to 14 Minutes,** stirring every 5 minutes, until hot and thickened. |

Pour hot pumpkin custard filling into prepared pie shell. **Microwave at Medium 22 to 25 Minutes,** rotating dish ½ turn after 12 minutes. The pie is done when the edges are set and the center is still slightly soft (very much like a conventionally baked pie). Let stand at room temperature about 15 to 20 minutes to set and cool before serving.

Makes 1 (10-in.) pie

2 PUMPKIN PIES: Prepare crust in 2 (8-in.) pie plates. Divide hot filling between pie shells. Microwave 1 pie at a time. **Microwave at Medium 12 to 14 Minutes,** rotating dish ½ turn after 6 minutes.

POWER LEVEL: **Defrost**

| TYPE | TIME MINUTES | COMMENTS |
|---|---|---|
| **Fruit or Nut Pie** whole (8-in.) | 8 to 10 | Rotate ¼ turn every 3 minutes. Let stand a few minutes before serving. |
| **Fruit or Nut Pie** wedge (1 or 2 slices) | 2 to 4 | |
| **Cream or Custard Pie** whole (14-oz.) | 2½ to 3 | Rotate ¼ turn every minute. |
| **Cream or Custard Pie** whole (26-oz.) | 5 to 7 | Rotate ¼ turn every 2 minutes. Let stand a few minutes before serving. |
| **Cream or Custard Pie** wedge (1 to 3 slices) | ½ to 1 | |

Chocolate Chip Bars

# Cookies

Brownies and bar cookies exemplify the best of micro-waving. Their taste, texture and appearance compare favorably with conventional baking and they can be ready to serve in 6 to 10 minutes. We don't recommend drop cookies for microwaving because the oven will not accommodate large batches. Instead, we've adapted some popular bar cookies for microwaving.

**Small** cookie has brown spots inside because cooking begins below the surface. Large cookie microwaves more evenly. Cookies are done when they are just set.

## CHOCOLATE CHIP BARS

| POWER LEVEL: High (10) | **Cook Code:** | 50 |
| --- | --- | --- |

MICROWAVE TIME: 5 to 7 min., total

| | |
| --- | --- |
| **½ cup (¼-lb.) butter, softened** | In small mixer bowl cream together butter and sugar, until fluffy. Add egg, milk, and vanilla. Mix well. |
| **¾ cup brown sugar (packed)** | |
| **1 egg** | |
| **1 tablespoon milk** | |
| **1 teaspoon vanilla extract** | |
| **1¼ cups unsifted all-purpose flour** | Stir together flour, baking powder and salt. Add to creamed mixture. Blend well. Stir in ½ cup choco-late pieces and nuts. Spread in greased 8-in. square dish. Sprinkle with remaining ½ cup choco-late pieces. **Microwave at High 5 to 7 Minutes,** rotat-ing dish ¼ turn every 2 minutes, until done. Cool and cut into bars. |
| **½ teaspoon baking powder** | |
| **⅛ teaspoon salt** | |
| **1 cup (6-oz.) semi-sweet chocolate pieces, divided** | |
| **½ cup chopped nuts (optional)** | |

Makes about 24 bars

## BASIC BROWNIES

POWER LEVEL: High (10)     **Cook Code:**  60
MICROWAVE TIME: 6 to 7 min., total

| | |
|---|---|
| **2 eggs** . . . . . . . . . . . . . . . . | .In small bowl at medium |
| **1 cup sugar** | speed on mixer, beat to- |
| **½ teaspoon salt** | gether eggs, sugar, salt |
| **1 teaspoon vanilla extract** | and vanilla, about 1 minute until light. |
| **½ cup (¼-lb.) butter,** . . . . . . **melted** | Add melted butter. Continue beating until thoroughly blended. |
| **¾ cup unsifted** . . . . . . . . . **all-purpose flour** | .Mix in flour and cocoa at low speed. |
| **½ cup cocoa** | |
| **1 cup chopped nuts** . . . . . | Stir in nuts. Spread evenly in greased 8-in. square dish. |

**Microwave at High 6 to 7 Minutes,** rotating dish ¼ turn every 2 minutes. When done, top looks dry and will spring back when lightly touched. Cut when cold.

Makes about 20 brownies

VARIATIONS: 1 pkg. (6-oz.) semi-sweet chocolate pieces, or 1 cup flaked or shredded coconut may be substituted for nuts.

Basic Brownies

## THREE-LAYER BROWNIES

POWER LEVEL: High (10)
MICROWAVE TIME: 6½ to 7¼ min., total

| | |
|---|---|
| **2 squares unsweetened chocolate** | .In small glass mixing bowl place chocolate and but- |
| **⅓ cup butter** | ter. **Microwave at High 2½ to 3 Minutes,** until melted. |
| **1 cup sugar** . . . . . . . . . . . | .Add sugar, eggs and vanilla. Beat 2 minutes. |
| **2 eggs** | |
| **1 teaspoon vanilla extract** | |
| **⅔ cup unsifted** . . . . . . . . . **all-purpose flour** | .Stir in flour and salt just until well blended. Pour into |
| **½ teaspoon salt** | greased 8-in. square dish. |
| **½ cup chopped nuts (optional)** | Sprinkle nuts over batter. |

**Microwave at High 4 to 4½ Minutes,** rotating dish ½ turn after 2 minutes. Remove from oven and cool while making icing and glaze.

### BROWNED BUTTER ICING    **Cook Code:**  50

In 1-qt. glass measure or medium mixing bowl place ¼ cup butter. Cover with wax paper. **Microwave at High 5 to 6 Minutes,** until butter is golden brown. Remove from oven and blend in 2 cups sifted confectioners sugar, 2 tablespoons milk and ½ teaspoon vanilla extract. Spread over top of brownies in dish.

### CHOCOLATE GLAZE    **Cook Code:**  20

In 1 cup glass measure place 1 square (1-oz.) semi-sweet or unsweetened chocolate and 1 tablespoon butter. **Microwave at High 2 to 2½ Minutes,** or until melted. Cool slightly and drizzle over icing on brownies. Refrigerate until cool and icing and glaze are set up.

Makes about 20 brownies or 8 to 9 dessert size portions

## BROWNIES FROM A MIX

POWER LEVEL: High     **Cook Code:**  60
MICROWAVE TIME: 6 to 8 min., total

| | |
|---|---|
| **1 pkg. (about 1-lb.)** . . . . . . . **brownie mix** | Prepare cookie dough as package directs. Spread evenly in lightly greased 8-in. round or square dish. |
| **Water** | |
| **Eggs** | |
| **Chopped Nuts (optional)** | **Microwave at High 6 to 8 minutes,** rotating dish every 2 minutes. When done, top feels firm when lightly pressed. To prevent |

dryness, do not overcook. Let stand directly on heat-proof counter or wooden board to cool.

Makes about 20 brownies

**Family Size Brownies:** Prepare cookie dough as package directs and divide between 2 8-in. round dishes. Microwave one dish at a time as directed above, except check for doneness after 5 minutes.

# PECAN LOGS

POWER LEVEL: High (10)
MICROWAVE TIME: 9 to 11 min., total

**½ cup (¼-lb.) butter** ..... In large mixing bowl place butter. **Microwave at High 1 Minute,** or until melted.

**1 lb. light brown sugar** .. Into butter, mix brown sug-
**2 eggs, well beaten** ar, eggs and vanilla. Stir
**3 teaspoons vanilla** well. Blend in pecans and
**extract** pancake mix, mixing thor-
**2 cups chopped** oughly. Pour batter into
**pecans** greased 12×8×2-in. dish.
**1½ cups pancake or** **Microwave at High 8 to 10**
**biscuit mix** **Minutes,** rotating dish ½ turn every 3 minutes. Center will not be quite set, but will firm upon cooling. When cool, cut into long thin bars.

**Confectioners sugar** .. Sprinkle top with confectioners sugar, or, cut into bars and roll in confectioners sugar.

Makes about 40 to 50 bars

# CHOCOLATE TOFFEE BARS

POWER LEVEL: High (10)
MICROWAVE TIME: 4 to 4½ min., total

**11 graham cracker** ...... In 12×8×2-in. dish ar-
**squares** range graham cracker squares to cover bottom.

**½ cup (¼-lb.) butter** ..... In 1-qt. casserole place
**½ cup brown sugar** butter and brown sugar.
**(packed)** **Microwave at High 2 Minutes.** Stir well.

**½ cup confectioners** .... Blend in confectioners
**sugar** sugar, cornstarch, salt,
**1 tablespoon** coconut and nuts. Spread
**cornstarch** evenly over graham crack-
**¼ teaspoon salt** ers.
**1 cup coconut**
**½ cup chopped nuts**

**1 cup (6-oz.)** .......... Sprinkle chocolate pieces
**semi-sweet** over top. **Microwave at**
**chocolate pieces** **High 2 to 2½ Minutes.** Let stand a few minutes, then spread chocolate over bars. Cool before cutting.

Makes 24 bars

# SWEET-TART LEMON SQUARES

POWER LEVEL: High (10)          **Cook Code:**    80
MICROWAVE TIME: 8 to 10 min., total

**1 can (15-oz.)** ........ In small mixing bowl stir to-
**sweetened** gether milk, lemon juice
**condensed milk** and rind, until thick and
**½ cup lemon juice** smooth. Set aside.
**1 teaspoon grated**
**lemon rind**
**(optional)**

**1½ cups graham** ....... Mix together crumbs, sug-
**cracker crumbs** ar and butter. Place about
**⅓ cup brown sugar** ⅔ of mixture in 8-in. square
**(packed)** dish and press firmly into
**⅓ cup butter, melted** bottom of dish. Add milk mixture and spread even-ly. Sprinkle remaining crumb mixture over top and pat down gently.

**Microwave at High 8 to 10 Minutes,** rotating dish ¼ turn after 4 minutes. Cut in small squares as cookies or in larger pieces as dessert.

Makes 16 to 24 cookies
or 9 desserts

# BUTTERSCOTCH BARS

POWER LEVEL: Medium (5)
MICROWAVE TIME: 16 to 21 min., total

**½ cup butter, softened** .... In a small mixing bowl,
**¼ cup brown sugar** cream together butter and
**(packed)** brown sugar. Add flour,
**1¼ cups unsifted** mixing well to make soft
**all-purpose flour** dough. Press evenly in bottom of 12x8x2 in. dish. **Microwave at Medium 6 to 8 minutes,** rotating dish ½ turn every 2 minutes. Let stand about 5 minutes to set slightly.

**2 eggs** ................. In large mixing bowl beat
**1 cup brown sugar** eggs, brown sugar, va-
**(packed)** nilla extract, flour, baking
**1 teaspoon vanilla** powder, and salt at me-
**extract** dium speed until well
**2 tablespoons flour** blended. Stir in coconut
**1 teaspoon baking** and ½ cup almonds.
**powder** Spread mixture over crust.
**½ teaspoon salt** Sprinkle remaining al-
**1 cup (3 to 4-oz.) flaked** monds over top. **Micro-
coconut** **wave at Medium 10 to 13**
**1 cup unblanched sliced** **minutes,** rotating dish ½
**almonds** turn after 5 minutes until set. Let cool before cutting.

Makes 24 bars.

# Cakes

## MICROLESSON

The growing popularity of microwaved cakes is indicated by the many new utensils being developed for cooking them. Microwave instructions are available from major cake mix manufacturers. Expect microwaved cakes to look different; they will not brown and the tops will be somewhat uneven, since they do not develop a dry crust to contain expansion. For this reason they are moist, airy, fluffy and have greater volume. Since most cakes are frosted or served with a topping you won't notice the difference in appearance but you appreciate the time saved when microwaving. Do not microwave angel food or chiffon cakes; they need the dry heat of the conventional oven.

## HOW TO MICROWAVE CAKES

**Cake Is Done** when a wooden pick inserted in the center comes out clean. There may be moist spots on the cake surface which will evaporate as the cake cools.

**Line Dish** with a single layer of paper towel, cut to fit the bottom, when you wish to turn cake out. For cake served from dish, grease but do not flour.

**Cakes Rise Higher.** This cake was baked using only 2 cups of batter. Plastic microwave cake pans are available with deeper sides.

**Pour** batter into microwave fluted ring mold, or make your own tube pan by placing a 4 to 5-in. high glass in a large glass mixing bowl. Pour batter around it.

**Prepare Dish** for fruit-topped cake by buttering sides well. Coat with finely ground nuts. Line bottom with circle of wax paper; pour in ½ can pie filling. Invert finished cake.

**Extra Rich Cakes** and mixes enriched with special ingredients cook last in the center and bottom. Cool directly on counter top and retained heat will complete cooking.

# MICROWAVING CAKES FROM COMMERCIAL MIXES

While some microwave experts recommend a reduction of the water called for on the package directions, we have found that the full amount of water results in a moist, eating quality cake and we recommend that cake batter be made following package directions exactly.

Amount of batter for 2-layer cake is too much for 2 round 8-in. cake layers because batter rises higher when microwaved than it does conventionally. Fill cake dishes only half full and use any leftover batter for cupcakes. You will get about ½ dozen extra cupcakes when using some mixes.

New microwave cake utensils made of plastic are designed to accommodate the greater expansion of cake batter. The round layer cake utensils hold half of batter from a 2-layer cake mix and the fluted and straight-sided molds hold all of batter from a 2-layer package. They are very convenient if you microwave cakes often.

Top appearance of microwaved cakes is uneven. Best shape may be obtained when 2-step method described below is used. However, for fastest microwaving, use High Power for all of cooking, reducing time by about 1 minute.

Immediately following this chart are recipes for some of the most popular cake mix variations. They may be microwaved according to the chart below.

| DISH SIZE | AMOUNT OF BATTER | MICROWAVE AT **Medium High** | ROTATE DISH ½ TURN FINISH MICROWAVING AT **High** |
|---|---|---|---|
| 12×8×2-in. (glass) | about 2½ cups | 3 Minutes | 3 to 3½ Minutes |
| 8-in. square (glass) | about 2½ cups | 3 Minutes | 3 to 3½ Minutes |
| 8-in. round (glass) | about 2 cups | 3 Minutes | 1½ to 2 Minutes |
| 9-in. round (microwave plastic or ceramic) | about 3 cups (½ pkg.) | 3 Minutes | 2½ to 3 Minutes |
| Tube Cake (from glass mixer bowl, see left) | about 2½ cups | 3 Minutes | 2 to 2½ Minutes |
| 16-cup Fluted or Straight-sided ring mold (microwave plastic or ceramic) | all of batter for 2-layer cake | For this cake **Microwave at High 11 to 14 Minutes,** rotating dish ¼ turn every 5 minutes. Let stand 5 to 10 minutes before inverting to cool. **Cook Code:** 110. | |

**Microwaved Cake** (second from left) looks different from conventional cake (above), until frosted or topped.

Whipped Topping with Drizzled Chocolate

Peach Upside Down Cake, page 264

## CAKE MIX VARIATIONS

Batters which start with packaged cake mix, microwave like regular cakes. You may have to cook to maximum time, or even 2 to 3 minutes over because extra ingredients add more volume. See chart, page 259. Let stand directly on heat-proof surface to cool. The heat retained helps cook the bottoms of rich cakes. Also see cupcakes, page 262. Each recipe makes 5 to 5½ cups batter.

### "MIX EASY" FRUIT FLAVORED CAKE

| | |
|---|---|
| **1 pkg. (2-layer) yellow cake mix** | ...In large mixer bowl, place cake mix, gelatin, eggs, water and oil. Blend on low speed of mixer until just moistened, then beat 4 minutes at medium speed. If desired, after microwaving, poke warm cake with fork and pour Lemon Glaze over top. |
| **1 pkg. (3-oz.) fruit flavored gelatin** | |
| **4 eggs** | |
| **¾ cup water** | |
| **½ cup cooking oil** | |

**Lemon Glaze:** Stir together ⅓ cup lemon juice and ½ cup sugar in 1-pt. measuring cup. **Microwave at High 3 to 5 Minutes,** until boiling. **Cook Code:** 30.

### "MIX EASY" SOUR CREAM CAKE

| | |
|---|---|
| **1 pkg. (2-layer) yellow cake mix** | ...In large mixer bowl place cake mix, eggs, sour cream, oil and sugar. Blend on low speed of mixer, just until moistened, then beat 4 minutes at medium speed. If desired, top batter with Easy Streusel before microwaving. |
| **4 eggs** | |
| **1 cup (8-oz.) sour cream** | |
| **¾ cup cooking oil** | |
| **½ cup sugar** | |

**Easy Streusel:** Stir together ½ cup finely chopped nuts, ¼ cup sugar and 1 teaspoon cinnamon.

### "MIX EASY" RICH NUT CAKE

| | |
|---|---|
| **1 pkg. (2-layer) cake mix, any flavor** | ...In large mixer bowl place cake mix, cream cheese, eggs, shortening, water and vanilla. Blend on low speed of mixer until just moistened, then beat 4 minutes at medium speed. |
| **1 pkg. (8-oz.) cream cheese, softened** | |
| **4 eggs** | |
| **⅔ cup soft shortening** | |
| **¼ cup water** | |
| **2 teaspoons vanilla extract** | |
| **½ cup finely chopped nuts** | ....Fold nuts into batter. After microwaving, top cooled cake with Quick Glaze and garnish with nuts if desired. |

**Quick Glaze:** Stir together 1 cup sifted confectioners sugar, 1 to 2 tablespoons milk or hot water, ¼ teaspoon vanilla extract and ⅛ teaspoon salt.

### "MIX EASY" PUDDING POUND CAKE

| | |
|---|---|
| **1 pkg. (2-layer) yellow cake mix** | ...In large mixer bowl place cake mix, pudding mix, eggs, water and oil. Blend on low speed of mixer until just moistened, then beat 4 minutes at medium speed. If desired, top cooled cake with Chocolate Glaze. |
| **1 pkg. (3¾-oz.) instant lemon or vanilla pudding mix** | |
| **4 eggs** | |
| **1 cup water** | |
| **¼ cup cooking oil** | |

**Chocolate Glaze:** In 1½-qt. casserole place 2 squares (2-oz.) unsweetened chocolate and 1 tablespoon butter. **Microwave at Low 3 to 4 Minutes,** until melted. Stir. Add 2½ cups sifted confectioners sugar, ¼ cup boiling water and ⅛ teaspoon salt. Stir smooth.

Powdered Sugar

Coconut Microwave
Topping, page 267

Cherry Pie Filling

Brown Sugar and Pecans

## FRUIT-TOPPED LAYER CAKE

*Some good flavor combinations to try with this technique are: yellow cake mix with peach pie filling, spice cake mix with apple pie filling and chocolate cake mix with cherry pie filling.*

POWER LEVEL: High (10)      **Cook Code:**  80
MICROWAVE TIME: 8 to 9 min., per cake

**1 pkg. (2-layer) cake mix**  ..Prepare cake mix according to package directions.

**1 can (20 to 22-oz.) pie** ... Cut wax paper to fit bot-
**filling**                 toms of 2 8-in. round dishes. Pour half of pie filling in-
to each dish. Then, pour 2
cups of prepared cake
batter into each dish. If
square dishes are desired,
batter can be divided
evenly between them.

Microwave one cake at a time. **Microwave at High 8 to 9 Minutes,** rotating dish ½ turn after 4 minutes, until tooth-pick stuck in center comes out clean. Let cake stand 10 minutes directly on heat-proof counter or wooden board.

If tops of cakes are not even, slice small amount from tops so they may be stacked. Invert 1 layer on serving plate. Invert and stack second layer on top. If desired, frost sides of cake with whipped cream or whipped dessert topping.

Makes 1 (8-in.) layer cake

## HOW TO MICROWAVE SPECIAL CAKE MIXES

1. Prepare batter according to package directions.

2. Pour batter into greased 8-in. round dish.

3. Microwave at High and rotate dish as described in chart below.

4. Cake is done when toothpick stuck in center comes out clean.

5. Let cake stand directly on heat-proof counter or wooden board to cool.

POWER LEVEL: **High (10)**

| CAKE | TIME MIN. | COOK CODE | COMMENTS |
|---|---|---|---|
| **Boston Cream Pie** | 5 to 7 ¼ turn every 2 minutes | 50 | Prepare custard filling and frosting as package directs. |
| **Pineapple Upside Down Cake** | 9 to 12 ½ turn after 4 minutes | 90 | To prevent spill-over, remove ¼ cup batter to make 2 cupcakes. |
| **Snackin' Cake** | 8 to 10 ½ turn after 4 minutes | 80 | If ring shape is desired, place drinking glass (2-in. diameter), open side up in center of dish. Reduce time by 3 minutes. |

## EASY CHOCOLATE CAKE

POWER LEVEL: High (10)      **Cook Code:**    70
MICROWAVE TIME: 7 to 9 min., total

| | |
|---|---|
| **½ pkg. (2-layer size)** ..... **fudge cake mix (about 2 cups dry mix)** **1 egg** **½ teaspoon vanilla extract** **⅓ cup cooking oil** **¾ cup water** | In bottom of ungreased 8-in. square dish place dry cake mix. Add egg, vanilla, oil and water. Stir with fork until smooth and creamy. |
| **½ cup semi-sweet** ....... **chocolate pieces** | Sprinkle chocolate pieces over top. |

**Microwave at High 7 to 9 Minutes** (no turns necessary). Serve warm or cool with ice cream or thawed frozen whipped topping.

Makes 1 (8-in. square) cake

## HOW TO MICROWAVE CUPCAKES

Select a recipe from this section, or use your favorite homemade recipe (except do not use angel food or chiffon batters). For best shape, spoon into paper lined microwave cupcaker or "paper forms" described for muffins, page 224. Fill paper liners only ½ full.

You may also microwave cupcakes in double or triple thickness of paper liners only (without cupcaker or "paper forms"), but shape may be uneven. Cupcakes microwave very quickly; check for doneness at minimum time.

## CUPCAKE COOKING CHART

POWER LEVEL: **High (10)**

| CUPCAKES | TIME MINUTES | COMMENTS |
|---|---|---|
| 1 | ¼ to ½ | If cooking more than 2, arrange in a circle on shelf. |
| 2 | ¾ to 1 | |
| 3 | 1 to 1¼ | When cooking several cupcakes, you may notice some will be done before others. If so, remove cupcakes as they are done and continue cooking the rest a few seconds more. |
| 4 | 1¼ to 1½ | |
| 5 | 2 to 2¼ | |
| 6 | 2½ to 2¾ | |

## ICE CREAM 'N' CAKE CONES

1. Spoon 2 to 3 tablespoons of chocolate or fudge cake batter from mix into flat bottomed ice cream cones. Press a cherry, nut half, caramel or a few chocolate chips into batter.

2. Microwave according to Cupcake Chart, above.

½ batter recipe makes 25 to 30 cones

## BASIC BUTTER CAKE

POWER LEVEL: High (10)      **Cook Code:**    80
MICROWAVE TIME: 8 to 10 min., per cake

| | |
|---|---|
| **2¾ cups unsifted** ....... **all-purpose flour** **2 cups sugar** **3 teaspoons baking powder** **½ teaspoon salt** | In large mixing bowl stir together flour, sugar, baking powder and salt. |
| **1 cup (½-lb.) butter,** ..... **softened** **1 cup milk** **1½ teaspoons vanilla extract** **1 egg** | Add butter, milk, vanilla and 1 egg. Beat 2 minutes at lowest speed of mixer, scraping bowl constantly for first ½ minute. |
| **3 eggs** ............... | Stop mixer and add eggs. Continue beating at lowest speed, scraping bowl often, 1 more minute. Batter will look curdled. |

Pour batter into 2 paper towel lined 8-in. round dishes; spread evenly. Microwave 1 cake at a time. **Microwave at High 8 to 10 Minutes,** rotating dish ½ turn after 4 minutes. Let stand directly on heat-proof counter or wooden board to cool 15 minutes. Cake may then be turned out on wire rack to complete cooling, if desired.

Makes 2 (8-in. round) cakes

**Nut Cake:** Stir 1 cup finely chopped nuts into finished batter.

**Marble Cake:** After mixing batter, take out about ⅓ (2¼ cups) plain batter and drop in small mounds over bottom of dishes. To remaining batter in bowl, mix in ¼ teaspoon red food coloring; take out ½ (2¼ cups) of pink batter and drop in mounds in dishes. To remaining pink batter in bowl add 2 tablespoons cocoa and ½ teaspoon cinnamon; mix well and drop chocolate batter in mounds in dishes. With small spatula, swirl 3 colors of batter as much as desired. Microwave as above.

## CHOCOLATE CHIP FILLED CUPCAKES

| | |
|---|---|
| **Batter from 2-layer** ...... **chocolate cake mix** **Chocolate Chip Filling (below)** | Prepare cupcake liners, if desired (left). To make each cupcake, measure about 2 tablespoons batter into liner. Cover with 2 to 3 teaspoons filling. |

Microwave cupcakes as shown on chart (left). As cupcakes cook, filling forms in center.

Makes 30 cupcakes

**Chocolate Chip Filling:** Stir together 1 pkg. (8-oz.) softened cream cheese, ⅓ cup sugar, 1 egg, ⅛ teaspoon salt, until well mixed. Blend in 1 pkg. (6-oz.) chocolate chips.

## OLD-FASHIONED BUTTERMILK CAKE

POWER LEVEL: High (10)          **Cook Code:** 110
MICROWAVE TIME: 11 to 13 min., total

| 2½ cups unsifted | In large mixing bowl blend |
|---|---|

**2½ cups unsifted all-purpose flour**
**¾ cup sugar**
**1 cup brown sugar (packed)**
**1 teaspoon nutmeg**
**1 teaspoon salt**
**¾ cup cooking oil**
.......In large mixing bowl blend together with pastry blender, flour, sugar, brown sugar, nutmeg, salt and cooking oil to make a crumbly mixture. Reserve 1 cup of this mixture for cake topping.

**2 eggs, beaten**
**1 teaspoon baking powder**
**1 cup buttermilk**
**1 teaspoon baking soda**
........To rest of crumbly mixture, add eggs, baking powder and buttermilk mixed with soda. Stir together until smooth batter is formed. Pour into greased 12×8×2-in. dish.

**½ cup chopped walnuts**
**3 teaspoons cinnamon**
........Over cake batter in dish, sprinkle the reserved 1 cup crumbs, then mixture of walnuts and cinnamon. **Microwave at High 11 to 13 Minutes,** rotating dish ½ turn after 5 minutes.

**¼ cup soft butter**
**1 teaspoon vanilla extract**
**1 cup confectioners sugar**
**3 tablespoons coffee**
.......While cake is cooking, stir together butter, vanilla, confectioners sugar and coffee.

When cake is done, let stand directly on heat-proof counter or wooden board to cool. After cake has cooled 10 minutes, pour butter-sugar mixture over top; it will soak into cake. Serve cake warm "as is", or cool cake to room temperature; finish with Drizzle Glaze, if desired.

Makes 1 (12×8×2-in.) cake

**Drizzle Glaze:** Stir together ½ cup confectioners sugar and 2 tablespoons milk until smooth. From tip of spoon, drizzle over cake in fine lines. Let cake stand a few minutes until frosting sets before serving.

## BANANA BUTTERMILK CAKE

Prepare Old Fashioned Buttermilk Cake, except omit nutmeg in cake batter and also reduce buttermilk to ½ cup. Add 1 cup (about 2 medium) mashed bananas along with buttermilk.

If desired, reduce cinnamon to 1 teaspoon and mix with reserved crumb mixture and nuts. Omit coffee in butter-sugar mixture.

## SPICY APPLESAUCE CAKE

*Good with Cream Cheese Frosting, page 267, or other favorite frosting, if desired.*

POWER LEVEL: High (10)          **Cook Code:** 100
MICROWAVE TIME: 10 to 12 min., total

**1⅓ cups unsifted all-purpose flour**
**1 cup sugar**
**1 teaspoon baking soda**
**½ teaspoon salt**
**½ teaspoon cinnamon**
**½ teaspoon nutmeg**
**¼ teaspoon allspice**
**1½ tablespoons cocoa**
**⅓ cup cooking oil**
**1 egg**
**1 cup canned applesauce**
.......In large mixer bowl place flour, sugar, soda, salt, spices, cocoa, oil, egg and applesauce. Beat 2 minutes at lowest speed of mixer, scraping bowl constantly for first ½ minute.

**½ cup chopped pitted dates**
**½ cup raisins**
**½ cup chopped nuts**
...Stir in fruits and nuts well.

Pour into 12×8×2-in. dish which has been greased on bottom only. **Microwave at High 10 to 12 Minutes,** rotating dish ½ turn after 5 minutes, until toothpick stuck in several places in cake comes out clean. Let cake stand directly on heat-proof counter or wooden board to cool.

Makes 1 (12×8×2-in.) cake

## CHOCOLATE BEAUTY CAKE

*Coconut-Nut Microwave Topping, page 267, is especially good with this cake.*

POWER LEVEL: High (10)          **Cook Code:** 80
MICROWAVE TIME: 8 to 10 min., total

**1½ cups unsifted all-purpose flour**
**1 cup brown sugar (packed)**
**¼ cup cocoa**
**1 teaspoon baking soda**
**½ teaspoon salt**
**½ cup water**
.......In mixing bowl stir together flour, sugar, cocoa, soda and salt. Add water and stir to a stiff shiny batter, about 100 strokes.

**½ cup water**
**⅓ cup cooking oil**
**1 tablespoon vinegar**
**1½ teaspoons vanilla extract**
..........Add additional ½ cup water, oil, vinegar and vanilla. Stir until smooth and well blended.

Pour batter into greased 8-in. round dish. **Microwave at High 8 to 10 Minutes,** rotating dish ½ turn after 4 minutes. Let stand directly on heat-proof counter or wooden board to cool. Finish with favorite frosting, or as desired.

Makes 1 (8-in. round) cake

Pineapple Upside Down Cake

## PINEAPPLE UPSIDE DOWN CAKE

*For variety substitute peaches for pineapple and almond extract for vanilla.*

POWER LEVEL: High (10)
MICROWAVE TIME: 9¾ to 13 min., total

| | |
|---|---|
| ¼ cup butter . . . . . . . . . . . | In 8-in. round dish place butter. **Microwave at High ¾ to 1 Minute,** to melt. Sprinkle sugar over butter. Drain pineapple (save liquid) on paper towels and arrange in dish. Decorate with cherries. |
| ⅓ cup brown sugar (packed) | |
| 1 can (8¼-oz.) pineapple slices | |
| 4 maraschino or candied cherries, cut in half | |
| 1¼ cups unsifted . . . . . . . all-purpose flour | In small mixer bowl place flour, sugar, baking powder, salt, shortening, egg, liquid and vanilla. Beat 3 minutes on lowest mixer speed, scraping bowl constantly first ½ minute. Carefully spread batter over fruit in dish. |
| ¾ cup sugar | |
| 2 teaspoons baking powder | |
| ½ teaspoon salt | |
| ⅓ cup soft shortening | |
| 1 egg | |
| Liquid from pineapple plus milk to total ½ cup | |
| 1 teaspoon vanilla extract | |

**Microwave at High 9 to 12 Minutes,** rotating dish ½ turn after 5 minutes. Some batter may run onto edges of dish, but will not spill. When done, toothpick stuck in cake comes out clean. Invert cake onto plate, let dish stand over cake a few minutes. Serve hot or warm.

Makes 1 (8-in.) round cake

## POPULAR CARROT CAKE

POWER LEVEL: High (10)      **Cook Code:** 130
MICROWAVE TIME: 13 to 15 min., total

| | |
|---|---|
| 1½ cups sugar . . . . . . . . . . | In large mixing bowl blend sugar, oil and vanilla. Add eggs and beat well. |
| 1 cup cooking oil | |
| 1 teaspoon vanilla extract | |
| 3 eggs | |
| 1½ cups unsifted . . . . . . all-purpose flour | In small bowl, stir together flour, salt, soda and cinnamon. Add to sugar-egg mixture and mix in. |
| ¾ teaspoon salt | |
| 1¼ teaspoons baking soda | |
| 2½ teaspoons cinnamon | |
| 2¼ cups raw grated carrots | Fold in carrots and walnuts. Pour batter into greased 12×8×2-in. dish. |
| ½ cup chopped walnuts | |

**Microwave at High 13 to 15 Minutes,** rotating dish ½ turn every 4 minutes. Let stand directly on heat-proof counter or wooden board to cool. Frost with Cream Cheese Frosting, page 267, if desired.

Makes 1 (12×8×2-in.) cake

## HONEY DRIZZLE CAKE

*This recipe won $5,000 in a recent microwave recipe contest.*

POWER LEVEL: High (10)      **Cook Code:** 160
MICROWAVE TIME: 16 to 18 min., total

| | |
|---|---|
| 5 eggs . . . . . . . . . . . . . . | Separate eggs. In large mixer bowl beat egg whites until foamy. Gradually beat in ¼ cup sugar and salt until fluffy. |
| ¼ cup sugar | |
| ⅛ teaspoon salt | |
| ½ cup sugar . . . . . . . . . . | In small bowl beat egg yolks, ½ cup sugar and vanilla until thick and pale. |
| 1 teaspoon vanilla extract | |
| 1½ cups chopped . . . . . . pecans | Fold yolk mixture into egg whites thoroughly. Blend pecans, wafer crumbs, baking powder and cinnamon; sprinkle over top. Fold all ingredients together well. |
| 1½ cups fine vanilla wafer crumbs | |
| 1½ teaspoons baking powder | |
| ½ teaspoon cinnamon | |

Pour into greased 8-in. square dish. **Microwave at High 8 to 10 Minutes,** rotating dish ½ turn after 4 minutes. Remove cake and cook Honey Syrup (below). Carefully pour syrup over cake. Serve in small pieces, warm or cold, with unsweetened whipped cream.

**Honey Syrup:** In 2-qt. casserole stir together 1½ cups water, 1½ cups sugar and ⅔ cup honey. **Microwave at High 8 Minutes,** stirring after 4 minutes. **Cook Code:** 80.

Makes 1 (8-in.) square cake

# PECAN SPONGE ROLL

*Fill Pecan Sponge Roll with vanilla ice cream instead of cream filling for a good make-ahead frozen dessert. Serve in slices with chocolate sauce.*

POWER LEVEL: High (10)          **Cook Code:** 80
MICROWAVE TIME: 6 to 8 min., total

Prepare paper on which to microwave Pecan Sponge Roll. Cut a sheet of wax paper (which is 12-in. wide) into a 28-in. long piece. Fold in half, making a double thickness of paper 14×12-in. in size. Cut a piece of brown paper (from grocery bag, if desired) same size and place under wax paper for added support. Generously butter top of wax paper.

| | |
|---|---|
| **4 eggs, separated** | In small mixer bowl, beat |
| **½ cup sifted confectioners sugar** | egg whites, until stiff. In large mixer bowl, beat egg yolks and sugar until thick and pale in color. Add va- |
| **2 teaspoons vanilla extract** | nilla. Mix pecans with bak- |
| **1½ cups ground pecans or pecan meal\*** | ing powder and fold into egg yolk mixture. Fold in |
| **¾ teaspoon baking powder** | stiffly beaten egg whites. |

Spread batter evenly on buttered wax paper to within 1-in. of edges. Handling carefully, place cake in microwave oven. **Microwave at High 6 to 8 Minutes,** until toothpick stuck in cake comes out clean. Let cake stand in microwave oven 1 minute, then carefully transfer to cooling rack. Cover with dish towel wrung out with cold water. Let cool.

When cool, remove towel and spread Vanilla Filling over cake. Roll up as for jelly roll starting at short side and peeling off wax paper as cake is rolled. Sprinkle with powdered sugar just before serving, or if desired, top with vanilla glaze.

Makes 12 (1-in.) slices

\*Ground pecans are found packaged at grocery stores, especially at holiday time. Or, if desired, whir pecans in blender until finely ground.

**Vanilla Filling:** In small mixer bowl, place 2 cups well-chilled whipping cream and 1 pkg. (3¾-oz.) instant vanilla pudding mix. Beat at high speed of mixer until thick and fluffy.

**Vanilla Glaze:** In small bowl stir together 1 cup confectioners sugar, 1 tablespoon corn syrup and 1 tablespoon water. **Microwave at Low ½ to 1 Minute,** just until lukewarm. Stir well and pour over Pecan Roll to glaze.

NOTE: To easily transfer batter and paper to oven, place a cookie sheet under the paper. Slide batter-topped paper from cookie sheet into oven. Same cookie sheet can be used to transfer baked cake from oven.

# ORANGE-GLAZED FRUIT CAKE

POWER LEVEL: High (10)          **Cook Code:** 140
MICROWAVE TIME: 14 to 16 min., total

| | |
|---|---|
| **1 cup (3 to 4-oz.) coconut** | In mixing bowl stir together coconut, flour, sugar and |
| **1 cup unsifted all-purpose flour** | baking powder. |
| **1½ cups confectioners sugar** | |
| **2 teaspoons baking powder** | |
| **¾ cup butter, melted** | Add butter, eggs and milk. |
| **3 eggs, beaten** | Mix well. |
| **½ cup milk** | |
| **2 cups chopped candied fruit** | Stir in fruit and nuts. Pour batter into greased 12× |
| **1½ cups chopped pecans** | 8×2-in. dish. |

**Microwave at High 14 to 16 Minutes,** rotating dish ½ turn after 8 minutes. Spoon Orange Glaze over hot cake.

**Orange Glaze:** In 1-qt. casserole stir together ½ cup sugar and 1 cup orange juice. Cover. **Microwave at High 3 to 5 Minutes,** until boiling. **Cook Code:** 30.

Makes 1 (12×8×2-in.) cake

# STEAMED PUDDING

POWER LEVEL: High (10) and Medium High (7)
MICROWAVE TIME: 17 to 19½ min., total

| | |
|---|---|
| **1 cup water** | Measure water into glass |
| **1 cup seedless raisins or cranberries** | measure. **Microwave at High 2 to 2½ Minutes,** until at rolling boil. Pour over fruit and let stand. |
| **2 tablespoons butter** | Beat together butter, sug- |
| **½ cup sugar** | ar, molasses and egg. |
| **½ cup molasses** | |
| **1 egg** | |
| **1½ cups unsifted all-purpose flour** | Stir together flour, baking soda and salt. Add flour |
| **1 teaspoon baking soda** | mixture and fruit with water to creamed mixture. |
| **1 teaspoon salt** | |

Lightly grease 2-qt. casserole, then place 2-in. diameter drinking glass (open side up) in center. Pour batter around glass. Cover dish well with plastic wrap. **Microwave at Medium High 15 to 17 Minutes,** rotating dish ½ turn every 5 minutes, until pudding appears set, but glossy. Remove from oven with pot holders.

Let stand 10 to 20 minutes; twist glass to remove. Unmold onto cooling rack. When cold, wrap well and allow pudding to age about a week before slicing. Serve with Hard Sauce or Citrus Sauce, page 269.

Makes about 10 to 12 servings

## EARLY AMERICAN GINGERBREAD

*Serve warm, topped with Citrus Sauce, page 269, or whipped cream, if desired.*

POWER LEVEL: High (10)      **Cook Code:**   50
MICROWAVE TIME: 5 to 6 min., total

| | |
|---|---|
| **1½ cups unsifted all-purpose flour** | In mixing bowl stir together flour, sugar, baking soda, ginger, cinnamon and salt. |
| **½ cup sugar** | |
| **¾ teaspoon baking soda** | |
| **½ teaspoon ginger** | |
| **½ teaspoon cinnamon** | |
| **½ teaspoon salt** | |
| **½ cup soft shortening** | Add shortening, egg, molasses and water. Beat 2 minutes on medium speed of mixer until well blended. |
| **1 egg** | |
| **½ cup light molasses** | |
| **½ cup hottest tap water** | |

Pour batter into greased 8-in. round dish. **Microwave at High 5 to 6 Minutes,** rotating dish ½ turn after 3 minutes. When cake is done let stand directly on heat-proof counter or wooden board to cool.

Makes 8 servings

## CONVENIENCE CAKE DEFROSTING CHART

Cakes packaged in foil should be removed from the foil and placed on a plate, or on an all cardboard lid. Frosted layer cakes can be defrosted on the styrofoam base.

Watch icing and frosting closely as they melt easily. Defrosted cakes should be cool and easy to cut. Let cakes stand 2 to 5 minutes before serving.

POWER LEVEL: **Defrost**

| ITEM | TIME MINUTES | COMMENTS |
|---|---|---|
| 2 to 3-layer, frosted (17-oz.) | 2 | |
| 1 piece, frosted | ½ | |
| 1-layer, frosted, filled or topped (12½ to 16 oz.) | 2 to 3 | Rotate ½ turn after ½ minute. |
| Pound Cake (11¼-oz.) | 2 | |
| 1 piece pound cake | ½ | |
| Cheesecake, plain or fruit topped (17 to 19-oz.) | 5 to 6 | Rotate ¼ turn every 2 minutes. |
| Crunch Cakes and Cupcakes (1 or 2) | ½ to 1 | |
| Crunch Cakes and Cupcakes (3 or 4) | 1 to 2 | |
| Crunch Cakes and Cupcakes (5 to 8) | 2 to 3 | Arrange in circle on plate. Rotate ½ turn after ½ minute. |

## BASIC CHEESECAKE

*Cheesecake, which is a custard rather than a batter, is especially appropriate for microwaving.*

POWER LEVEL: High (10) and Medium (5)
MICROWAVE TIME: 24¾ to 28½ min., total

| | |
|---|---|
| **3 tablespoons butter** | In 8-in. round dish place butter. **Microwave at High ¼ to ½ Minute,** to melt. Stir in crumbs and sugar. Press mixture on bottom and sides of dish. **Microwave at High 1½ to 2 Minutes,** rotating dish ½ turn after 1 minute, until set. |
| **1 cup fine crumbs (graham cracker or chocolate cookie)** | |
| **2 tablespoons sugar** | |
| **4 eggs** | In blender container place eggs, sugar, cream cheese, vanilla and salt. Blend on high speed 1 minute until smooth. (If mixed with electric mixer, use large mixer bowl and mix at high speed 3 minutes.) Pour over back of spoon into crust.* |
| **1 cup sugar** | |
| **2 pkg. (8-oz. each) cream cheese** | |
| **2 teaspoons vanilla extract** | |
| **¼ teaspoon salt** | |

**Microwave at Medium 23 to 26 Minutes,** rotating dish ¼ turn every 7 minutes, until center is almost set. Refrigerate at least 3 hours before serving. Garnish with Whipped Cream Cheese Topping (below) and chocolate curls, if desired.

Makes 1 (8-in.) cheesecake
8 to 12 servings

*Pouring over spoon prevents crust from breaking.

**Whipped Cream Cheese Topping:** In small mixer bowl place 1 pkg. (3-oz.) softened cream cheese, ½ cup whipping cream and 2 tablespoons sugar. Beat until fluffy. Serve in dollops or spread over top.

## VERY CHOCOLATE CHEESECAKE

Prepare recipe above with Chocolate Cookie Crust. Add 2 squares (2-oz.) unsweetened chocolate, melted, to filling. For light chocolate, use 1 square of chocolate.

## CREME DE MENTHE CHEESECAKE

Prepare recipe above with Chocolate Cookie Crust. Omit vanilla, add ¼ cup green creme de menthe to filling.

## IRISH COFFEE CHEESECAKE

Prepare recipe above with Graham Cracker Crust. Omit vanilla, add 1 teaspoon instant coffee powder and ¼ cup Irish mist liqueur to filling.

## REFRESHING ORANGE CHEESECAKE

Prepare recipe above with Chocolate Cookie Crust. Omit vanilla and add ¼ cup orange juice concentrate, undiluted, and 1 tablespoon grated fresh orange peel.

## EASY FUDGE FROSTING

POWER LEVEL: High (10)　　Cook Code:　30
MICROWAVE TIME: 3 to 4 min., total

**1 cup sugar** . . . . . . . . . . . .In 1½-qt. casserole com-
**¼ cup butter**　　　　　　bine sugar, butter and
**¼ cup evaporated milk**　evaporated milk. **Micro-
**　　　　　　　　　　　　wave at High 3 to 4 Min-
**　　　　　　　　　　　　utes,** uncovered, stirring
　　　　　　　　　　　　after 2 minutes, until
　　　　　　　　　　　　bubbly.

**1 cup (6-oz.)** . . . . . . . . . . . .Add chocolate pieces,
**　semi-sweet**　　　　　marshmallow creme and
**　chocolate pieces**　　vanilla to hot mixture. Stir
**1 cup marshmallow**　　until well blended. Excel-
**　creme**　　　　　　　lent on brownies or plain
**1 teaspoon vanilla**　　cake layers.
**　extract**

Makes about 2 cups frosting

## BASIC CONFECTIONERS SUGAR FROSTING

POWER LEVEL: High (10)　　Cook Code:　10
MICROWAVE TIME: 1 to 2 min., total

**1 pkg. (1-lb.)** . . . . . . . . . .In 1½-qt. casserole place
**　confectioners sugar**　sugar, milk, salt and vanilla
**¼ cup milk**　　　　　　and stir just to blend slight-
**¼ teaspoon salt**　　　ly (mixture is too stiff to mix
**1 teaspoon vanilla**　　thoroughly). Add butter on
**　extract**　　　　　　　top.
**¼ cup butter**

**Microwave at High 1 to 2 Minutes,** until mixture can be beaten smooth.

NOTE: Add additional 1 to 2 teaspoons milk if mixture is too stiff.

Makes enough frosting for
2 (8-in.) round or square layers

## BUTTERCREAM FROSTING

Using above recipe decrease milk to 2 tablespoons and increase butter to ½ cup. Microwave as above. If mixture gets too hot, it will be runny and may run off cake. Let frosting stand in bowl a few minutes, stirring occasionally, before icing cake. As it cools, it thickens.

## COCONUT-NUT FROSTING FROM A MIX

POWER LEVEL: High (10)　　Cook Code:　10
MICROWAVE TIME: 1 to 1½ min., total

**1 pkg. (9.9-oz.) coconut** . . .In 1-qt. casserole place
**　nut frosting mix**　　frosting mix, milk and but-
**Milk**　　　　　　　　　ter (use amounts on pack-
**Butter**　　　　　　　　age). **Microwave at High
**　　　　　　　　　　　　1 to 1½ Minutes,** until mix-
　　　　　　　　　　　　ture can be stirred smooth.

Easy Fudge Frosting

## COCONUT MICROWAVE TOPPING

POWER LEVEL: High (10)　　Cook Code:　20
MICROWAVE TIME: 2 min., total

**1 cup brown sugar** . . . . .In 1-qt. casserole blend to-
**　(packed)**　　　　　　gether brown sugar, corn-
**1 tablespoon**　　　　　starch and milk. Add but-
**　cornstarch**　　　　　ter. **Microwave at High 2
**2 tablespoons milk**　　**Minutes,** stirring after 1
**2 tablespoons butter**　minute.

**½ cup flaked coconut** . . . .Stir mixture well, then stir in
　　　　　　　　　　　　coconut. Pour over cooled
　　　　　　　　　　　　cake.

Makes enough frosting for
2 (8-in.) round or square layers

**Coconut-Nut Microwave Topping:** Add ¼ to ½ cup chopped nuts (walnuts, pecans or peanuts) along with coconut.

## CREAM CHEESE FROSTING

POWER LEVEL: High　　　　Cook Code:　10
MICROWAVE TIME: 1 min., total

**1 lb. confectioners** . . . . . .In 2-qt. casserole place
**　sugar**　　　　　　　sugar. Put cream cheese,
**1 pkg. (8-oz.) cream**　butter and vanilla over top.
**　cheese**　　　　　　　**Microwave at High 1 Min-
**6 tablespoons butter**　**ute,** just until ingredients
**2 teaspoons vanilla**　can be beaten together.
**　extract**　　　　　　　For a fluffy frosting, beat
　　　　　　　　　　　　with electric mixer.

This recipe makes a very generous amount of frosting for top of 12×8×2-in. cake. If you desire thin layer of frosting, reserve leftover in refrigerator or freezer for another cake.

# Dessert Sauces

Delicious, smooth and creamy dessert sauces microwave with exceptional ease and speed. With conventional cooking, they require care in melting chocolate or dissolving sugar mixtures, and constant stirring to prevent scorching and lumps. With microwave cooking, stirring is minimal and sauces are ready in 2 to 7 minutes.

## QUICKIE CHOCOLATE SAUCE

| POWER LEVEL: High (10) | Cook Code: 20 |
|---|---|
| MICROWAVE TIME: 1½ to 2½ min., total | |

| | |
|---|---|
| ½ cup light corn syrup<br>1 pkg. (6-oz.)<br>semi-sweet<br>chocolate pieces<br>1 tablespoon butter | . . .Into 1-pt. glass measure, measure syrup. Stir in chocolate and butter. **Microwave at High 1½ to 2½ Minutes.** Stir until completely smooth. |
| ¼ cup dairy half & half<br>or milk<br>¼ teaspoon vanilla or<br>rum extract | . . .Blend in half & half and vanilla. Serve warm or cold. |

Makes about 1½ cups

## SCRUMPTIOUS BUTTERSCOTCH SAUCE

*Its name describes how it tastes.*

| POWER LEVEL: High (10) | Cook Code: 40 |
|---|---|
| MICROWAVE TIME: 3½ to 4½ min., total | |

| | |
|---|---|
| 1 tablespoon<br>cornstarch<br>1¼ cups light brown<br>sugar (packed)<br>½ cup dairy half & half<br>2 tablespoons light<br>corn syrup<br>⅛ teaspoon salt<br>¼ cup butter | . . . . . . . . . .In 1½-qt. casserole stir together cornstarch and brown sugar. Stir in half & half, corn syrup and salt. Add butter. Cover. **Microwave at High 3½ to 4½ Minutes,** stirring after 2 minutes, until thickened and sugar is dissolved |
| 1 teaspoon vanilla<br>extract | . . . . . .Add vanilla and stir until smooth and well blended. Serve warm or cold. |

Makes 1½ cups

## WONDERFUL MAPLE NUT SAUCE

Prepare recipe above, substituting 1 teaspoon maple flavoring for vanilla. Add ⅓ cup chopped nuts if desired.

Scrumptious Butterscotch Sauce

## CRUNCHY CHOCOLATE SAUCE

POWER LEVEL: High (10)          **Cook Code:**   30
MICROWAVE TIME: 2½ to 4 min., total

| ¼ cup milk | In 1-pt. glass measure, measure milk. Drop in chocolate. **Microwave at High 1½ to 2 Minutes.** Blend chocolate and milk. |
| 1 square (1-oz.) unsweetened chocolate | |
| ¾ cup light brown sugar (packed) | Add sugar; stir to blend. **Microwave at High 1 to 2 Minutes,** until mixture boils. |
| ¼ cup crunchy peanut butter | Add peanut butter and vanilla and stir until well blended. Serve warm or cool. |
| ¼ teaspoon vanilla extract | |

Makes 1 cup

## FUDGE SAUCE

*The kind which mounds from a spoon.*

POWER LEVEL: High (10)          **Cook Code:**   50
MICROWAVE TIME: 5 to 6 min., total

| 1 cup sugar | In 3-qt. casserole stir together sugar, salt and milk, until blended. **Microwave at High 5 to 6 Minutes,** until boiling hard. |
| ¼ teaspoon salt | |
| 1 can (5.3-oz.) evaporated milk | |
| 2 squares (2-oz.) unsweetened chocolate | Into boiling mixture stir in chocolate until completely melted. Stir in butter and vanilla. |
| 2 tablespoons butter | |
| 1 teaspoon vanilla | |

Makes about 1½ cups

## FESTIVE RICH BUTTER SAUCE

POWER LEVEL: High (10)          **Cook Code:**   30
MICROWAVE TIME: 2½ to 3½ min., total

| 1 cup sugar | In 1-qt. casserole stir together sugar and half & half. Add butter. Cover. **Microwave at High 2½ to 3½ Minutes,** until sugar dissolves. Stir vigorously to combine. This rich sauce may separate slightly on standing. If so, stir again. |
| ½ cup dairy half & half | |
| ½ cup (¼-lb.) butter | |

Makes 1½ cups

NOTE: If desired, ½ teaspoon rum extract or 1 tablespoon brandy, rum, sherry or fruit flavored brandy may be stirred into sauce after cooking.

## CINNAMON SUGAR SAUCE

POWER LEVEL: High (10)          **Cook Code:**   30
MICROWAVE TIME: 3 to 4 min., total

| ½ cup sugar | In 1-qt. casserole stir together sugar, cornstarch, cinnamon and water, until completely smooth. Cover. **Microwave at High 3 to 4 Minutes,** stirring sauce after 1½ minutes. |
| 1½ tablespoons cornstarch | |
| 1 teaspoon cinnamon | |
| 1 cup hot tap water | |
| 2 tablespoons butter | Stir in butter until well blended. Serve warm. |

Makes 1⅓ cups

## CITRUS SAUCE

Prepare recipe above, omitting cinnamon. Stir 1 tablespoon lemon or orange juice and 1 to 2 teaspoons finely grated lemon or orange rind into sugar mixture.

## HARD SAUCE

POWER LEVEL: High (10)          **Cook Code:**   10
MICROWAVE TIME: 1½ to 2 min., total

| 1 pkg. (1-lb.) confectioners sugar | In small glass mixer bowl or 1½-qt. casserole place sugar, salt and rum. Place butter on top. **Microwave at High 1½ to 2 Minutes.** |
| ¼ teaspoon salt | |
| ¼ cup rum or brandy* | |
| ½ cup (¼-lb.) butter | |

Beat on highest speed of mixer until smooth. Sauce will be soft and creamy after beating. If a true hard sauce is desired, refrigerate until hardened. Serve over plum pudding or other baked fruit puddings, or with fruit cake, gingerbread, applesauce cake, etc. Or use as "frosting" for fruit cake.

*Or use ¼ cup milk with 1 to 2 teaspoons vanilla, rum or brandy flavoring (or use orange or lemon extract).

Makes 2 cups

## TOASTED ALMOND SAUCE

POWER LEVEL: High (10)
MICROWAVE TIME: 7 to 9 min., total

| ½ cup (¼-lb.) butter | In 1½-qt. casserole place butter. **Microwave at High 2 Minutes.** |
| 3 pkgs. (2⅞-oz. each) sliced almonds | Add nuts and stir until well coated. **Microwave at High 5 to 7 Minutes,** stirring well after 3 minutes, until bubbly and golden brown. |
| 1 jar (1-lb.) honey Nutmeg | Stir in honey until evenly mixed. Sprinkle generously with nutmeg. Serve hot. |

Makes about 12 servings

## TRUE BLUEBERRY SAUCE

| POWER LEVEL: High (10) | **Cook Code:** 50 |
|---|---|
| MICROWAVE TIME: 5 to 7 min., total | |

**1 tablespoon lemon juice**
**2 tablespoons cornstarch**
**¼ cup sugar**
**⅛ teaspoon salt**
**1 can (16-oz.) blueberries**

In 1-qt. casserole stir together lemon juice and cornstarch. Add sugar and salt. Stir in undrained blueberries. **Microwave at High 5 to 7 Minutes,** stirring every 2 minutes, until sauce is thickened and clear. Serve over ice cream, pancakes or unfrosted cake such as pound cake.

Makes about 1½ cups

TO USE FROZEN BLUEBERRIES: Place 1 (10-oz.) pouch package of blueberries in microwave oven. **Microwave at Defrost 5 to 7 Minutes,** just until berries can be separated. Substitute for canned blueberries. Add ½ to ¾ cup water for liquid, increasing cooking time, if necessary.

Mint on Mint Sundaes

## CINNAMON GLAZED PINEAPPLE SAUCE

| POWER LEVEL: High (10) | **Cook Code:** 60 |
|---|---|
| MICROWAVE TIME: 6 to 7 min., total | |

**1 can (13½-oz.) pineapple tidbits**
**2 tablespoons sugar**
**1 tablespoon cornstarch**
**¼ teaspoon cinnamon**
**2 tablespoons butter**

In 1-qt. casserole place pineapple. In small cup mix together sugar, cornstarch and cinnamon. Add to pineapple, stirring well. Cut butter in 2 pieces and place over top. Cover.

**Microwave at High 6 to 7 Minutes,** stirring well after 3 minutes. Serve hot.

Makes 1⅔ cups sauce

## MINT-ON-MINT SUNDAES

*Chocolate mint sauce is also delicious on plain chocolate or chocolate ripple ice cream.*

| POWER LEVEL: Medium (5) | TEMP: 140° |
|---|---|
| APPROX. MICROWAVE TIME: 2 to 3 min. | |
| | **Cook Code:** 25 |

**1 pkg. (6½-oz.) chocolate covered mint patties\*\***
**¼ cup whipping cream**

In 1-pt. glass measure place unwrapped mint patties. Add cream.

Insert temperature probe so tip rests on center bottom of cup. Cover with plastic wrap arranging loosely around probe to vent. Attach cable end at receptacle. **Microwave at Medium. Set Temp, Set 140°.**

When oven signals, stir sauce smooth. Serve warm chocolate mint sauce over mint ice cream.

\*\*6½-oz. package contains about 24 patties, about 1¼-in. diameter each.

Makes about 1 cup sauce

## HOW TO WARM COMMERCIAL SUNDAE SAUCES

Commercial sundae sauces and syrups seem special when warm. Pour sauce or syrup into microwave oven-proof pitcher or measure. Avoid heating in original glass containers which might not be heat tempered.

To soften a 12-oz. jar of cold sauce topping from the refrigerator, **Microwave at High ½ Minute.** For hot fudge or butterscotch, heat about 1 minute more.

Try canned pie fillings as sundae toppings. Cherry or blueberry pie fillings are great favorites.

# Jellies, Jams & Relishes

Like all fruits and vegetables cooked by microwaves, jellies, jams and relishes retain their sparkling fresh flavor. Because microwave energy heats from all sides, not just the bottom, sugar mixtures do not scorch and need very little stirring. As with range top cooking, they boil up high, so be sure to use a large casserole. Since fruit juices do not evaporate in microwaving, we recommend using fruit pectin to thicken jellies, jams and preserves. You will also obtain a greater yield for the same amount of fruit.

## GENERAL RECOMMENDATIONS FOR JELLY AND JAM MAKING

1. Use High Power on all recipes.

2. Whenever pectin is added – add gradually, stirring very well.

3. Use pot holders as sugar mixtures get very hot.

4. Avoid steam burns by lifting lid away from you when removing.

5. Pour jelly into hot sterilized jars or glasses; wipe off rim well, then seal with hot sterilized lids or paraffin. Sterilizing should be done in pot of boiling water on surface unit. Paraffin manufacturers recommend melting paraffin in a double boiler.

6. If you live in a warm or humid southern climate, the United States Department of Agriculture recommends that you water-bath process the filled and sealed jars of chunky preserves and jams for about 5 minutes.

## APPLE JELLY

POWER LEVEL: High (10)
MICROWAVE TIME: 17 to 21 min., total

| | |
|---|---|
| **2 cups bottled unsweetened apple juice**<br>**3½ cups sugar** | In 3-qt. casserole stir together apple juice and sugar. Cover. **Microwave at High 12 to 14 Minutes,** stirring after 6 minutes, until boiling. |
| **½ bottle (6-oz.) liquid fruit pectin** | Stir in pectin, mixing thoroughly. Cover. **Microwave at High 4 to 6 Minutes** more, until mixture returns to boil. **Then, time for 1 minute of boiling.** Stir and skim off foam if necessary. Ladle into prepared glasses. Seal.<br><br>Makes about 3 cups |

Fresh Peach Jam

## GRAPE JELLY FROM FROZEN JUICE

*It is very important to mix pectin well with juice before microwaving.*

POWER LEVEL: High (10)
MICROWAVE TIME: 15 to 18 min., total

| | |
|---|---|
| **1 can (6-oz.) frozen grape juice concentrate, defrosted**<br>**1 pkg. (1¾-oz.) powdered fruit pectin**<br>**2 cups hot tap water** | In 3-qt. casserole, blend together grape juice and pectin. Stir in water. Cover. **Microwave at High 8 to 9 Minutes,** stirring well after 4 minutes, until bubbles form around edge of dish. |
| **3¾ cups sugar** | Add sugar, mixing well. Cover. **Microwave at High 6 to 8 Minutes,** stirring well after 4 minutes, until mixture boils. **Then, time for 1 minute of boiling.** Stir and skim off foam with metal spoon. Ladle into prepared glasses. Seal.<br><br>Makes about 4 cups |

## SPARKLING CHAMPAGNE JELLY

*Other wines such as red, rose, burgundy, port and white may be used in this recipe.*

POWER LEVEL: High (10)
MICROWAVE TIME: 9 to 11 min., total

| | |
|---|---|
| **1¾ cups champagne wine**<br>**3 cups sugar** | In 3-qt. casserole, stir together champagne and sugar. Cover. **Microwave at High 8 to 10 Minutes,** stirring after 4 minutes, until mixture begins to boil. **Then, time for 1 minute more of boiling.** Stir. |
| **½ bottle liquid fruit pectin** | Gradually stir pectin into hot mixture, mixing well. Ladle into prepared glasses.* Seal. |

Makes about 4 cups

NOTE: Other wines such as red, rose, burgundy, port and white may be used in this recipe.

*For gift giving, place a washed bunch of fresh grapes in each glass before adding jelly. Especially pretty when sealed in custard cups with parrafin and unmolded on plate for serving. Use immediately; grapes show age after about 1 month.

## FRESH STRAWBERRY JAM

POWER LEVEL: High (10)
MICROWAVE TIME: 17 to 21 min., total

| | |
|---|---|
| **4½ cups crushed fresh strawberries (wash and stem before crushing)**<br>**1 box (1¾-oz.) powdered fruit pectin** | In 3-qt. casserole place berries and pectin. Stir well. Cover. **Microwave at High 8 to 10 Minutes,** until mixture is at a full rolling boil. |
| **7 cups sugar** | Add sugar to boiling mixture and stir well. |

**Microwave at High 8 to 10 Minutes,** uncovered, stirring after 5 minutes, until mixture reaches a full rolling boil. **Then, time for 1 minute of boiling.** Skim off foam with metal spoon, stirring jam about 5 minutes before ladling into prepared glasses. Seal.

Makes about 8 cups

## STRAWBERRY JAM FROM FROZEN BERRIES

*This spread can be made year round.*

POWER LEVEL: High (10)
MICROWAVE TIME: 21 to 27 min., total

| | |
|---|---|
| **3 pkgs. (10-oz. each) strawberries in plastic pouch** | Place unopened packages in microwave oven. **Microwave at High 4 to 6 Minutes,** checking at minimum time and rearranging fruit if continued defrosting is necessary. |
| **2 tablespoons water**<br>**½ box (2½ tablespoons) powdered fruit pectin** | Remove fruit from pouches and place in 3-qt. casserole. Crush the fruit. Add water and pectin, stirring well. Cover. **Microwave at High 8 to 10 Minutes,** or until mixture is at a full rolling boil. Stir. |
| **3 cups sugar** | Add sugar to boiling mixture and stir well. |

**Microwave at High 8 to 10 Minutes,** uncovered, stirring after 5 minutes, until mixture reaches a full rolling boil. **Then, time for 1 minute of boiling.** Skim off foam and stir jam about 5 minutes before ladling into prepared glasses. Seal.

Makes about 4½ cups

## APPLESAUCE BUTTER

*Start with about 1-qt. of applesauce to make this recipe. It is very good made with microwaved applesauce, page 240.*

POWER LEVEL: High (10)
MICROWAVE TIME: 18 to 22 min., total

| | |
|---|---|
| **1 qt. (4 cups) applesauce (or 2 cans, 16-oz. each)**<br>**1 pkg. (1¾-oz.) powdered fruit pectin**<br>**1 tablespoon pumpkin pie spice**<br>**1 teaspoon cinnamon** | In 3-qt. casserole stir together applesauce, pectin, pumpkin pie spice and cinnamon. Cover. **Microwave at High 8 to 10 Minutes,** stirring after 5 minutes, until mixture boils. |
| **4½ cups sugar** | Add sugar to hot mixture, stirring well. Cover. **Microwave at High 9 to 11 Minutes,** stirring every 5 minutes, until mixture reaches a full boil. **Then, time for 1 minute of boiling.** Stir well. Ladle into prepared glasses. Seal. |

Makes about 6 cups

# FRESH PEACH JAM

POWER LEVEL: High (10)
MICROWAVE TIME: 16 to 20 min., total

**4 cups peeled, pitted and finely chopped peaches**
**2 tablespoons lemon juice**
**1 box (1¾-oz.) powdered fruit pectin** . . .In 3-qt. casserole place peaches, lemon juice and pectin. Stir well. Cover. **Microwave at High 8 to 10 Minutes,** or until mixture is at a full rolling boil. Stir.

**5½ cups sugar** . . . . . . . . . .Add sugar to boiling mixture, stirring well. **Microwave at High 7 to 9 Minutes,** uncovered, stirring after 4 minutes, until mixture reaches a full rolling boil. **Then, time for 1 more minute of boiling.** Skim off foam and stir jam about 5 minutes before ladling into prepared glasses. Seal.

Makes about 7 cups

# PEACH CONSERVE

POWER LEVEL: High (10)
MICROWAVE TIME: 17 to 19 min., total

**3½ cups peeled, pitted finely chopped peaches**
**½ cup dark seedless raisins**
**¼ teaspoon grated lemon peel**
**2 tablespoons lemon juice**
**¼ teaspoon cinnamon**
**1 box (1¾-oz.) powdered fruit pectin** . . .In 3-qt. casserole place peaches, raisins, lemon peel, lemon juice, cinnamon and pectin. Mix together well. Cover. **Microwave at High 10 Minutes,** stirring after 5 minutes.

**5 cups sugar** . . . . . . . . . .Add sugar to hot mixture mixing thoroughly. Cover. **Microwave at High 6 to 8 Minutes** more, stirring after 4 minutes, until mixture reaches a full boil. Stir then **time for 1 more minute of boiling.**

**½ cup brandy**
**1 cup sliced, unblanched almonds** . . . . . . . .Immediately stir in brandy and nuts. With metal spoon skim off foam if necessary. Ladle into prepared glasses. Seal.

Makes about 8 cups

# SWEET CITRUS MARMALADE

*Be sure to remove half of white portion of orange rind so sweet, most natural orange flavor can be obtained.*

POWER LEVEL: High (10)
MICROWAVE TIME: 31 to 33 min., total

**3 medium oranges**
**2 medium lemons** . . . . .Prepare rind portion from oranges and lemons first; peel rind from fruit in quarters. Laying rind white-side up, scrape about half of white layer from rind and discard scraped material. With sharp knife or scissors, slice remaining rind crosswise very thin.

**1½ cups water**
**⅛ teaspoon baking soda** . . . . . . . . . .In 2-qt. casserole place rind with water and baking soda. Cover. **Microwave at High 12 Minutes,** stirring after 6 minutes. While rind is cooking, section fruit, removing and discarding white membrane and seeds. Chop. Add this pulp and juice to the undrained cooked rind. Cover. **Microwave at High 6 Minutes.**

**5 cups sugar** . . . . . . . . . .In 3-qt. casserole measure 3 cups fruit mixture. Add sugar, blending well. Cover. **Microwave at High 12 to 14 Minutes,** stirring after 6 minutes, until mixture comes to a full boil. **Then time for 1 more minute of boiling.**

**½ bottle (6-oz.) liquid fruit pectin** . . . .Stir in pectin, mixing thoroughly. With metal spoon, skim off foam and stir 5 minutes to cool slightly. Ladle into prepared jars. Seal. If sealed with metal lids and band, turn upside down to prevent floating fruit.

Makes about 5½ cups

## PORT WINE CONSERVE

POWER LEVEL: High (10)　　　**Cook Code:**　80
MICROWAVE TIME: 8 to 10 min., total

| | |
|---|---|
| **1½ cups port wine** . . . . . .<br>**1 cup chopped raisins**<br>**3 cups sugar** | In 3-qt. casserole stir together wine, raisins and sugar. |
| **3 large cinnamon sticks** . . . . . .<br>**1 tablespoon grated orange peel**<br>**¼ teaspoon whole cloves**<br>**½ teaspoon cardamom ground** | Prepare spice bag by placing cinnamon sticks, orange peel, cloves and cardamom on a square of cheesecloth. Fold cloth around contents and tie securely with string. Add bag to wine, stir and let stand 5 minutes. **Microwave 8 to 10 Minutes,** stirring well after 5 minutes, just until bubbles appear around edge; do not boil. |
| **½ bottle liquid fruit pectin** . . . . . . | Remove spice bag. Immediately stir pectin into hot mixture. Ladle into prepared glasses. Seal. |

Makes about 3½ cups

## CUCUMBER SANDWICH PICKLES

POWER LEVEL: High (10)
MICROWAVE TIME: 27 to 29 min., total

| | |
|---|---|
| **2 qts. ¼-in. slices small to medium cucumbers**<br>**½ cup salt**<br>**2 qts. water** | In large mixing bowl place prepared cucumber slices. Sprinkle with salt. Add water and let stand 2 to 3 hours. Drain and rinse. |
| **1 cup vinegar** . . . . . . . . . .<br>**1 cup water** | In 2-qt. casserole place cucumber, vinegar and water. Cover. **Microwave at High 10 Minutes,** stirring after 5 minutes, until tender. Drain. |
| **2 cups vinegar** . . . . . . . . .<br>**1 cup hot tap water**<br>**1 cup sugar**<br>**1 cup light brown sugar (packed)**<br>**½ teaspoon mustard seed**<br>**½ teaspoon celery seed**<br>**½ teaspoon turmeric** | In 3-qt. casserole mix together vinegar, water, sugar, brown sugar, mustard seed, celery seed and turmeric. Cover. **Microwave at High 6 Minutes.** Stir well. |

Add cucumbers. **Microwave at High 11 to 13 Minutes,** stirring after 6 minutes, until mixture reaches full boil. Immediately pack into sterilized jars, leaving ⅛-in. headspace. Seal. Let stand at least 24 hours before serving.

Makes about 3 pints

## SHORTCUT WATERMELON PICKLES

*You will need about ¾ of a medium, round-shaped watermelon to produce 3 quarts prepared pieces for recipe below. This new recipe cuts hours of soaking time.*

POWER LEVEL: High (10)
MICROWAVE TIME: 85 min., total

| | |
|---|---|
| **3 qts. chunks white portion of watermelon (see below)**<br>**2 cups water** | In 3-qt. casserole place watermelon. Add water. Cover. **Microwave at High 30 Minutes,** stirring every 10 minutes. Let stand, covered, while cooking syrup. |
| **1 tablespoon mixed pickling spice**<br>**2 cinnamon sticks, broken**<br>**1 lemon, sliced thin**<br>**3 cups sugar**<br>**1½ cups white vinegar**<br>**1 cup water** | Prepare spice bag by placing pickling spice, cinnamon sticks and lemon on a square of cheesecloth. Fold cloth around contents and tie securely with string. Place bag with sugar, vinegar and water in 2-qt. casserole. Stir and cover. **Microwave at High 20 Minutes,** stirring very well and uncovering after 10 minutes. |

Just before syrup has finished cooking, drain off water from watermelon. Pour syrup, including spice bag, over watermelon in 3-qt. casserole. Cover. **Microwave at High 35 Minutes,** stirring every 10 minutes. Chunks should be tender and somewhat transparent; they will become more transparent after standing. Immediately ladle hot watermelon pickles into hot sterilized jars and seal with sterilized vacuum lids.

Makes about 5 cups

TO PREPARE WHITE PORTION OF WATERMELON: Work with ¼ of watermelon at a time. Scoop almost all of red portion from watermelon, but leave ⅛-in. of red for color. Cut rind into 1-in. strips. Cut green peel from strips, leaving white portion. Cube into about ½-in. pieces.

## WHY HOME CANNING IS NOT RECOMMENDED FOR MICROWAVING

Canning should still be done on the range top and is not recommended for either the conventional or the microwave oven.

Special range top canning utensils rapidly bring the water and jars to a boil, and maintain consistent heat to each jar during the canning process. When pressure canners are used, temperatures above boiling are developed to preserve low acid or non-acid foods.

While it is an excellent appliance to use for cooking jelly and preserve mixtures, the microwave oven is not efficient in processing the canning jars.

## COLORFUL CORN RELISH

POWER LEVEL: High (10)
MICROWAVE TIME: 20 to 22 min., total

| | |
|---|---|
| **1 cup sugar** | In 3-qt. casserole stir together sugar, cornstarch, minced onion, mustard seed, celery seed and turmeric. Gradually add vinegar and water, blending well. Cover. **Microwave at High 5 Minutes.** Stir well. |
| **2 tablespoons cornstarch** | |
| **1 tablespoon instant minced onion** | |
| **1 tablespoon mustard seed** | |
| **1 teaspoon celery seed** | |
| **¼ teaspoon turmeric** | |
| **1 cup vinegar** | |
| **¾ cup hot tap water** | |
| **3 cans (12-oz. each) whole kernel corn with chopped peppers, drained (about 5 cups)*** | Add corn to sauce. Cover. **Microwave at High 15 to 17 Minutes,** stirring well after 7 minutes, until mixture boils. Stir well. Ladle into prepared glasses. Seal. |

Makes about 5½ cups

*Sold as Mexicorn or Corn 'n' Peppers.

## YEAR ROUND FRESH TOMATO RELISH

*Delicious on hamburgers.*

POWER LEVEL: High (10)
MICROWAVE TIME: 3 min., total

| | |
|---|---|
| **1 tablespoon prepared mustard** | In 1½-qt. casserole stir together mustard, brown sugar, vinegar and salt. **Microwave at High 1 Minute.** |
| **1 tablespoon brown sugar (packed)** | |
| **2 teaspoons white vinegar** | |
| **½ teaspoon seasoned salt** | |
| **2 cups finely chopped tomato** | Add tomato, celery, green pepper and onion. **Microwave at High 2 Minutes,** uncovered. Stir well and refrigerate at least 1 hour before serving, to blend flavors. Store leftovers in refrigerator. |
| **½ cup finely chopped celery** | |
| **½ cup finely chopped green pepper** | |
| **¼ cup finely chopped green onion** | |

Makes about 3 cups

## SPICY COLESLAW RELISH

*Serve hot over hot dogs, Polish sausage or bratwurst.*

POWER LEVEL: High (10)
MICROWAVE TIME: 7½ to 9½ min., total

| | |
|---|---|
| **2 tablespoons butter** | In 2-qt. casserole place butter. **Microwave at High ½ Minute,** until melted. To butter add cabbage, green pepper, onion, tomatoes, vinegar, mustard, Worcestershire sauce, salt, pepper sauce and pepper. Mix together well. Cover. **Microwave at High 7 to 9 Minutes,** stirring after 4 minutes. Refrigerate leftovers. |
| **2 cups finely shredded cabbage** | |
| **1 chopped green pepper** | |
| **1 small onion, chopped** | |
| **2 medium tomatoes, chopped** | |
| **2 tablespoons vinegar** | |
| **2 teaspoons prepared mustard** | |
| **1 teaspoon Worcestershire sauce** | |
| **½ teaspoon salt** | |
| **¼ teaspoon hot pepper sauce (tabasco)** | |
| **⅛ teaspoon pepper** | |

Makes about 4 cups

## SEALING AND STORING RELISHES AND PICKLES FOR FUTURE USE

Proper procedures should be taken in sealing jars of relishes and pickles to assure their wholesomeness after storage. If relishes and pickles are to be stored on the shelf at room temperature, they must be vacuum sealed in glass jars with 2-piece metal lids available for that purpose.

Sterilize the jars and lids in a kettle of boiling water and keep in hot water until just before filling. Ladling the boiling hot relish or pickle mixture into hot jars and sealing with hot lids is the best way to assure a good vacuum seal. Be sure rim of jar is clean before adding lid; wipe with damp cloth just before sealing. To completely assure proper seal, the U.S. Department of Agriculture recommends processing all relishes and pickles in water bath canner 10 to 15 minutes.

If you do not use the type of jars which may be vacuum sealed, store relishes and pickles in the refrigerator after they have cooled. Glass jars saved from purchased foodstuffs may be used as refrigerator storage jars, but do not use them for on-the-shelf storage at room temperature. Or, for gift giving, ladle relishes or pickles into attractive re-usable serving containers or glasses such as brandy snifters, unusual serving bowls, champagne glasses, etc. Cover with plastic wrap and store in refrigerator until giving.

# Beverages

Heating beverages is one of the most popular uses of the microwave oven. Whether brewed or instant, it takes only 1¼ to 1½ minutes to heat a cup of coffee or tea. These water-based beverages can be heated at High.

When heating more than 4 cups, arrange them in a circle for even heating. Use a 3 to 4-qt. casserole for large quantities.

**Do Not** attempt to defrost or heat beverages in narrow necked bottles. Pressure builds up in the lower part of the bottle, causing it to shatter.

### CALIFORNIA COCOA

POWER LEVEL: High (10)          **Cook Code:** 60
MICROWAVE TIME: 6 to 7 min., total

| | |
|---|---|
| **¼ cup cocoa** | In 1-qt. glass measure combine cocoa and sugar. Add about ½ cup milk to make a smooth paste, then stir in remaining milk, orange rind and almond extract, blending thoroughly. |
| **¼ cup sugar** | |
| **3 cups milk** | |
| **2 teaspoons grated fresh orange rind** | |
| **¼ teaspoon almond extract** | |
| **Cinnamon sticks** | **Microwave at High 6 to 7 Minutes.** Pour into mugs and add cinnamon sticks for flavor and for stirring. |

Makes 4 servings

### WASSIL

*The traditional English holiday drink.*

POWER LEVEL: High (10)          **Cook Code:** 150
MICROWAVE TIME: 15 to 18 min., total

| | |
|---|---|
| **1 quart apple cider** | In 3-qt. casserole place cider, allspice, cloves, nutmeg, cinnamon sticks, orange juice, lemon juice, sugar and apples. **Microwave at High 15 to 18 Minutes,** until hot. Strain and serve. |
| **1 teaspoon allspice** | |
| **½ teaspoon ground cloves** | |
| **¼ teaspoon nutmeg** | |
| **2 cinnamon sticks** | |
| **½ cup orange juice** | |
| **2 tablespoons lemon juice** | |
| **½ cup sugar** | |
| **2 tart medium apples, thinly sliced** | |

Makes 8 to 9 (½ cup) servings

**Use** the temperature probe, set at Medium and 140°, when heating cocoa and other milk-based beverages which boil over easily. Add marshmallow ¼ minute before cocoa is done. To heat by time, allow about 1½ to 2 minutes per cup. Time is longer than for reheating coffee because starting temperature of refrigerated milk is probably lower. Use cocoa mix or heat chocolate-flavored milk for fast cocoa.

# TWIN BERRY SHRUB

*Shrubs are old-fashioned sparkling punches made with berry juice and carbonated beverage.*

POWER LEVEL: High (10)
MICROWAVE TIME: 13 to 16 min., total

**2 pkg. (10-oz. each) frozen strawberries in pouch**
**2 pkg. (10-oz. each) frozen raspberries in pouch**
Place all 4 packages of berries on oven shelf. **Microwave at High 12 to 14 Minutes,** turning packages over and rearranging after 6 minutes. When berries have completely thawed, sieve to remove all seeds.

**1 can (6-oz.) frozen lemonade concentrate**
In small glass bowl place lemonade. **Microwave at High 1 to 2 Minutes.** Add to the sieved berry syrup. Chill.

**2 qt. club soda, well chilled**
Just before serving, blend berry juice mixture with club soda in festive glasses or in punch bowl. Decorate with lemon slices if desired.

Makes 3 quarts

# IRISH COFFEE

POWER LEVEL: High (10)          Cook Code:   10
MICROWAVE TIME: 1½ to 2 min., total

**3 tablespoons (1½-oz.) Irish whiskey**
**1 to 2 teaspoons sugar**
**1 tablespoon freeze dried or instant coffee**
**Water**
In 8-oz. stemmed glass, mug or coffee cup, place whiskey. Add sugar and coffee. Add water until container is about ¾ full. Mix well. **Microwave at High 1½ to 2 Minutes.** Mixture should be very hot but not boiling. Stir to dissolve all sugar.

**Whipping cream**
Whip cream until almost stiff. It should be stiff enough to pour from the bowl over a spoon, onto the surface of the coffee without blending.

Fill glass to brim with cream. Do not stir. Coffee should be sipped through the layer of cream.

Makes 1 serving

**Irish Mist Coffee:** Use Irish Mist Liqueur instead of Irish whiskey. This variation makes a very smooth, sippable drink.

# HOT BUTTERED RUM

POWER LEVEL: High (10)          Cook Code:   10
MICROWAVE TIME: 1½ to 2 min., total

**1 to 2 teaspoons granulated or brown sugar (packed)**
**¼ cup (2-oz.) light or dark rum**
**Water**
In tall mug or cup place sugar and rum. Add water to ⅔ full. **Microwave at High 1½ to 2 Minutes,** until mixture is very hot but not boiling.

**Butter**
**Nutmeg**
**Cinnamon stick**
Add about ¼-in. thick slice butter. Sprinkle with nutmeg and serve with cinnamon stick for stirring.

Makes 1 serving

**Old Boston Buttered Rum:** Substitute apple cider for water and use lower amount of sugar.

# KENTUCKY MINT JULEP

*This is a tradition every year during the Kentucky Derby.*

**To make each drink:** Pour 1 tablespoon Mint Syrup (below) into tall glass filled with very finely crushed ice. Slowly add 2-oz. Kentucky bourbon whiskey. Garnish with sprig of mint and add straw.

**Mint Syrup:** In 1-pt. measure mix together 1 cup sugar and ½ cup water. **Microwave at High 4 to 4½ Minutes,** until hot and sugar is dissolved. Stir well. Add 1 bunch (18 stalks) mint. Stir well. Strain into small glass jar. Cover tightly and refrigerate. **Cook Code:** 40.

# SOURS

*Vary the liquor to change the character of the drink.*

POWER LEVEL: High (10)          Cook Code:   10
MICROWAVE TIME: 1½ min., total

**1 can (6-oz.) frozen lemonade concentrate**
**Water**
**Liquor (see below)**
Remove concentrate from can to glass, microwave ovenproof pottery or stoneware pitcher. **Microwave at High 1½ Minutes,** until melted enough to stir. Add water and liquor and, if desired, ice cubes.

Makes about 4 drinks

**Liquor:** Use rum for daiquiris; bourbon for whiskey sours; or Scotch, orange slices and cherries for Scotch old-fashioneds.

# Index

# Defrosting Guide POWER LEVEL: Defrost

| MEAT | AMOUNT | FIRST HALF TIME/MINUTES | SECOND HALF TIME/MINUTES | COMMENTS |
|------|--------|------------------------|--------------------------|----------|
| **Bacon** | 1 package | 2 to 3 per lb. | 2 to 3 per lb. | Place unopened package in microwave oven. Turn over after first ½ of time. Microwave just until strips can be separated. |
| **Franks** | 1 pound | 3 to 5 | none | Place unopened package in microwave oven. Microwave just until franks can be separated. |
| | ½ pound | 1½ to 2½ | none | |
| **Ground, Beef & Pork** | 1 pound | 3 | 3 | Scrape off softened meat after second ½ of time. Set aside. Break up remaining block, microwave 2 to 3 minutes more. |
| | 2 pounds | 6 | 6 | Scrape off softened meat after second ½ of time. Set aside. Break up remaining block, microwave 5 to 6 minutes more. |
| | 5 pounds | 12 | 12 | Scrape off softened meat after second ½ of time. Set aside. Break up remaining block, microwave 11 to 12 minutes more. Second scraping may be needed. |
| **Roast, Beef, Lamb, Pork & Veal** | 1 roast | 5 to 6 | 5 to 6 per lb. | Place wrapped roast in microwave oven. After first ½ of time, shield warm areas with foil. Turn over and place in roasting dish. Defrost for second ½ of time. Let stand 15 to 30 minutes. |
| **Spareribs, Pork** | 1 package | 2 to 4 per lb. | 2 to 4 per lb. | Place wrapped package in microwave oven. Turn over after first ½ of time. After second ½ of time, separate pieces with table knife. Let stand to complete defrosting. |
| **Steaks, Chops & Cutlets; Beef, Lamb, Pork & Veal** | 1 package | 2 to 4 per lb. | 2 to 4 per lb. | Place wrapped package in microwave oven. Turn over after first ½ of time. After second ½ of time, separate pieces with table knife, let stand to complete defrosting. |
| **Sausage, Bulk** | 1-lb. tray | 3 | 3 | Scrape off softened meat after second ½ of time. Set aside. Break up remaining block, microwave 2 to 3 minutes more. |
| | 1-lb. roll | 2 | 2 to 3 | Turn over after first ½ of time. |
| **Sausage, Link** | 1 pound | 2 | 1 to 2 | Turn over after first ½ of time. |
| **Sausage, Link,** | 8-oz. | 2 | 1 to 2 | Turn over after first ½ of time. |
| **Sausage, Patties** | 12-oz. pkg. | 1 | 1 to 2 | Turn over after first ½ of time. |

| POULTRY | AMOUNT | FIRST HALF TIME/MINUTES | SECOND HALF TIME/MINUTES | COMMENTS |
|---------|--------|------------------------|--------------------------|----------|
| **Chicken, Broiler-fryer, cut up** | 2½ to 3½-lb. | 7 to 8 | 7 to 8 | Place wrapped chicken in microwave oven. After ½ of time, unwrap and turn over. After second ½ of time, separate pieces and place in cooking dish. Microwave 2 to 4 minutes more, if necessary. |
| **Whole** | 2½ to 3½-lb. | 9 to 11 | 9 to 11 | Place wrapped chicken in microwave oven. After ½ of time shield warm areas with foil. |
| **Cornish Hens** | 1 | 3½ to 4½ per lb. | 3½ to 4½ per lb. | Place wrapped package in microwave oven. Turn package over after first ½ of time. After second ½ of time, unwrap and shield ends of legs with foil. Microwave 3½ to 4½ minutes more. |
| **Duckling** | 1 | 2 to 3 per lb. | 2 to 3 per lb. | Place wrapped duckling in microwave oven. After first ½ of time, unwrap and turn over into cooking dish. Shield warm areas with foil. |
| **Turkey** | 1 | 2½ to 3 per lb. | 3½ to 3 per lb. | Place wrapped turkey breast side down in microwave oven. Rotate ½ turn after first timing. After second timing, unwrap and shield warm areas with foil. Turn turkey breast side up and repeat timings. |